MURDER

AT THE

ADELPHI

*A rehearsal diary of the original London
production of the musical Sunset Boulevard*

By Peter Gale

FIRST EDITION

ISBNs
eBook: 978-1-80227-521-6
Paperback:978-1-80227-520-9
Prepared by PublishingPush.com

Also by Peter Gale:
Stella and the Yellow Cello
Published by Centaur Press (imprint of Open Gate Press) 2014

I Shudder to Think, Therefore I Am
Published by Yes Oh Yes Press.
Hardback 2004.
Paperback 2008

Foreword

Dear reader, I wrote this diary when I was a dedicated thespian – not a medicated lesbian, as spell checker suggested. The word "thespian" stems from Ancient Greece, when Nicholas Thespis recited narrative poems on his handcart to shoppers buying fruit and veg in Athens' market. Nicky was paving the way to great theatrical tragedies, like *Antigone* by Sophocles, *King Lear* by William Shakespeare and *Coronation Street* by Tony Warren.

Part 1: Setting the Scene

Studios 2 and 3, Riverside Studios, Hammersmith

We worked for four and a half weeks with our director Trevor Nunn on the London premier of Andrew Lloyd Webber's 1993 spectacular musical *Sunset Boulevard*. Each morning, I woke about 5 a.m., scribbled an account of the previous day, went for a jog, washed, breakfasted, tubed to Riverside, rehearsed, zipped home, polished my invisible Oscar, cooked, ate and hit the sack about 10 p.m.

Part 2: Break a Leg

Adelphi Theatre, the Strand, London

We rehearsed in the beautifully redecorated theatre for four and a half weeks on John Napier's spectacular sets. There then followed our dress rehearsals, public previews and the first night in front of a star-studded audience.

The Savoy Hotel, the Strand, London

The first night party was held at this beautiful hotel but it was dreadful because the management chopped the company into two halves, seated on different floors.

In the Abraham Lincoln Room were our stars, Patti LuPone and Kevin Anderson, plus six other leading actors, our director Trevor Nunn, the composer/producer Andrew Lloyd Webber, the writers Don Black, Christopher Hampton and Tim Rice, and RUG's production team. Also with them was Billy Wilder, the co-writer and director of the 1950 Paramount movie on which the show is based, plus many other specially invited VIPs and celebrities.

Seated in the equally elegant Riverside Room a floor below them were supporting actors (like me) and the production team. There we dined with our more humble guests wondering where on earth everyone had gone.

This diary describes our show's mixed press reviews, followed by further sporadic daily entries. It ends two years later when I bade the show farewell and ran screaming into the eponymous sunset.

My schedule in *Sunset* was full-on: eight shows a week, understudy rehearsals and my duties as the Equity deputy. Why in the name of Nicky Thespis did I volunteer? I had to organise company discussions, supervise votes, attend meetings at the British Actors' Equity office, draft and type out reports, pin them on the company noticeboard, photocopy updates, distribute them to the artists' dressing rooms, and help the cast and stage management with any problems, including grumbles about inadequate (i.e. vanishing) tea breaks during rehearsals. I was later asked to mend the seismic rift between our aggrieved leading lady, Patti LuPone and her exasperated producer/composer, Andrew Lloyd Webber.

It was then irreparable and took them twenty-four years to settle the angry mess amicably.

Murder at the Adelphi has been written and published without the help of Andrew's company, the Really Useful Group (RUG). When I rang them and asked if they would collaborate on the book, their response was like opening a refrigerator and sticking my head inside. Far from offering help, they expressed no interest whatsoever, hence no glossy production photos. RUG has, of course, copyright control over all such material which I respect. This book, however, is my "intellectual property", the correct official phrase.

I must say thanks to Alexander Bermange, the poet, songwriter and playwright who encouraged me to keep going when he saw me sobbing over some scribbled notes in our local Cafe Nero in Radlett. I also thank two other coffee buddies, Jill and Malcolm Steene, who gave me their beautiful original *Sunset Boulevard* programme and souvenir brochure. Mine disappeared in the hurly-burly of my fabulous showbiz career, otherwise known as lost somewhere amongst a pile of old papers.

Finally, all details are as accurate as possible and I apologise for any mistakes involving names, dates or times. I have eschewed (as dear Shakespeare used to say) kiss-and-tell gossip, being always the last person to hear about sexy shenanigans – even when I'm directly involved. Which is odd.

Speaking of which, my love life suffered a frustratingly dull patch during the show's pre-production months and opening weeks. Needless to say, I afterwards made up for lost time with my current hot stuff, Dave, and when that happened, he didn't know what hit him. Dave is not his real name so calm down and be quiet.

I also sincerely apologise for any factual errors, including the precise location of bodies buried under the M25.

Contents

THE ORIGINAL 1993 LONDON CAST OF
SUNSET BOULEVARD

ARTIST	ROLE
Patti LuPone	Norma Desmond
Kevin Anderson	Joe Gillis
Daniel Benzali	Max von Mayerling
Meredith Braun	Betty Schaeffer
Michael Bauer	Cecil B. DeMille/ Ensemble/1st Understudy to M. von Mayerling
Gary Snook	Artie Green
Harry Ditson	Sheldrake/Ensemble
Nicolas Colicos	Manfred/Ensemble
Kate Arneil	Ensemble
Gerard Casey	Ensemble/Understudy to J. Gillis
Anita Louise Combe	Ensemble/Understudy to B. Schaefer
Steve Devereux	Ensemble
Alisa Endsley	Ensemble/2nd Understudy to N. Desmond
Nicola Jane Filshie	Ensemble
Peter Gale	Ensemble/2nd Understudy to C. B. DeMille
Liz Greenaway	Ensemble
Simon Hayden	Ensemble

Mark Inscoe	Ensemble/Understudy to A. Green
Adam Matalon	Ensemble
Sasha Millard	Ensemble
Larissa Murray	Ensemble
Daphne Peña Pardy	Ensemble/Swing Girl
Richard Purro	Ensemble
Bernard Sharpe	Ensemble
Dawn Spence	Ensemble
Nadia Strahan	Ensemble
Sandy Strallen	Ensemble/Swing Boy
Richard Tate	Ensemble/Understudy to Sheldrake
Carol Duffy	1st Understudy to N. Desmond

PRODUCTION TEAM

Composer	Andrew Lloyd Webber
Lyrics and Book	Don Black & Christopher Hampton
Director	Trevor Nunn
Choreographer	Bob Avian
Orchestrators	David Cullen & Andrew Lloyd Webber
Musical Supervisor	David Caddick
Musical Director (conductor)	David White
Sound Designer	Martin Levan
Lighting Design	Andrew Bridge
Set Designer	John Napier
Costume Designer	Anthony Powell
Trevor Nunn's assistant	Mary-Lee McNulty
Ass. Musical Director	Andrew Friesner
Ass. Director	Andrew McBean
Associate Choreographer	Maggie Goodwin
Company Manager	Richard Oriel
Production Manager	Alastair Smith
Production Stage Manager	Pippa Shaw
Stage Managers	Stephen Burnett & Debbie Cronshaw

Assistant Stage Managers	Lee Fowler, Lee Kean & Nigel Wright
Vocal Coach	Joan Washington
Head of RUG	Allan Benson
RUG Merchandising Manager	Sue Watts
Rehearsal Pianists	Leslie Hayes, David White & Carol Woods
Equity Contacts	Rachel Carter & Hilary Strange

PART 1

Setting the Scene
Riverside Studios

Chapter 1

JANUARY 1993

THURSDAY 7th January 1993

10 a.m. Dance Works, 16 Balderton St. W1

I auditioned for *Sunset Boulevard*, Andrew Lloyd Webber's shiny new West End musical. It's based on the terrific 1950 Paramount Studios movie. *Sir* Andrew was knighted last year in the Queen's Honours List.

Trevor Nunn (director) held the audition with David Caddick (musical supervisor). Trevor has won many awards for his productions of plays and stage musicals, including *Nicholas Nickleby*, *Cats* and *Les Miserables*.

David Caddick was music director at the Royal Shakespeare Company and for several hit shows in London, including *Cats, Evita* and *Miss Saigon*.

I had to do a speech from an American play and sing a song.

MONDAY 11th January 1993

1 p.m. King's Head Theatre, Islington

The first public performance of *The Secret Garden*. I am playing Lord Archibald Craven in a musical adaptation of Francis Hodgson Burnett's 1909 book by Steven Markwick and Diana Morgan. Archibald is a recently bereaved widower; he sings sadly about the death of his beloved wife, "lovely, lively Lillian."

The King's Head is a pub that houses a very popular theatre in its back room. The stage is tiny but plays work astonishingly well here. We run for the next three weeks.

FRIDAY 15th January 1993

10:30 a.m. Dance Works

My second *Sunset* audition. We were taught a brief dance. Later, I rang my agent, Roberta Kanal.

"Forgive my curiosity, Roberta, but could you ask Mr Webber's company what part I'm auditioning for?"

"I'm sorry, Peter. They're being very secretive about the whole thing. No details." Roberta then used the c word. "Chorus and understudy are all they are willing to say at this point. Sorry."

The secretive "they" are the two producers of *Sunset* – Lloyd Webber's The Really Useful Theatre Co. (part of RUG) and Paramount Pictures, the studio who made the terrific 1950 film on which this stage version is based.

MONDAY 18th January 1993

2:20 p.m. Royalty Theatre

My third audition for *Sunset*.

Chapter 2

MARCH 1993

WEDNESDAY 17th March 1993

10:45 a.m. Home

My agent rang me. "First, the good news, Peter. They want you."

Oh, those magical words… *They want you!*

"The *Sunset* previews start at the Adelphi Theatre on June 18th; that's in three months' time. The world premiere is scheduled for 22nd June."

"Thanks, Roberta. Yes, that's very good news. Okay. Now I'm bracing myself for the bad news."

"Still no specific role, I'm afraid. Only chorus and understudy. And the basic salary is £300 a week. Sorry about that, but you'll get an extra £25 a week for covering the role of Cecil B. DeMille."

So, at the ripe old age of fifty-one, I have finally made it to the chorus.

In Roberta's negotiations, she has used the more diplomatic word "ensemble", but in my contract it would say chorus – if I sign.

With its pros and cons, this job is a double-edged sword. Grappling with it, blood splashes all over my newly fitted carpet. Speaking professionally, it would mean a big step down for me after enjoying a fairly high-profile over the past thirty years in TV, film and theatre. But all acting careers have peaks and troughs.

"Can I see a script, Roberta? That might help me decide."

"No, I'm afraid not. They said, 'Tell Peter that we can't send him one for security reasons.' Also, they want you to sign a year's contract. What I suggest is this: think about it, and call me back."

Misgivings crowded round my ankles. They snapped like terriers but I shooed them away. This job ticked excellent boxes, including the money box. The basic salary is poor, considering it's a spectacular West End show, but here's the bottom line. I sorely need to earn regular dosh because I'm still financially recovering from the tax bill I paid when my partner Paul Hardwick died of a sudden heart attack ten years ago.

When we bought our house, we agreed Paulie would pay the mortgage and be the property's sole owner. I would spend my savings and earnings on extensive house repairs. It was in a shocking state. Everything needed seeing to: from the cracked chimney stack down to the rising damp and the broken drains.

In his will, Paul left his entire estate to me. We had lived together for almost twenty years but we were not a heterosexual wedded couple, and so, in accordance with Capital Transfer tax laws, Her Majesty's Revenue and Customs took all Paul's savings and most of mine.

Ten years later, I am still struggling to recover financially and *Sunset Boulevard* pretty well guarantees me a year's paid work. So, suck it up, Pete.

Needing friendly advice about doing the show, I rang my chum the actress Bronwen Williams. She said, "Well, that's very exciting, Peter. Congratulations, darling. All I would simply add is a word of warning. This job might be depressing after the leading roles you've played in the past in the West End, and working with Spielberg and appearing in masses of TV productions. I presume your new agent knows about all that. Here's the thing, Peter. If you accept *Sunset*, you've got to think positive. That's the only way to approach it, darling. Think positive!"

"Point taken, Bronnie. I badly need a steady job so I shall thank my lucky stars for every wage packet and think positive if it kills me. Talking of money, our two leads Patti LuPone and Kevin Anderson are rumoured to be getting a big slice out of *Sunset*'s budget. £20,000 a week. Each. Do you think that's possible?"

"Good heavens. Well, I've no idea, but Lloyd Webber's accountants aren't famous for throwing their money about. That said, Broadway stars often receive salaries roughly double those paid to leading actors in London."

"Oh well, I'm getting twenty-five quid each week for understudying DeMille. It's better than a poke in the eye with a sharp stick as Jane Austen used to say."

MONDAY 29th March 1993

1 p.m. The King's Head Theatre, Islington

This was the first performance of the play *Gatsby* that I've directed at the King's Head. The cast were excellent. Bravo everyone!

Syd Golda runs the lunchtime slot in this little theatre. A few weeks ago, he sent me a new stage adaptation of F. Scott Fitzgerald's terrific novel *The Great Gatsby*.

He said, "Will you direct it?"

"Yes, I would love to! Thank you, Syd. On one condition. I've just read the book. Now, I realise what all the fuss is about. It's terrific. But you must let me rewrite this adaptation. As it stands, it's incomprehensible and unworkable. It begins in a morgue! Everyone's dead, lying on slabs!"

Syd gave me the go ahead. The official adaptor approved of all my rewrites but at the last minute refused to allow me any credit on the programmes or posters. Yes, it's just another fringe theatre play in the back room of a pub with a stage the size of a beer mat, the actors suited and booted on an even smaller budget. But a modest "co-adaptor" would have been nice. Oh well. It's been great to do and I love the cast.

Chapter 3

APRIL 1993

SATURDAY 17th April 1993

2:30 p.m. The King's Head Theatre, Islington

Today was the last performance of *Gatsby* that I directed. To celebrate the end of our three-week run at the King's Head, I threw a little party back at my pad for the cast and stage management.

Our low budget play has finished on a high. Good press reviews pulled in full houses. Time Out Magazine's theatre reviewer Bonnie Greer even put us in their Critic's Choice section. After praising the actors, she wrote, "Peter Gale's elegant, moving production never makes a wrong move." A cheering accolade for everyone! Ms Greer particularly liked the monologues. They were all mine, not copied from the novel but faithfully adapted.

Syd Golda is a wonderfully surprising character. He looks like a retired wrestler and talks with a Cockney accent. His colourful early life included doing time in prison. He also won a case he brought against the UK government to give prisoners the right of access to a solicitor. Later, Syd got a job at RADA, became hooked on the magical world of theatre and opened the first London fringe theatre at The Spice of Life, a 200-year-old pub in Cambridge Circus.

For years, Syd has been putting on lunchtime plays at King's Head which is the city's second oldest fringe theatre, founded by Dan Crawford in 1970. Syd shares all profits equally between the cast and the stage management, taking nothing for himself and living solely on his pension. Syd loves plays and actors and he helped me to dress and light our dishy *Gatsby* cast to look like drop-dead gorgeous Hollywood stars.

Andy Granger was the tall, handsome adventurer, Jay Gatsby. Laurissa Kalinowsky played the classy Daisy Buchanan, a rich, married Jazz Age flapper who sets their illicit passion ablaze. Their friend Nick Carraway is the sharp-eyed, cool narrator of the whole affair. He was played by Mark Gillis, and Stephanie McNamara was a deliciously beguiling Jordan.

In the novel, Tom Buchanan sneers jealously at Gatsby: "He wears pink suits!" Our invisible-to-the-naked-eye budget wouldn't stretch to suits of that colour and so I changed the line to: "He wears pink shirts."

I braced myself for angry letters in The Times. Not one. Whew!

MONDAY 19th April 1993

2:30 p.m. Palace Theatre, Stage Door

I said to the stage door keeper, "I'm here for a costume fitting for *Sunset Boulevard.*"

"You're the first to arrive. Take the lift. I'll phone and tell them you're on your way up."

As the lift gates opened, I was greeted by Bob Worth. Over the years, Bob has kitted me out with outfits for many theatre and TV roles.

I smiled at him. "Hello Bob."

He frowned back at me like a stern headmaster. "What are *you* doing here?" His tone implied this job is a professional comedown for me.

I rose above it. Bronnie's advice echoed in my head… "Think positive, Peter."

"Thanks for the welcome, Bob. Funny you should ask me that question. To be honest, I haven't the foggiest idea why I'm here today, except to have some sort of fitting. But what for? Lloyd Webber's production office has kept me completely in the dark. No script. No music. No cast list details. Nothing. Even my agent doesn't know what parts I'm playing in *Sunset*. All it says in my contract is ensemble and understudy. Nothing else."

I felt dazed and confused. How could today be a fitting? Nobody had even measured me yet.

"I don't even know why we're in this theatre, Bob. You work at Bermans and Nathans Costumiers. Why aren't we over there?"

"You'll see. Follow me." Bob led me along the corridor. "I'm assisting Anthony Powell who is designing all *Sunset's* costumes."

Ah, memories! They bounced around in my head like washing in a tumble dryer. Seems like only yesterday Bob was measuring me for my togs in *Maggie* at the Shaftesbury Theatre, a musical based on J. M. Barrie's play *What Every Woman Knows*. My co-star Anna Sharkey played Maggie and won the 1977 SWET Award. The Times critic called my John Shand "a handsome, virile presence." Very perceptive.

In 1981, I played John Dashwood in BBC TV's mini-series *Sense and Sensibility* based on Jane Austen's novel. In 1987, I was Mr Victor in Steven Spielberg's epic film *Empire of the Sun* and in 1991, I was Mr Shell in Yorkshire TV's *The Darling Buds of May*, starring David Jason and a new kid on the block, Catherine Zeta-Jones.

I didn't care what I was doing at the Palace. Why should I? RUG's high security treatment makes that pointless. It's "classified information". Heaven forbid I should ask any *questions*. Alarm bells might go off. So, I did.

"Bob, why are we here backstage at the Palace? I don't get it."

"Because Andrew Lloyd Webber owns it. He bought the Palace in 1985. This is where a lot of the costumes worn in his shows are now stored. According to newspapers, he paid £1.3 million for it when he produced *Les Mis* here. Rumour hath it, he had this whole floor redecorated as an ensuite flat for him and Sarah Brightman."

"Ah! That explains this fancy wallpaper!"

"Yes. This was their love nest. Only married for six years. Got divorced three years ago. If these walls could only talk."

I was pretty glad they couldn't.

On one speechless wall, I noticed faded block capital letters of a previous occupant: FOURTH FLOOR, EMILE LITTLER.

Mr Littler became a theatrical legend as the producer who ran the Palace Theatre from the 1940s till the 1980s. It seats 14,000 people and his smash hit musicals included *The Student Prince*, *The Desert Song* and *Annie Get Your Gun*; they all became big, beautiful, technicolour Hollywood films. He presented more than two hundred pantos in London and around Britain. This floor was the flight deck of Emile Littler's Starship Enterprise.

I said, "We are walking on hallowed ground, Bob."

He showed me into a surprisingly pretty side room. It had red wallpaper and pink fringed curtains with dinky tassels. On the wall were framed black and white photos of glamorous 1930s

Hollywood movie stars, like Myrna Loy in her MGM Studios prime. Was this a spare bedroom in Sir Andrew and Sarah's flat?

"I just don't get it, Bob. In most shows, they usually take my neck, chest and inside leg measurements *before* I have a fitting. So far no one's come near me with a tape measure."

His young assistant was sitting on the floor, checking a pile of paperwork. He looked about ten years old. He ignored me completely and just muttered, "It's okay, Bob," in a bored monotone. "He's come to the right place."

"Good to know." I gave him a friendly smile.

He glanced up, glared at me glumly, then returned to his notes.

Bob said, "I'll explain, Peter. It's quite simple. You're here today to try on this gold breastplate." He indicated a piece of armour on a clothes rack. "It was made for *Technicolour Dreamcoat*."

"Would I wear it in *Sunset*?"

"Maybe. Made of plastic. Not heavy."

"But what on earth is it for? What role? I'm completely baffled."

"At one point, you're a Hollywood actor working on a biblical epic."

"Oh, I see. Well, thanks, Bob. At least I've learnt something today."

Just then Anthony Powell breezed in. Anthony is our jolly, chubby costume designer on *Sunset Boulevard* – aged fifty-eight and the winner of three Oscars, one for the film *Death on the Nile*.

He greeted me with a cheery, "Hello, Peter! How are you?"

"I'm fine, thanks. Just completely bewildered. Can you shed some light on what I'm playing in *Sunset*? Lloyd Webber's RUG company won't even send me a script."

"Yes, I'm sorry about that. Things are a bit confusing for all of us at the moment." Anthony referred to a list. "Now let me see... Ah, yes! You're the one with all the instant costume changes in the first scene. I've no idea how we're going to do those. First, you're a policeman. Then a newspaper reporter. Then a security guard at Paramount Studios. Then you're an actor working in DeMille's movie *Samson and Delilah*. Hence this gold breastplate! And then you're an assistant to DeMille. You've got a busy first half!"

There it was. Bit parts. My heart sank, but Bronnie's advice echoed in my head. "Peter, you have got to think positive!"

As they measured and photographed me (face forwards, profile and full length), the corridor filled with other ensemble actors who seemed equally bemused, including Richard Tate, a short, fifty-year-old guy. I tried to share my "think positive" attitude with him.

"Exciting, isn't it?" I said. "Being in a big new West End musical."

No reply; he just beamed up a friendly smile.

Another actor arrived who I happened to know, Lancashire-born Bernard Sharpe. Bernie has also accepted ensemble and understudy in *Sunset*. We recently worked together in a show called *Give a Dog a Bone* at the Westminster Theatre. He played the eponymous pooch and I was Mr Spaceman. Amazingly, Bernie is crazy about the army and ten years ago, he bravely volunteered to serve in the Falklands War in which a thousand Argentinian and British soldiers were killed. Let's hope *Sunset* has fewer casualties.

As I was leaving, Michael Bauer arrived – an actor/opera singer with a strapping physique and a deep, growly bass-baritone voice. Only two years ago, Michael and I played leading roles in *HMS Pinafore* at the Chichester Festival Theatre and at London's Barbican Theatre. Michael was Dick Deadeye and I had great fun as Sir Joseph Porter – "The very model of a modern Major

General."

I said, "Michael, do you know what you're playing in *Sunset*?"

"Cecil B. DeMille."

A plum cameo role. No busy show for him. This put a wee dent in my "think positive" grin.

3 p.m. Palace Theatre, Stage Door

Tanya Franks was waiting to tell me some exciting news. Tanya and I recently worked at the King's Head Theatre in Islington, playing the leads in J. M. Barrie's witty play *The Twelve Pound Look* written in 1914. It is a witty war of words between Harry Simms (me), a pompous, money-grubbing capitalist who is about to be knighted, and Kate (Tanya), his ex-wife, who reveals that she left him when she managed to save up £12 to buy a typewriter and thus gain her independence working as a typist. Tanya is in her mid-twenties and a very attractive, enterprising actress, full of energy and plans.

"Peter, I have set up a theatre production company called Stock-pot and I want to present a series of rehearsed readings of plays by Bernard Shaw. If you're free, would you direct *Widowers' Houses* for me? That reading is going to be at the Theatre Museum on a Sunday in October."

"I'd love to, Tanya. Many thanks. *Sunset* should have settled in by then. One of my favourite roles was in Shaw's *Mrs Warren's Profession*. I played Frank in a production at the Theatre Royal, Windsor."

TUESDAY 20th April 1993

7:30 a.m.

A gloriously warm spring day. I cleared up after my jolly *Gatsby* company party, returned the wine glasses to Waitrose and then sunbathed in my little front garden on my rickety old sun lounger.

2 p.m.

Had lunch and then, with a regular salary coming in, I stormed Ikea. I bought two small carpets, a desk lamp, two cassette stackers and a blizzard of small cushions. Well, only three. But in my frugal world, it felt like a blizzard.

I've learnt a harsh lesson over the years about possessing "stuff". I've been burgled three times. You don't possess objects. They possess you.

On a more light-hearted note, when I worked with the actor George Cole, I said to him, "By the third robbery, there wasn't much left for anyone to steal. They even took my duvet and the hoover."

George said, "It must have been a woman."

WEDNESDAY 21st April 1993

No rehearsal call.

I can't help it. Waking each morning, it hits me. I am a fifty-one-year old chorus boy. So, I have to give myself a good talking to.

Peter, get a grip. It's a paid job.

Yes, okay. But it feels like my career is taking a big step back.

Listen, stupid, you are lucky to be working.

I'm only saying that doing this feels… uncomfortable. I've played good parts and had excellent reviews for performances in West End theatres and fringe venues.

Okay then, stupid. Don't do Sunset.

I've got to. I've no choice.

Really? And why is that, stupid?

For three reasons. And stop calling me stupid.

The first reason is the money. Here's what happened.

In 1964, I met the actor Paul Hardwick at Stratford-on-Avon in its quarter centenary festival season, called "The Wars of the Roses". It celebrated Shakespeare's 400th birthday with performances of all his history plays. I was twenty-two and Paulie was forty-four, a lot older than me but despite the age difference, we became devoted to each other.

After renting flats for eight years, we bought a house in West Hampstead, only affordable because it needed extensive (expensive!) restoration and had no back garden. Here's the deal Paulie and I made with each other.

He took care of the mortgage and the rates, and I paid for everything else. I took driving lessons, passed my test, bought a second-hand car and became Paul's chauffeur. I renovated the entire house. Everything needed mending or replacing – the chimney stack, the roof slates, the window frames and the cracked drains. To stop the rising damp, I had a damp-proof course installed and by having two walls removed, I created an open jolly kitchen/dining room. That was important for Paulie because he was head chef.

Upstairs, I had another wall taken out, creating a combined office and living room. I bought furniture, carpets, curtains, a TV, a record player, a radio and a recording sound deck. Being a carpenter, I built many shelves for my large collection of books and had the entire house redecorated. Also, I designed and planted a pretty front garden. Every penny I earnt went on creating a happy home for us. It was a labour of love.

Here comes the kicker. When Paul made his will, he kindly named me as the sole beneficiary. However, my home improvements increased the house's property value. This meant that, if Paulie died before me, it would raise the inheritance tax bill I'd have to pay. Which is exactly what happened.

Ten years ago, on October 22nd 1983, Paulie died of a sudden heart attack, aged sixty-four. I suffered a double nightmare – grief and Capital Transfer Tax, otherwise known as Death Duties.

One day, an official from Her Majesty's Revenue and Customs arrived to evaluate the crap out of my possessions, i.e. my "goods and chattels" (that word once meant cattle). All "contents" in the house formed a part of Paul's "estate", i.e. the total cash and property a person owns.

My problem? All the contents were mine – Paulie didn't buy a single thing, let alone any cattle. I've since heard that dishonest people hide their stuff in a warehouse before such inspections. I wish I had.

She was a nice lady doing a nasty job, going from room to room, poking about with her biro and notebook, listing every knick-knack I collected over the years in antique shops and junk shops while acting around Britain; each picture I'd had framed; each coaster, candlestick, cup, saucer, vase, clock, standard lamp, lampshade, light fitting, mirror, ash tray and ornament – like my two Staffordshire flat backs – and every stick of furniture I bought when Paulie and I set up home. Nothing was left out: the curtains, carpets and gas stove, the TV, fridge, bookcases, fitted shelves that I made and my heavy beloved Edwardian typewriter. Even a toothbrush cabinet I bought at John Barnes!

She pointed to my coffee table. "That's nice. How much did it cost?"

"I didn't buy it. I made it. I'm a carpenter. If you don't believe me, I'll show you the tools I used. They're in the garage. I bought the planks in the Kilburn High Road wood store, carried them here on my shoulders because they were too long to fit in my Mini Minor. I can't remember how much I paid for them. Those are Minton tiles on the top of the coffee table. I bought them in an antiques shop in Church Street."

"Very nice coffee table. I'd say it would cost about £150 to buy."

And down it went on her stinking list.

She said, "I shall try to keep the evaluation as low as possible but it has to be credible to my employers, otherwise they'll get suspicious and send an inspector, who will charge you a lot more. I really am sorry, Mr Gale. This is difficult for both of us."

My heart bled for her.

Soon after, I was hit with a bill that swallowed every penny of Paul's savings and all but a fraction of mine. I was even forced to pay tax on the pergola near our front door. I built that with old banister poles. Paulie called it our bower of bliss. What with the hideous hell of grief, the fight went out of me.

As I woke each morning and remembered I'd never see Paulie again, before I opened my eyes, tears trickled down my face. I even considered suicide but Toby our darling nine-year-old Welsh Border Collie kept me here. Bless his heart, I couldn't abandon Tobes. Paul's disappearance made him very fretful. Luckily, I found enough acting work to pay my day-to-day bills, but now I must earn regular dough, and lickety-split.

My second reason for doing ensemble in *Sunset* is to work with Trevor Nunn, one of Britain's finest theatre directors. His stage, film, TV credits and awards are staggering. They include *The Life and Adventures of Nicholas Nickleby* and Andrew Lloyd Webber's worldwide success *Cats*.

My third reason is to have this show on my CV. The 1950

movie it's based on won nine Academy Award nominations, two Oscars and was voted a landmark film by America's National Film Registry. The lyrics are by Don Black (he won an Oscar for *Born Free*), the book is by Christopher Hampton (a Tony Award for *Dangerous Liaisons*) and the music is by Andrew Lloyd Webber, a phenomenally successful composer, producer and award-winner. His hit shows include *Joseph and the Amazing Technicolor Dreamcoat, Cats, Evita, Jesus Christ Superstar* and *The Phantom of the Opera*.

All showbiz careers are upsy-downsy. Here's a couple of my upsies. When I was twenty-nine, I played Dickie Winslow in a classy West End revival of Terence Rattigan's play *The Winslow Boy*. Rattigan attended some of the rehearsals. Sir Kenneth Moore played the barrister and Annette Crosbie was my elder sister, Catherine Winslow. My younger brother, the eponymous Ronnie, was excellently played by thirteen-year-old Stephen Pacey. It was a great honour to work with Rattigan and I treasure the letter he wrote to me.

My second upsy is a kiss-and-tell. Literally. In 1972, I kissed Sir Noel Coward. It was the first night of *Cowardy Custard*, a revue at the Mermaid Theatre, featuring Coward's words and music, directed by Wendy Toye and starring Pat Routledge and John Moffat. The Master (Sir Noel's affectionate nickname) attended the premiere with Wendy. After our final bow, the celebrity-packed audience chatted their way to the bar. The cast were told to form a line on the stage to be presented to Sir Noel.

The next moment, the Master himself was offering me his sun-browned hand to shake. I thought, *This is the very hand that wrote all those plays, musicals, films and songs. I can't just shake it.* So, I kissed it.

The next day, Wendy said, "He was very touched by the gesture."

After a matinee performance of *Cowardy Custard*, the sixty-one-year-old Oscar-winning actress Ginger Rogers appeared in the corridor while I was taking a cup of tea to my dressing room.

"Oh darling," she exclaimed, "I've been looking for you. I had to come backstage and say how much I loved your tap dance. I just wanted to get up and dance alongside you."

My mouth opened but words wouldn't form. "I Like America" was my only solo number in *Cowardy Custard* and I wanted to explain that when choreographing it with Wendy, I included a step Miss Rogers performs with Fred Astaire in the 1936 film *Swing Time*. It's a comedic number called "Pick Yourself Up", and here was Miss Rogers, thirty-six years later, talking to me!

As a child, I loved watching Fred and Ginger dance routines in TV re-runs of their classy RKO musicals. My mum, Alice, duly took me to tap classes at the Anne Greenwood School of Dancing in Slough High Street. Sweaty work but terrific fun. To pay for those classes, Alice scrubbed floors in local shops and at the Horlicks factory, but a few quid danced back into her purse when I was booked to perform song-and-dance numbers at local garden parties.

I couldn't tap dance on their manicured lawns so they laid something called a dance mat on the grass, made of slippery slats of polished wood. I hated it. But worse was performing in working men's clubs where the air was thick with cigarette smoke that stung my eyes.

Chatting to John Malkovich one day while filming Spielberg's 1987 *Empire of the Sun*, I told him about Ginger Rogers' backstage visit.

"That's amazing," he said. "You should've got her to dance a few steps with you. Then you could've said, 'I danced with Ginger Rogers!'"

"Yes, I know. But as she smiled at me, I couldn't think of anything to say except, 'Do you live in London?' She said, 'Oh no, darling, I live in Los Angeles, but I love coming over here to see the theatre. It's so wonderful.' You're right, John. I could've done a quick time step with Ginger Rogers. Now that would've been a swell showbiz anecdote to bore everyone to death with!"

THURSDAY 22nd April 1993

First full company rehearsal.

4 a.m.

The great day arrived! Got up. Wrote. Went for a run. Had breakfast.

8:30 a.m.

Left the house. Caught the tube at West Hampstead.

Sunset Boulevard – a tale of love, madness and murder. Ain't that the truth? On the first day, I was nearly killed.

9:40 a.m. Hammersmith Tube Station

I noticed a map on the wall near the ticket office showing the street exits. It looked like a snakes and ladders board game. Which exit should I use for Riverside Studios? I made a guess and chose the wrong one.

Emerging at street level, I faced the traffic whirlpool from hell, otherwise known as Hammersmith Roundabout – a raging torrent of cars, trucks, lorries, vans and buses. My only clue was the word Riverside. Unable to find a pedestrian crossing, I aimed for the River Thames on its opposite side, braving a ferocious torrent of vehicles but encouraged by helpful honks from furious drivers. I was born in Slough. It's a Slough thing.

And I wasn't alone. Just ahead of me was a gorgeous young

lady also risking life and limb – yet strangely not from Slough. I later discovered her to be Kate Arneil from Glasgow, a fellow ensemblical. We both jumped out of our skins as a cyclist zoomed past, bashing our arms, a bloody sight too close. A few inches closer and there really would've been a bloody sight.

I thought, *Pete, for Pete's sake. Tomorrow, find the right exit for Riverside Studios. And use it. No more dicing with death!*

10 a.m. Riverside Studios Reception Area

As Kate and I entered the lobby, a tall young man bounced up to us.

"Hello, I'm Nigel Wright, assistant stage manager. Here are your identity badges. Please try to remember to wear them at all times."

"Sure, but why? I've never had to wear one at a rehearsal before."

"It's for security; to show at the reception desk every day when you arrive. We need to stop newspaper reporters sneaking in and snooping around for gossip. Sir Andrew has suffered a lot of nasty harassment from the press."

"Really? That's shocking. Journalists have no respect for privacy. What sort of gossip, Nigel? I want to hear every filthy disgusting detail."

He smiled. "And this is your script." He handed it to me and then gasped with almost orgasmic achievement. "Oh, the relief! Thank heavens for that! I've delivered the lot of them now."

I guess he would have suffered death by a thousand cuts if a single script went AWOL.

In the canteen, I sat with the delightful Kate who told me she is on the very same pay deal as me, a basic £300 a week. Kate is twenty-one years old and the youngest member of the ensemble, fresh out of Guildford Drama College, whereas I am fifty-one, with three decades of stage, TV and film work under my belt. Doesn't that warrant an extra tenner?

Sitting in the canteen nearby, I recognised Michael Bauer. He is playing DeMille, one of the six principals in the show.

He said, "Trevor's been speaking to us for two days. He's done amazing research, all of it fascinating but it's made considerable demands on our attention spans. Not to mention our bladders."

10:30 a.m. Studio 2. A Full Company Call for Trevor's Introduction

Studio 2 is the large rehearsal room on the ground floor. The twenty-eight actors sat in a circle with Trevor Nunn and Sir Andrew Lloyd Webber. Sitting behind us in a semicircle were the production team, stage management, crew and office personnel.

Andrew spoke first, simply to introduce himself and say welcome. "I shall now hand over to our leader."

Trevor nodded and smiled as everyone chuckled.

When Andrew had left, Trevor said, "I would like to begin by asking each one of you to introduce yourselves in turn – starting with Patti."

Did this mean a two-page CV? No.

"Patti LuPone, playing Norma Desmond."

"Daphne Peña-Pardy, Swing Girl."

"Gerard Casey, ensemble."

"Kate Arneil, ensemble."

After a while, Trevor said, "People seem to be avoiding using a certain word."

And so, when it came to my turn, I said, "Hello everyone. I'm Peter Gale, and in my contract, it says I'm in the chorus." It got a small laugh.

Trev is a bewitching master of ceremonies. If the Olympic Games hosted a talking event, he would be a multiple gold medallist. Using his extensive preparatory work, he spoke for an hour and three-quarters – without referring to notes!

"Who amongst you here today was alive in 1950 when the film *Sunset Boulevard* was made?"

A silent exchange of glances. Four raised their hands: Harry Ditson, Michael Bauer, Daniel Benzali and me. I was only nine years old that year.

Trevor described the political climate of the late 1940s and 50s, McCarthyism and the shameful Hollywood studios witch hunts for "pinkos", i.e. communists. Cruel "reds under the beds" attacks were led by two rabid right-wing gossip column reporters – Hedda Hopper and Louella Parsons. The playwright Arthur Miller brilliantly savaged their self-righteous, lethal persecutions in his 1953 play *The Crucible*.

"The ensuing court proceedings," Trevor explained, "were more like vicious attacks. Some aggressive cross-examinations seriously harmed the careers of first-rate directors and actors – in certain cases even destroyed them. Several, including the director Joseph Losey, were forced to move to Britain to find work. Other victims were Paul Robeson, the black actor and singer; Leonard Bernstein, the conductor and composer; Charlie Chaplin, the actor, clown, writer, composer and film director; Lena Horne, the actress and singer, and Elia Kazan, the film director. Plus many more."

Trevor then turned to the collaboration of Billy Wilder and Charles Brackett who almost furtively wrote the script of *Sunset Boulevard*.

"Their screenplay was far from the cheery vision of Movieland celebrated in the song 'Hooray for Hollywood!'. They paint an astringent portrait of a narcissistic industry where money-grubbing bosses manufacture entertainments on conveyor belts and callously dump talent once it becomes unprofitable. Wilder and Brackett kept their project under wraps using the smokescreen title 'Can of Beans'."

Trevor then described how the female leading role was cast. "In their script, Norma Desmond is a fictitious silent screen goddess who has faded into middle-age and obscurity. This fate befell several popular Hollywood stars in real life, such as the celebrated 'It Girl', Louise Brooks, and Theda Bara, an anagram of Arab death! Wilder and Brackett approached these and several other retired silent screen idols – Pola Negri, Mae Murray and Mary Pickford, but one after another, they turned it down because of Norma Desmond's unsympathetic, domineering character. Even Mae West was approached – a daringly raunchy leading lady and scriptwriter in the early talkies. She famously boasted, 'I make sex witty and wit sexy.' After expressing strong interest in playing Norma Desmond, Mae West added, 'There's just one condition. I would, of course, have to rewrite the entire screenplay myself, according to my customary practise.' Her proposal was politely rejected. No. In the film, Norma doesn't do suggestive wisecracks and isn't given the glamorous soft-focus treatment.

"Finally," Trevor added, "Gloria Swanson accepted the role. She was fifty years old when she shot the film. In fact, one of the secrets behind Gloria Swanson's stunning performance is that she relishes Norma's darker side and consequently shines in the role. Fred MacMurray was offered the part of Joe Gillis but he was unavailable."

This elicited much guffawing from some young female company members, which slightly irked me. True, MacMurray excelled in several comedies, but only six years before *Sunset Boulevard*, he had starred opposite Barbara Stanwyck in Billy Wilder's gripping murder drama *Double Indemnity*, giving a first-rate performance in a film that was nominated for seven Oscars.

"Wilder and Brackett," Trevor continued, "Had written the leading role of Joe Gillis in *Sunset Boulevard* specifically for the handsome twenty-four-year-old Montgomery Clift. He accepted the role but, only two weeks before shooting began, Clift pulled out. It was rumoured he was living with an older woman and felt the character of Joe Gillis uncomfortably mirrored his own private life. I personally doubt that was the reason. I get the impression that for the male lead it was the kind of project that has 'do not touch' stamped all over it. Joe is an anti-hero, a weak loser who becomes the unpaid servant and live-in lover of a rich, domineering woman – a faded, silent-movie goddess. And basically, it is her film. What leading male screen actor would want that? *And* he gets killed in the first reel!

"It was offered to William Holden, aged thirty-two. He had appeared in twenty films, including the highly acclaimed film adaptation of Thornton Wilder's play *Our Town*. Holden accepted. As it turned out, *Sunset Boulevard* was showered with eight Academy Award nominations – including both Gloria Swanson's Norma Desmond and William Holden's Joe Gillis.

"The main point I wish to stress," Trevor continued, "Is that this show is based *very* firmly on the film and we should make no apology for that. Feel free to watch the movie," he suggested. "Even ask for it to be shown to you here at Riverside Studios and use it to base your work on – not to copy, necessarily. No major alterations to the story will be made, but enlargements of details will certainly be worth exploring, especially where they offer theatrical possibilities. Oddly enough, when stage plays are adapted for the screen, the usual complaint is that the camera clumsily opens up the story to make it cinematic. Our version does the opposite. It encloses it for the stage, ingeniously I think, using exterior colours and textures to contrast with the claustrophobic, oppressive interior of Norma Desmond's opulent house."

With absolutely no disrespect to Trevor, his softly muted voice carried us towards the two-hour mark and I began to wonder if we needed to know all these fascinating facts. Having been up since 4 a.m., I was fighting the dreaded drooping eyelids as I sat in my chair. Even so, I do feel terrifically excited to be a part of this brand-new, spectacular major West End theatre production.

12:15 p.m. Riverside Studios Canteen. Tea Break

The atmosphere was friendly and relaxed. We exchanged names and shared jokes and reminiscences. Our leading lady Patti LuPone, playing Norma Desmond, is delightfully outgoing and accessible. Her raucous, infectious laugh dispels any trace of the *grande dame*.

"I'm a broad," she said to me, using the self-deprecating term with a roguish smile. In fact, Patti is a great deal more than that. Aged forty-four (her birthday was yesterday), she is a hugely popular Broadway star of plays and musicals, and the winner of three Tony Awards, three Drama Desk Awards and a Laurence Olivier Award.

As we chatted, she mentioned RUG's frugality. "Last year, Andrew asked me to be in a rehearsed recital version of *Sunset* for backers at the Sydmonton Festival. No one in the cast was paid a penny." She gave me a gorgeously wicked smile. "We did it for the honour, apparently. I never dreamt RUG would offer me the lead when the show was produced in London. Seriously. I assumed Andrew would use a big British star name."

12:30 p.m. Studio 3

This is a smaller rehearsal room, one floor above Studio 2.

Trevor talked to us in here for another hour. He finished by saying, "This afternoon, you will have models of the stage sets displayed and explained to you by John Napier in Studio 2, the main rehearsal room. So, *please,*" he exhorted us, "*Don't* go in there *yet.*"

1:30 p.m.

We broke for lunch.

Chatted to Kevin Anderson, our boyishly handsome Joe Gillis, he said, "My acting career began with the Steppenwolf Company in Chicago. It was set up by John Malkovich."

"What a small world!" I replied. "I worked with John, six years ago – in Spielberg's *Empire of the Sun.* John was very friendly and funny. His wife Glenne Hedley joined him for a holiday and he hired a car and they drove Miranda Richardson and me around southern Spain for a few days. I was playing Miranda's husband in the movie. One evening, John invited Miranda and me to dinner in a restaurant in Seville, and he did a hilariously camp impersonation of Faye Dunaway playing the Hollywood star Joan Crawford in the film *Mommie Dearest.* Miranda and I hadn't seen it so we were treated to the rare sight of John Malkovich being Faye Dunaway being Joan Crawford being an adoptive mother from hell to her daughter Christina!"

Kevin said, "I didn't get to act with Malkovich in his Chicago theatre company, Steppenwolf. He'd left by the time I joined. But I was lucky to be in a play there called *Orphans* and that turned into a magic carpet! Carried me to New York, then to London with Albert Finney. Later, when David Caddick was casting *Miss Saigon* in New York, I auditioned for him and he offered it to me but instead I took *Orpheus Descending* on Broadway. However, when David Caddick became the musical supervisor on *Sunset,* I had more meetings with him and they led to this. And here I am!"

2:30 p.m. Studio 2

On a table in the middle of the room was a black box. The front of it was the proscenium arch of the Adelphi Theatre stage. Instead of a curtain, the stage was concealed by the show's wonderfully evocative front cloth. It has a gold background and a Los Angeles street sign saying, "SUNSET BLVD" with the red shadows of palm trees falling on it.

Ever since I was a child, models of stage sets have bewitched me and I had great fun making scenery for several daft little puppet theatres. When my family or neighbours bought a new pair of shoes, I begged them not to throw away their cardboard shoebox because I would turn it into a little theatre, either for hand puppets or for cut-out characters. I slid them on from the side, speaking all the voices. But today – here was the real grown-up article!

Trevor introduced John Napier to the cast. He is our production designer, the winner of international theatre and film designer awards – tall, dark and handsome, with an engagingly diffident manner.

"Having wrestled with the lack of space problem at the Adelphi," Trevor explained, "John is a much older and wearier man than he was before taking on the task. His big – *small!* – problem is the Adelphi's narrow wings space and upstage area. There's nowhere for any scenery to go – except up into the flies. So that's what he has done."

We had heard about an extraordinary set that would descend from the grid, but nothing could have prepared us for the moment when John Napier removed the proscenium arch front cloth revealing an empty stage. He then lowered, by cantilevers, the interior of Norma Desmond's house in all its opulent detail, including a magnificently baroque staircase. The real thing will weigh nine tons. To murmurs of "Wow", all of us applauded.

John Napier then showed us other set designs for *Sunset*:

The enormous golden Paramount Studios gates.

The office of Sheldrake, the Paramount Studios film producer.

The grand interior of Norma Desmond's house.

The poolside in her garden.

Joe's little guest room.

The garage for Norma's and Joe's cars.

The backlot at Paramount Studios.

The huge exterior doors of Soundstage 18 at Paramount.

Betty's office at Paramount Studios.

A film set at Paramount of a street corner with shopfronts.

The interior of Schwab's Drug Store.

John Napier's design for this set is based on photographs taken by Paramount Studios designers for the original 1950 film. Schwab's was demolished in 1988 to make way for a shopping mall and a cinema multiplex.

In its heyday, Schwab's was the favourite drinking hole for Hollywood folk to relax and network. Basically, it was a chemist shop with a counter that served coffee, ice cream and snacks. According to early Hollywood movie legend, it was here that a talent scout spotted Lana Turner working behind the counter. However, she was in fact spotted when aged sixteen by Billy Wilkerson, the founder of The Hollywood Reporter, Hollywood's first daily entertainment newspaper. Lana was skipping a school class to enjoy a Coke with friends at the nearby Top Hat Malt Shop.

John's last model set was the Soundstage 18 inside Paramount Studios. This is where DeMille is seen shooting his biblical epic film *Samson and Delilah* on the Temple of Dagon set. All John's beautiful little model stage sets were terrific and we felt privileged to be given a private preview of them.

There is something endearing about a stage designer at this vulnerable moment. The results of countless hours of extensive research and work are laid bare for the company to see and judge.

Trevor was, as ever, warmly supportive, playing the master of ceremonies while John revealed set after set to an awestruck, admiring cast.

3 p.m.

When John had safely removed his stage models, Trevor took us through a series of improvisations, all except Patti.

"Patti won't be with us," Trevor explained, "Because these exercises aren't exactly appropriate for her character."

Improvisations are basically "let's pretend" games – like charades. Often, theatre directors use improvs early on to break the ice and to help a company interact with one another. Sorry. I should say "bond". Bond is the buzzword these days. The purpose of improvs is to break down barriers of shyness to help actors work together, sometimes very intimately.

In the hands of a bad director, they can be a colossal waste of valuable time but if well-devised, they help a cast to interconnect freely and to let go. They can encourage a group of strangers to throw off their inhibitions and have fun relating to each other in imaginary situations. Well, that's the idea, anyhow. Otherwise, rehearsals can be tentative and awkwardly diplomatic.

Today, we worked on *Sunset Boulevard* with Trevor Nunn, one of the most brilliant directors in the world, and I was happy to go along with his ideas.

"I want to ask each one of you, on your own, to choose a favourite cartoon character and to demonstrate that individual's physical attributes and mannerisms in a short scenario."

My mind went blank. I could only think of Olive Oyl with her comedic, sticky-out elbows and the hilariously hapless scrapes she gets into with Popeye. Yes, she's female, but isn't that more of an imaginative stretch?

The company began to crawl, beg, threaten, chase, pounce, laugh and scowl, as if someone spiked our coffees and teas at lunch with hallucinogens.

"Now I'd like you to develop your impersonation into a thirty-second scenario." We did.

"Now, I'd like you to perform it with sounds."

Okay. So, I was Olive Oyl happily stirring a cake mixture. "La-la-la!"

The bully Bluto suddenly jumps through my window. Shocks me! Aagh!

Oh no! I drop the bowl onto the floor. Smash!

Bluto grabs me. Help!

Popeye comes to my rescue and I watch in horror as he is bounced back and forth by the bully Bluto. Boing! Boing!

A brainwave! I open a tin of spinach. Pour it down Popeye's throat. His muscles grow bigger!

Popeye grabs Bluto, twists him into knots and flings him away!

Goodbye Bluto!

"Oh Popeye, my hero!"

Trevor continued with his instructions, "Now, compress your scenario into thirty seconds."

"Now, join into couples and perform that scenario to each other, again with sounds."

"Now, both of you tell each other a story at the same time."

"This time repeat your partner's story back to them, imitating their delivery as they simultaneously repeat back your story."

Warning: this exercise can induce a splitting headache.

"Next, I want you to choose a movement of some kind and a sound – for example, a shrug and a growl, and combine the two accurately."

My partner was Nicholas Colicos, a thirty-one-year-old, six foot five tall Canadian.

Looking down at me, he exclaimed, "You're so small!" as if I was a gnat. I wouldn't call five feet eleven inches small. Was he joking?

"Now I want you to copy these movements in groups of four."

We obediently squeaked, giggled, waddled and lurched around.

"And now in groups of eight."

More improvs followed, containing sudden changes of feeling. First, we were a gathering of friends, whispering as we planned a secret party for an unsuspecting chum who was just about to arrive. And then... "Surprise–surprise! You didn't know, did you? I bet you thought we forgot!"

Then we were despairing shipwreck survivors in a lifeboat. We spotted a helicopter and tried to gain its attention.

Finally, we were a celebratory crowd arriving at a railway station – horrified to see our last train leaving.

The afternoon was exhausting but very enjoyable. I still haven't the faintest idea yet if I've a decent role in *Sunset Boulevard* but I'm determined not to let that bother me for now.

Arrived home. Felt wiped out.

The actress Tanya Franks rang and invited me to see a late-night show with her. It sounded good, a one-man revue about Cole Porter performed by Lewis Holt at the Players Theatre in Villiers Street.

I apologised to Tanya. Too bushed.

11 p.m.

Hit the sack.

FRIDAY 23rd April 1993

Happy birthday, Bill!

5 a.m.

On this day in 1564, our beloved William Shakespeare was born. We think. The problem is we've no clear evidence exactly when little wee baby Bill arrived on this planet, but he was baptised on 26th April and most christenings took place three days after the child's birth.

When Paulie and I bought our house in West Hampstead, I sowed a rosemary seed in a flowerpot and left it on a sunny window sill. It germinated and today he is a welcoming five foot tall gatekeeper. Paulie loved Shakespeare's genius with a passion and each year, in honour of Will's birthday, he pinned a sprig of rosemary to his lapel.

In "Hamlet", Ophelia says, "There's rosemary. That's for remembrance."

Happy birthday, Will!

10 a.m. Riverside Studios. Studio 2

More fun and games for the ensemble. This morning, Trevor took us through a fascinating and highly concentrated one: the mirror exercise.

Actor A stands looking at himself in an imaginary full-length mirror.

Actor B is the mirror image. B has to reflect A's stance, gestures and facial expressions as perfectly as possible.

At first, Trevor told A to demonstrate a happy greeting, and then later an angry response. Both reactions were copied exactly by B. We changed partners three times.

Afterwards, Trevor said, "I am astonished at the extraordinary ability of some of you to create almost faultless mirror images of each other, down to the exact width of space separating your fingers. Now, I want you to choose a number from one to ten and to stick with it."

I chose ten.

"Now, walk around revealing your level of personal confidence and self-esteem that the number you chose would indicate – one being the most meek and ten the boldest."

I was about to trade in my number because ten is pretty easy. However, Trevor insisted we should not.

For several minutes, we demonstrated our number's walk and physical bearing.

Trevor said, "Okay. Now, I now want you to form a queue and place yourselves in your numbered order. Number ten should head the queue here, in front of the banked seating. The end of the queue should be furthest away."

Several people marched straight to the front. I assumed they were tens and squeezed myself into third position. When the line was finally assembled, I asserted my ten status, firmly but politely, by gesturing to the two people ahead of me to move out of my way. I then stood on the first step of the banked seating.

Trevor then asked us to reveal our numbers. I was the only ten.

"Next, I want you to choose a new number."

I chose three.

"This time, imagine that you're at a party. I'd like to see how you explore the problems of associating with strangers, trying to assess their level of importance and self-esteem."

I decided that I was a next-door neighbour. "Hello. I've received an invitation to your housewarming. We've never met. Are you the newly arrived family? No? You're not? Oh well, it's good to meet you. Do you know where the host is?"

It turned out that nobody was the host. No one knew the host or had even *met* the stupid host. Hey! Some weird party, man.

Trevor stopped the exercise and told us to reveal our numbers. The person I finally happened to be talking to was also a three.

"This exercise will have a direct bearing in the opening scene at Paramount Studios in which your status is all important. For example, it will affect how you deal with someone who only wants to be with you because you could be useful to them. Or maybe you are approaching a person for what you can get out of them."

After this, Trevor gave us a specific character to improvise.

"Peter, you are an actor working at Paramount Studios, playing the role of a priest in an Old Testament epic movie. You are with three actresses playing vestal virgins. We see the four of you inventing a bit of business for the next shot, a big crowd scene. After a quick discussion, you all grab a coffee from the studio refreshments cart. Joe Gillis, a script writer that you know, walks past you on the set. You recognise him and greet him. Then, according to your character, you might or might not say hello to whoever else you happen to meet."

After this exercise, Trevor said, "That went well. I really enjoyed the impression of hyperactivity you all created. We shall now repeat this improvisation and, during it, at some unspecified point, the film's director, Cecil B. DeMille (Michael Bauer) will walk across the stage, directly through you, as you're gathered on the studio lot. Keep in mind what Peter said about being able to tell where Steven Spielberg was on a film set. He was like a source of heat to which everybody was drawn. I want the same effect to take place during this improvisation. One by one, you should realise who is walking past you. The illustrious Cecil B. DeMille! Too high status for lowly crowd artists to approach, but he attracts your attention like iron filings drawn to a magnet."

Well, Michael walked through us twice and no one as much as

turned a hair. There was barely time to notice him. It's a tricky one.

"Okay," Trevor said, "Now, I'd like you all to sit in a circle."

We collected chairs and settled down.

"Can somebody describe what the first day of working on a movie is like? The general atmosphere, what happens, who you meet, how people behave."

Kevin Anderson was very useful in this discussion because he had made films in California, though obviously not in the early 1950s. This opened a floodgate of observations which went on for longer than Trevor had anticipated.

For example, I mentioned that Americans claim they don't have a snobbish class system ("like you Brits") but they certainly have a financial hierarchy – from the poor, down on the lowest rungs of the ladder, to the moneyed and successful, up on the top. I've met people at both ends. There is serious poverty and unemployment in slum areas but high-status people and wealthy big shots occupy gated properties.

For example, the likes of Norma Desmond mix mostly with other prosperous people. In the Paramount film, Norma Desmond lives almost like a recluse in palatial luxury, only inviting into her house a few cronies from her silent movie days to play card games with her. These once famous screen stars of that time appear in the film as themselves, amongst them the Swedish born actress Anna Q. Nilsson (in 1928, she received 30,000 fan letters a month!), and also the great comedic actor/director Buster Keaton.

1:05 p.m. Lunch Break. Riverside Studios Canteen

Sat with Bernard Sharpe and Peter Rutherford. I've worked with both before. Peter is fifty-six years old, has a rugged face and a heavy build which hide a warm, often engagingly camp sense of humour. In *Sunset*, he is playing the Hollywood producer Sheldrake.

Back in 1981, Peter acted in a play I wrote called *The Unspeakable Crime of Maud Allan* at the Kingston Overground Theatre. The dialogue was taken straight from a notorious trial for "obscene libel" at London's Central Criminal Court in 1918, concerning a private production of Oscar Wilde's banned play *Salome*. Witnesses used new-minted sexual terms like "clitoris" and "orgasm" that left the jury bewildered.

Peter played a real Harley Street doctor, Dr Arthur Cooke, who seemed oddly misinformed.

At one point, the judge asked him, "What is an orgasm?"

Doctor Cooke's reply was cut from the published report as too indecent, but his following comment beggars belief.

He claimed the great actress Sarah Bernhardt, who famously played the role of Salome in Wilde's play, had to be a sadist. "Any actress performing the role must have a perverted mind. It would be a lunatic asylum for her within a week." And to top it all, he added, "It is natural for men to have orgasms but not women."

Orgasms at the Old Bailey! Whatever next? What with the catastrophic First World War still raging in Europe and female orgasms being called unnatural, the jury didn't know if they were coming or going.

"Has your play been done anywhere else?" Peter asked me.

"Yes. You won't believe this. In Moscow of all places! A friend of mine took a copy of it there when he was on business and showed it to a theatre manager. Russians love confrontational drama so *The Unspeakable Crime of Maud Allan* was translated into Russian and the Arts Council flew me over to direct it at the Sphera Theatre in Chekhov Square."

"Good gracious!" Peter exclaimed. "Do you speak Russian?"

"No, but their Russian translator did a good job, as far as I could tell. All except for one line. It puzzled the cast."

"Which line?"

"During the actual trial, Maud Allan is asked to justify naughty dialogue Princess Salome speaks in Wilde's play. She refers to the pleasures of sadism. Maud felt cornered. She explained to the judge, 'Sometimes, when you act, it's not what you say but the way that you say it.' She then added, 'Take, for example, a nursery rhyme. You could say, "Mary had a little lamb", and you could read that in a good many different ways.' This raised a few titters in the Old Bailey courtroom.

"But in Moscow, her line puzzled the actors. They said to me, 'Why did the people laugh, Peter? Who is this Mary? And why does she have a lamb?' I realised then that the Russian translator had been too literal, so I said to the Russian actors, 'Maud was quoting a very well-known English nursery rhyme about a child called Mary and her little pet lamb. You must replace it with an equivalent Russian nursery rhyme.' They conferred. 'Ah! Yes!' they exclaimed. 'We have one!' Maud's line in Russian finally ran, 'You could say, "The old lady loved her goat", and you could read that in a good many different ways.' This got a big laugh from our

Moscow audiences."

Peter Rutherford and I exchanged some anecdotes about making films. One specially amused me.

Peter said, "I played an opera singer in Zeffirelli's 1988 film, *The Young Toscanini*. It starred Elizabeth Taylor, cast as a prima donna, Nadina Bulichoff. In one scene, she was presented to the opera cast. We all stood in a row. As Elizabeth Taylor finally came face to face with me, I had to greet her with this immortal line: 'Ah, my dear, what a mistake not to have married you in Turin!' This made Elizabeth burst out screaming with laughter, causing me and everyone to join in. Elizabeth had been married eight times. Her reply to me finally came, 'If I had married you in Turin, where would we be now?' At which, we all broke up again."

I then told Peter and Bernie how lucky I was to work with Steven Spielberg on his film *Empire of the Sun*, set in a Japanese internment camp in Hong Kong during World War II. Christian Bale played the lead, a fourteen-year-old boy, Jamie, who gets separated from his parents in the chaos when the Japanese soldiers invade Shanghai. He has to share a hut with a British couple, Mr and Mrs Victor, played by Miranda Richardson and me.

"For one scene," I told Bernie and Peter, "Steven directed Christian to run into our hut to tell us some news, but he finds us sitting on our bed feeling far from well. Before we shot it, Steven whispered to us, 'Christian takes his work so seriously, which is good, but I'm trying to make him break up during a take. Next time we do it, when Christian enters, would you two suck your cheeks in and roll up your eyes like that little girl in the movie *Airplane*?' We were happy to oblige. On 'action', Christian ran into our hut, but when he clocked our silly faces, he was not amused. He just stared at us as if we were stupid. Critics widely praised Christian's performance but Steven hasn't worked with him again since."

Bernie said his favourite anecdote was about Alfred Hitchcock directing a scene in *Lifeboat* in 1944. "The female star was Tallulah Bankhead and it was well known she never wore knickers. When the crew complained to Hitch, he said, 'I don't know if that's a problem for the wardrobe department or hairdressing.'"

I said, "I've another anecdote my partner, Paulie, told me. He was in a production of *King Lear* at Stratford. Sir John Gielgud was playing Lear. One evening, Paulie was standing in the wings next to Gielgud who was about to do the king's famous mad scene on the blasted heath, in which Lear shouts at the tempest and curses his cruel daughters for throwing him out of his castle without a raincoat. He calls them unnatural hags and detested kites. Just before he went on, Gielgud shuddered. 'Oh Paul. Christmas with the Lears must have been dreadful.'"

As us oldies sat laughing over our lunch, some of the younger actors in *Sunset Boulevard* gave us puzzled looks.

"Oh dear," I said to Bernie and Peter. "They've probably never heard of John Gielgud. We're in our anecdotage."

2:20 p.m. Riverside Studios. Studio 2

This afternoon, we sat round the piano to learn "Let's Have Lunch". This is the huge opening production number of *Sunset Boulevard*. It's amazingly complicated so we began to learn each of the voice parts one section at a time.

Here's the scene's basic setup. The year is 1949. A young film script writer called Joe Gillis (played by Kevin Anderson) arrives on a sound stage at Paramount Studios where Cecil B. DeMille's epic film *Samson and Delilah* is being shot.

I recognised the main melody from the dance audition – a cool, laid-back tune with a swing jive rhythm and a jagged running bass undertow.

In the clever lyrics, two great Hollywood film makers' names are rhymed: Zukor and Cukor. Adolph Zukor emigrated to America from Hungary when he was twenty-two years old and later founded Paramount Studios, where *Sunset Boulevard* was shot. And George Cukor famously directed more than fifty films, including Greta Garbo in *Camille* in 1937 and Ingrid Bergman in *Gaslight* at MGM in 1944, for which she won an Oscar.

Trevor Nunn began to cast provisional roles. "… and Peter, I want you to be Sammy, an actor who is playing a priest in *Samson and Delilah*."

At last, I have a named role! Go Sammy!

4:30 p.m.

Andrew Lloyd Webber arrived. He sat facing us and we sang through "Let's Have Lunch" for him. He immediately started to troubleshoot. He isolated problems, analysed and solved them, altered keys, reshaped vocal lines to suit voices more comfortably, and then played around with note values, tempi and rhythms.

5:20 p.m.

Andrew said to us, "Now, for my own purposes, I'd like to tape record a bash through of 'Let's Have Lunch', faults and all, so that I can get a general impression of it. I hope nobody minds. It's only for me; not for public consumption."

No one objected.

6:15 p.m.

We broke.

Our next call is Monday. Act One at 10:30 a.m.

SATURDAY 24th April 1993

No call. Had the day off. Caught up with household stuff.

My chat yesterday with Peter Middleton and Bernard Sharpe stirred other memories of working with Steven Spielberg in Spain on his 1987 movie *Empire of the Sun*. Miranda Richardson and I played a British couple called Mr And Mrs Victor.

One day, Steven directed us in what he playfully called "my first love scene". The set was a hut in a Japanese prisoner-of-war camp for British civilians during World War II.

As the lights were being fixed, Steven said, "Peter and Miranda, could you come onto the set? I want to speak to you in private. I feel a bit embarrassed. I have two confessions and an apology to make to make."

Miranda and I followed Steven into the Victors' prison camp hut. We all sat on the bed and I wondered what on earth was coming. The first thing that happened was that the bed collapsed and we all laughed. A perfect ice-breaker. Loose blocks of wood had been propping up the bed, ready to frame the next shot.

When Steven, Miranda and I had settled down, he said, "My confession is that I've never directed an intimate kind of scene like this before. It's my first actual love scene."

I couldn't believe my ears. I thought back. No, Harrison Ford doesn't smooch leading ladies in his rollercoaster action movies. I briefly worried that he might ask us to take our clothes off but felt sure he wouldn't stray into that territory with a fourteen-year-old child as the leading character.

"Here's my first apology," he continued. "I'm sorry but this isn't going to be a traditional Hollywood love scene with tender kisses beautifully framed in Hollywood-style close-ups. Far from it. You are both malnourished and exhausted. Mr Victor simply wants to have an intimate moment with his wife. So, Peter, you discreetly begin to touch and kiss her, hoping she'll respond to your needs. Then you notice the boy, Jim, is watching you through the ragged curtain that you hung up, puzzled by what you're doing. A few seconds later, there are flashes of light through Jim's window and the boy shouts out to everyone that a bombing raid has started. That's all it is. We're shooting without a mike because there's no dialogue. I can add atmospheric sounds later, like the breeze moving the ragged curtain. Are you both happy about that?"

We said it would be fine.

"Okay. Here's the other apology. I feel a bit embarrassed. Will it be okay if I ask you and Miranda to be physically intimate like this with each other? I want to run the camera and when I say action, I'd like to get a selection of shots of you touching your wife's breast, Peter, and trying to place your lips on hers as she moves her face away slightly. It's just for editing purposes. Is that okay with you both?"

We said it would be fine. There would be no problem at all.

And so, I found myself lying on a bed with Miranda Richardson as Steven Spielberg said to me, "Okay, Peter, your right hand goes over to the left breast, Peter. Now fondle the breast, Peter. Not too roughly, Peter. That's good. Now do that again, Peter."

I had no lines to remember, I was working with a world-famous director and I was being paid a lot of money, by my standards.

"Now," Steven added, "I have to make a confession." He had our undivided attention. He gave us a twinkly grin. "Many years ago, I got involved in making a porn movie."

For two seconds, I was speechless. "What? You were… You're kidding. How on earth did that happen?"

"I was at college, working on an English course at California State University at Long Beach. Some students were shooting an amateur porn film and asked me if I would help them."

"But Steven, what did you…?" I couldn't help smiling. "Exactly *how* were you involved? Did you... perform in it?"

"No." Another playful grin. "I was the sound guy."

"I don't understand. You say you were studying English? Weren't you on a film-making course?"

"No. I didn't get the necessary high school grades for that, so,

while I was doing the English course, I kind of created my own film study programme. That's when I made a short called *Amblin*."

Amblin won awards at film festivals from Atlanta to Venice. Steven was only twenty years old.

Two days later, he greeted me with that same cheeky grin. "Last night, I looked at the rushes of the love scene we shot. What you did with Miranda was so hot, Peter!"

"Maybe you could put it back in the director's cut one day."

"Good idea. Trouble is that would make the movie longer. I don't want to lose anything but I'm already worried its running time is too long for the distributors. They like ninety-minute movies they can show three times a day to make more money."

The finished movie runs exactly two hours and thirty-four minutes.

SUNDAY 25th April 1993

The world premiere of *Empire of the Sun* was held in March 1988 at the Leicester Square Odeon in aid of the Cinema and Television Benevolent Fund.

My invitation read, "In the gracious presence of Her Majesty the Queen and His Royal Highness the Duke of Edinburgh." Dead posh.

I am proud to say one of my few lines got a good laugh. In the Victors' hut, Jim prattles to them about the benefits of eating weevils.

"They provide valuable protein," Jim points out, picking the beetles from his food and munching them. As if things weren't bad enough!

Mr Victor's response is to mutter in exasperation, "Oh, for heaven's sake."

The audience laughed sympathetically. The weevils were superbly acted by lentils.

That Christmas, I received a poignant "Seasonal Greetings" card from the Spielbergs. I still have it. On the front is a photo of Steven, his wife, the actress Amy Irving and their young son Max. I say "poignant" because two years later, Amy filed for divorce – an "amicable separation" after only four years of marriage. According to press reports, Amy received a settlement of a hundred million dollars, one of the largest in history at that time and roughly half of Steven's wealth.

MONDAY 26th April 1993

10 a.m. Riverside Studios, Studio 2

Maggie Goodwin, our associate choreographer, prepared us with a few gentle stretches and physical exercises, then our conductor David White followed with a vocal warm-up.

10:30 a.m. Act One

Before starting to work with us, Trevor gave us a brief heads-up. "We shall be rehearsing in this large studio for the next five weeks while the scenery is being built. In the sixth week, we'll move to the Adelphi Theatre and start working on the sets – if they're ready by then."

10:45 a.m.

Patti and Kevin disappeared upstairs to go through their songs in Studio 3 with our conductor David White. Trevor stayed with us as our musical supervisor David Caddick took us vocally, and very helpfully, through the words and music of the labyrinthine opening number, "Let's Have Lunch".

Trevor explained, "Everyone in the ensemble who sings a solo line in this number will also be required to play other non-singing characters. Otherwise, it will look as if only sixteen people are working at the film studio."

I have three roles. First, I'm briefly a police cop, then Sammy, a film actor working on *Samson and Delilah* at Paramount, and then I'm Jonesy, the security guard who checks Joe in at the studio's huge front gate.

David Caddick is a tall, handsome, lanky guy. I said to him, "You remind me of the young Gary Cooper." Boy, does *that* date me!

To pull everyone together musically, David sharpened our vocal delivery with fierce concentration and nervous intensity. The rhythm of "Let's Have Lunch" has an edgy drive and it's quite a challenge for us to interweave our fragmentary statements in this number. The lyrics overlap in counterpoint as bar values jump brilliantly from 3/4, to 2/4, to 4/4, to 6/4.

Trevor heard a vocal run-through of the number and said, "I now want to go upstairs to work with the principals on their solos and duets as they happen in the context of their scenes. Bob Avian, your choreographer, will take over and begin to sharpen the staging of 'Let's Have Lunch'."

Before Bob began, he confided in us. "Trevor's brief to me was, I quote, 'No actual dance', as such. What he wants is a physical style. Definition. Not an easy task. I don't want it to look campy," he pointed out, using the American version of our "camp". "I want a dynamic feeling in your activity, rather than everyone just slouching or wandering around. Move in rhythm to the music. Give it some urgency, then we'll contrast that with a few people walking *out* of rhythm – maybe slowly pushing along big props on trollies, or whatever."

Bob immediately picked up on something I've had to correct when directing a few young actors – physical economy. Without knowing it, some of them look unfocused because they move or shift about needlessly, or repeat a gesture as they speak. It communicates insecurity, uncertainty and a diffused energy. They might be exploring options but they were often simply unaware of what they were doing.

There was a lot of this when I directed *Gatsby* at the King's Head, Islington. During rehearsals, some actors delivered a line and then looked down at the floor, or changed their weight from one foot to another for no reason, or took a step closer to the person they were addressing. It blurred their image and made them look insecure. I'm not saying actors should stand stock still and obediently face the person they are addressing, but during conversations in real life (whatever that is) people often fiddle with their fingernails, noses or necks, their ears, their hair, chins, shirt collars, cuffs, bra straps or ties, or scan the sky, the horizon or the floor while searching for a word. It's fascinating, for example, to watch how people needlessly repeat a gesture or scratch themselves in every conceivable place, including a bus. The difference is that good actors, without being distracting, use these movements in an economical and telling way – perhaps unconsciously revealing anxiety, shyness, boredom, fear, delight or vulnerability. Or maybe their character is trying to cover up a thumping bare-faced lie.

The same principle applies to pauses. To use one pause at the right moment is compelling. To use several, Mr Worthing, looks like carelessness.

11:30 a.m. Tea Break

To help actors rehearse a play, stage management usually draw a map of the set on the floor with white chalk. This indicates, for example, where the doors, walls or stairs will be located. A second colour might show the positions of chairs, tables or other furniture.

On the enormous floor of Studio 2, our stage managers have used seven different coloured tapes to mark out the ground plan of our many sets, pieces of scenery and furniture: green, white, orange, red, blue, yellow and purple. Some colours outline the position of different sets on moveable pallets (rostrums). Others indicate the location of travellers (black curtains) and also the two tall towers which will contain stairs leading to an upper level for actors to enter and exit above stage level. Another coloured tape shows the position of the wings.

Most importantly, the yellow tape outlines the huge interior of Norma Desmond's house, with its imposing, baroque staircase dominating the entire stage area. It also indicates the positions of pieces of furniture. This entire set will descend from the flies as a single unit.

11:45 a.m.

We continued working with Bob Avian. *Sunset Boulevard*'s ensemble is full of highly talented young performers, each with their own individual personality.

One of them, however, Nadia Strahan, keeps pulling my attention. She is a tall, gorgeous-looking girl and a bewitching dancer but she seems unable to stand still or sit quietly. While she waits at the back of the rehearsal room to enter during a run of the opening number, Nadia sometimes breaks into dance steps completely unrelated to the show.

Bob Avian gestured to her to cut it out. "You're distracting my eye." Nadia simply needs to be more self-contained and to focus.

In an idle moment, I asked Maggie Goodwin (assistant choreographer) if she could remember who else was at my second audition when we had to dance. Maybe someone I knew.

"Sorry, no, I can't. There were so many!"

"You mean – at the dance auditions?" I asked.

"Oh yes! And that was what really separated the sheep from the goats. You'd be surprised how many actors can't even walk in rhythm, never mind learn a couple of simple steps."

1:15 p.m. Canteen

I noticed the American actor Daniel Benzali was having lunch alone. Forty-three-year-old Daniel has worked with the Royal Shakespeare Company and seven years ago, played Juan Peron in Andrew Lloyd Webber's musical *Evita* in London. He later starred in *Holiday* with Mary Steenburgen at the Old Vic. In *Sunset*, Daniel is playing Max von Mayerling, Norma's butler and the director of her silent movies.

I invited Daniel to sit at my table. A trio of egg-heads – Daniel (playing Max), Peter Rutherford (Sheldrake) and me.

The cast is now complete. Twenty-nine altogether, I think.

2:30 p.m.

Trevor began to give us wonderfully intricate moves for the first half of the ensemble's big opening number, "Let's Have Lunch". The setting is the gated entrance to Paramount Studios where the script writer Joe Gillis (Kevin) arrives and greets his colleagues and friends. The entire company is milling around, playing film stars, extras, technicians and studio staff.

Trevor is amazing to watch at work. His preparation is all embracing. He knows everyone's name, their skills and where he can deploy them. He thinks fast on his feet and moves the company around the space with a brilliant eye for shape and dynamics.

He picked up on several ideas pooled yesterday, including what I said about my partner Paul filming *The Prince and the Showgirl* with Marilyn Monroe. Sasha Millard, playing Hedy Lamarr, will be sewn into her figure-hugging dress before each shot by the wardrobe people. And he also used what I said about working with Steven Spielberg: "You could always tell where Steven was because he was like a source of heat to which everyone was drawn."

3:45 p.m. Tea Break

Peter Rutherford and I discovered that for the auditions we chose to do exactly the same speech from Neil Simon's comedy, *Plaza Suite*. We probably weren't the only ones.

4 p.m.

I have noticed something curious about the young female ensemble. Many of them wear the same kind of shoes – black army boots. Bizarre! At the end of their lovely legs, they stick hulking great big, thick-soled, lace-up boots.

Today, most young women wouldn't be seen dead wearing anything else. In my prissy fashion, I suggested to a couple of them, "It might be a good idea to rehearse in high heels because that's what you'll be wearing in the show."

I thought it could also help them to get the feel of the period. My well-meant suggestion was met with a silent, stony-faced stare. In other words, mind your own business. Oh well. When we start rehearsing on the stage, many things will have to change anyway.

I remember hearing Beryl Reid talking about choosing her characters' footwear in an interview. She was the wonderful comedic actress who starred in the play and the film *The Killing of Sister George*. She said, "When I start to find my way into a role, I always begin with the shoes. Once I get the shoes right, the rest of the person follows."

Just as the right shoes can help in rehearsals, so can a long cloak or a walking stick. But I guess each actor has their own individual method of finding their way into a character, just as each role has its own approach to the actor. Some parts have jumped at me fully formed, as if greeting me like an old friend. Others have been standoffish, and a couple have cut me dead completely. Very hurtful.

5:30 p.m.

We broke.

TUESDAY 27th April 1993

10:30 a.m. Riverside Studios, Studio 2

A sunny, windy day.

All morning, we sat on chairs as David Caddick, our musical supervisor, repeatedly hammered us through the big opening number "Let's Have Lunch" – and by the end of three hours, lunch was exactly what everyone desperately needed.

11:15 a.m.

Andrew Lloyd Webber walked into the rehearsal room just as Peter Rutherford (playing the film producer Sheldrake) delivered his line that closes the opening number: "Joe, what the fuck brings you here?" A nice welcome!

When Andrew appears in the rehearsal room, he never greets anyone, not even a general wave to the company. Also, he has a curiously haunted, hunted look about him, almost furtive.

All books were down and we sang "Let's Have Lunch" specially for Andrew. We finished. Silence. Nothing. What was his reaction? We waited for a comment. Nothing to us.

He turned to Trevor Nunn and David Caddick. In a whisper, he immediately began to diagnose problems and weaknesses.

After fifteen minutes, Andrew faced us. He turned over pages of the score and said, "The early section of the number, particularly I feel, sounds nicely complex but not clear enough to understand, not even roughly. Too muddy and muddled. And later on, it sounds a bit too dull and naked. And here! Someone's taken out the 'swing feel'. Why is that?" He pointed to the page. "Look! He's even written in, 'Not swing!' Who said he could do that? I want it swing all the way through."

Trevor and David offered reasons for this defacement to Andrew but they were found wanting. "No! I want that funky quality to be sustained."

The un-hip bars were readjusted to their former groovy glory.

Andrew then scrutinised the music in the three vestal virgins' repeated line, "This is the greatest film ever made". The virgins lost their triplets – simplified to plain crotchets.

We sang the entire sequence again and waited to hear Andrew's verdict.

Silence. He turned to Trevor. "Is it muddled enough now?"

Everyone laughed.

11:45 a.m. Canteen. Coffee Break

A couple of actors complained, "Andrew could at least have said 'well done' after we sang the number for him."

I wasn't much bothered. He's clearly single-mindedly focused on trouble-shooting, like any composer worth his salt. But I took their point. Noblesse oblige. We did our best for him and shyness or insecurity doesn't excuse a lack of human warmth and common politeness. Many actors are also shy and insecure to some degree but must learn to deal with it.

12 p.m.

We continued vocally shaping "Let's Have Lunch" with Andrew. To sing an exposed solo phrase in this bewilderingly intricate number at exactly the correct moment (especially in front of the composer!) can be a paralysing terror for any actor who might not feel confident in the singing area.

All of us are desperately counting ourselves in and pitching slippery notes. I consider myself pretty adept musically but it's no picnic for me by any means, modest as my contribution is.

1:30 p.m. Lunch

As we sat eating, the following barb came from another ensemble actor. "Andrew might have thanked us for working so hard on 'Let's Have Lunch'. It wouldn't have *cost* him anything."

The money issue is a sensitive area…

2:30 p.m. Studio 2

Bob Avian (choreographer) said, "Okay everyone. Now that Trevor's blocked this number, put your chairs aside and I'll work in physical detail on a later section. I need to shape and refined your movement."

As far as I can see, it really is already beginning to look wonderful – dazzlingly fluid. It lobs the audience's eye focus back and forth like a tennis ball in a mixed-doubles at Wimbledon.

4 p.m. Tea Break

It's gruelling to work in that stuffy studio so we went outside in the alley to bask in the brilliant sunshine, buffeted by a refreshing April wind. The cast have to choose two Equity deputies. Absolutely no offers. It's a modestly paid job and delivering actors' grievances to the management can be a poisoned chalice.

"Our problem in this show," someone explained, "Is similar to what happened on *Joseph*. Andrew's company, RUG, seized the first £75,000 of the LP record sales' profits to pay off the cost of the publicity."

As far as I could understand, this meant that Andrew, as the record company owner, was taking the sales money out of his right pocket and putting it in his left pocket.

My colleague added, "This caused a big row between Andrew and the *Joseph* company, so he'll probably try to avoid that with a special clause in our contracts for the *Sunset* recording. Whoever offers to be our Equity deputy will have to fight that sneaky clause and Andrew won't thank them for it. Our Equity deputies on *Joseph* received a very snotty-nosed letter."

Well, people don't get rich by being generous and the man is certainly rich. He has five hit musicals playing in London and heaven knows how many all over the world. In fact, Sir Andrew is reported to be one of the wealthiest composers alive and one of the most financially astute theatre producers. But massive success often attracts criticism and jealousy. Even hate.

A younger actor appealed to us eight older members. "Somebody with experience ought to be Equity deputy."

I said, "I take your point, but surely this is an opportunity for two young people who've never done it to accept the job and learn. I've done it twice."

No one volunteered. Here's their problem in a nutshell. How do we sort out the ensemble's share of the record sales? Tomorrow, at 9:45 a.m., we're having a meeting with an Equity official when the whole thing will at last be thoroughly confused. Sorry. I mean, clarified.

4:15 p.m.

We rehearsed the scene that follows the show's big opening extravaganza. The hyperactive set calms down and Jonesy, the security guard (me), allows Joe Gillis (Kevin) to enter Paramount Studios' front gate.

For this moment, I like to wear my peaked baseball cap and 1950s sunglasses, and I wipe the sweat off my neck with a handkerchief to convey the hot morning sun. Trevor commented favourably on the feeling of heat. I'm not blowing my own trumpet. I'm just saying it's rewarding to work with a director who expresses his appreciation of detail. And, yes, dear reader, I'm a sad bastard, pathetically grateful for any crumb of praise.

5:30 p.m.

We broke after doing more than an hour's work on "Let's Have Lunch" and not reaching the end of it. This is the middle of week two and our choreographer is still setting this opening number. But what a number.

Bob Avian gathered us together and made an admission. "I feel frustrated," he admitted. "My problem, as I told you, is that I can't choreograph dance, as such. That was specified in the brief Trevor gave me. What I am aiming for is an impressionistic effect which certainly seems to be working. So, thank you, everyone, for all your hard work. I feel much better about the way the whole sequence is shaping up. It's looking really good. I'm very pleased, people."

So are we.

Security is on warp speed. Leaving the front reception area today, we were each handed a typed memo: If you need to go to the lavatory, please use the toilets upstairs through Studio 3.

However, if people are rehearsing in Studio 3 you must be specially seen through the combination lock door that goes through to the public area.

That loo is the one used by mere mortals. By the time you reach it, you've probably wet yourself.

And at lunchtime, we have to: exit and re-enter the building through the front entrance by the canteen.

All this is to avoid letting in snoopers. So far not one has been spotted hanging around near the place.

This reminds me of my partner, Paul Hardwick, when he filmed *The Prince and the Showgirl* in 1957 at Pinewood Studios with Marilyn Monroe and Laurence Olivier.

"One day," Paul said, "Larry noticed a hefty gentleman always lurking about the set, so Larry asked an assistant who he was. The answer was, 'One of Marilyn's bodyguards.' So, Larry went over to the slab of muscle and said, 'Thank you but your presence here is quite unnecessary. Our security is extremely efficient.' To which the minder replied, 'You never know. Miss Monroe might be attacked by a sex-crazed carpenter.'"

WEDNESDAY 28th April 1993

9:45 a.m. Riverside Studios, Studio 2

An Equity meeting. Not a complete cast turnout. Two of our leads stayed away – Patti (Norma Desmond) and Daniel (Max). One of the most important jobs for a lead actor in a show is, unsurprisingly, to lead a company. Hence the word "lead", I guess. Their absence this morning doesn't bode well.

Today's company powwow was supervised by Hilary Strange, our West End union representative. Primarily, she came to find out if we had chosen two Equity deputies. So far, no one has volunteered. It's an infernal headache because it swallows up so much of your valuable free time – organising and chairing meetings, drafting, typing out, photocopying and distributing reports and notices, etc.

I am tempted, partly because of my friend Bronnie's advice, "You've got to be positive about this job, Peter", but also because I feel someone should look after the interests of the younger cast members.

It's a tricky one for them. As I said yesterday, they are naturally nervous about appearing like bolshy unionists. It might put them in the firing line with the management, especially the big nobs – Trevor Nunn, Andrew Lloyd Webber and his company RUG (the Really Useful Group) – and possibly sour their prospects of being re-employed by them in the future. Who wants to engage a rulebook-thumping troublemaker? Personally, I don't much care what Trevor or RUG think of me.

There are three important issues for the ensemble to discuss and agree on before negotiating with RUG:

1) Our fees for video shots of rehearsals shown in a TV documentary – and possibly used in a sold video.
2) Our fees for an original cast album record.
3) Our fees for video shots of us in News Access clips.

Equity has already approached RUG but RUG hasn't responded to Equity's offer of terms – except that they said "No" to standard rates.

Negotiating the cast album deal is extremely important to members of the ensemble because royalties of £3,000 per year (or even more) are possible – handy for anyone struggling financially. Several cast members who were in *Miss Saigon*, *Joseph* and *Aspects* have tales of woe to tell.

Hilary said, "All of you have to decide amongst yourselves as a company what kind of a royalty points deal you will accept."

She outlined our two options…

a) Both the actors and stage management could share the royalty points equally – very egalitarian and "all for one and one for all". Pretty rare, apparently.

b) Or we could split the points into a varying scale of shares.

As she spoke, I was vividly reminded of a musical I was in at the Theatre Royal Drury Lane, way back in 1971. A re-vamped revival of the old 1925 show *No No Nanette* was produced at the Theatre Royal Drury Lane in London. I was thirty years old and I played the leading young man, Tom Trainor. It didn't enjoy a long run but I sang "Tea for Two" for 277 performances without a throat mike, accompanied by a full orchestra.

Before we recorded the LP, the *Nanette* cast held a meeting and we unanimously voted to share the royalty points equally – all of us except sixty-seven-year-old Dame Anna Neagle (playing Aunt Sue). She adamantly refused even to attend the meeting.

Protecting her star status, Anna shook her head, smiling sweetly, "I've always had more points than anyone else and I can't change that. I have to have more points." And off she went.

I wanted to break the exciting news to her that there's a first time for everything. Sadly, I didn't.

The *Nanette* company faced deadlock. I was horrified.

"I really want to make this recording," I said. "It's a fantastic opportunity for me so I'll give Anna some of my points."

Tony Britten, Anna's forty-five-year-old co-star, kindly galloped to the rescue. "No, Peter. I shall relinquish some of my points to Anna. That will settle the problem and save hours of bargaining."

Dear Tony garnered a shed load of brownie points from his fellow actors – especially me. But as for those LP disc royalties, I haven't received a penny to this day.

Our leading man, Kevin Anderson (Joe Gillis), arrived at today's Equity meeting but no Patti (Norma Desmond) or Daniel (Max). As we gathered, I explained to the younger ensemble the chief issue to be discussed.

"According to our Equity contact, this points sharing could be a real problem. Our Equity contact Hilary Strange told me that if our leads want to protect their lions' share of the points – let's say it plainly, if they wish to be *greedy* – they could take out not only a sizeable lump of the royalties on the album, but they could also grab a sizeable chunk of any remaining percentage points, leaving just a small percent of a small percent for the rest of us to share amongst ourselves."

I wanted to add that if this does happen the prune tart will hit the fan and the show's two Equity deputies will be in for a bumpy ride, steering a rocky route between RUG, the ensemble and the leads. Like many essential and worthy responsibilities, the deputies' job on this production could prove to be a time-consuming, tedious pain in the backside. Yes, it would have been kind of me to mention this. But also crazy. So, I didn't.

Nick Colicos said, "We need an outside auditor's help but I strongly doubt if one would be allowed to inspect RUG's royalties share-out. I was in *Joseph*. No qualified auditor was permitted to check the royalties distributions."

Hilary said, "I assure you, RUG can be trusted. That's how business is carried out – on trust."

A loud burst of jeers and guffaws from the company greeted her naïve claim.

"It's true!" Hilary insisted. "And anyway, RUG will make the record through Polydor, so if anyone is going to get screwed by anyone, it will be there."

Another ensemblonker pointed out, "I was in *Joseph* too. Our problem was that RUG promoted the show with an expensive TV commercial. Then they charged the cost of making the commercial to the LP record sales, even though we strenuously objected."

Someone else agreed. "Yes. RUG seems to have creative accountants who work hard for RUG but not for actors employed by RUG. And here's another odd thing about *Joseph*. We couldn't find out why full royalties were paid on the sale of LPs but not on the sale of CDs. And yet CDs are far more expensive. Shouldn't the same proportion of points be shared out on CDs as on LPs?"

We seemed to be getting nowhere. As my mind wandered, I thought, *LPs are almost extinct now.* Gone with the dinosaurs.

Author's note: *How wrong I was! LPs have since made an impressive comeback. To paraphrase Mark Twain: "Reports of the death of LPs have been greatly exaggerated."*

Another interesting fact was voiced by an actor. "I was in *Aspects of Love* and we were told by Equity that sales of LP cast albums are higher abroad than in Britain."

Nick Colicos wryly added, "Yes, that's what we were told in *Joseph*. And we still didn't get our percentage."

Hilary replied, "You *did* get it but you *didn't* get it."

I'll never fathom what that exquisite piece of Equity Union logic meant because Hilary's attempt to explain was drowned out by a babble of protest, derisive laughter and chatter. But Hilary resolutely struggled to maintain her credibility in a somewhat hostile environment.

"The deal we made with Cameron Mackintosh's management on behalf of the *Miss Saigon* company for the sale of show LPs abroad was the best so far."

"It wasn't a good one," came the complaint.

"It was the best achievable so far," Hilary responded, implacably.

Nick Colicos said, "Our being videotaped during *Sunset* rehearsals should also be looked into. RUG used clips of the company rehearsing *Joseph* to beef up a video single, but the ensemble weren't paid a penny because no deal had been struck. And the points arrangement was so lousy for the *Aspects of Love* company, none of them turned up on the first day of recording the show! That forced RUG to renegotiate in their favour."

A brave crew.

By the end of our *Sunset* meeting, I was hovering on the brink of volunteering to be Equity deputy. No one else had. We clearly need somebody who will take the job seriously but try to keep a sense of humour while trudging through the tangled undergrowth of points shares, LPs and CDs percentages, TV documentary fees, cast album and news video extracts deals and royalties distributions.

"Whoever does it," Hilary suggested, "Should come to the negotiations we have with RUG and see what that's like. It's quite an eye-opener."

This certainly whetted my appetite in my old age. I've always hated seeing people or animals getting screwed over by powerful, wealthy groups of any kind.

Just as I decided to open my mouth and say, "I'll do it", Nadia Strahan, a fellow ensemblator, was cornered into accepting the job by a couple of her young chums. Nadia was in *Joseph* and she must have had a taste of the fray. I now definitely decided to volunteer. I couldn't stand back and watch the poor girl struggle with the task on her own. It will entail the following.

The tough leverage which RUG could use to blackmail us into accepting their terms is this double threat:

1) They could feature (and pay) only four or five leading members of the cast in a TV programme or a video single.
2) They could use session singers to record the whole album. For heaven's sake!

I was truly staggered at the grasping meanness of these stand-down tactics and the pusillanimous, jelly-boned weakness of our union. Where *is* Equity in this game of bluff? What are we paying our Equity fees *for?*

Someone then expressed an outright lack of faith in Hilary's skill to negotiate the best terms with RUG, to cope with the pressure of doing so and her courage to call RUG's bluff. I wasn't impressed by her reply.

"Of course, I am able to cope, because I'm determined to get the best achievable results." Which, in fact, is no answer at all. Was she conflating the problem with the finesse she needed to deal with it?

If only Hilary had said that Equity would get an ace professional lawyer's advice and a top accountant to examine the contractual terms, she would have inspired more confidence. Wake up at the back there!

10:15 a.m.

The meeting ended. My dander was up. Here we go! I had to save the entire future of human civilisation as we know it from complete annihilation. So, I went to Hilary Strange and offered to partner Nadia as co-Equity deputy.

10:25 a.m.

Hilary left and Nick Colicos gave me a word of warning, "We have little faith in what Hilary says. My colleagues in *Aspects of Love* are still fighting for their rightful share of the LP recording royalties. They might even hire a lawyer and sue Equity because

Hilary failed to notice a clause in the agreement inserted by RUG, allowing RUG to seize profits made on the record to pay for TV adverts promoting *Aspects*." Oh brother!

Nick added, "Hilary talks as if she's worried about antagonising RUG. But if we hire a lawyer, it's no skin off Hilary's nose. Equity would pay our legal fees. In other words, the acting profession would pay! Hilary herself wouldn't be financially liable."

10:30 a.m.

On with the rehearsal.

The entire morning was spent ironing out wrinkles in "Let's Have Lunch". This opening number has become my bête noire. Trevor reblocked the middle section's action to add character and motives to our moves. Bob Avian then refined and shaped the chaotic ebb and flow of us Paramount workers going about our movie business.

By the end of the morning, it was feeling really amazing but we still haven't reached the third and last part. However, Bob and Trev decided they can't finalise that yet because it's going to be altered musically.

11:30 a.m. Tea Break

I ran upstairs to use the gents by going through Studio 3, the smaller rehearsal room. It looked completely deserted. I then noticed a small person lying on a table. In a split second, I realised no one could be resting comfortably like that. I moved nearer to find out what was wrong with them.

To my horror, it was a stuffed monkey wrapped in a white knitted shawl. This is an important prop, Norma Desmond's beloved dead pet chimpanzee that she sings a sad goodbye to. It gave me quite a turn.

1 p.m.

Lunch

2 p.m.

New sheets of music arrived to insert in our clip-binders. We sat *all afternoon* relearning more revised melodies and harmonies.

4:30 p.m.

Sir Andrew arrived, listened to the changes and then – hey presto! – completely emerged from his shell! He left his chair, joined us as we sat round the piano and started to supervise refinements with on-the-spot additions. He also expressed his enthusiasm for the progress we'd made. Very gratifying to the whole company, because…

5:30 p.m.

… one hour later, we felt as if we'd been singing "Let's Have Lunch" since the dawn of creation. It felt especially exhausting because we're not all musically literate and able to sight read harmonies instantly (I'm not), particularly harmonies that are constantly being altered. After learning several variations of a phrase, it gets very tricky to re-jig your vocal melody and timing.

For example, Sir Andrew landed Richard Tate with a particularly dodgy change of a solo phrase. Richard clearly felt uncomfortable, struggling to place the re-adjusted notes in front of everyone – and with the composer conducting him! Sir Andrew then expressed dissatisfaction at the glumness of my solo line about Oscar nominations.

"It sounds dull," he said. "It needs more brilliance."

"Shall I sing it an octave above?" I suggested.

"Sorry. No."

Okay. What exactly was the problem? Me or his music? Andrew

wouldn't specify. This made me look stupid and feel incompetent.

"And more people should be saying, 'Let's have lunch', and 'You look great'. Also, I'm still not hearing the three repetitions of the name Sheldrake. Why is that?"

There was a pause.

Somebody said, "Because Nick Colicos isn't with us."

"Where is he?" Andrew asked.

"He's doing the matinee of *Joseph*," they replied.

This is a certain musical composed by Andrew himself!

"Oh, I see," Andrew replied. "In that case, it's coming *incredibly* well. All I can say is, 'be encouraged', because it really is sounding great already. And it's quite the most complex number I've ever written. So well done!"

And there was the pat on the back, at last. Thanks, Andrew.

Trevor now asked David Caddick, the musical supervisor, "Shall we get everyone on their feet and incorporate these harmonic changes into the staging of the number?"

"It's 5:40. I think they're all wiped out and we should call it a day."

Music to our ears. I thought, *Bless you, David.*

THURSDAY 29th April 1993

10:15 a.m. Riverside Studios, Studio 2

A lovely spring morning! A full company call and we started off with a vocal warm-up.

10:30 a.m. Schwab's Drug Store

Trevor painted a clear picture of this popular Hollywood showbiz hangout, mentioned in many a movie legend.

"Basically, it was a humble chemist shop, but during its 1930s to 1950s heyday, they also served coffee, ice cream, magazines, newspapers and books, and was a popular hangout for film folk to network, useful to swap professional tips and gossip." Lots of drinking and reading business for us!

"Its address was 8024 Sunset Boulevard – a twenty-two-mile long road. Schwab's Drug Store was eventually pulled down in 1983 to make way for a shopping complex and cinema. To shoot important scenes for Billy Wilder's 1950 film *Sunset Boulevard*, Paramount Studios built an exact copy of Schwab's interior on the backlot. A nice Hollywood myth claimed that a talent scout discovered the screen goddess Lana Turner in Schwab's serving at the soda fountain counter. That's only partly true. In fact, she worked at the Top Hat Cafe, also on Sunset Boulevard.

"What we are depicting in this scene," Trevor explained, "Is the egalitarian, classless society of America. There, unlike in Britain, it is widely accepted that an actor might work, for example, as a waiter or waitress to make ends meet but without losing dignity or self-esteem. In fact, it's something of a tradition for American actors to have what they call a day job while looking for film, TV or stage work. So, in Schwab's, we see all kinds of people in the moviemaking industry getting snacks and soft drinks, networking, exchanging news and gossip or just hanging out.

"The main action here shows the growing relationship between the ambitious writer Joe Gillis (Kevin) and Betty Schaefer (Meredith). Betty is a script reader working at Paramount Studios who might be able to help him, but I want to frame their deepening friendship within a busy, convincingly detailed environment."

He allocated our characters. Some of us are the same as in the opening number "Let's Have Lunch" at Paramount. Again, I am Sammy, a struggling, middle-aged actor and a friend of Joe Gillis, played by Kevin. He arrived today sporting a very becoming haircut of the period, nicely graded to a neat line along the back and the sides, but full on top. Very 1950s. I imagine his designer stubble will go too. It's a fashionable look these days but wouldn't be right for Joe; back then it usually meant that a man hadn't been home all night or was on the skids financially.

Richard Tate is playing a new character. He is Buddy, the "soda jerk" behind the bar in Schwab's, serving us coffee and soda drinks.

Trevor gave us situations to launch all the activity. We did two improvisations, inventing relationships inside the complex web of our movie community. For example, I know Buddy serving behind the bar, and I've met Artie, an assistant director (played by Gareth Snook}. I was interviewed by Myron, a B movie director (Nicolas Colicos), and Mary (Kate Arneil) is a would-be screen actress.

We began to improvise. Mary (Kate) turned to me and smiled. "Did you say you're an actor?" she asked.

"Yes, I am," I replied, "But not working right now. Waiting to hear about something."

"Who is your agent in Los Angeles?"

"Steve Marcus," I replied, snatching any old name out of my brain's lucky dip. "But I'm not happy with Steve. I'm hoping Morino Associates will take me on their books. Can I buy you a coffee?"

After a while, Trevor stopped us. He suggested, "Maybe this time Dawn will be Lana Turner. Or... maybe we won't play that as an in-joke."

We began. I was standing near Dawn and as I caught her eye, she said, "Can I help you? I work at this bookstall."

"Yes, please. I'm looking for a book. I've forgotten the title.

Paramount are planning to make a film based on it."

She replied, "That doesn't give me much to go on, sir, but I shall try to help you. Is it a comedy, or a thriller or…?"

"Excuse me. Are you an actress? I'm sure I've seen you playing a good supporting role in a movie. Could you remind me of your name?" And so on.

Trevor seemed pleased with our beehive of chatter and activity.

We then sat down. Pages of fresh recitative to open this scene were handed round.

Trevor said, "When Andrew has heard all this new sung dialogue and has finalised it to his satisfaction, I shall incorporate it into the blocking."

11:30 a.m. Tea Break. Riverside Terrace

Some of us went outside and sat on the pavement, basking in today's glorious sunshine. The weather remains sensational – a powder blue sky.

Again, we admired Andrew Lloyd Webber's long, sleek, black limousine. He had just arrived. In fact, as I was returning to the rehearsal room, I noticed him walking towards me along the narrow corridor. We haven't been personally introduced yet but as he approached, I gave him a friendly, "Good morning."

He completely ignored me and walked past without any kind of response at all.

When we sing through a number for Andrew, he has a fascinating habit. He stares ahead at nothing with a fixed, unblinking gaze, oblivious of all about him. I know this state well. Your mind enters a sound-world, blocking out your vision.

Yesterday, in the rehearsal room, he was looking fixedly at me. After tentatively smiling back at him for a few moments, I realised he wasn't actually seeing me – wasn't even in the room. He was inside his head, mentally scrutinising the music playing at that moment. And his eyes are extraordinary; the actual iris is coloured a deep blue, as if it is one large dark pupil. His stare reminds me of the disconcertingly direct, unflinching gaze of a baby.

I must introduce myself to him. Or should I? So far, I don't think he's offered a personal hello to any member of the ensemble. But I might be wrong. Maybe he has, to those who've acted in his other musicals.

11:45 a.m.

We returned to the opening number "Let's Have Lunch". Bob wanted to see what condition its final section was in and how he could complete it.

At the end of it, I re-enter from upstage as Sammy, the Hollywood film actor, playing a Babylonian priest in DeMille's movie *Samson and Delilah* and dressed in a long robe. With me are my three vestal virgins – Anita Louise Combe, Sasha Millard and Dawn Spence. Bob choreographed them to gyrate and lunge like temple dancers in a corny biblical movie. I have decided *not* to carry a sacrificial bowl or an altar cloth because it could bugger me up if Bob adds new gestures or complex business in the final moments.

Jung coined the term, "the collective unconscious". Well, while performing "Let's Have Lunch", we share "the collective headache". This entire number is a fragile house of cards – a web of broken phrases, sung solo but often overlapping another artist's phrase. We each listen for the end of someone else's line in order to deliver our following statement, which in turn becomes the cue for the next actor. If anyone falters, or comes in even a single beat too early or too late, the whole edifice cracks, teeters and falls apart – just like the massive Temple of Dagon in *Samson and*

Delilah which beefy biblical Samson sends to its crashing special effects doom.

Time and again either David Caddick (musical supervisor) or David White (conductor) shouts, "Stop!" because someone fouled up a vocal entry and tipped the recitative into incoherent chaos. I confess, during a run I came in late by one single crochet – oh, the shame! – and was responsible for nigh-on broken limbs in the ensuing disintegration.

Bob Avion (musical staging) is giving each of us eye-catching gestures to "texture the picture", as he says, and to pull the audience's focus on our individual line. They will certainly be helpful later – when we know the number backwards! But right now, they make it even more of a brainteaser – like patting your head and rubbing your stomach at the same time.

Richard Tate finds one of his phrases so devilishly tricky to place, he said to me, "I have to start it on the beat after your line ends, Peter. Could you tap me on the back exactly as you sing your last word?"

Being a nice person underneath all the filth, I said, "Yes, okay, Richard. I'll do it. We can sort the money out later."

Did I forget to tap the little chap on his back? Of course, I did. Give me a break. Talking of which…

1:30 p.m. Lunch. Canteen

Trevor always eats his lunch sitting with the leading actors and production team. Today I was delighted to consume my nosh eagerly in the company of our utterly unflagging rehearsal pianist, Leslie Hayes. For a petite, pretty person, she thumps the knickers off that joanna like a good 'un.

2:30 p.m.

The rest of the afternoon we continued to reblock and polish the end of "Let's Have Lunch", including a move downstage for the ensemble to clear the screens. These descend to hide a set change that will then happen upstage.

As we all exit (in four separate groups), Sheldrake's pallet slides on from stage right, carrying the Paramount Pictures producer Sheldrake sitting at his office desk. No big finish or applause. Sheldrake neatly dovetails into his dialogue. After endlessly repeating this and in a state of brain death…

5:40 p.m.

… we all gladly dovetailed into a bus or tube.

8:30 p.m.

Off to a party!

Walking along my little front garden path, I was closely watched by two blackbirds. They were sitting in their nest only inches away from my eyes as I passed them, having set up home in the scented honeysuckle climber that I planted years ago. They were snuggled together like a honeymoon couple. Feathered romance is definitely in the air.

Today, my friend Gay Hamilton is fifty – two years younger than me, and she never lets me forget it. Her closest friends, the actors Tom and Kara Conti, had said to Gay, "Because it's your special birthday, we'll throw a party for you here in our ballroom."

Tom and Kara live in Hampstead in a beautiful house called the Wabe. And yes, it has a ballroom. Its weird name, the Wabe, comes from Lewis Carrol's poem "The Jabberwocky":

"T'was brillig, and the slithy toves

Did gyre and gimble in the wabe."

Exactly why its original owner/architect chose the name Wabe is a mystery. As eccentric as he was rich, he designed the house in a mix of several styles – Arts and Crafts, Art Nouveau and Scottish Baronial.

Gay's friendship with the Contis began when they were all three drama students at the Royal Scottish Academy of Music and Drama in 1962.

Tom and Kara's party for Gay was very jolly and I chatted with several friends. As we sat on the veranda, the sunny sky calmed to a soft brilliance. People were avidly interested in *Sunset Boulevard* but answering the same questions about it dozens of times grows a bit tiresome. Yes, it's tough at the top. However, one of them irritated me.

"You are lucky to be in that show!" she said.

"Well, maybe, but I've worked hard to get this job. Did three acting, singing and dancing auditions for Lloyd Webber and Trevor Nunn. Had to learn a dance routine at one of them. And I'm not playing a good part in *Sunset*; only walking on and understudying, but I need the money. The tax office took all my savings when Paulie died."

"But you *are* lucky!" she insisted. "You're *working*! I can't tell you what it's like to be unemployed for months on end."

I let it go but this seriously hacked me off. Of course, I know what it's like. Soul destroying. That's why I've never waited for the phone to ring. I've written a novel, a book of poetry and devised many programmes for BBC radio. I wrote and toured a one-man play called *Hopkins!* and also a cabaret-style song and dance show called *Being Alive*. I composed a song cycle and even orchestrated it! Never just sat on my arse waiting for the phone to ring.

Talking of *Being Alive*, it featured our human upsy-downsy ride in this pome wot I rote...

"Life, however sweet, soon discloses

That sometimes you get hurt, sometimes sick.

Even if it's one long bed of roses,

You have to put up with the occasional prick."

FRIDAY 30th April 1993

10 a.m. Riverside Studios, Studio 2

A call for physical and vocal warm-ups.

Our leading young man Kevin Anderson joined us, completely clean-shaven for the first time. He looks good. Also, for the past few days he's been wearing a light jacket with generously padded shoulders; it helps to give him the 1950s feel.

We haven't seen much of Patti. She's been mainly upstairs in Studio 3, rehearsing her scenes and songs with Trev.

10:15 a.m.

We kicked off with a seated vocal check-up of the big opening company number on Paramount Studios' backlot, "Let's Have Lunch". It still sounds a bit ragged but improving.

Trev joined us to judge how it was progressing. After several runs, our conductor David White added a quiet full-stop after the last sung bar. "Terrific."

Trevor replied, "That's the word I want to hear. Terrific."

Trev left us to work upstairs again with the principals.

10:30 a.m.

We hoisted the big opening number "Let's Have Lunch" onto its sexy hind legs. Our choreographer Bob Avian added more moves.

After twenty minutes, he said, "It's beginning to look good. I'm fairly pleased with the work we did on it yesterday but I'd like to incorporate a rather important detail. I'd like to see DeMille walk straight through all the extras on the Paramount backlot as he goes to Stage 18 where he's directing *Samson and Delilah* – passing directly through the middle of the crowd."

Was this addition because Trevor picked up on the comment I made about Steven Spielberg being like a heat source in a throng of actors and film crew, all faces turning to him?

Bob looked round the cast. "And someone can say, 'Good morning, Mr DeMille.' Just in case the audience wonders who the fuck he is."

Well, during the next run, nobody said it to him. So, the following time I wished him good morning as he walked past me. It felt right because I had sung dialogue at that moment and it helped me to "pull focus", as everyone says now. Also, at that point I am playing Sammy, an actor with a role in DeMille's picture who would be keen to ingratiate himself with the great director. But no.

After two more rehearsals, Bob commented, "I don't think a supporting actor like Sammy would say good morning to DeMille. The choreographer would be working closer with the director and he'd be more likely to say it. So, Sandy, you say it."

But was he right? Even an extra, like Sammy, might very likely offer a polite hello to the great DeMille. Oh well. It's nice for Sandy, but I couldn't help feeling a sting of disappointment. All of us in the ensemble are grabbing any scrap of acting moment we can find and clinging onto it tightly.

11 a.m.

Trevor returned from upstairs and sat next to Bob. We performed "Let's Have Lunch" for him. A breathless silence ensued.

"Well done," Trevor murmured to us softly. Then he turned to Bob, fondled the back of his neck and rewarded him with a quiet,

"Bravo."

11:15 a.m. Tea Break

As we left the rehearsal room, Gerard Casey muttered, "A terrific would have been acceptable."

I had to agree with him. It's impossible for us to judge if the number's working effectively. After this long hard haul to get "Let's Have Lunch" to this stage, we just hope and pray it's looking good from the outside because it still *feels* like bloody chaos from inside.

Richard Tate amused me, "You're very busy in this scene, Peter. You're in and out like a dog at a fair."

Here's a strange thing. During our tea break, we stood outside in the alley to enjoy the warm sun, leaving behind our pretend world of film studios, crews, cameras and props in the rehearsal room.

Suddenly, someone said, "Look at that!" and pointed directly across the road. A BBC film unit's vehicles were parked on the street corner. I went over and asked what they were working on.

"It's a scene in a new BBC TV police drama series called *Between the Lines*. We're shooting in a flat on that council house estate."

Not a Hollywood DeMille epic, maybe, but filming on camera, the real thing. Nice. In fact, I've heard that *Between the Lines* is one of very few TV dramas to include a gay character, played by Siobhan Redmond, who shares a same-sex kiss with a colleague. Excellent.

As I took my coffee cup back to the refreshments table, I noticed Sir Andrew was walking towards me in the corridor. He saw me, stopped, turned away and looked behind himself for someone to talk to. No one was there. So, he continued to approach. I smiled and opened my mouth to say "Hello," but he kept his face averted, obviously not wishing to speak to me. Oh well. I was only going to propose marriage anyway.

Chatting to Peter Rutherford, I said, "I feel a bit sorry for Andrew. I tried to say 'good morning' to him but he sort of cut me dead."

"I wouldn't take that personally, Peter. It's only his guarded manner. He's shy. His whole body language is extraordinarily defensive and tight. You can see he's afraid to open himself to the company. He's never once said hello to any of the cast. Have you noticed that, even when he arrives at a rehearsal, he barely greets Trevor Nunn or Bob Avian. And yet people say he's very worried about this standoffish image he projects; and he closely monitors the way he's reported in the press."

"The trouble with such defensive behaviour," I said, "Is that it encourages the attention it's trying to avoid. I'll probably end up chasing him along corridors yelling his name as he desperately flees from me like a frantic bat into the distance."

Peter Rutherford laughed. "You're right."

Maybe Andrew wants to be outgoing and popular but just hasn't got the hang of it. Every coin has two sides and fame sometimes acts like an inhibitor, isolating a celebrity in a prison of self-protection. Who can I trust? Who is my enemy? Are people trying to use me? Will they pester me? This was shown recently in a TV interview with Michael Jackson who came over as a delightful person, struggling for air inside a solid gold straightjacket. Well, a prison is a prison, even if it's a high-security luxury mansion.

11:30 a.m.

After tea break, we sat round the piano and were handed more new pages of music for the evening scene in Schwab's Drug Store in Act One. Sir Andrew has revised some of the sung dialogue. It's a welcome relief to work on this reprise of the show's opening number "Let's Have Lunch" because it's written in a less hectic style, with phrases shared between couples who are meeting to chat over a quick coffee.

The section ends with Richard Purro singing this fascinating order on the coffee bar menu: "Six broiled dogs."

Richard said, "I was born and raised in America, worked in Seattle, Providence, Milwaukee, all over, and I cannot remember ever seeing 'broiled dogs' on any menu in the States. 'Hot dogs', yes."

This triggered a big discussion with escalating hilarity as more and more outlandish alternatives were voiced. "How about six Big Macs?"

I chipped in with, "Or six veggie burgers?"

"Doesn't rhyme and doesn't scan," Trevor joked. I think he enjoys these moments of light relief – always quick to spot irony in a situation. Trevor's great reputation for being an actor's director is founded on his humour, humanity and dazzling directorial ability. I have never known a director so wonderfully responsive with motives and images to fuel a performer's imagination and to nourish their inventiveness if they are floundering in rehearsals. He listens closely to their problem, offers a new idea, adapts it if necessary or offers alternative suggestions.

For this show, Trevor's *paramount* (get it?) insistence is that whatever anyone does or how they move should be justifiable in terms of their character. The reason for this? Sir Andrew, it seems, issued an edict. Any shade of a "musical comedy" must be avoided. This means Bob Avian can't give us actual dance steps to perform.

"Trevor's adamant instruction to me was this," Bob explained to us, "He said, 'I don't want anyone on the stage to look like a good dancer at any point.'" Then Bob smiled and added, "But with that swing-shuffle riff and the running bass motoring the first number, it's pretty difficult for me to resist the temptation."

"Here's an idea, Bob," I said. "Maybe we should all stomp about out of rhythm, like awful dancers."

Bob slid me a sideways grin of "thanks for the suggestion but no thanks". Then he said, "See you tomorrow," and left.

Sunset Boulevard is the second musical I've done in which I do not dance one single step (so far). And yet I had to learn a routine at the auditions! A tragic waste. My other non-dancing show was *Maggie* at the Adelphi Theatre in 1979. It was based on J. M. Barrie's wonderful play *What Every Woman Knows*. I was the leading man, an ambitious Scottish politician, John Shand – a fine orator but too dour to dance. Och! Nay! Hoots, mon!

Ironically, a friend of mine who came to see *Maggie* said, "You know that bit when Anna Sharkey (playing Maggie) invited you to waltz with her and you stumbled about for a few moments and then gave up? I heard a woman sitting behind me say, 'That's Peter Gale. Huh! I thought he was supposed to be able to dance.'"

I said, "You should've told her it's something called acting. She probably thinks Christopher Reeve in *Superman* actually flies about between New York skyscrapers."

Oh well, in *Sunset Boulevard* a lot of things are probably going to be changed before we open – including this other rude c word (to join "chorus"): choreography! Now here's a great idea! There is a moment in the show when a bit of *real dancing* might be appropriate. During the New Year celebrations at Artie's apartment, Artie and Betty could teach their party guests to do the cha-cha-cha round the room, a very popular dance in the 1950s. That might cheer things up.

1 p.m. Lunch

Kevin Anderson, our leading man, sat with us. He's a really easy-going, likeable guy; he joins in our vocal and physical warm-ups and has made friends with the whole company.

2 p.m. A Male Ensemble Call

We sat down and embarked on learning the words and music of "The Lady's Paying". In this number, Norma gives Joe a wardrobe makeover. She invites Manfred into her home – a high-class gentlemen's outfitter. Manfred (played by Nick Colicos) arrives with his team of male assistants (including me). He supervises us while we dress a sullenly uncooperative Joe Gillis in a completely new wardrobe, beginning with a formal evening dress suit – white tie, black tails and patent leather evening shoes.

After listening to the music, Trevor allotted solo lines and spent the afternoon blocking the number.

"At some point," Trevor said, "More space needs to be given for Norma to respond to Joe's initial, rather brutal rejection of her sartorial makeover."

David Caddick immediately offered to extend the music by a couple of bars. "With Andrew's approval, of course, but I'm sure it's possible."

"Is Andrew with us?" Trevor asked a few people sitting in the stalls. "Can we check with him?"

There was a brief pause.

"No. He's not here," someone responded.

"Where is he?" Trevor enquired.

"He's gone to France," came the murmured reply.

6:10 p.m.

By now, Trevor had vocally sketched out the shape of the complex storyline in "The Lady's Paying". This means that next week we'll be ready for Bob Avian to choreograph the action.

6:15 p.m.

As I left, yet more pages of music for this number were handed to me by Emily Fuller, one of our delightful young stage managers.

"Why do we need more copies of these dots?" I asked her. "They look identical to the ones we've already been given."

"No, they're not. The previous ones weren't stamped with the red identification code number. Andrew won't be pleased unless you destroy all pages of music that haven't been stamped."

But how on earth can they check whether we've dutifully obeyed Sir Andrew's paranoid instructions? I do, of course. Every night I shred all naughty unstamped pages of music, boil the scraps for two hours with onions, carrots, mint, marjoram, fresh garlic and basil, and then sling it out of the window.

Chapter 4

MAY 1993

SATURDAY 1st May 1993

10:30 a.m. Riverside Studios, Studio 3

A call for gentle stretches and a vocal warm-up.

10:45 a.m.

Before rehearsals begin, I repeat my plea to stage management, "Could you open one of the two dock doors for a bit of cool air?"

So far this has been disallowed by Sir Andrew for security reasons but today it was decided his rule could be relaxed. For the first time, both big doors were opened, welcoming in blessed sunshine and allowing breezy fresh air to circulate! At long last!

As we did the warm-up, I noticed Nadia Strahan hadn't arrived. She finally appeared an hour late. That's the second time this week. I am intrigued by this. Nadia wastes a lot of time and energy during rehearsals larking about, making silly jokes, breaking into distracting dance steps and then saying, "I'm just not together!"

I asked my three vestibule virgins if they've worked with Nadia before.

Anita said, "A friend of mine has, and the Useful Group think she's wonderful."

"But does she always carry on like this?"

Sasha said, "Yes. To me, it's just affectation. It's all put on."

Dawn agreed. "It grates on your nerves when you know it's only attention seeking; just done to show off."

Anita added, "Bob (our choreographer) sees right through it. He doesn't like it. But Andrew's fooled by it, and so are all the others at RUG."

Till now, both Trevor and RUG have been very accommodating to Nadia's irritating lack of focus. Okay, anyone can be late. But twice in eight days? So far, the rest of the ensemble have been on time and I sense a terrific impetus to be with the work and to do it well.

For an hour, Bob Avian polished "Let's Have Lunch", the opening number, and let's hope it's starting to shimmer and shine! He decided that several people should say, "Good morning, Mr DeMille", instead of just Sandy. It does look right. More natural.

11:45 a.m. Tea Break

And now it was *my* turn to be late! After downing a nice cuppa earlier, I desperately needed a pee. I belted to the upstairs loo, obeying the official warning: You must use the upstairs toilet when no one is rehearsing in Studio 2.

But today, both doors leading to that area were locked – even chained! So, I quickly dashed back down again, my bladder almost bursting, and – mea culpa – I went through the security pass door to use the loo in the reception area. Oh, just in time! My relief was ineffable. Nay, sublime. And no one missed me.

Riverside Studios has a fine history. Many popular British movies were filmed here. For example, *The Seventh Veil* starring

James Mason and Ann Todd. It won the Oscar for Best Screenplay in 1945. And in 1950, there was the hilarious British comedy, *The Happiest Days of Your Life*, starring the wonderful Alastair Sim and Margaret Rutherford. In that one, Joyce Grenfell plays an endearingly posh, gawky schoolteacher. Her line, "My name's Gossage. Call me sausage," was often quoted with much laughter.

12 p.m.

Bob rehearsed the ensemble scene in Schwab's Drug Store. To help us "pull focus" as we each sing a solo line, Bob gave us a gesture. This number is nowhere near as complex as "Let's Have Lunch" that opens the show. However, our problem is to remain in character but quietly animated as Joe Gillis and Betty Schaefer have a private conversation downstage and sing their duet, "Girl Meets Boy". Difficult not to distract as we keep our mimed chatter bubbling along and silently network in the background.

1:15 p.m.

Bob released us, bless his heart. Our next call: Tuesday 10 a.m.

It's been an enjoyable but tiring week for everyone. Because of the heat in the rehearsal studio, I've simplified my threads to Bermuda shorts and a sleeveless vest. However, when we run a number, it helps me if I don trousers and a shirt. This attracts mocking comments, including, "How many changes of clothes do you *have?*"

My reply is a grin and a shrug. That's me. Always quick with a snappy one-liner.

Didn't hang around for lunch.

Sitting on the tube train going home and facing the prospect of another bank holiday Monday alone, I felt myself suddenly engulfed by a stomach-clenching wave of self-pity. All my friends are with families or staying at hotels. Tears were sternly ordered back.

At Baker Street tube station, football fans burst onto the train. Burly lads with tattooed arms, bellowing and hollering incoherently. One of them sat next to me. I decided to confuse him. Using my poshest southern English voice, I asked, "Am I mistaken or is there a football match on?"

"Yeah. Wembley," he replied, staring straight ahead.

"Ah, I see. Who's playing?"

He looked terrified. "Wigan versus Widnes."

"I hope you have a very good time and enjoy the game."

"Thanks," he muttered in profile, still refusing to catch my eye, as if I was about to pounce on him and smother him with grateful kisses.

Home

I collapsed in front of a terrible Sylvester Stallone movie, a bank holiday weekend treat for the viewers. Drank half a bottle of red wine and had a good cry. Still miss Paulie who died ten years ago.

Talking of wine reminds me of an amusing friend of ours, the English stage and film actress Dulcie Gray. In my twenties, I worked with her in a Theatre Royal Windsor touring production of Pinero's comedy *Dandy Dick*. Dulcie, then in her late forties, told me that she could never drink much alcohol, let alone the vast amounts actors reputedly necked in those days. And she certainly never took drugs.

"I'm so naïve about such things," she said. "My darling husband Michael (Dennison) and I were once guests at a glamorous cocktail party in some principessa's palazzo in Rome. All very 'La Dolce Vita'. A waiter approached us carrying a huge silver tray. I was expecting a few tasty canapés but instead I was astonished to see hypodermic needles, pills, marijuana cigarettes and all sorts of drugs. My automatic response was extremely polite. 'No, thank you. I haven't eaten yet. Might spoil my appetite.'"

SUNDAY 2nd May 1993

5 a.m.

Up to write this deathless document.

7:30 a.m.

Went for a short run round the streets. Weather dismal, cold and cloudy. But of course. It's a bank holiday weekend.

10:40 a.m.

Took a train to Swanley, Kent.

12:30 to 6:00 pm. Roundel Studios

Did a voiceover promotion tape for Peter Middleton's company, Proactive Marketing. Missed lunch. Fee £180.

7:30 p.m.

Arrived home and ate out. Treated myself to an over-priced Italian meal. Still hate to eat alone in a restaurant.

Writing yesterday about leading British movie actors, like James Mason, reminds me that I have three connections with the Hollywood star Marilyn Monroe.

The first is an American film actor Ben Lyon who started Marilyn's career and also kicked off mine. As a young man, Ben starred in silent movies and even worked with Gloria Swanson (twenty years later, she played Norma Desmond in the film *Sunset Boulevard*). In 1931, Gloria and Ben co-starred in the crazy comedy *Indiscreet* but eventually Ben became a casting director at 20th Century Fox in California where he interviewed Norma Jeane Mortenson, a pretty, would-be movie actress. He gave her a screen test, a studio contract and a new name: Marilyn Monroe.

In 1951, Ben moved with his family to London to work for Fox as a talent scout.

Ben used to have his hair cut in the gents' barber shop at the Cumberland Hotel at Marble Arch. My dad worked there as a shoeshine and receptionist and he enjoyed chatting to the customers.

One day Ben Lyon said to him, "Hi Reg. How are the kids?"

"Fine, thanks, but my twelve-year-old boy's very disappointed. He failed his Eleven Plus exam so he can't go to the local Slough Grammar, like his brother. He's been sent to a secondary modern school and not happy there."

"That's the boy who learned to tap dance and likes Hollywood musicals, isn't it? Why not send him to a stage school?"

"We couldn't afford the fees."

"No problem, Reg. Try Arts Educational. They have an agent who finds acting jobs for the kids. The salaries the kids earn pay the school fees. In the morning, they do acting, singing and dance classes, and in the afternoon, they have regular school lessons."

And so, I went to Arts Educational.

That's my first Marilyn connection. Thanks to Ben Lyon, her mentor, aged twelve I starred as the Boy David in the 1953 BBC TV play *A Little Stone* – broadcast live! It was a children's teatime biblical drama about David and Goliath. To soothe King Saul's savage breast, I sang a lovely setting of "The Lord Is My Shepherd" in my childish soprano, plucking a rubber-stringed lap harp. All TV pictures were black and white back then but to give it a sheen, mine was gold-painted. My harp-plucking skills were a cheat, of course. Seated just off-camera was the great Russian harpist Maria Korchinska, playing her magnificent concert harp.

My second connection with Marilyn came only four years later when her mentor, Ben Lyon, offered my dad an extraordinary job.

"Hey, Reg, Marilyn is coming over here to make a movie with Larry Olivier at Pinewood Studios. It's called *The Prince and the Showgirl*. Would you like to be Marilyn's butler?"

When Dad came home and told us about this, we all said, "Fantastic, Dad! Say yes! You must be Marilyn Monroe's butler!"

"Of course, I can't. I've never been a butler; wouldn't know where to start. Anyway, after a few weeks she'll fly back to America and my job at the Cumberland Hotel will have gone to someone else. When the rent man knocks on our front door every Friday that money has to be waiting for him on the mantlepiece, otherwise we're all out on the street."

While Marilyn was making *The Prince and the Showgirl*, she stayed for four months at Parkside House in Englefield Green at Egham – quite near Slough where we lived! I've often wondered who her butler was.

I shall describe my third, closer connection with Marilyn tomorrow...

MONDAY 3rd May 1993 – Bank Holiday, May Day

And here it is. My partner, Paul Hardwick, acted with Marilyn in the 1957 film *The Prince and the Showgirl*. Marilyn played the chorus girl Elsie Marina and she also produced the film. Her co-star was Laurence Olivier.

Terence Rattigan based the screenplay on his original West End stage comedy called *The Sleeping Prince* produced at the Phoenix Theatre in London in 1953. Paul had played the Major Domo and it starred Laurence Olivier and his wife Vivienne Leigh. Paulie repeated his role in the film version, now more sexily retitled *The Prince and the Showgirl*. Olivier was again Charles the prince regent of Carpathia, but now Marilyn Monroe was Elsie, the American chorus girl the prince invites back to his apartment at the embassy for a bit of nookie. Larry also chose to direct the film.

Paul said to me, "I was paid two salaries. One for playing the Major Domo, and another for acting Larry's role while he directed each scene before we shot it. I knew his dialogue because I understudied him in the stage version," Paul said. "One day, Larry and Marilyn rehearsed their canoodling scene on the sofa. Then Larry said to me, 'Paul, I want you to play this scene with Marilyn now so that I can watch it through the camera lens.'

"I stretched out on the sofa, Marilyn lay on top of me and we ran through it. When Larry was happy, he said to her, 'Okay, baby, off you go to make-up and we'll shoot it. Paulie, while she's gone, I need to rehearse my dialogue. You know Marilyn's lines. This time you be Marilyn and I'll be me.'

"Larry stretched out on the sofa and I got on top of him, being Marilyn, and we kissed and cuddled our way through the scene. For those thirty minutes, I was the envy of the entire sexually active population of the world. But it wasn't a happy film to work on. Marilyn was constantly late and she had awful trouble remembering her lines."

"That's unfortunate, Paulie, but the fact is she's wonderful in the film. And so what if she was late? She was the producer. She paid everyone's overtime."

"I must admit one day Dame Sybil Thorndyke gave Larry a stern telling off for swearing at Marilyn and being angry about her lateness and constant drying."

Dame Sybil was seventy-seven years old, playing the dowager duchess of Carpathia in *The Prince and the Showgirl*. She had known Larry for years. She was famously Larry's mother Jocasta to his Oedipus in *Oedipus Rex* at the Old Vic theatre.

"Dame Sybil said, 'I've been to see the rushes, Larry, and that darling girl knows more about working in front of a camera than everybody in this studio put together. She's charming, beautiful and completely natural. You must remember she's in a foreign country, away from her own home. You should be more considerate and patient.' Larry wasn't pleased."

I said to Paul, "I agree with Dame Sybil. Marilyn has a delightfully spontaneous and vulnerable quality. She makes Olivier look wooden."

"I admit it's true. Personally, I got on very well with Marilyn and when we finished the film, she wrote me a very sweet letter."

I looked at him in stunned silence for a few seconds. I couldn't believe my ears. "Sorry, Paul. Did you say… Marilyn wrote you a letter?"

"Yes. It was very charming of her."

"But you've never mentioned this before. You mean Marilyn actually wrote you this letter? It wasn't just a typed and signed one? It was written in her own handwriting."

"Oh yes. I was quite surprised. She didn't need to."

"What was it about?"

"Just how much she'd enjoyed working with me. Thanked me for being patient with her. Apologised for her lateness and said she'd been going through a difficult time. Very sweet of her, really."

"But you've never shown me this letter, Paulie. Where is it? Can I see it, please?"

"I've no idea where it is now. I gave it away."

Another stunned silence. "You did what? You gave away a hand-written letter, to you, from Marilyn Monroe?"

"Well, I didn't think much of it at the time. I never keep letters anyway."

"I don't understand, Paulie. This wasn't just any old boring letter. Why on earth would you give it away?"

He began to get a bit testy. "Well, I hardly knew who she was in those days. I hadn't seen her films, too busy working at Stratford most of the time. Besides, Hollywood stars weren't taken seriously by English actors. She was regarded as just a glamourpuss. A sex symbol."

"Paulie, she was a lot more than that. She was a massive star and an extremely good comedienne. She was brilliant in *Gentlemen Prefer Blondes*. Okay, she never won an Oscar but she might have done if she hadn't died so early; only thirty-six. She made the world a happier place and still does to this day because her work hasn't dated. She has a unique charm, a vulnerable quality. Don't you think she was delightful in *Bus Stop*?"

"Yes, she was. Wonderful."

I smiled. "You know how much that letter would be worth now?"

"Worth?" That grabbed his attention. "You mean valuable?" Paul was from Yorkshire where folk are rumoured to have deep respect for money.

"Of course. Collectors pay high prices for a celebrity's signature – even more for one of their letters."

This hit home. "Good Lord. I didn't know that."

What astonished me was that Paulie had worked closely with countless stars including Vivienne Leigh, Laurence Olivier, John Gielgud, Edith Evans, Paul Robeson, Anthony Quayle, Sybil Thorndyke, Anthony Quinn, Peggy Ashcroft, Diana Rigg, Judi Dench, Franco Zeffirelli, Trevor Howard, Charlton Heston, etc. Did he throw away all their letters and first night "Good Luck" cards?

"So, Paulie – Marilyn's letter. Can you remember who you gave it to?"

"A little boy in Bridlington."

"You gave Marilyn's letter… to a child? Why?"

"One of our neighbour's children had Down's syndrome and was very sweet. His hobby was collecting famous people's autographs."

The moment Paulie said this, I fell in love with him all over again. During World War II, he was captured and held for two and a half years in a German prison camp. It left him with a bruised, complex view of the transience of this life. Even so I must confess I sometimes wonder where Marilyn's letter is today… and how I could get the darn thing back!

And now, through the miracle of Vista-Diary-Scope, we hurtle forwards to 1993, and, alas, more grim matters. No, not *Sunset*.

BBC Radio 4 Today

They said the IRA bomb that devastated London City two days ago caused a billion pounds worth of damage. One person was killed and forty people injured, most of them security guards, builders, maintenance staff and employees who had come into their offices to work on Saturday. The heart-breaking, cold-blooded cruelty of such an attack is unspeakable. I understand our troubled British-Irish history, but will it never end? Murderous violence achieves nothing. It only perpetuates misery, negativity, loathing, bitterness, grief and futile revenge.

As Churchill said, "Jaw-jaw is better than war-war."

TUESDAY 4th May 1993

10 a.m. Riverside Studios, Studio 2

Vocal warm-up.

10:15 a.m.

We sat and sang through the big opening company number, "Let's Have Lunch". After rehearsing it for six days, it still remains a tricky high-wire act for me. I can only do it by using my fingers to count the number of bars and notes, trusting that the person I took my first count from finished their last note exactly on cue. Even so, in the final run, I mistimed my vocal entry and began to sing a beat early. Aaagh!

10:30 a.m.

Trevor said, "I now need you to put your chairs aside and run through the whole number for me. And find, if you can, a way for each one of you to exit more in character. Don't just leave the stage on cue."

I now check my wrist watch to see how long I have before my interview at Paramount, suspected the time it's showing is wrong, put it to my ear. It has stopped! Afraid I might lose a film part, I get the hell out.

We then ran the ensemble number set in Schwab's Drug Store. It begins as a lively reprise of "Let's Have Lunch" and gently softens into a muted background for ensuing intimate duologue between Joe and Betty (played by Kevin Anderson and Meredith Braun), followed by their duet, "Girl Meets Boy".

"I am slightly foxed," Trevor confessed, "As to how to treat this problem of damping down the background tone of the coffee shop to a more mellow feeling, short of making Schwab's one of those places where the happy hour is signalled by the lights being dimmed to create an intimate atmosphere."

Someone quietly whispered a suggestion to me. "It could be closing time and we could all just leave." Not an altogether serious proposal. Certainly not one to share with Trevor.

The life blood of (that dreadful c word) the chorus is humour. What else keeps you sane? For example:

"Okay. Everyone spread out and form a group."

"Let's go from the cuntrapontal section."

A: "Ouch. You trod on my toe!"

B: "You can always teach."

Sandy Strallen gave me this nice one: "Things are getting ugly. I'm staying."

11 a.m.

We began rehearsing a new number: "This Time Next Year". It is set in two places simultaneously – one is above and the other below.

Down at stage level is Artie's apartment. Artie (played by Gareth Snook) is an assistant movie director, throwing a jolly New Year's Eve party for friends and work colleagues. A lot of animated chit-chat and action. Fractured phrases are sung and flung back and forth, building up to a rowdy, celebratory climax, all of us merry-making our socks off.

Meanwhile, in stark contrast, hovering just a few feet above us is the splendid living room of Norma Desmond's huge house. It weighs seven tons!   Norma is completely alone, pacing back and forth, forsaken by her live-in lover, Joe Gillis, and tortured with jealousy.

We sat around the piano. Trevor distributed solo lines sung by the ensemble at Artie's party. Then we bashed through the dots to hear how they sounded. The final choral section is tricky and sits uncomfortably high for the tenors. For the first time, I notice that the name David Cullen is printed at the bottom of every page in the score.

"Who is David Cullen?" I whispered to someone.

"Sir Andrew's co-orchestrator," I was told.

Having broken the seal on the music, we *improvised!*

Trevor outlined the action and away we went, enjoying a fun party in Artie's flat for all we were worth. The door opens and Joe Gillis (Kevin) appears. He is presented with the wonderful world of living, breathing, spontaneous young people who welcome him back to full-bloodied humanity.

Well, mostly young.

I got a few laughs from the stage management with some improvised wisecracks. I asked Peter Rutherford, "What is your New Year's resolution?"

"To be in an Esther Williams movie," Peter joked.

I said, "I thought you were Esther Williams."

"Next year, I want a juicy part," said Sasha.

"There's nothing like a juicy part!" I cried. Ooh. Very saucy.

And playing DeMille in the party skit, I shout loudly, "Ready when you are, everyone!"

That's a misquote from a well-known old joke about DeMille directing an elaborately spectacular battle scene involving hundreds of extras. It is so complicated they can only shoot it in one take with four cameras rolling. The whole sequence goes brilliantly.

At the end of it, DeMille yells, "Cut!"

To his horror, three of the four cameras had technical problems.

"Sorry, no good." But all is not lost.

DeMille yells to the fourth cameraman, perched at the top of a hill. "Did the shot look okay?"

The man waves back to him and shouts, "Ready when you are, Mr DeMille!"

And later, during Artie's party, I announce, "Coming soon to a screen near you! A truly medieval spectacle! A thousand chariots! Elephants! Camels! Chipmunks!"

And when I am asked what I want next year, I punch the air and shout, "To be a star!" Someone had to say it.

11:30 a.m. Tea Break. Canteen

After a cloudy bank holiday, the gloriously sunny skies are clear blue – in strict accordance with Sod's Law.

11:45 a.m. Studio 2

Andrew Lloyd Webber joined us. We all sat down and he asked us to sing "This Time Next Year" for him. And so, we did.

Afterwards, he appeared oddly agitated.

"Why has it been changed?" He sounded surprised. "These chords are totally inaccurate."

We exchanged worried glances with each other like suspects in a creepy murder whodunnit. Who was the mysterious culprit?

"And the chorus harmonies must all be re-adjusted to what they were. It sounds terrible." His indignation puzzled me. Didn't he write them?

Andrew thumped out phrases and harmonies on the piano. "At that point, it's supposed to be G minor over A."

This wicked crime involves three suspects, all three called David. Did David *Cullen* commit the offence, slightly embarrassing for us to witness? It can't have been him. As the co-orchestrator, he must have collaborated in fine detail with Sir Andrew on the score and we are rehearsing with a direct piano transcription of their work.

Suspect number two is David *Caddick*, the musical supervisor. Is he the culprit? But surely Mr Caddick also worked closely alongside Andrew.

The third suspect is David *White*, our conductor and musical director. It's unlikely that his job would also include writing the piano transcription.

Andrew Lloyd Webber was red-faced – obviously infuriated. I must confess our singing hadn't done full vocal justice to the vocal arrangement (whoever wrote it) because we aren't faultless sight-readers.

Trevor tried to restore things to a more good-humoured even keel with something akin to the old joke, "Apart from that, Mrs Lincoln, how did you enjoy the play?"

This helped to calm Andrew down. At least he seemed fairly happy with the way Trevor has re-allocated some lines amongst the ensemble but said he still felt that more music is needed here, less there. He then added, "And the DeMille parody section should be cut." That's my comedy skit material.

"You don't mean lose it altogether?" Trevor asked, a bit anxiously.

I held my breath, awaiting Andrew's reply.

"No. But it needs to be trimmed," Andrew replied. "There's too much sand dance music."

I breathed again.

1:30 p.m. Canteen

I had lunch with Alisa Endsley, an extremely pretty American actress. Alisa, like me, is having a busy time in the ensemble playing several supporting roles. She is also the second understudy to Norma Desmond.

"I have seven wigs," she confided. "And I think I get the record for the most number of changes."

During these rehearsals, we are being individually released to have costume and wig fittings with Anthony Powell in one of Riverside Studios' offices.

Peter Rutherford, fresh from a fitting, joined us at our table and described the colour of the suit he had just been measured for. "It's going to be something called greyge, according to the costumiers."

"You mean a mix of grey and beige?"

"Yes. Otherwise known as elephant's breath."

2:30 p.m.

After lunch, we worked with Trevor on blocking Artie's party, so that Bob Avian could later refine it in more detail.

3:45 p.m.

We ended the afternoon with the three vestibule virgins having a jokey bump-and-grind dance choreographed for them during the skit they perform at Artie's apartment. It parodies their slinky Philistine routine in the film *Samson and Delilah*. Then Adam and Sandy worked on a comical Ancient Egyptian sand dance and a jokey "Samson Kills the Lion" sketch.

6 p.m.

We headed home, walking our weary ways to Hammersmith tube station. I said, "Was anyone else surprised by Andrew's grumpy reaction to the wrong chords in our vocal run of 'This Time Next Year'?"

"The reason for that petulant outburst was that he gets someone else to write down the piano arrangement, so it's not always exactly what he ordered."

This really baffles me. The man is obviously a gifted musician. Doesn't Andrew write down his own music on paper accurately and then give it to the arrangers to copy exactly? I don't mean this disparagingly. Many highly successful and talented composers, like the great Irving Berlin, our own Lionel Bart and even Noel Coward weren't very strong in the scoring department, but they were able to indicate exactly the melodic line, the treatment and harmonies they wanted.

And as for being charming, well, Richard Rodgers (*Carousel*) never won popularity prizes, and Arthur Sullivan (*HMS Pinafore*) could be notoriously cruel when it pleased him. Here's a quote from a book by H. Sullivan & N. Flowers: "Being painfully shy doesn't excuse Sir Arthur for being so insensitive to other people's feelings."

Andrew is clearly working under great stress. I just hope that, once he sorts out the ensemble numbers to his greater satisfaction, he might be able to relax with us a little more. Maybe even say a simple "Hello" to me in passing. But maybe not.

WEDNESDAY 5th May 1993

10 a.m. Riverside Studios. Studio 2

A full company physical and vocal warm-up with David Caddick.

Daniel Benzali never joins in. Nor does Patti, who has her own idiosyncratic exercise – a penetrating little musical phrase she delivers on the move, contributing to her bird-like persona. It's a rolled r sung up and down a fifth, very fast and brightly, often heralding her arrival in the rehearsal room, like an exotic parrot winging its way through a jungle treetop canopy.

These three tongue twister warm-ups are new to me…

"Wicked cricket critic." Repeat faster and faster.

"I rattled my bottles in Rollockson's yard."

"Equity deputy, Equity deputy."

We then sang through "Let's Have Lunch", naturally, but David, our musical supervisor, stressed the need for constant vigilance to keep it vocally fine-tuned. We sang the entire number five times until early morning errors were eliminated.

"You see, everyone?" David commented. "It takes that amount of work to polish it up to performance level."

We sang it again several more times, walking round in circles clockwise and then (to stop ourselves getting dizzy) anti-clockwise. After that, we performed the number using all the complex moves Bob Avion added yesterday. Inevitable mistakes led to traffic jams that fouled up the whole thing again. Will it ever come together, we wondered? What didn't help was a couple of actors being absent for fittings.

We then ran the Schwab's Drug Store scene. That didn't present as many problems, but Andrew wasn't entirely happy with the way it sounded.

"Modifications will arrive from Andrew at a later date," we were told.

When I arrived this morning, I noticed the addition of new props in the rehearsal room – huge lights on wheels, the kind used in early motion picture studios known as arc lamps. I think today film crews call them brutes.

They featured in the next scene we rehearsed, when Norma Desmond visits Paramount Studios to meet DeMille and discuss him directing her *Salome* script. We don't have substitute props yet to act as a movie camera or a sound boom. The boom is a long extendable metal rod with a microphone hanging from its far end. However, Gerard Casey (playing the sound operator) has cleverly improvised a boom by linking two scenery braces together and attaching a white plastic cup to the end to represent the microphone. This comes in very handy for a significant moment later when Norma Desmond, once a silent screen goddess, reacts with distaste to the mike when it hangs too near her face, as if it's giving off a nasty smell.

Trevor described the ensemble's participation in this scene. "Try to imagine what it would be like if Sir Laurence Olivier visited us here today and walked into this rehearsal room. Whether you are familiar with his work or only know of him through his famous name and publicity photographs, the impact would be infectious and overpowering."

Patti then said, "Could I ask you a very important question about the number I sing in this scene, Trevor? I need to know – is it an interior monologue or is it delivered as a speech to everyone in the studio? I feel 'As If We Never Said Goodbye' is very private in feeling."

"Oh no. It is definitely addressed to everyone around you, I'm sure of that. Maybe it's a kind of combination of the two, but it's definitely a disclosure you openly share with everyone around you."

Their exchange fascinated us because we hadn't yet heard this song, although it's one of two knock 'em dead hit numbers in *Sunset* already recorded by Barbra Streisand.

To help Patti perform it, Trevor then described in detail Norma's feelings about baring her soul in front of DeMille's film cast and crew. "She *is* nervous and she admits it. She's returning to a world with which she was once very familiar, but it has suffered a sea change. In fact, there's a wonderful moment in the film which we must try to preserve, when she's sitting in the studio. By chance, the microphone slides across her field of vision. She immediately reacts with contempt and swats it away as if it was a huge insect. 'Get that hideous invention out of my sight!'"

The moment has come for Gerard's white plastic cup tied to the end of wooden braces to perform a brief but significant role – the small but deadly enemy that has destroyed Norma's glorious silent screen career.

"No, Norma is not afraid to admit her nervousness about returning to Paramount Studios because she has been recognised and accepted so warmly there by everyone on the platform of her previous cinematic achievements."

Trevor outlined the staging of this very complex scene, and began to allocate the parts we play and the individual lines we speak or sing. For example, Heather, DeMille's secretary (played by Daphne Peña Pardy) has several lines of dialogue at the end of the sequence which Trevor decided would be more appropriate spoken by Mr Sheldrake, the Paramount producer.

Trevor then added, "And, to set anyone's mind at rest, this is in no way a comment on Mr Sheldrake's private life," which got a laugh from the cast, not least from Peter Rutherford, playing Sheldrake.

The irresistible image of the mighty movie mogul, "Heather" Sheldrake (as Peter's character was immediately nicknamed), seated in his Paramount office wearing a lilac summer dress and toying with a string of pearls, was too good to skim over.

1 p.m. Canteen

Over lunch, I asked two of the American actors in our cast, Adam Matalon and Richard Purro, if their male colleagues in the States enjoyed the same "camp", uninhibited sense of humour as we Brits, knowing full well what the answer would be.

"Definitely not!"

American actors are widely thought here to take themselves deeply seriously. It's all to do with preserving and protecting their image. Making a camp joke would be highly corrosive to masculine dignity, if that's your professional persona. "Persona" was originally a Latin word that meant a mask, or a character in a play. Our less solemn approach may account for the fact that American actors are better than British actors in certain respects. A too keen sense of the ridiculous can be a bit of a hindrance during improvisation exercises. For example, our TV show *Spitting Image* has satirised Dustin Hoffman doing a method acting exercise in a drama class not only impersonating but also actually *becoming* a green cos lettuce.

2 p.m. Riverside Studios, Studio 2

After lunch, we put together some individually rehearsed sections of the scene at Paramount when Norma Desmond returns to her old studio.

When it came to the moment for Patti to sing her main number, "As If We Never Said Goodbye", she was unable to do so because of the emotion generated by the warm welcome Norma had received from her fellow actors and crew at Paramount. Patti's eyes flooded with tears and she choked on the words of the song.

Before we embarked on a full run of the whole scene, Trevor asked Patti to push her way through the song if she could. It proved quite an uplifting moment for us when Patti sang this song in its context and improvised a few moves because today is the first time we've heard any of the principals perform one of their solos. And somehow this particular one is central to all the work we've been doing. In a sense, it is why all of us are here, on more than just one level. The song generates the whole plot, describing Norma's joy at visiting her beloved Paramount Studios, the very heart of her past glories. Plus, it also seems to be uniting all of us – both as characters in her story and as actors here today in this rehearsal room.

Patti clearly had to struggle not to break down during the song, which made it all the more moving to hear Norma sing that she is "trembling", that she feels as if she "had come home at last", that the bad old days of being alone are "all in the past".

After the number ended, there was a hushed silence for several seconds in the rehearsal room, followed by a heartfelt round of applause from everyone.

Patti later confessed, "I felt really nervous about performing that song in front of you all."

We re-assured her that her anxiety didn't show and was completely unnecessary. In fact, her vulnerable, slightly hesitant delivery of the song impacted on us emotionally all the more.

Trevor said, "In the actual performance, I want you to wait a respectful moment after the final words of her song and then to respond with gentle applause as you cluster round and make a respectful fuss of her."

I strongly suspect that any subtle, hesitant response from us will be lost in the audience's immediate applause, but, of course, our delayed reaction will only add to the general acclaim. Some might call this moment schmaltzy but I am very pleased Trevor hasn't short-changed it. More than anything else in the world, Norma Desmond wants at this point to be welcomed back into the caring, nourishing family of "movie folk", and to taste again the old magical mixture of success, loving friendship and glory. It is Norma's dream but sadly this one brief visit to her beloved Paramount Studios is the closest she will come to realising that dream.

The spontaneous display of admiration for Norma by her professional colleagues feels absolutely authentic to me. I witnessed a real-life example of it in 1981 when my chum, the actress Julia McKenzie, was the subject of an episode of *This Is Your Life* on Thames Television. I was invited to guest on the programme having worked with Jules in two hit shows in London at the Mermaid Theatre: *Cowardy Custard* and *Cole*.

The award-winning film actress Lee Remick was the special star guest at the end of the programme. Julia had appeared with Lee in the TV series *Ike: The War Years*.

After the transmission, Lee was surrounded and fussed over by the other guest actors, expressing their heartfelt admiration and affection – exactly like Norma returning to Paramount in *Sunset*.

As we rehearsed *This Is Your Life*, I remember seeing Laurel Ford, who had worked with Julia in *Cowardy Custard*, sitting next to Lee Remick; the two chatted away for quite a while. Lee was clearly as approachable and friendly as she was talented and beautiful.

In 1974, my partner Paulie had appeared with Lee in *Jennie*, the TV series based on the life of Jennie Churchill, Winston Churchill's mother. Paul said, "Lee was a joy to work with."

The performance won Lee a BAFTA, an Emmy and a Golden Globe award.

THURSDAY 6th May 1993

No morning rehearsal

The men were given this morning off. Bob Avian worked with the girls on Patti's complicated scene with Norma and her beauticians.

I made phone calls, paid bills, looked at the score, went for a run round the streets, did a work-out and then spent an hour sunbathing nude. This caused much hilarity amongst the lads at work when I described what happened…

Be patient. First, the boring stuff.

Received a brusque letter this morning. A few weeks ago, I was invited to appear in a charity show at the Lyric Theatre on 16th May in aid of the London Lighthouse Aids Hospice. Would I perform a Noel Coward number? I wrote back saying I'd be delighted to – on just one condition. I would like to see a statement showing the box-office takings, the names of those paid and the amount they received in expenses and salaries.

This morning comes a curt negative reply. "The musicians and arrangers will receive fees for their work. We assume, in principle, you would disagree with this."

His attitude seriously pissed me off. When I was nineteen years old, I received a Slough Council grant to go to drama college, so that year I supported my first charity, Amnesty International; I am still helping them. Over the years, I have added thirty other charities on my direct debits list. Also, since 1974, I have organised annual Christmas fundraising charity shows called *Bah! Humbug!* and *A Bob of Cherries*. The first was at St. Paul's Cathedral, then at St. Martin-in-the-Field Church and the last at St. George Church, Hanover Square, all in aid of the vicars' Christmas Appeal.

Every penny the public put in the collection box went to those in need or financial distress. I charged no fee and the churches allowed us free use of their premises. The stars received no salary or expenses whatsoever, not even bus fares. Over the years, these artists included my partner Paul Hardwick, Diana Rigg, Judi Dench, Michael Williams, Dorothy Tutin, Janet Suzman, Derek Godfrey, Bernard Miles (who created the Mermaid Theatre), Derek Jacobi, Julia McKenzie, Alec McCowen, Paul Chapman, Penelope Keith, Gwen Taylor, Clive Swift, Gary Raymond and Paul Eddington. The first pianist was John Burrows and later Geoffrey Bowyer.

The solo singers included Marilyn Hill-Smith, Kenneth Nelson, Clifton Todd, Jenny Wrenn and Susan Bullock.

I've discussed fundraising with someone who works for a big charity.

"You're right, Peter. When we put on fundraising events, we don't always get much profit from tickets sales after expenses are paid. Some charities fly Hollywood stars over first-class and put them up at top hotels. But big names generate publicity and that raises a charity's profile which increases public support for us."

Having no back yard, this morning I stretched out on my tummy in my little front garden, my bare botty soaking up the rays. I heard the voices of two ladies chatting as they were walking along the pavement.

One said, "This is such a pretty front garden. These flower boxes are always a pleasure to see."

They stopped as her friend replied, "Yes, I agree, they are. I often lean over the wall to admire the clematis and honeysuckle on the pergola. And look at that lovely… Oh!"

The rest was silence.

1 p.m. Gate Restaurant

I arrived early and ate at the Gate. It's just a few yards away from Riverside Studios, run by the Christian Society and it offers a veggie menu. I felt I should explain to the waiter that I'm not a practising Christian but a pleasant enough bloke. It seemed to put his mind at rest.

As I was eating, I heard a man at a nearby table quote a proverb, new to me: "By walking it will be cured."

I said to him, "I like that; it's very good. Old sayings fascinate me. Never heard that one before."

"A very old Latin maxim. A Roman emperor probably invented it to justify sending his troops on long, gruelling marches."

"I'm an actor. We talk about doctor theatre in the same way. You may be feeling rotten but if you can get to the theatre and go onstage, you often forget what's ailing you because the adrenalin kicks in and helps you recover. And that's like another motto: 'Energy creates energy'. Dancers are famous for working through injuries and pain because it sometimes helps a muscle to heal more quickly than by resting it. But only sometimes. It's a question of balance and not pushing the injury too hard too soon."

"Very good," he said. "Here's a gardener's saying for you. 'You can't tame nature. You can only hold it at bay.'"

I smiled. "Ah, yes. A wealth of wisdom there."

2:30 p.m. Riverside Studios, Studio 3

We sat round the piano and worked on Act One's closing number, "This Time Next Year", learning Andrew's new harmonies. We play a crowd of happy chums enjoying the New Year's Eve party at Artie Green's apartment, and we wish each other good luck in the year ahead.

Bob Avian, our American choreographer, said, "And now I'd like you to put your chairs to the side and perform the whole scene for me so I can see what kind of state it's in."

We went for it and improvised the living daylights out of our bustling interactions. I play Sammy, a movie actor who is a friend of the host, Artie (played by Gareth Snook), an assistant film director. During this party, the writer Joe Gillis (Kevin) meets and is attracted to Betty Schaefer (Meredith), a script editor at Paramount Studios. Sammy briefly cuts into their conversation when he presents a jokey cabaret show to entertain his exuberant film studio colleagues, featuring skits that make fun of DeMille and his grandiose epic Old Testament movie. It includes a comical

Egyptian sand dance from the lads, and three vestal virgins (Sasha, Anita and Dawn) perform a sexy bump-and-grind routine. The scene finishes with a full-throated chorus from everyone at the party, hoping that our dreams of success at Hollywood will be granted by "This Time Next Year"! End of Act One. Interval.

4 p.m.

Don Black (lyricist) arrived to watch us run this scene again and, wouldn't you know? I completely loused up my lines during the party cabaret.

The final chorus still feels uncomfortably high for the tenors but we bashed it out countless times as Bob choreographed more detailed business for us. "People, try to keep your action as consistent as possible so that I can reject or improve or simply preserve what you are doing."

5 p.m. Tea Break

We went outside and stood in the alley to enjoy the sun. Sir Andrew arrived in his midnight blue Mercedes Benz. It looks like a vast, glossy, blue-black olive.

As he walked into Riverside's entrance, I faced him directly, smiled and determinedly said, "Good afternoon."

Andrew looked at me with a startled half-smile and murmured "Hello" (I think) without pausing in his tracks for one second.

Well, I finally managed to exchange a greeting of sorts. I shall limit our wedding guest list to only six or seven hundred.

5:20 p.m.

We performed the rowdy New Year's Eve party again for Andrew and his musical supervisor David Caddick. They particularly wanted to check out how the song "This Time Next Year" sounds in context. At the end we awaited in silence for Andrew's verdict.

Pause…

"I've finally worked out what this number most urgently needs," Andrew announced. "The final chorus must be put up into a higher key."

Immediate murmurs of shock-horror from the company.

Dear David Caddick discreetly appealed on our behalf. "Yes, I see exactly what you mean, Andrew," he began diplomatically. "The problem is that everyone, the tenors especially, are already blasting away at their upper limit."

Andrew immediately trod on David's point, as if it was a petty detail. "That may be but it's got to happen."

David was faced with an uncomfortable deadlock, but he very politely and patiently struggled to accommodate the two conflicting positions.

"I know exactly what you're saying, Andrew. Let me see. What we could possibly do, perhaps, is rescore the harmonies and—"

"It *must* happen," Andrew insisted, "Because one also wants to hear the sopranos clearly in their upper register at the end of that section."

"Yes, of course, Andrew. It's just that the tenors are having to hold the A flats and A naturals over a sustained number of bars. We'll simply have to restructure the whole harmony. But yes, it can be done. Maybe, if we slightly—"

"It *must* be done!" Andrew firmly interrupted, "Because it's quite obvious *that's* what's needed! What else? Various things. The DeMille cabaret section is clearly too low, and Artie's solo about buying the rambling old house with the apple tree and a swing for the kid, that needs to be put in double time. It's got a leisurely, romantic feeling that's wrong in that context. It holds everything up." He then chose several vocal sequences and began to examine them, one after another.

As David Caddick played the relevant bar sections on the piano, Andrew asked him to modulate them into various keys to hear how they would affect the final chorus of "This Time Next Year". David instantly played each bar for Andrew to consider.

"Now, play it in F sharp... Now, modulate into G... Now, modulate up to G sharp..." Andrew finally decided. "G natural. That sounds all right. Yes, G natural. That'll be the one."

Having fixing that, Andrew asked the cast to stand up and perform the whole New Year's Eve scene again, including the final chorus. Afterwards, we awaited Andrew's verdict...

"Well done, group."

Andrew's Now-Do-This, Now-Do-That treatment makes us feel like brainless shop window dummies being shoved around.

An actor muttered to me, "Sir Andrew ought to work more closely with the musical director and the orchestrator. This basic problem of the right key could've been sorted out much earlier."

Bob Avian expressed his approval of my corny shouted interjections in the cabaret, mimicking the director Cecil B. DeMille: "Lights! Camera! Action!", "A truly medieval spectacle!", "Cut! Print! Terrific!" and, "The – End!"

He said, "Very good, Peter, but I must warn you that it's not for me to say if our writers will be so keen on them. That's their department, not mine."

He then expressed his doubts about the way he choreographed the sand dance in our cabaret skit.

I said to Bob, "I've an idea Andrew is thinking of an old English music-hall act called 'Wilson, Keppel and Betty'. They performed a silly, comical dance routine looking like Ancient Egyptian hieroglyph figures wearing loin cloths and head dresses made of tea towels; and they did lots of rude pelvic thrusts."

"That's interesting. You see, in the States," Bob explained, "A sand dance is something totally different. More a soft shoe shuffle. I think I'm going to have to change that."

Looking around the room, I noticed Andrew had vanished again. I said to Simon Hayden, "Andrew is constantly disappearing. Do you know where he goes?"

"He's absent all the time because he has to attend important meetings – six today, apparently. Some are only a few hundred yards apart, but, because he's so well-known, walking through London streets is not an option for Sir Andrew."

Poor soul. Did I say poor? Andrew is mega-rich, amongst the top few British multimillionaires. He has five hit musicals currently running in London, and Lord knows how many productions playing in theatres around the world. What a weirdly narrow view of life the wealthy have, softly cocooned inside posh homes, cars, restaurants, hotels, private jets and helicopters. Maybe Andrew should write a musical called King Midas. He knows better than anyone how it feels to have the golden touch.

This reminds me of a poem I wrote…

"King Midas was given the golden touch

But didn't enjoy it much, as such.

'You can't feed seed to a solid gold parrot,

Or munch an eighteen-carat carrot.'"

6:15 p.m.

We broke.

FRIDAY 7th May 1993

10 a.m. Riverside Studios, Studio 2

A physical warm-up call.

I love beginning the day with the stretches we're given by Maggie Goodwin (assistant choreographer). I change in the gents and wear my blue singlet and pink and yellow candy-striped Bermuda shorts – bought in my local Pound Shop in Kilburn. I really enjoy the freedom of practise gear, especially doing the shoulder work. Far cooler and more comfortable. But it has earned me a notoriety for changing my clothes on the hour every hour from sheer overweening vanity. My vanity used to be under-weening but I took night school classes for that.

10:15 a.m.

David White led a vocal warm-up. David is our splendid conductor and musical director, only in his mid-twenties, charming to work with, boyish-looking, bespectacled and very talented.

This morning's schedule is to check all the ensemble numbers with David and polish them till they sparkle – we hope. Before we began, David answered several questions, particularly this one: "Should we continue to learn this material, fixing it solidly in our minds? Or is it going to be changed? – as Andrew implied last week."

This put David slightly on the spot. He grinned. "My advice is to do what Mark Inscoe suggested the other day. In his words, 'Stay in an attitude of flux.' You've seen how many changes Andrew has already made and incorporated into numbers, and no doubt others will follow. He can only see what he wants to alter when he watches and hears the numbers performed. So, what I suggest is this: let's use today to get the work as solid as possible. *But* keep in mind Mark's 'Stay in an attitude of flux.'"

I didn't hear Mark say that but I'm now hell bent on adopting a one hundred percent attitude of flux. If it ain't flux – I don't want it!

David then clarified another problem Sir Andrew is keen to tackle. "Andrew has some worries about 'Let's Have Lunch'. Several counterpointed phrases aren't coming over clearly. He thinks it might be just a question of simplifying the writing. The audience must immediately understand the words you are singing so they can be recognised when you echo them again throughout the number."

10:30 a.m.

So! We launched on a thorough wash-and-brush up of that fiendishly elaborate but beautifully written opening routine. Everyone has problems counting themselves in for individual phrases. Our aim today was to troubleshoot a lot of these tricky musical and physical moments. Generally speaking, we did extremely useful work.

The company's mood is extraordinarily lively and exuberant. The company feels relaxed and yet terrifically on the ball, mainly because the absence of the production top brass has taken the pressure off us. Both David and Maggie are wonderful to work with – delightfully good-humoured, patient, as well as tremendously professional and helpful.

This is in no way a criticism of their immediate superiors, Trevor and Bob Avian; in fact, a very positive reflection on them. My Paulie used to say, "Whatever the atmosphere in a rehearsal room, it always comes from the top."

11:30 a.m. Coffee Break

After an hour and a half, David smiled engagingly and announced, "We'll take a rest. This is in marvellous shape now. I'm sure if you can perform the number like that on Monday for Andrew and Trevor, there'll be no need to simplify any more musical phrases."

11:45 a.m.

We sat round the piano and did more detailed vocal work with our conductor David White on the scene in Schwab's Drug Store, including all the spoken and sung dialogue.

Andrew said, "I've re-adjusted several lines. Some of them are *too* fractured and impressionistic for their own good."

We then attacked the New Year party in Artie's apartment, especially the closing chorus, "This Time Next Year", with its crunchy harmonies and high tessitura, all of us cheerfully screaming our heads off about hopes for big breaks in the New Year: to get bigger salaries, to work with fine directors, to live in nicer apartments with plumbing that works, to make useful contacts, to land starring roles in Oscar-winning movies and enjoy lifelong careers in the film industry.

David reassured us later, "This number will not be reset in a higher key. That's a promise."

"How about," I suggested, "a clever modulation that sounds like it's going up but actually goes down?"

I received no response from David except a smile. Perhaps I was again trespassing on private property. But skilled orchestral arrangers know how to work this trick effectively. I was a happy bunny when some low-pitched lines I sing in the DeMille party sketch were shifted up slightly by Andrew to be less growly for me. And the lyrical section between Joe and Betty in Artie's party was given a sharper definition to lovely effect.

We all stood up, put our chairs aside and performed the reprise of "Let's Have Lunch" in Schwab's.

After repeating it several times, the girls were released for lunch.

12:30 p.m.

"The Lady's Paying". The men sat down again and David gave this dressing number a vocal makeover, applying the necessary spit and polish to our dotted quavers.

An hour later they glittered like icicles dangling in a moonlit Norwegian forest. Oooh!

1:30 p.m. Lunch

By now, our salesmen's sartorial onslaught upon Joe sounded pretty ritzy. Bob Avian hasn't choreographed "The Lady's Paying" in detail yet so we left it for his closer attention next week.

2:30 p.m.

The girls worked on the beauticians number with Bob.

3:15 p.m.

The ensemble sat round the piano and made sure the detailed vocal work we did this morning on the show's opening number, "Let's Have Lunch", hadn't vaporised. Yes and no. But mainly no, thank goodness. And in fact, our *final* sing through of it this afternoon was the best ever! Very encouraging in more ways than one because an amazing thing happened at this point.

Someone had been watching us without our knowing. Sir Andrew was standing by the tiered seating, leaning over the handrail. He heard the whole number and now walked onto the rehearsal floor looking very cheerful!

"That is going to work," he said, with a beaming smile. "That is going to work *very* well."

Most of us weren't even aware Andrew was still in the building. Perhaps a good thing.

4 p.m. Tea Break

Being a beautiful May day, several of us gathered on the pavement entrance outside Riverside Studios to catch the rays. We were also treated to the whiff of the drains from the manhole in the road.

"Ah, how it takes me back to those romantic nights in Spain," I sighed. "Sweet-scented flowers mingling with the pong of sewage."

Parked near us was Andrew Lloyd Webber's chauffeur-driven car and as Andrew emerged from the Studios, he caught sight of us and came over, full of enthusiasm and praise for the vocal performance we'd given of the opening number, "Let's Have Lunch".

"It's started me thinking of further possible improvements from my end. We might be able to make all of it more syncopated, which could be very interesting. And even add some funny rhymes in those repeated phrases."

We were overwhelmed by his extraordinary charm and enthusiasm. I haven't stood so close to him before and found the warmth of his smile completely overwhelming. In fact, it was like meeting a different person. And there was more.

"I've also got some news for all of us which *could* be good, could be bad. It all depends. Variety Magazine, the Hollywood show business trade paper, has announced it's going to devote an entire edition to this show – something it has never done before in its whole history."

"That's marvellous," I said. "But why could it be bad news?"

"Well, because it might raise expectations impossibly high, I suppose."

This was a really stunning piece of information. Coming on top of Sir Andrew's disarmingly friendly behaviour, it rendered most of us gobsmacked.

Gerard Casey's next remark showed how well he knew his way round RUG's road system. "I'm sure Cameron Mackintosh will read Variety's announcement with interest."

To which Andrew and everyone (except me) burst into full-throttled laughter.

I was puzzled but unfortunately Andrew had no time to elaborate.

"I must go. I have to attend a band call and check the arrangements. I'll be just across the river, so give a shout if you should need me."

And off he purred in his Mercedes Benz.

As we all made our way back to the rehearsal room, I asked Nick Colicos to clarify Gerard's jokey comment about Variety. "Why did it made everyone laugh? Particularly Andrew?"

"There's a friendly professional rivalry between Cameron Mackintosh and Andrew," Nick explained. "For the first night party of *Miss Saigon* two years ago, Cameron laid on a boat to ferry the company and their guests down the Thames to the restaurant. For *Sunset*, Andrew wants to create a Californian boulevard lined with palm trees, beginning outside the Adelphi Theatre and going all the way along the Strand to the Savoy Hotel. That's where *Sunset*'s opening night party is being held. It's going to be really something."

4:15 p.m. Studio 2

Tea break over. A full company call to work on the final scene.

Trevor, Patti, Kevin and Daniel joined the rest of us in the big rehearsal room downstairs. We sat and listened as Trevor described the end of the show, based closely on the film's famous final scene.

After Norma's murder of Joe Gillis, her house is now full of police, news reporters, film cameramen and press photographers. Unexpectedly, Norma appears at the top of the sweeping staircase and looks below at all the intruders. The once great movie star is now mad as the sea wind.

At first, she recoils, confused and afraid to see so many strangers. Max reassures her that the magnificent dream she cherished of filming her script of *Salome* has actually been realised and he coaxes her to walk down the stairs because studio technicians and cameramen have arrived and are now ready to film her performing the role of Princess Salome under DeMille's direction. Norma's mind tumbles from its fragile pedestal as she makes her final descent, both tragic and triumphant, lost in her fantasy world of unattainable stardom.

"And here's the thing we have to think about," Trevor explained. "This scene could appear to be a brutal invasion of Norma's home by the police and a horde of noisy parasites – cold-blooded reporters with their newsreel cameras and questions, snooping about, seeking colourful copy and exposé pictures, their comings and goings, a hubbub of quiet chatter, gossiping and joking, and so on. However, that is *not* what is reflected in the music. Listen to this."

David Caddick then played what I recognised as Norma's lullaby to her dead chimpanzee: "Surrender". It is the same slow waltz which accompanies DeMille's song, praising Norma's youthful beauty and hopes, "when all of her dreams were new". But the music David played today was a delicate echo of that melody – and it certainly seemed curiously at odds with the callous activity of the police in Norma's house, now a crime scene, casually looking for clues.

"It deceptively sets a gentle tone," Trevor continued, "For the horrible shock that is to come – Norma's sudden entrance at the top of the sweeping staircase, irretrievably lost in her mad dream of great stardom. So, what you've got to do is to bring this scene to life, convincingly but without overpowering that strangely delicate music. We want to see these Hollywood Babylon buzzards picking over the bones after the kill, eager to record any sordid, dirty details to sell for hard cash to gossip magazines. Another lurid exposure of a sordid crime of passion, this time a movie star's downfall from untouchable glamour to the squalid degradation of the gutter. Today, Ronald Reagan is the latest big name to receive this feet of clay treatment. The press have just accused Mr Reagan of having been a secret FBI agent."

As Trevor spoke, I was reminded of recent claims concerning the private life of Walt Disney, based on documentary proof of his extreme right-wing Republican politics and his alleged covert involvement with the House of Un-American Activities Committee. There was even a rumour that Disney refused to lower the American flag at Disneyland to half-mast after the assassination of the Democrat President John F. Kennedy in 1963. A whole industry has been built on the sale of books divulging "shocking truths" about famous names linked to the Hollywood film industry, prompting litigation that has fuelled an enormously profitable business for lawyers.

"We first need to see you realise," Trevor continued, "That the poor woman is deranged. Your initial shock might then change to distress, or to embarrassment, maybe cynicism, as her tragedy affects each one of you differently. But a few moments later, we must also see you respond more sympathetically when she is persuaded to act what she thinks is a scene in her *Salome* movie directed by Mr DeMille. Okay. Let's just do it without any further fuss on my part."

Patti expressed a slight concern. "Trevor, after I shoot Joe, there's a blackout and I exit off stage right and climb the gantry to the upper level of the set while it is descending and moving forwards. Up there, I do an *entire* change of costume and make-up in a matter of a few seconds and then re-enter at the top of the staircase. Added to this, the place where I exit is crowded with seven or eight other actors waiting to enter."

"Don't worry about that now," Trevor replied. "We shall address all these logistical problems in due course."

"I must tell you an awful story," she continued.

"Must you? I don't know that I want to hear it!"

"It happened because two understudies were on, and they hit face to face in the dark and broke their jaws, their noses and their teeth."

"Yes, well, I've got to counteract that story with one about the impossibly quick change that we had to deal with in *Les Miserables*, when the entire company of twenty-three actors found themselves having to switch costumes in a matter of seconds in a tiny back room at the Palace Theatre, measuring about five feet by seven. It appeared a total impossibility, and yet a few weeks later, once it had been properly organised and become a routine, they found they had time for a sit down and a quick fag! So, let's do the scene."

4:45 p.m.

And we did. Today, for the first time, actors playing press photographers were able to use authentic-looking flash cameras we've seen in so many American films – those big, heavy, square jobs with black concertina fronts, but without the flashbulbs actually going off yet. I play a press reporter in this scene; Sasha Millard is my cub reporter; other ensemble are police officers, news film camera people, forensic experts and gossip columnists.

Patti briefly walked through the end of the preceding scene when she shoots Joe. She was alone because Kevin was upstairs, working on his songs in Studio 3. She simply marked her moves by walking on the ground plan – a huge map drawn on the rehearsal floor with strips of coloured sticky tape.

Norma (Patti) is standing in the middle of the staircase. She shoots Joe (Kevin) with the prop gun. Click (one shot). She then moves down to the bottom of the stairs. Click (another shot). Then she takes two more steps down to the pool at the front of the stage. Click (the final shot).

"Blackout," Trevor said, quietly.

Patti turned and quickly marked climbing the stairs to exit stage right – still walking on the ground plan.

As the orchestra plays Norma's fragile lullaby again, the rostrums will move upstage and the huge house set will descend to stage level and then travel forwards several feet. And, exactly like the opening of the show, the body of Joe Gillis (played by Sandy Strallen) is again hauled out of the pool (the orchestra pit) to be identified by the police. The ensemble quietly enter, playing newspaper reporters, photographers, a TV broadcast crew and other outsiders; they wander around Norma's house and casually pick over the bones of a scandalous murder, hoping to get an official statement from the police or some juicy gossip.

Norma Desmond's butler Max (Daniel Benzali) is quietly conferring with the Chief of Police (Peter Rutherford). When Trevor was directing their conversation earlier, he looked at Peter and Daniel's completely shaven bald heads and said, "It's like the meeting of two Martians!"

An abrupt interruption. All attention is suddenly pulled to the top of the staircase where Norma has appeared. Patti, still referring to a page of script, sings Norma's rambling, confused thoughts. Max, standing at the bottom of the staircase, mounts the lower two steps and encourages her to descend, telling her that Mr DeMille's cameras are ready to shoot her last scene in *Salome*, the movie she has written.

Patti cast the script aside and delivered Norma's final speech in the show, explaining to Mr DeMille and the studio crew that she can't continue to act because she is "too happy". Tears poured down Patti's cheeks.

It was all the more moving because Patti was working in her everyday clothes – wearing her black dome crowned hat, like a rimless bowler, and her round framed spectacles. And yet, like a transparent ghost superimposed by special effects, Norma Desmond was also standing there, unmistakably.

Patti gave Norma's final speech, declaring how wonderful she feels to be making a picture. This will always be her life. Nothing else exists. Only the studio, the crew, the film cameras and "all you wonderful people out there in the dark". The crowd who has invaded Norma's house are stunned into silence. The exotic music is played and they watch the great silent movie star walk down the staircase, using her silk veil to enhance Princess Salome's oriental dance gestures.

When she reached downstage centre, Leslie played the closing piano chords. Patti turned in profile and, using her own scarf as Salome's veil, she struck her final exotic Norma Desmond pose. A long breathless silence…

Trevor broke it softly with, "Blackout."

The company rewarded Patti with cheers, praise and warm applause.

"We are, by good fortune, on schedule," Trevor said, winding up our third week of rehearsal. "We'll be working here in Riverside Studios for a further two weeks and then move, hopefully, into the Adelphi Theatre to rehearse for the last three weeks on the completed set. It sounds a deceptively generous amount of time but we have a vast technical puzzle to work out and we'll need every second to get it right. So, next week, we shall start with a run-through here for the production team to see what kind of over-all shape the show is in."

Patti asked, "Could we do a run-through before that? Just for us?"

"Of *course,* you can, but let it be understood that none of the work done by yourselves in these rehearsals will ever be received by the production team in a judgmental way."

Point taken. However, Patti's request was highly appreciated by everyone. The pressure on us actors facing that array of observers will be pretty daunting for us.

Today was the first time we heard the piano transcription of the music played in the final scene. I have to admit – oh, sacrilege and sedition – I detected lovely shades of Delius, Ravel and Rachmaninov, whose 2nd Piano Concerto's slow theme is glancingly but distinctly echoed. Maybe Sir Andrew's arrangers have coloured some chord sequences that make unconscious reference to those composers?

5:45 p.m.

We broke. Next call: 10 a.m. on Monday 10th May. Tomorrow off!

SATURDAY 8th May 1993

5:30 a.m.

Woke up to write.

8:30 a.m.

Went for a run. Did a workout and then sun-bathed nude again in my front garden – cheeky! Wonderful weather with a fresh northeast wind, but it didn't chill my naturist sun trap.

Alas, my weekend was blighted. The Theatre Writers Union rang to say I've no legal right to stop *my* re-edited stage adaptation of Fitzgerald's novel *The Great Gatsby* from being claimed as the property of the first adaptor and of the producer at the Kings Head Theatre in Islington. Both are selling the script as theirs which some legal agreement permits. They are also flying to Sweden to oversee a production there, using my script, of course. The cast I directed at the King's Head are sweetly sympathetic and supportive.

"Peter, we've kept copies of the first adaptation to show people how awful his was compared to yours and how much you improved it."

Well, I'd need a lawyer to fight this piddling battle for me, and lawyers cost. Out of the question.

I can hear my Paulie advising, "Rise above it, Petey."

7 p.m.

I collected my next-door neighbour Jill and drove her over to Ann Wakefield's flat in Little Venice for dinner. They have been great pals for years.

Annie played vivacious Mad-cap Maisie in the original 1953 production of Sandy Wilson's musical *The Boy Friend*, set in the 1920s. Her song and dance number "Won't You Charleston with Me?" stopped the show every night.

After opening successfully at the Players Theatre, *The Boy Friend* transferred to the Wyndham Theatre and enjoyed a huge success for five years! I was then aged fifteen and, by coincidence, acting in a play at the New Theatre (now the Noel Coward Theatre). It was a comedy by Liam O'Brien called *The Remarkable Mr Pennypacker*, starring Nigel Patrick and Elizabeth Sellars. I played one of their seven Pennypacker children. My stage name back then was Richard Peters. Our New Theatre stood back-to-back with the Wyndham's and we kids in our top floor dressing room often waved to the actors in their dressing rooms across the dividing alleyway. One of them might have been Annie!

Jump forwards thirty-six years to today and Annie has just moved into a neat little council flat in Lisson Grove – without furniture, carpets or fridge.

The moment I arrived, she said, "Peter, can you help me? I've bought a portable clothes horse to dry my washing on and it needs putting together. All the parts are in this box."

"No problem." I opened the box. It contained metal rods, screws and wheels which, under my unerring supervision, Jill and I assembled perfectly and then threw away the leftover bits. Annie was thrilled. Her vivacity and charm remind me of a famous film star.

I said, "You are the Katharine Hepburn of Little Venice." Tickled her pink.

This evening an old friend of Annie joined us, Robert Huke. Bob, as Annie calls him, was the cameraman on countless marvellous high-profile films, including the James Bond movie *You Only Live Twice* directed by Lewis Gilbert. Bob also filmed David Lean's *Ryan's Daughter* which won an Academy Award for Best Cinematography. He is now seventy-three years old and looks very tired and worried. Poor soul, his wife is suffering badly from Alzheimer's disease.

We all sat on the floor to eat. Yes, our backs were against the wall, but we merrily munched and laughed our way through a very jolly dinner. My contribution was a chocolate cake from M&S, a big hunk of cottage cheese and sweet cicely leaves, freshly picked from my front garden.

Bob spoke fascinatingly about working with David Lean. "It took Lean five years to make *Ryan's Daughter*. For a whole year, he kept the cast and crew shooting on location at Dingle Bay – Ireland's rainiest area!"

"Oh yes!" I said. "That scene on the beach with dark clouds

and a ferocious tempest lashing down. You could see it was the real thing, not back projection. But as I watched it, Bob, one thing puzzled me. How on earth did you keep the rain off the camera lens?"

"Have you ever stood on the bridge of a ship in a thunderstorm?"

"Funny you should ask. No."

"When the rain is fiercely lashing down, the steersman at the helm looks through a round glass panel in the window. That glass panel is spinning at very high speed so that, as the rain lands on it, the water is immediately flung off, giving a clear view ahead. We adopted exactly the same principle for the camera. We put a spinning glass window in front of the lens. Of course, the camera was also covered with a protective hood. And so were we!"

SUNDAY 9th May 1993

5 a.m. Home

Up to write. Rain. Each Sunday is still a desolate hell without my Paulie so…

11 a.m.

I went to the Quaker Friends Meeting House in Hampstead with a friend of mine, the actress Richenda Carey. We were in the TV series, *The Darling Buds of May*. Richenda played Lady Buff-Gore and I was Mr Shell, the tedious tax inspector. We then had a coffee in Dome's Cafe and I told her how shabbily I was treated by the Kings Head Theatre when I directed *Gatsby* there.

She was sympathetic but added, "Peter, I strongly advise you to leave it behind. Chalk it up to experience and let them stew in their own juice."

I knew immediately this was the advice I needed to hear and thanked Richenda from the bottom of my heart.

Lunched alone at Surya, the vegetarian Indian restaurant in West End Lane. The Sunday Times kept me good company.

Went home and watched my video of Hitchcock's terrific *Spellbound*. I love Ingrid's psychiatrist, Dr Peterson. One of the reasons she won three Oscars and four Golden Globes career was that she chose her film roles very carefully.

For example, she was asked to be in the 1977 film, *The Poseidon Adventure,* an award-winning film but not the kind that attracted Ingrid.

Her friend and favourite stage manager Griffith James said to me, "Ingrid is often asked to be in these star-studded disaster movies they're making now. It's always a character who falls in the water and drowns. She says to the producer, 'Thank you very much, but no, I don't think so.' It's not because Ingrid can't swim but because the role is usually a badly-written cardboard cut-out."

Ingrid once said to me, "I never make a movie just because they offer me a lot of money. If I like the part and the budget is small, I accept a lower fee." One was the 1973 film *The Hideaways* about an eccentric old lady. She made it when she was fifty-six years old.

Griff said, "Her character was supposed to be much older and the make-up people had trouble trying to age her. They put her in a grey wig and frosted her eyebrows but it didn't work. She still looked wonderful."

And way back in 1947, she even persuaded Lana Turner to swap roles with her in MGM's *Dr Jekyll and Mr Hyde*. She said, "I preferred to play the cockney barmaid Ivy instead of another boring, virtuous wife."

And in the 1974 film *Murder on the Orient Express*, Ingrid exchanged roles with Wendy Hiller.

"The producer wanted me to be the Russian princess but I said I would rather play the dopey missionary." Ingrid had a lot of fun as Greta Ohlsson, gave her a comical Swedish accent and bagged an Oscar for Best Supporting Actress.

Ironed shirts. Did desk work. Snoozed on the sofa…

MONDAY 10th May 1993

10 a.m. Riverside Studios, Studio 2

Vocal warm-up.

Our musical director David White is off ill with a throat infection so David Caddick the musical supervisor took charge. Our rehearsal pianist, Leslie Hayes, did the warm-up. Nice one. But, with the whole production team watching, the final exercise pushed us up into our highest registers.

David soon jumped to his feet and told us to stop singing. He looked red-faced and very cross. "You all sound like people undergoing some horrible torture, as if those high notes were being dragged out of you with the utmost reluctance."

An awkward pause followed. We awaited his helpful advice on how to warble the dulcet tones he sadly craved. We were all silently thinking, "Leave your problems at home, Mr Grumpy. It's Monday morning. Help us out, please."

Finally, our pianist Leslie asked him, "Do you want to continue with the warm-up, David?"

"No." David snapped at Leslie, ungraciously. "Let's get to work."

10:15 a.m.

And then, what else, but the opening number "Let's Have Lunch" – for two solid hours. Trevor and Bob Avian forensically re-examined details to make sure each move and gesture added up to a complex but clear visual clear statement.

But even after two hours, there were unexpected traffic jams caused by some of us (me included) being slightly inconsistent getting from A to B. Some hitches were caused by tiny re-adjustments that Bob or Trevor made, altering an actor's position or the timing of a step, and these created a domino effect on other people's cues, lyrics and moves.

But the whole company remains buoyantly good-natured. We are hoping and praying this sequence is looking better because we are heartily sick of bashing through it endlessly. We'll happily work hard on a number if we think it's improving, but this routine still feels like an explosion in a body parts warehouse. A crazy shambolic mess.

Bob Avian questioned my exit at the end of this opening number.

I said, "You told me to delay my exit to the next line. So, I did."

"But you were the only person leaving the stage at that moment."

"In a baby pink spot," Nick Colicos added.

"Exactly," I replied. "It's in my contract." As if anyone didn't know.

12:15 p.m. Coffee Break

We exchanged theatrical anecdotes.

I said, "Back in the 1970s, I was on *The Good Old Days*, the BBC TV Victorian Music Hall variety show. One day, the actor Sir Bernard Miles and I stood in the stalls watching an amazing trio of acrobats. One twirled rings on his arms. A second stood on the first one's shoulders, juggling balls. A third balanced on the second one's shoulders upside down on his hands, playing instruments with his feet. Bernard said, 'Look at them. Too bloody lazy to learn a song.'"

Another anecdote was about the actress Coral Browne. She was a friend of my partner, Paulie. He said, "She converted to Roman Catholicism. One day after holy communion, she emerged from the church, looking for a taxi. A man was already there at the kerb waiting for one. As a cab pulled up Coral said to the man, 'Piss off. I'm in a state of fucking grace.'"

12:30 p.m.

Trevor blocked the very opening moments of the show. His idea is a marvellously effective trick of the eye – a *trompe-l'oeil* as it's called in cultured circles. Can we make it work?

The Paramount Studios movie opens with the camera at the bottom of a swimming pool looking up at Joe Gillis' dead body floating on the surface of rippling water. Police cops are seen standing on the edge of the pool. One is holding a long pole with a hook on the end which he uses to tug Joe's corpse to the pool's edge so others can haul him out of the water.

Our show begins in the same way. A group of policemen (I'm one) are standing on the upstage rostrum, and one of them, Gareth Snook, is holding a long pole. We are glancingly lit by flashing blue lights from a Los Angeles police car parked offstage. Gareth Snook is just about to use the pole to pull Joe Gillis' body to the pool's edge.

Trevor said, "Can I ask your group standing upstage to lean back. I want the audience to get the impression they are viewing you from the bottom of the pool. It might feel odd, but think superior thoughts, as if you were looking down at some doo-doo floating in the water."

And so we *do* do.

"It works!" Trevor exclaimed.

This action overlaps with exactly the same activity being performed by one of them down at the edge of the stage by a similar group of cops. Near them is a chrome bathing pool handrail and they haul Joe's dead body out of the pool (the orchestra pit). As they do this, the lights fade on us cops upstage and we bugger off and the dead man himself, Joe Gillis (Kevin Anderson) emerges from the downstage group, faces the audience and begins to narrate the entire story, describing, ironically, the moment of his own death, saying that the time was about 5 a.m., the cops had been called, and so on.

Trevor linked these two identical pieces of action by getting a reporter (Richard Tate) to hurry across the upstage rostrum. He stops as he sees the body, then walks towards it. And at the same time, Adam Matalon performs that same action down at the edge of the stage.

The lights fade and the set opens up, moving the location to the forecourt of Paramount Studios, outside one of the big soundstages. I exit left, climb down the stairs and have a very quick costume change into Jonesy the security guard at Paramount's front-gated entrance. When Joe arrives, I check his name on my clipboard and wave him through.

We then ran this entire complex opening number.

1:25 p.m. Lunch

Adam Matalon (ensemble) had permission to leave our rehearsal to attend the Fringe Awards Ceremony at the Hackney Empire, hosted by Lily Savage. Adam recently appeared with four other actors in a highly acclaimed play, *Porcelain*. Their show was nominated for five awards. Our fingers are crossed for him. He is a very talented young actor, writer and producer in his mid-twenties, I guess.

Before Adam was born his mother, Elizabeth Seal, starred as the first Irma in the 1858 musical *Irma La Douce* in London. She then wowed Broadway in the 1960 transfer to New York, winning a Tony Award for the Best Actress in a Musical.

2:30 p.m.

Bob Avian spent two hours on "This Time Next Year", the ensemble number we sing at the New Year's Eve party in Artie's apartment. This baby is physically and vocally complex like the opening number, involving the whole company, apart from Patti (Norma) and Daniel (Max).

Trevor reshaped groups and retimed moves, asking us to keep our action consistent in order to fix the blocking. He then asked us to quieten down our background hubbub as Joe and Betty exchange intimate dialogue and sing, "I'm Too Much in Love to Care". This is always a problem for the ensemble because we have to retain the same level of energised activity but without making any sound – or leaning towards each other to whisper, "What the hell are you saying?"

After rehearsing this effusively rowdy party for two hours, I was in a muck sweat, however the scene felt better, especially Bob's grouping for the final moment – raising our drinks to each other and hoping things will be better "this time next year".

4:30 p.m. Coffee Break

Richard Oriel, our company manager, distributed copies of a letter of agreement from the Really Useful Group to Equity regarding the fees the ensemble will receive for a proposed video documentary. It would use extracts to describe the making of this show. Also, RUG have included a suggestion for a payment deal if rehearsal clips are screened in TV news reports.

Nadia Strahan and I held a quick consultation with the cast

and then I rang Equity and gave Hilary Strange the company's general response to the terms of agreement proposed in the letter sent by RUG to Equity.

Hilary said, "You'll need to hold a proper meeting about this, Peter."

I duly then asked Bob Avion if the cast could have a few moments for a quick powwow.

He very kindly said, "Sure, Peter. I can allow you fifteen minutes of my rehearsal time before I look at the girls' beauticians number."

During our meeting, we generally decided, most importantly, that RUG's letter of agreement is far too ambiguously worded and lacking in detail. We need to draw up a settlement that deals with every specific point about the sale of filmed material. It seems barbaric to me that this has to be handled by the actors through Equity without the help of our individual agents. As far as I can make out, it gives RUG's accountants a huge advantage. In theory, they can confuse or obscure the deal by using last minute tactics if they are unscrupulous.

That said, our brief, hastily assembled meeting seemed to address the pertinent problems quite single-mindedly, given that we are a many-headed beast – and a tired one at that.

All the cast and stage management were there – except Patti, Daniel and Kevin. I was told they were either busy elsewhere or had gone home. Their lack of cooperation slightly worried me because it looks as if their American agents are advising them to keep their distance.

Nadia Strahan and I promised the company we would ring Hilary tomorrow and report the company's reaction back to her.

5 p.m.

After our discussion the men were released and Bob moved on to the beauticians scene with the girls.

I heard later that Adam Matalon's play won four out of the five Fringe Awards for which they were nominated – a terrific achievement. It shows how much talent there is in this company.

TUESDAY 11th May 1993

Riverside Studios, Studio 2

All the men called to rehearse the number, "The Lady's Paying". We now refer to it as the "Bona Frock" scene. Ooh, matron!

10 a.m.

First, a physical warm up with Maggie Goodwin, and then our sweet pianist Leslie Hayes led a vocal *Rise and shine!* warm-up. Our young conductor David White is still nursing a throat infection and barely able to speak – his voice reduced to a husky pianissimo.

10:15 a.m.

Bob Avian overhauled the blocking and business in "The Lady's Paying" – without Patti. She was rehearsing upstairs with Trevor in Studio 3 but our Swing Boy, Bernard Sharpe, kindly offered to play Norma. His book-held performance was very helpful.

Peter Rutherford said later over lunch, "It was a rare pleasure to see Norma Desmond as if played by Gracie Fields in her inimitable Lancashire accent, welcoming the outfitters to her villa in Capri."

Bob devised a way for us Mr Manfred's tailors to strip Kevin down to his vest and underpants and then to completely reclothe him in full evening tails – all in less than forty seconds! I begin by removing his jacket. Then another outfitter takes off his shirt. Then his slacks and sneakers come off, and on go his evening dress trousers, shoes, shirt, tie and waistcoat (Bob calls it his "vest"). And finally – his tails coat. *Et voila!*

11 a.m.

Patti returned to rehearse "The Lady's Paying" with us, but again she left out the central section. At this point in the film, Norma Desmond performs an elaborate, comical routine, doing three impressions of famous silent screen stars to amuse Joe. Patti appears as Charlie Chaplin, waddling about with a stick-on moustache, taking a hat and cane from the clothes rack we bring on. Then she impersonates Douglas Fairbanks sword-fighting, and lastly Rudolph Valentino, as the romantic Arab Sheik vowing undying love.

In the film, all these parodies are played with considerable flair and humour by Gloria Swanson, who has, of course, the luxury of quick editing from one character to another. Patti, however, is less than enamoured of the sequence and resists all encouragement to embark on it. She even jokes that it would make an effective cut if it were completely removed!

12:30 p.m.

Most of the girls had arrived by now and for the first time they watched us run "The Lady's Paying". They laughed a lot and applauded at the end, which was supportive and encouraging.

"Okay, people," Bob said, "After lunch, we'll be doing this number for Andrew, so try to remember everything we've worked out."

12:45 p.m.

Coffee Break

1 p.m.

Two run throughs of the high-spirited New Year's Eve party number, "This Time Next Year". It feels like an exhausting mess of unfocused energy released by everyone in a hit or miss fashion. My feeling is that to keep the ebullient party celebration looking fresh and spontaneous, we need more precision and consistency than most of the ensemble can retain.

After the second run, Bob Avian (choreographer) conferred with David White (musical director) and Andrew McBean (Trevor's assistant) as if we weren't in the room.

Their discussion ended thus. "Okay, people. We can't go any further with the cabaret section till we hear what Sir Andrew wants to change. He said he might give DeMille's line in the cabaret about the Philistines to the three temple virgins."

This made me sit up. I would lose a valuable lyric, but I wasn't personally referred to.

One of my fellow actors sympathised. "To them, Peter, we're just insensible objects to be shoved around and obey orders."

Trevor arrived and watched a run through of the boisterous New Year's Eve party number, "This Time Next Year". It really caught fire and took off.

"That had a wonderfully alive quality," Trevor said. "Try to remember exactly what it was you all did because we'll be running it for Andrew this afternoon and what tends to happen is, the moment he's in the audience, rigor mortis sets in and you all freeze solid."

1:35 p.m. Lunch Break

Back in an hour.

2:35 p.m.

Sir Andrew arrived. With Trevor's rigor mortis plea in mind, we ran "This Time Next Year" for Andrew, plus a whole group of other people watching with him, most of whom I didn't recognise, but amongst them was David Cullen (orchestral arranger). He reappeared having been busy with the band calls which Andrew pops off to attend.

Before we began, Trevor's instruction to us was, "Give the number all you've got."

We did. It finished. No response. We waited.

The usual awkward silence followed as the production team quietly conferred. The usual long uncomfortable pause followed, till…

"Okay," Trevor said. "We'll do the number again. This time, let's see if you can be less rowdy during the quiet dialogue between Kevin and Meredith (playing Joe and Betty). Remember, you mustn't lose your energy but you've got to drop out vocally so that we can hear what they are saying. Also, there's an inconsistency of level in the singing of your various lines. Try to keep an even volume otherwise our ears have to adjust very quickly from one of you to another."

We ran the number again. Another hushed conference between Trevor, Andrew, David Cullen, David White and our other invited audience members.

Trevor at last turned to us and said, "I must apologise to you all for discussing your performance as if you weren't present. I shall give you Andrew's alterations later. Let's now look at 'The Lady's Paying.'"

We performed the Bona Frock number for Andrew. Silence.

Andrew's only one comment was, "It sounds very low. I think the final chorus section should go up a tone to G."

Trevor said to him, "In all fairness, I must point out that they have only just rehearsed the moves and might not yet be giving the music full value."   "Yes, I understand," Andrew replied, "But I'd like to hear it again, this time singing it a tone higher."

Clenching our buttocks, we obeyed.

Andrew's only comment was, "I'll have a look at it. It isn't vocally right yet. What I would like to do now is ask you all to sit down again and do a vocal run for me of the opening number 'Let's Have Lunch'. I want to give this a more boogie, syncopated feel."

After we sang it through for Andrew, David Caddick (our handsome, mid-thirties musical supervisor) said, "Be aware that you have to attack your individual solo lines with more energy, otherwise the whole number becomes uniform, dull and flaccid. And, as you know," he added with a playful grin, "If something becomes flaccid, we don't have anything to do with it."

Well, frankly I was shocked. The things young people come out with nowadays. There should be a law.

Andrew kindly gave us a bit of information. "At the band call last Friday, I heard the orchestral arrangement of this number for the first time. It sounds amazing. You'll be knocked out when you hear it – full of percussive effects and bongo drums. It's got a really edgy, driving jazz feel to it, so you must be aware of that when you sing your individual lines."

This was a deliciously rare moment for us, being treated as more than just blocks of wood and mechanical robots being tinkered with and carrying out endless orders. It would be nice to be told what's going on more often.

Meanwhile, in another part of the score's forest, David Caddick and Andrew added jazz syncopations to a few vocal entrics, i.e. singing a fraction earlier than on the beat. And there came a moment when just one perfectly innocent little crotchet was removed from a bar – smaller than a needle in a haystack. I've no idea where because I didn't go looking for it.

Bob Avian appeared more cheerful this afternoon. He said,

"Good news! I can start applying this jive feel to your movement in the number because I have *at last* been given permission to give you some dance steps. This will help me to establish the choreographic language within the whole show. Nothing ostentatious, just a low-slung, understated Lindy feel."

I knew what he meant, having directed the Jiving Lindy Hoppers in *The Cotton Club*. It was a fun show Andrew Meadmore produced at the Barbican in 1991.

4:15 p.m. Tea Break

Nadia Strahan and I rang Rachel Carter at Equity to talk about the terms of agreement RUG have offered for the proposed TV documentary and for the sale of filmed extracts shown in TV news broadcasts, chat shows and suchlike. This made us a bit late returning to Studio 2 but Bob was okay with that.

Parody lyrics: "Gotta run," has become "Got the runs."

"We are down on knees outside Grauman's Chinese," has become "We are down on our knees with a deadly disease."

Maggie Goodwin, our assistant choreographer, reminded us all of the dance audition routine which she taught us months ago at Dance Works. Very simple, very hip-based. Bob amusingly refers to one of the moves as a "ka-ching", meaning a simple step-ball-change. It's his shorthand moniker for describing the casual style he wants.

4:35 p.m.

The rest of the afternoon was given over to Bob who examined everyone's individual moves in the final "counterpointed" section of the number, adding more turns and "ka-chings" to our footwork.

"But whatever I show you, you must take and use what feels most natural and easy. And all of you, please, never lose your character and become just an anonymous dancer in the scene."

6 p.m.

Come 1800 hours and Bob dismissed the company, saying, "That's all I can do today. I'm suffering from brain death."

So was I.

Entering the tube station, I showed my weekly pass to a newspaper seller. He gave me a puzzled but sympathetic look.

WEDNESDAY 12th May 1993

5 a.m.

Wrote for three hours. Ran round the streets. A cloudy sky and humid but trees and bushes are budding and front gardens are flowering beautifully. Did a workout with weights.

11:15 a.m. Riverside Studios, Reception Desk

11:30 a.m.

The full company call is at 12 but I arrived early to ring Hilary Strange at Equity. We need her to clarify negotiations going on between Equity and RUG about the proposed filming of us during rehearsals, and the use of that footage in a proposed TV documentary or in TV news reports.

The girls' call began earlier and I assumed they were still working on the beauticians scene in Studio 2. But I was wrong. The big rehearsal room was empty!

"Where is everyone?" I exclaimed. The silence was uncanny.

Canteen

I sat with our choreographer Bob Avian.

Over coffee, he explained to me what happened. "You're right. The girls' original call was earlier but there was a hasty phone-around and they were asked to come in later and work with the men at 12. Apparently, all but a couple were contacted."

"Why was it changed? What's going on, Bob?"

"I'm not exactly sure but rumour hath it, things are being discussed. It seems Andrew is concerned about the musical non-flow in the 'New Year Party' scene. And he wants to cut the sand dance interpolation."

Andrew wrote mock oriental music to accompany the Wilson, Keppel and Betty routine Bob choreographed for Sandy and Adam during the party cabaret.

"If it sounds right to Andrew, it looks right, but first it's got to make *musical* sense to his ear. And let's face it, he knows. He doesn't have a string of huge hits all over the world for nothing. And he hates the other melodic parodies in 'The Lady's Paying' number for the same reason, when Norma Desmond does those impersonations of movie stars. I've cut them down to just one – Chaplin – but even that may get the chop. And I don't think Patti will be too sad to see it go."

I called Equity to speak to Hilary Strange.

"Sorry, Peter. Both Hilary and her co-organiser, Rachel Carter, are in meetings and unable to come to the phone."

So, I left a message. "Could you ask Hilary to ring me back later this afternoon? Thanks."

I gave Patti and Daniel copies of a brief letter written by Alan Benson to Equity regarding a possible TV documentary. Alan is head of production at Andrew's Really Useful Picture Company.

Patti seemed unhappy. "Don't tell anyone yet, Peter, but I have to admit I've a few misgivings about the whole thing. Alan came to see me at my house in Connecticut months ago. He said the TV documentary showing *Sunset Boulevard* in rehearsal would be about the Los Angeles production with someone else playing

Norma, not about this one. What are they doing? I'll have to ring my agent. I'm not going to be in a documentary that has two Normas in it! We are creating the original *Sunset Boulevard* musical here in London. The documentary should only be about the making of this premiere production."

I guess RUG's idea is that US TV viewers would be more interested to see an American production being rehearsed, but Patti's concern is perfectly understandable. The Los Angeles news has hit her on the morning Barbra Streisand's recordings of Norma's two solo numbers "With One Look" and "As If We Never Said Goodbye" are being played on British radio. It means that those songs are now up for grabs if RUG allows, and yet Patti – the first stage Norma – has yet to record her version. Red warning lights are flashing in my head. Clearly, all is not sweetness and light between Patti and Sir Andrew.

Patti confirmed this. Chatting to her during rehearsals, she gave me a wicked smile. "I promise you, Peter, on the first night, when it gets to the moment for me to launch into 'With One Look', I'll turn to the audience and say, 'And now, ladies and gentlemen, here is the song everyone's been singing! Altogether!' And then I'll conduct the entire audience in a big chorus."

I was suddenly reminded of Bette Davis' warning to her party guests in the film *All About Eve*: "Fasten your seat belts. It's going to be a bumpy night."

I longed to ask Patti to explain what had soured her relationship with Sir Andrew but thought it wiser to keep a safe distance and avoid any toxic radioactive fallout.

12 p.m. Studio 2

Trevor changed this call to include both the female and male ensemble singing "This Time Next Year" at Artie's New Year party. It ends the first act.

After our lunch break, Trevor wanted to show Sir Andrew a considerably tweaked and rearranged staging of this number, hoping it would gain his approval.

For the next hour and a half, we repeatedly ran the whole New Year scene as Trevor cut out the sand dance altogether and turned the DeMille comic cabaret skit into one unbroken sequence. He then lifted Joe and Betty's sung conversation and placed it at the end of the scene. Trev added fresh details to our rowdy activity during the party which greatly clarified what us guests are getting up to. His improvements instantly worked.

Peter Rutherford was absent today, organising the funeral of a friend. Trevor gave me Peter's one solo line he sings in the number, "Till his next project", during our jokey DeMille skit. I'm sure this will prompt a typically droll comment from Peter when he returns tomorrow.

Trevor said that he loved my improvised comments as DeMille:

"Ready when all of you are!"

"A truly medieval spectacle!"

"You look wonderful this morning, Hedy."

"Bring on the camels! The horses! The penguins!"

"But," he added, "You mustn't forget the new line Christopher Hampton has given you to say when you introduce the fight between Samson and the lion: 'Coming soon to your neighbourhood theatre! Lights! Camera! Action!'"

Trevor's masterful gift for story-telling focuses the audience's attention exactly where it needs to be, immediately matching the action with a relevant pictorial statement.

He said, "I like the way Gareth and some others are mixing amongst people at the party holding their drinks above their heads. But it doesn't work if there isn't anyone near you, so we must make sure those kinds of images are used within groups."

Trevor's high respect for the dialogue's writer was clearly demonstrated when he asked Chris Hampton's permission to alter one word. "Instead of saying the phone is *over* there as he points to the floor beneath the drinks table, could Artie say *under* there?"

Chris Hampton's sense of responsibility as the book's co-author (with Don Black) reached awesome dimensions with his reply, "Leave it with me. I'll think about it and let you know."

1:40 p.m. Lunch

By the time we broke, the scene had become much easier to play, highly energised as it was, because the action is now more consistent and specific. Hallelujah!

I lunched with Joan Washington, the leading voice and accent coach. She is going to repair any wayward American accents.

"I've been working at the National Theatre," she said, "Helping

them with their cockney accents in *Sweeney Todd*. They're all very tired."

"Yes, I know," I said. "My chum Julia McKenzie is playing Mrs Lovett. She said they've been rehearsing from 10 in the morning till 9 at night and getting huge overtime pay, which the National can well afford, of course."

2:45 p.m.

After lunch, we ran "This Time Next Year" several times until it was finally ready for Sir Andrew to come in and watch.

We bashed through it for him.

Silence. As usual. Then the customary big powwow ensued between Trevor, Bob Avian, David Caddick and Sir Andrew. We quietly awaited the outcome.

Trevor finally spoke. "Listen up, everyone. For the next forty-five minutes, I shall be working with Patti, Kevin and Daniel. The rest of you can relax."

3:30 p.m.

During this unexpected free time, a football materialised from somewhere and several of the lads had a kick around in the alleyway outside Riverside Studio's entrance, greatly endangering Sir Andrew's immaculate midnight blue Mercedes Benz. The people at the reception desk came out and had a word. The guys duly transferred their game onto a small patch of grass by a nearby block of flats.

One of the RUG management arrived and sat in the back seat of Sir Andrew's car with the engine running and enjoyed the benefit of the cool air conditioning inside it. However, this meant that as we stood outside enjoying the fresh air, the car's exhaust fumes enriched the stink from the drains.

One of the staff at the reception desk came out and announced, "There's a phone call for Peter Gale."

It was Hilary Strange at Equity. "Hello, Peter. Can you ring me tonight at 9 p.m.? We need to sort out a time to meet face to face for a proper discussion about payment for the proposed TV documentary."

4 p.m. Studio 2

We were all called back inside. For two hours, we repeatedly ran "This Time Next Year" over and over and over, as Trevor modified and honed moves, positions and lines, again and again and again.

Finally, Sir Andrew seemed happy with the number's smoother, newly polished shape.

6 p.m.

Everyone now felt fairly knackered but more confident that the scene is cooking well.

9 p.m. Home

I rang Rachel Carter at Equity.

"Peter, I'll come in and have lunch with you at Riverside Studios next Monday 17th to give you details of Alan Benson's proposed payment for the TV documentary. You'll need to type out a summary of it and make photocopies for everybody to examine. And then we'll organise another full company meeting one day early next week, which I will attend with my colleague Hilary Strange. The Really Useful Company must give the company time during a rehearsal to do this," Rachel stressed, "Because it's part of the show's production." Rachel stressed this point. She then added a warning. "But don't make yourself unpopular with the director or the choreographer."

Hmm… Okay. Tricky.

I typed a notice for the company noticeboard. Here's the summary:

"Our Equity contact Rachel Carter will be coming into the theatre Monday 17th to give Nadia Strahan, *Nigel Wright and Peter Gale details about the proposed contract terms which the Really Useful Group has offered the company for a TV documentary about the show to be filmed, and for the use of extracts from it to be used in TV news programmes.

(*Nigel Wright is our stage management spokesman.)

When I had typed it out, I used coloured pencils to draw the *Sunset Boulevard* logo at the top.

I ended with, "We hope you consider this to be totally bona. Love you all to distraction."

I don't see why I should lose my sense of humour just because I am the Equity rep. But yes, I know. Business and pleasure don't mix.

THURSDAY 13th May 1993

10:15 a.m. Riverside Studios, Studio 2

Call for stretches and a physical warm-up with Maggie Goodwin and a vocal warm-up with Leslie Hayes.

I pinned my Equity update to the noticeboard.

10:30 a.m.

Trevor accompanied Andrew Lloyd Webber, who said, "I've decided that the men's number in the first act, 'The Lady's Paying', sounds too low, as well as too operetta-ish."

We duly sat round the piano and sang it through for Andrew. He began to cut out all harmonies and tried new higher keys, which took everyone (including Patti) by surprise as we all reached for unreachable notes and clutched intimate parts of our anatomy for support. Alas, oft-times to scant avail.

We ensemble quietly discussed the final raised key. I said, "That last note is so high only bats can hear it."

"Bats and homosexuals," came the dry correction.

Afterwards, Trevor said, "I'd now like to hear you sing it again in the old key. I appreciate that this is a pernicious request but it is quite ghastly to hear you straining your voices to achieve those upper notes. For the purposes of this rehearsal, let's work the numbers in their lower keys."

A wise and gratefully received request. My vocal cords are so bashed up this morning I can't sing anything above E over C anyhow.

Trevor now asked us to put our chairs aside and perform "The Lady's Paying" so that he could take a close look at all our physical flurry as we salesmen transform Joe's appearance from a bum to a toff.

After watching it, Trevor said to Bob Avian, "Could I ask you to add much more hustle and bustle of activity the moment the outfitters are given the signal to burst into action with their boxes and garments."

Personally, I feel that a whole morning spent on achieving this effect was making heavy weather of it, but at least it was done.

1 p.m. Lunch Break. Canteen

As we sat with Patti, she made this announcement. "I'd like you all to know I am having natural orange juice and milk delivered to my front door every morning!"

She was astonished when we told her that she could also order dairy products, plus bread, potatoes or chicken – even a Christmas pudding in December if she so desired. Maybe that's one service you *can't* get in New York.

2 p.m. Studio 2

The girls rehearsed the beauticians number.

Riverside Studios Entrance

During our extended lunch break, the men stood in the alley outside and discussed the ensemble's possible royalties if the BBC TV documentary is shown in America. It would be only about thirty percent of our daily pay and probably amount to £30.

Somebody pointed out, "This is Sir Andrew's car. It's a Mercedes Benz. It cost him £93,000."

Several of us were leaning against it.

"He apparently bought another two this morning," someone added.

Suddenly, the £30 royalties we'd been offered for the US TV documentary looked pretty meagre.

On a lighter note, Peter Rutherford said to me, "I officiated at my friend's funeral yesterday, Peter. It went off extremely well, dare I say. Several people asked me if I would organise theirs. It opens up a whole new career for me!"

Our conversation caught the attention of other cast members who named the music they'd like played at their burial. Oddly enough, an article was published in yesterday's Guardian about that very subject.

I said, "Marilyn Monroe chose 'Over the Rainbow'. Mine is Peggy Lee singing, 'Jump for Joy' with the Nelson Riddle Orchestra. I want everyone to get up and dance and have fun. It ought to be a celebration."

Bernard Sharpe, who is crazy about the army, said, "I've chosen 'The Dam Busters March' by Eric Coates, written for the 1955 film."

I said, "Brilliant! And they could bounce your coffin down the church aisle like the Barnes Wallis bombs in that movie."

Canteen

After Patti and the girls ran the beauticians number for Trevor, Sir Andrew and David Caddick, we were all told to relax in the canteen while Trev, Andrew and David had a secret discussion about further changes or improvements.

We call these tripartite conferences either Single or Double Door Meetings, depending on whether both the old soundproof Studio 2 doors are shut or just one. Today was a top security Double Door meeting from which the company was excluded, so Patti and the girls joined us outside.

We are still completely excluded from Trevor's rehearsals of book scenes involving Patti, Daniel and Kevin upstairs in Studio 3.

"Not ready yet for public consumption," Trevor had said.

This banishment also includes Bob Avian, our American choreographer, and Maggie Goodwin, his assistant. They joined us in the alley with cups of tea and coffee. Bob seemed a bit peeved.

"Friends ring and ask me how it's doing and I say, 'I don't know. I'm just sitting around most of the time, enlarging my behind!'"

As we were chatting, a lady from the entrance desk approached. "I've been given a car registration number. Do you know whose vehicle it belongs to? Because it's been broken into."

Sadly, it was owned by Sandy Strallen, our dance captain. A couple of local youths had smashed the car window and stolen his mobile phone which he had left on the front passenger seat. He is fully insured but the inconvenience for him is a pain in the neck. Sandy runs a theatre entertainment business in Sheffield and needs to use that phone constantly.

There is a curious coda to this story. Sandy often gives Richard Tate a lift home and as they were waiting till 7 this evening for the car window replacement people, they witnessed a blazing row in the alleyway. It was between Patti LuPone and a middle-aged couple who live in the block of flats directly opposite the rehearsal studios door. Something to do with the couple's lorry blocking Patti's chauffeur-driven car.

Sandy said, "I've heard my fair share of crude language, like most

of us in this business, but Patti's was spectacular."

"Listen," Patti said to me later, "I'm a New Yorker. Anyone shouts at me and I fire back with everything I've got. She didn't know what hit her. And he couldn't speak afterwards."

3:40 p.m.

This coffee break gave me a chance to grab a quick word with Peter Rutherford.

"Peter, I've awful news for you. I hate to say it but while you were away yesterday at your friend's funeral, Trevor gave me your solo line to sing during 'This Time Next Year' at the New Year party."

"I'm not in the least heartbroken, dear Peter. You are more than welcome to have the line. I am standing there, all dressed up as a Latin American speciality dancer in some film, sporting a Gilbert Roland moustache, trying vainly not to be recognisable as Mr Sheldrake, the Paramount film producer, otherwise known as Heather, and I come out with four words about DeMille, 'Till his next project', sung in a plumy South American accent, which wouldn't fool anyone – even if they understood it. So, I have no concerns about losing the line. Though it does demonstrate the danger of asking for time off to attend a funeral."

4 p.m.

The rest of the afternoon was spent checking the "ka-chings" in Bob's newly jived-up version of the opening company number, "Let's Have Lunch". He also added some cute stiff-legged bounces to the final moments, which gave the choreography a bit of style to match the apparently terrific arrangements which we still haven't yet heard.

Bob examined this number in detail, conferring with us one by one.

As I waited my turn, I saw Adam Matalon picking up paperclips from the floor (discarded from new script pages) and linking them into long necklaces. I wasn't pleased. I've been doing the same thing, collecting these silvery orphans to keep on my writing desk. What sad fate awaits these little chaps? To become jokey necklaces? Bracelets? Brooches? Badges? Earrings? Hair-clips? I mentioned this to Mark Inscoe and he reassured me my fears were groundless. He said Adam is an industrious writer, like me. He'll find each one a happy home.

6:10 p.m.

We broke.

FRIDAY 14th May 1993

10:15 a.m. Riverside Studios, Studio 2

A call for vocal warm-up exercises with David White.

10:30 a.m.

Trevor said, "I want to run the scene in Act 2 when Norma Desmond visits Paramount Studios to see Cecil B. DeMille. He's directing a movie on Stage 18 and she greets her old friend to ask him if he would direct her in her film, *Salome.* Up till now, Patti, when you've sung 'As If We Never Said Goodbye' in this scene, you have moved amongst the cast, touching the arm of someone briefly as if greeting a dear friend, and then focusing on another person for a few seconds."

"Yes, I really feel I need to at the moment."

"Of course. However, for today's run, before you begin to sing the number, Patti, I'd like you to sit on the stool when it's offered to you. Remain seated there, more isolated. Internalise the song."

After another run, he said, "Well, that was a very rough approximation to what we did last time. The most important point for you all to remember is that, when Norma is singing her reflective thoughts, you have to stay physically animated but begin, very gradually, to quiet down your conversations. Don't suddenly go silent, like switching off a radio, otherwise the magical moment doesn't happen."

Not easy. When Patti starts singing, my back is turned to her. I'm talking to Mark Inscoe, who is playing the props man.

I said, "Mark, can you give me a cue when to dwindle my chat volume button?"

He did.

Patti sang through the number again as Trevor described, a self-reflective monologue, delivering her final words to the audience, "We taught the world new ways to dream".

The fade-out of the company's chat was better and Trevor was happy with the result. Even so someone was heard speaking improvised dialogue on his own.

He said, "Do be aware that crowd scenes like this can be notoriously dangerous. If all the actors turn off their hubbub volume too abruptly, one person might be left speaking improvised dialogue in a loud voice on their own. This reminds me of something that happened in a production of *Julius Caesar* at Stratford. Mark Anthony called out his famous plea to the assembled Roman crowd: 'Friends, Romans, Countrymen, lend me your ears!' There was a sudden drop in the crowd noise, but a single voice was heard ringing round theatre, shouting, 'Use your own fucking ears!' This got a big laugh from the audience." It also received a hearty chortle from us.

Trevor added, "Of course, after that, the problem was that all the Roman citizenry went into frozen shock, too terrified to shout or even mutter a single improvised word during the rest of the scene." More laughs amongst the company.

Patti surprised us by pointing to the floor. "This insect," she said, "Has survived the whole number!"

A busily marching little brown oval person had been bravely acting out its own private drama through the entire scene, bang centre stage. Right under our feet!

"Of course, it survived," Trevor said. "It feels safe in the company of true-minded Buddhists who have respect for all forms of life – even weevils."

He gave me a brief glance. I wondered if Trevor was referring to something I told him years ago. When my partner Paulie died, I was advised by a friend to go to Buddhist meetings on a Sunday to help relieve the devastating loneliness. The best advice I was ever given.

Mark Inscoe scooped up the stage-struck tiny thespian with great care and placed it in the scene dock, well out of harm's way, to general approval.

Before we ran Norma Desmond's Act One arrival at Paramount again, Trevor sorted out the timing of various details, such as the important exchange of dialogue that Hog-eye (Richard Tate) has with Norma Desmond (Patti). Hog-eye is the electrician who calls down to Norma from the gantry. Sitting at the top of the stage right tower, he warmly welcomes Norma back to Paramount and then switches on his spotlight.

During the orchestral intro to Norma's song, Hog-eye moves the beam of his spotlight around the stage. It has to hit Norma just as the music reaches its crescendo.

Trevor also fine-tuned the movement of the big black panels which slide on and off. They create a huge black wall that masks the upstage area. It contains one important gap – the doorway into Stage 18 at Paramount.

1 p.m. Lunch at Riverside Canteen

Talking of Stage 18, Patti privately advised me that I'm mispronouncing the word "eighteen" when I play Jonesy, the security guard outside Paramount Studios gates.

She said, "In America, people say 'Paddy' for Patti, and 'Peder' for Peter. But when they say the word 'eighteen', the t is retained.

It's not pronounced 'eigh*deen*.' "

I consulted Joan Washington, our dialect coach. Joan clarified the point beautifully. "In America, the letter t is pronounced as a t if the following syllable is stressed – for example in the word 'striptease'. But if the next syllable is unstressed the t becomes a d. This means, for example, they say 'Paddy' for the name Patty, but 'can*teen*' and not 'can*deen!*'"

I said to Joan, "Yes, you're right. Patti says 'Noo York Siddy'. But this can be a bit ambiguous. If an American says, 'My wife's a great rider,' he could mean she's either a great horsewoman or a great author."

2 p.m.

After lunch, we were given new music for the opening of Schwab's Drug Store.

Andrew has made it shorter.

After looking at that, Bob Avian (choreographer) experimented with the idea of bringing the company on as a group *before* the pallets slide into their positions. These pallets are low rostrums that carry furniture and bits of scenery on and off the stage.

Bob's phrase for calling us to heel is, "Okay, people!" To sharpen our company entrance into Schwab's Drug Store, Bob tried out variations of the basic moves which we learnt at the *Sunset* dance auditions.

Trevor uses the phrase, "Listen up, everyone!" to gather our collective attention. Today, he added more details revealing a character's behaviour or motivation, and described the necessary rhythm of an individual's or a group's movement. Trevor's filigree work (as I call it) is tireless and, in my theatre experience, unequalled. For Trevor, every movement is an opportunity to enrich the telling of the story and is never wasted or left generalised.

"You are a terrific director!" Patti exclaimed during the note session, as Trev painted images and interior journeys to fuel everyone's performances. "I think you'd direct us if we were dying!"

Trevor considered this double-edged compliment. "I worked at Stratford with a fellow director called John Barton. After a play's final performance, he went round to all the dressing rooms giving notes to the cast."

"What the hell for?" Patti asked, amidst sniggers and exclamations of disbelief from the cast.

"He said to them, 'You never know, my comments might come in useful if you do the play again.'"

I worked with John Barton at Stratford-upon-Avon in the 1964 quarter centenary celebration of Shakespeare's birth. I was twenty-three years old, playing a tiny role, Young Talbot in *The Wars of the Roses*. Back then, it was weirdly rumoured that John Barton chewed razor blades. "The mind boggles!" people used to say, "And the body cramps," was the reply.

It was claimed that actors working at Stratford either had affairs, got married or divorced. I met the actor Paul Hardwick there and we lived happily together for nineteen years till Paulie made his final exit from this world's stage. So, it wasn't all pretend battles and fake blood. Some of it was real. Just kidding; we were devoted partners.

3 p.m. Canteen

The company were turfed out of the rehearsal room so that Trevor could work privately on the two-hander scene between Joe Gillis (Kevin) and Betty Schaeffer (Meredith) at Paramount Studios.

Sir Andrew arrived looking reasonably cheerful.

Somebody said, "You can always judge Andrew's state of mind by the colour of his chauffeur's tie."

And this afternoon, Jan's tie had a jolly multicoloured pattern.

3:30 p.m. Act Two, Scene Two

We worked on the short scene between me (playing Jonesy, the security guard at the gates of Paramount Studios) meeting Patti (Norma), Kevin (Joe) and Daniel (Max) as they arrive at Paramount's gates, seated in Norma's car. I was slightly flustered. I knew the lines but had never rehearsed the scene and wasn't sure when to enter, exactly how to run the dialogue or where to stand. Did I dry stone dead? Of course, I did.

Also, there is this "device". Norma (Patti), Max (Daniel) and Joe (Kevin) are downstage right sitting in the front seats of her car, the Isotta Fraschini Tipo 8A. It is a cut-out section of the vehicle, facing the audience. Max is behind the steering wheel. I am Jonesy, the older Paramount Studios guard. When I speak to Norma, Trevor has put me standing downstage left. The younger security guard (Gerard Casey) is downstage centre, both of us facing front. Gerard tries to stop Norma entering the studio but I tell him to let her car drive through, "You heard Miss Desmond."

Trevor said, "During this exchange, Peter, I want both you and Gerard to keep facing the audience as you talk, and not look at each other."

This feels very odd indeed. I'd like to discuss it but Trevor says, "Run the scene now."

We do.

He says, "That looks good."

So, I'm happy.

5 p.m.

We then ran the whole first scene outside Paramount Studios.

At the end, Trevor filled the ensuing customary graveyard

silence with an almost whispered, "Well done. That's beginning to look much better."

In the middle of this, David Caddick, our musical supervisor, brought in an orchestral recording of David Cullen's arrangement of the opening number, "Let's Have Lunch". Everything stopped as we listened to his terrific big-band swing version. Several cast members said it reminded them of "When You're a Jet" from Bernstein's *West Side Story*. It sounded absolutely glorious and gave us all a tremendous boost.

6 p.m.

Bob Avian said, "We'll call it a day. I would've preferred to continue for another hour or so but that would take us into overtime. So, let's finish there for the weekend."

Thank goodness we did. My voice sounds like a rusty drainpipe. Feels rough too.

As we packed up, one of the female ensemble said to me, "I'm glad Bob's letting us go. We only got £9 for working overtime the other day. It's hardly worth it."

The ensemble aren't called till 2:30 p.m. Monday afternoon – free to frisk the whole weekend long!

Yikes! I forgot that I arranged a hot Equity date with Rachel Carter at Riverside on Monday morning at 9:30 a.m. with the other company deputies. I must ring her and reschedule. Thank goodness I remembered.

Latest news: The reason the set is behind schedule is because it's so complicated to construct. The Adelphi stage management crew were due to start a "dry tech" (a technical run without actors) next Monday. It's now rescheduled to start the following Thursday.

In my Evening Standard it said, "The first public preview of *Sunset Boulevard* has been pushed back three days, from June 18th to the 21st."

SATURDAY 15th May 1993

Went out for a run, did a late spring clean, exercised and gardened.

Lunch

For light relief, I watched *Belle of New York* on TV, the 1952 Hollywood musical set in 1900, starring Fred Astaire and Vera Ellen. Great fun. It opens with Fred throwing a lavish party for his many ex-girlfriends, bidding goodbye to them and his Lothario ways before getting spliced…

"Who wants to kiss the bridegroom

On his last night out?

Next time you bring champagne on,

I'll have the ball and chain on."

I also taped another Astaire film, *Silk Stockings* (1957), with a score by Cole Porter. It was an expensive flop, took four and a half months to rehearse and shoot, and cost MGM $1.4 million. A ton of dough back then. It was Fred's farewell to twenty-four years of dazzling tap routines. He was aged fifty-eight. His leading lady Cyd Charrise was twenty-three years younger than him. In Hollywood casts, a young male star was never paired with an older female star. *Sunset Boulevard* was a notable exception.

After lunch, I popped next door to see my neighbour Jill Beck. Jill used to work for a publishing company called Scripts. It was set up and run by the actor Victor Madden. She typed out professional-looking copies of plays, books and film scripts that were hand-written by the likes of Tom Stoppard, Laurence Olivier, Harold Pinter and Edna O'Brien.

On Jill's kitchen table was another pile of pages – a new novel by Joan Collins. I looked at the top one.

"Good Lord, Jill. I can't make this out at all. How on earth can you decipher her writing? It's just rows and rows of loops!"

"Joan says that I'm the only person who can read her handwriting."

We had a jolly cuppa tea in her leafy back garden. Just the job.

Shopped at Sainsbury's.

Went to see my friend Richenda Carey in *Redeeming Vices* by Michael Browning at the Hampstead New End Theatre. That building began life as the local mortuary. A corpse hotel!

Richenda and I first met two years ago acting in the TV series *The Darling Buds of May* directed by Rodney Bennett. A twenty-two-year-old actress named Catherine Zeta-Jones played the daughter, Mariette Larkin.

Rodney said to me, "When we were casting the role of Mariette, our production office was inundated with photographs of beautiful young actresses sent to us by their agents. There was a pile of them on a table. One photo immediately caught my eye. I pointed to it. 'Bring her in,' I said. It was Catherine."

SUNDAY 16th May 1993

I drove over to see my friend and neighbour, the actress Bronwen Williams.

"You're such a generous hostess, I want to wish you 'A Happy 50th Birthday!' by treating you to a delicious, eat-what-you-like buffet spread lunch at Surya, the new Indian vegetarian restaurant in West End Lane."

Bronnie is currently starring with Barry Cryer and Willie Rushton in their comedy show, *Two Old Farts in the Night.*

Extremely funny.

7 p.m.

I rang Rachel Carter, our Equity *Sunset Boulevard* negotiator. We rescheduled our Equity meeting tomorrow.

We'll lunch at 12 p.m. At 1 p.m., we need to discuss how much the ensemble actors and stage management will be paid by RUG for appearing in a TV documentary about *Sunset Boulevard* the BBC are planning to make.

MONDAY 17th May 1993

No morning call

7:30 a.m. BBC Radio News

A report says the Bosnian Serbs have rejected the Owen-Vance Peace Treaty. Never mind that. We have a show to put on!

10:45 a.m.

My backpack is pounds lighter since I stopped carrying the entire script and stacks of music to work. Every day, we get handed more pages, mostly new copies of the same five numbers whose lyrics or keys have been altered or cut. How many more forests have to bite the dust?

Good news. I'm deeply relieved that my voice has returned to normal after feeling scratchy and sounding hoarse by the end of last week. I won't belt out my stuff in rehearsal any more. My singing teacher, Gladys Lack, warned me. She was elderly and frail but in her younger days she had sung in the chorus at Covent Garden Opera.

"Chorus work can be helpful," she said. "You can stand close to a singer you admire and hear how they produce the sound. The problem is that a vocal technique that works for them might not work for you. Also, amongst many others you might not be able to hear your own voice and unknowingly slip into bad habits – poor intonation, for example. And being told repeatedly to increase your volume could tempt you to strain your vocal cords."

12 p.m. Riverside Studios Canteen

I met my two Equity contacts Rachel Carter and Hilary Strange for a chat over lunch.

1:30 p.m. Studio 2. Equity Meeting

In the big rehearsal room, we were joined by Nadia Strahan (my Equity co-representative) and Nigel Wright, the stage management spokesman.

We all sat down and Rachel began.

"I shall outline for you the financial terms Sir Andrew's company RUG has proposed for making a TV documentary about the show, and for using film clips of the show in news programmes – it's called News Access. RUG has made the company an offer. They will also pay you royalties if they use the original sound recording of *Sunset Boulevard* in any of those clips."

I am trying hard to be nice to Nadia but I find her manner infuriating. She either disagrees violently with any suggestion I make or patronises me unbearably. Here's an example. When the Equity meeting ended, I asked her to help me clarify a technical point about the percentage of the recording sales for the summary I was hastily jotting down.

She walked away briskly, saying, "We'll discuss it later. No need to bother about that now."

Her reply puzzled me and I suspected she was avoiding the subject.

2:30 p.m. Riverside Studios, Studio 2

Sir Andrew watched Bob Avian rechoreograph parts of the number in Artie's party, "This Time Next Year". We then performed the whole number for him.

Afterwards, Andrew shortened:

a) the three temple virgins' sexy oriental dance routine
b) the *Samson and Delilah* jokey cabaret mime at Artie's party
c) and a section of lyrics we sing there about DeMille.

All good cuts, I think.

The phrase I sing, "Till his next project", (inherited from Peter Rutherford last Wednesday) that also went.

Nobody sings it now. Nobody has a lovely voice. Sounds unearthly.

Bob then examined the opening of Schwab's Drug Store. A group of us enter in a tight clump and simultaneously travel downstage centre performing three different dance steps, and then begin the next vocal section. That move lasts barely twenty seconds but we spent an hour and a half polishing it. We rehearsed/checked/changed it. Rehearsed/checked/changed it. Rehearsed/checked/changed it, again and again and again and again and again and again.

This is the only way Bob Avian can see what works. He sweetly explained his problem. "I'm searching to establish a conformity of style for all the ensemble numbers which is not overtly dance but physically reflects the high-octane quality of the jazz arrangements. I must respect Trevor's insistence that there should be no choreographic shift towards 'musical comedy dance routines', as such. So, I want to see you mime everything – chatting, walking in rhythm, holding a pose or using enlarged gestures and so on, and then I can see what combination of them looks best at what point."

After that, we worked on the opening number, "Let's Have Lunch". At the mere mention of it, the company groans, "Oh no."

On the newly revised music handed to me, I noticed someone had written, "More BOOGIE than previously." It replaces "Shuffle Jive" written on earlier sheets. But it looks as if we are finally getting to grips with the number's physical, musical – and "wordal" complexity, as someone called it. I ain't never heard of no wordal before. Looked it up. No such wordal in my dictionary. Absurdal!

Just one thing bothers me. During this opening number, I play the film actor Sammy dressed as a Babylonian priest for the epic movie at Paramount Studios. A photograph taken at the fitting shows me in this costume looking like a walking Christmas tree. On my head is a tall gold crown. Round my chops a long beard with curly ringlets dangles down. I have a shiny gold breastplate and a floor-length robe made of upholstery material. From my shoulders hangs a huge cloak with a long train that drags behind me. I wonder, will the audience even recognise me when I re-appear as Sammy at Artie's party dressed in my civvies? In the opening number, all this floor-length fabric will hide all my snazzy "ka-chings" from the audience. A tragic loss.

Bob Avian added more activity in the loud, brassy central section of the music. This is when tall black panels (called the runners) slide off to reveal the back lot at Paramount. That spectacular set will fill the whole stage. At Riverside Studios, substituting for the runners, we have coat rails on wheels hung with black masking material. Tall steel towers will also move onstage and offstage carrying studio lights.

DeMille (Michael Bower) and his camera crew (Mark Inscoe and Nick Colicos) will be seen perching on top of one of these towers and will climb up and down them as part of the action. Today at Riverside Studios, standing in for the towers we have tubular steel frames on wheels. Our stage management team are pushing them about to give us an idea how the set will work around us.

When we get to the technical rehearsal at the Adelphi Theatre and perform with the actual scenery – well! That's really going to be something. I can't wait!

Before a final run of "Let's Have Lunch", David Caddick (our musical supervisor) made a request. "As the majority of you leave the stage at the end of this number, would the people who work in the next scene keep going so that we can see how the action flows from one into the other."

As the ensemble left the stage singing the last phrase of "Let's Have Lunch", Joe, the movie script writer (Kevin Anderson) begins to plead with Sheldrake the producer (Peter Rutherford) for money for all the writing he has done on spec. Betty (Meredith Braun), the studio's script reader, then enters and gives a very negative report on Joe's submitted outline, but makes a date with Joe to discuss it with him further. We have only rehearsed chorus numbers for four weeks. This is the first actual scene performed by the principals that we've been allowed to watch.

It turns out Kevin, Peter and Meredith have scarcely worked on the scene at all with Trevor. What do they do upstairs in Studio 3? Listen to Trev talk, I suppose.

5:50 p.m.

We broke.

As we began to leave, David Caddick said, "That was very good everyone. Just to let you know, we'll be rehearsing further vocal changes tomorrow, because Sir Andrew is constantly revising the musical texture of the piece. So, bear with us please. And thank you for your hard work and patience." That was nice.

I caught Nadia's attention on the way out. "Before you go, Nadia, could you help me clarify a point about the percentage of the recording sales royalties? I'd like to make sure I jotted them down right."

To my astonishment, Nadia smiled and treated the whole matter as a joke. Without stopping, she said, "To be honest, I haven't got the faintest idea what any of it meant and didn't make any notes. Let's not bother about it now. We'll work it all out later."

I was warned that she was sacked by RUG on a previous show for unprofessional behaviour, whatever that means. It doesn't surprise me.

Worryingly, one of her female chums said to me, "RUG has re-employed Nadia in this show under probation." In other words, she expects to be paid for doing this job but is glad to dump all the work involved on me. What the hell?

6 p.m.

Going home, the tube train was full of hairy young people wearing black leather jackets and Iron Maiden T-shirts decorated with ghoulish monsters climbing out of graves.

I asked one of them sitting next to me what the occasion was. He was swigging on a beer bottle wrapped in a plastic bag. I think he told me to fuck off.

So, I asked another fresh-faced tribe member. He kindly explained that they were all attending a rock concert at Wembley. Rain was lashing down outside.

"Won't you all get wet?" I asked in my Mary Poppins schoolmarm tone.

"It's covered," he replied.

God, I'm old.

TUESDAY 18th May 1993

5 a.m.

Wrote this.

8 a.m.

Ran round the streets, then did a workout.

10 a.m.

Rang my agent about claiming royalties on my rewrites of *Gatsby* that I directed at the King's Head theatre back in March.

"Peter, I do understand how angry you feel at the shabby way they've treated you. But I suggest in the long run it would be better to forget about a co-adaptor credit on posters in future productions or in the programmes, let alone a claim for royalties."

I'd like to shrug it all off because it's been so horrible. But I felt I should make some gesture of protest and not allow them to walk all over me. But what? A letter to the Stage. Wow! That *would* show them.

"Here's the bottom line, Peter. You don't have a literary agent to fight your corner. Legal advice would cost you a fortune. Nor can Equity help you because the play wasn't produced on Equity contracts. It's awful, I agree with you, but my best advice is to chalk the whole thing up to experience and focus on *Sunset Boulevard*. Sorry."

She's right. It would be less trouble just to drop it.

10:30 a.m.

Nigel Wright rang me. He is the *Sunset* stage management spokesman.

"Hello Peter. I've tried to contact Hillary Strange but she's at Stratford-upon-Avon, visiting the RSC company."

"That's okay, Nigel. I rang my other Equity contact last night, Rachel Carter. We cleared up a couple of points and I've typed them out on a statement for the whole company to read. This afternoon I'll bring it to Riverside and pin it on the company noticeboard. It summarises Equity's three proposed payment terms. One, for the TV documentary; two, for the News Access clips, and three, for the recording."

12 p.m.

Lunched at home.

2 p.m. Riverside Studios, Reception Hall

I dutifully pinned the statement on the noticeboard and told everyone I would make photocopies to give them. I also suggested there should be a company meeting about it tomorrow.

I then had a personal word with Kevin and Daniel. "This afternoon, the company has to agree over their share-out of the recording royalties at a meeting. So, you and the other principals, Patti and Meredith, will have to discuss amongst yourselves what proportion of the points you'll agree to take."

This royalties issue is a tricky mess. I hope sorting it out doesn't drive me nuts.

2:30 p.m. Studio 3. Music Call

We rehearsed upstairs in the smaller Studio 3, where the company first gathered three and a half weeks ago.

David Caddick (musical supervisor) gave us Andrew's revised vocal parts for "This Time Next Year". The vocal arrangement now has fewer harmonies and a clearer melodic line. The tenors and baritones are praying that it won't sit any higher for them than it already does, but I think several more top A's have been added to a few of their phrases.

The weather is lovely but it makes this room sticky hot for us to work in. And a loud echo doesn't help much either.

Sir Andrew joined us, listened to his reworked version and seemed pleased. "What I'm trying to do is to avoid making you all sound like a chorus out of the *White Horse Inn*."

That was a hugely successful 1930s German operetta, very old-fashioned now. In London, one song was called "Happy Cows"! On Broadway, it was changed to "Cowshed Rhapsody". Mooody.

"*Also*," Andrew continued, "We want to aim for a clearly sung statement about your hopes for the New Year, to preserve the party atmosphere but not let it degenerate into a rowdy, yelling football crowd."

"It's attitude," said David Caddick, our musical supervisor.

"Attitude" seems to be the buzzword these days.

"Whatever you're doing," David continued, "Drinking, dancing or lounging on the sofa, you must preserve that level of energy and accuracy through the whole number, otherwise it slides into a lazy, soggy delivery which becomes quickly boring. And when you make that final statement, hoping that you won't be saying all these things 'This Time Next Year', don't drop your energy level! Keep pushing it through to the final note."

This "attitude" was queried. The original idea was, for a moment, to make our penultimate sung statement reflective and ironic, before we repeated a big full-stop statement: 'This Time Next Year!' We tried to point out to Andrew that Bob Avian had told us to face the audience for one brief, private "thinks" moment to ourselves, before we turn back to each other, raise our glasses and make the final, big, emphatic toast.

"No," Mr Caddick insisted. "That moment mustn't be reflective."

Okay. Now we were really confused.

"You mean more like the Hitler Youth?" offered Richard Tate.

There was a stunned silence. And then the room exploded with echoing laughter and chatter. Sir Andrew stared at Richard in complete bafflement. Or disbelief?

Richard struggled to elucidate. "Like in *Cabaret*, when they sing 'Tomorrow Belongs to Me'." But his efforts to explain were completely wasted in the hubbub. I knew exactly what Richard meant and he was spot on, although his comment did sound suspiciously like a wisecrack.

Conflicting directions from a production team inevitably occur in a many-headed beast like a musical – the director wants one thing, the choreographer wants another, the producer wants another and the musical director another. You have to juggle them as best you can. That's what made rehearsing *No No Nanette* at Drury Lane in 1973 such a nightmare. They all constantly disagreed with each other.

Sir Andrew and David Caddick left. We continued to polish the singing with David White, our conductor. He struggled valiantly to drill us into high-precision phrasing and diction but our concentration was cracking and crumbling beyond help.

"Hold the vocal sounds till the end of the note, 'Thi-i-i-i-i-i-i-i-i-is time'. And begin the word 'we' with the 'ooo' sound, before the 'eeh' right on the beat. Ooo-Wee."

Well, Ooo-Wee did our best but it became a schoolroom of high-spirited kids singing that they needed to go for a Ooo-Wee. Just then, Ooo-Wee were called downstairs to rehearse the end of the show with Trevor.

Good timing.

3 p.m. Riverside Studios, Studio 2

Before looking at the show's final scene, Trevor explained, "The whole atmosphere in Norma's house is now very low key. The ladies and gentlemen of the press have gathered and are quietly waiting for the police to give them information about the murder."

We ran the scene several times accompanied by a loud banging of drums from next door.

Trevor explained. "It's a company of Japanese taiko dancers rehearsing for their forthcoming show at Sadler's Wells."

Patti coped skilfully with their thuds and thumps counterpointing Norma Desmond's final crazy aria.

In his note sessions, Trevor sometimes uses the word "miserating" to describe the very opening scene of the show when the police pull the body out of the pool at dawn. It's a new one on me. I've looked it up. Miserating means depressing. Trev also asked for Norma's lullaby music which introduces the final scene to be played slower.

David Caddick said, "I'm sorry, Trevor, but Andrew specifically asked for it to be played faster this last time. That's why I've tried to push it along at a quicker tempo."

There followed a fascinating pause. We held our breath, awaiting the outcome of this direct conflict of desires.

Trevor smiled. "I think I'd better cut my tongue out."

We ran the final scene. Patti, who always weeps real tears, delivered her final speech about making a comeback movie an even more emotional confession to the world. Terrific!

Trevor updated us on the rest of the week's schedule. Tomorrow: a run of Act One. Thursday: a run of Act Two. Friday: a full run.

"When will we be getting into the theatre?" Alisa Endsley asked.

"Monday," he replied. "We are *just* on schedule, so that's all going

well, fingers crossed. Why do you want to know? Do you have special

arrangements to make?"

"No. Just curiosity."

"Well, the proper answer to that is mind your own business."

We all laughed. But as we dispersed, Alisa asked me if Trevor was being serious.

"I'm not sure, exactly. I assumed it was meant as a joke, but it was a pretty ungracious one."

"But was I wrong to ask? Did I say something I shouldn't have? Is it because I'm American? Don't you ask questions like that over here?"

"I guess we're more passively obedient. I'm pretty sure it's a question everyone would like to ask, and there's no real reason why we shouldn't. I'm sorry Trevor made you feel uncomfortable."

The whole company is eagerly looking forward to getting into the Adelphi Theatre and sorting out their costumes and dressing tables and cupboard spaces. And it's a specially exciting moment when a performer can finally walk into a theatre or studio, get a feel of the acting space and use the actual props and furniture, after coping with make-do bits and pieces in a grubby, sometimes echoey church hall.

And yet... A special atmosphere is often created in that room or hall where actors have improvised makeshift props or clothing, and coped with whatever furniture is available, however rough and ready. And, sometimes, the final run-through there can have a vivid immediacy never quite recaptured in the theatre. The soul of the work has grown organically from nothing, occasionally producing lovely subtle, intimate details that might later evaporate with the addition of a big stage, elaborate costumes, wigs, props and scenery. Not always, of course, but sometimes.

Our company manager Richard Oriel has organised a full company call for tomorrow morning: 10 a.m.

Let's hope we can solve the recording royalties problem amicably.

WEDNESDAY 19th May 1993

8:45 a.m.

Today, a full company Equity meeting at 10 a.m.

Left the house bang on "a quarter of nine", as they say in Noo York.

A show's Equity deputy cannot be late!

Oh yes? Little did I know what awaited me.

9:20 a.m.

Reader alert! This diary entry is strictly for fans of Charles Pooter's *Diary of a Nobody* by George and Weedon Grossmith.

"Today, I told my wife Carrie that a bomb scare paralysed Green Park's underground tube. Most tiresome. Passengers were instructed to vacate their carriages and leave the station! I complained to a ticket barrier official. 'This is most inconvenient. I am an actor, rehearsing a musical by Sir Andrew Lloyd Webber. I am also the cast's union rep, and at 10 a.m., I'm chairing an important Equity conference at Riverside Studios. I have even bought a new rail pass!' The station employee shrugged and asked me if I would rather die in an explosion and be sent home in a wooden box. He then produced a handkerchief and blew his nose, loudly. I told Carrie that I was mortified but managed to hail a taxi. Then, of all things, in the Cromwell Road we became stuck in a traffic jam. The cab fare was now £3.60. I stepped out of the vehicle and gave the driver £4.00 which included an adequate tip. No word of thanks, of course; only a surly grunt. At Gloucester station, to my intense relief, the Metropolitan line was working and I went three stops to Hammersmith station. Proceeding on foot, I crossed two busy traffic lanes and hastened along Queen Caroline Street to Riverside Studios in Crisp Road. After describing this to Carrie, I heard her snore loudly. She had nodded off and was fast asleep in her chair. I prodded her. She woke up and said, 'Where am I? Oh yes. Sounds like you had a nice day, dear. What's the time? Did you remember to buy the celery?'"

10 a.m. Equity Meeting. Riverside Studios, Studio 2

Only twelve company members arrived (out of twenty-eight). After waiting five minutes, we discussed the terms of the proposed filming agreement. It was generally found acceptable.

Adam Matalon asked, "Will we have any control over the use of the documentary in all countries outside Britain and USA? What about those royalties?"

I said, "I raised this matter with Rachel at Equity. She said that on balance the terms seem okay. There's no extra work involved for us. It isn't going to be a film version of our show. It's a documentary about the creation of the musical, featuring a series of interviews with the adaptors. Nor will it be an elaborate commercial advert for the production, otherwise *Omnibus* (BBC TV's arts documentary series) wouldn't touch it."

Another decision we considered at the meeting was about making a record. But, until the agents who represent our lead actors have settled their clients' contract deals with RUG, we can't get those performers' votes on the royalties (or points) question. It means that no choice of options could be made about an LP.

Anyhow, today's discussion was useful. People aired all the questions they wish to raise at tomorrow's meeting with Rachel and Hilary. I made a list of the questions, rang Hilary during the afternoon coffee break and gave them to her secretary for Hilary to consider.

10:30 a.m.

Trevor began to examine the entire first act, running it section by section. Us lot in the ensemble watched the book scenes for the first time. There was a sense of occasion and an avid interest seeing the principals work.

However, there is also a distinct feeling of grievance amongst the ensemble about the way we are being treated. David Caddick (musical supervisor) scolded us for singing one particular phrase sloppily at the end of "This Time Next Year". It is the number at Artie's party that closes Act One with that very same phrase, "this time next year".

We have rehearsed the wretched little creep with Mr Caddick and David White (our conductor) till we are boss-eyed. Sung it quick. Sung it slow. Brighter. Softer. Every which way except out of our backsides. Now Mr Caddick decides to change it again. Much faster this time. He should fix it separately and not interrupt this rehearsal with such a piddling detail. Besides which, we are also trying to remember numerous re-revised harmonies we were given only yesterday for this song.

Another irritating moment was Trevor's complaint. "On the last line of that number, you all faced front." Indeed we did, for a simple reason – because we were told to do precisely that by our choreographer, Bob Avion. Yes, he was the dastardly perpetrator of this criminal offence who had specifically, nay, *laboriously* rehearsed us to face front. And, what's more, he was sitting right in front of us, next to Trevor! This made Bob our chief witness for the defence.

Bob graciously pointed this out. "Trevor, it's my fault."

"No, it's not your fault," Trevor insisted, as if he was dealing with a bunch of intractable brats. But since we are hoping to be employed again by Mr Nunn nobody dares utter a word of protest.

We then rehearsed the scene in Schwab's Drug Store which comes earlier in the first act. It opens with the ensemble's arrival. Today, our cue to enter was changed yet again. And get this. Singing a reprise of the show's opening song, "Let's Have Lunch", we now enter on the *first* beat of the *second* bar containing *six* beats, that's after the *first* bar containing *seven* beats, instead of on the *fourth* beat of the *second* bar containing *six* beats. Are you with me? Please pay attention.

Also, we *had* been told to stop bouncing on our toes with stiff legs on the word "hold" during "Hold the fries!". *Now* we halt on "fries".

And today, Trevor wants us to be less stylised and to start chatting to each other earlier. We've rehearsed so many variations of moves, lyrics and harmonies, it is hard to remember which one was the most recent.

This also applies to the principals. At one point in "The Lady's Paying" (the gentlemen's outfitters' number), Patti said to David Caddick, our musical supervisor, "I need to ask you an important question, David. Which version of the song do you want me and Kevin to sing?"

David smiled impishly. "The latest," came his helpful reply.

1:15 p.m. Lunch

2:15 p.m.

During Trevor's notes session on "The Lady's Paying", David admonished us gentlemen's outfitters for not singing the full

189

chorus strongly enough.

"You must sing *at least* three times louder to give it the brilliance Andrew wants."

All right, all right, for pity's sake. He seems to forget that we are trying to remember recently revised business, altered harmonies and revised melodic lines. In fact, we're all totally hacked off with being treated like a bunch of lazy school kids instead of experienced, talented actors.

We ran "The Lady's Paying" several times, during which Patti galloped to our rescue. She introduced a hysterical note into the number. As she sang some lines about not being "a platinum blonde bitch", she did an extremely funny imitation of Ethel Merman, the legendary brassy-voiced star of Broadway musicals like *Gypsy* and *Anything Goes*. At least someone was keeping a sense of humour.

3:15 p.m. Coffee Break

Trevor seems a bit peeved. Is it because his funnies aren't going down well with the company today? I'm still his number one fan but his dismissive way of over-riding actors' tentative comments or suggestions can be demeaning. And at times, he impatiently grips you by the elbow and shunts you into a different position, making you look and feel stupid.

Here's a small example. I asked an assistant stage manager if the bar stool I sit on in Schwab's Drug Store is moveable.

She said, "No. They will all be fixed to the pallet, which slides on and offstage."

However, I had earlier nipped out for an urgently needed leak. Big mistake.

I later discovered that while I was gone, Trevor said, "For the purposes of today's rehearsal, as you exit Schwab's Drug Store, I want you to pick up the stools you've been sitting on and take them off with you, just to facilitate the scene change."

Consequently, not having heard this, Peter made his exit from Schwab's Drug Store and blithely left his bar stool where it was. Oh dear. Naughty Peter must choose better moments to strain the potatoes.

Trevor said, "Okay. We'll run the scene again. And this time, Peter, it would help if you take your stool off with you as you exit." He then added, "We know how you hate moving furniture, Peter."

Was this a joke? A barbed comment on my work attitude? It might have been a dig at my being the Equity dep. and trying to claim extra "push and pull" money for ensemble artists who are directed to move props or furniture during a scene change in full view of the audience. They are entitled to and should have "push and pull" payment clauses in their contracts.

At the end of the coffee break, Sir Andrew passed me on his way to sit in his chair. Once again, we came face to face. I smiled and said, "Hello."

He could barely look me in the eye, let alone reply. I think he murmured, "Hi."

Maybe he thinks I'm a trade union book-thumping troublemaker.

4:15 p.m.

Trevor said, "I'd now like to rehearse the end of that number in Schwab's Drug Store. Then we'll run the whole scene from the top and continue to the end of Act One before we break for coffee."

An aghast silence. The cast and stage management glumly prepared to carry out his ambitious plan.

Trevor added, "You obviously don't find the idea amusing."

Was it intended to be? If continuing to work for another hour and forty-five minutes was meant to be funny, we missed the joke.

A fellow actor quietly muttered to me, "Sorry, Trevor, but you frequently work us for two and a half hours without a coffee break."

This is a complaint I often have to pass on to the stage management as the company Equity dep.

Before we ran the whole of Act One, the New Year's Eve party number was changed again. A section that was removed yesterday was now put back.

Trevor said, "Who cut it? I wasn't even aware it had gone."

I was glad it was kept because it included one of my lines in the party cabaret when I mimic Cecil B. DeMille boasting that each of his chorus girls "is a genuine Philistine". And wait for this. I was given the next lyrics to sing as well! Visions of star billing stirred in my crazy, stage-struck heart.

5:50 p.m.

Our schedule was to finish at 6 p.m.

"Okay, listen up everyone!" Trevor said. "We'll set up for the opening and run Act One again. We'll probably get through about two thirds before we have to stop."

This announcement did not please the company who like to be informed if we will be working late.

6:45 p.m.

Fifty-five minutes later, Trevor stopped us before we sang the number at Artie's New Year's Eve party; we had rehearsed that earlier. He expressed approval of the work achieved.

"Very good indeed. Tomorrow, we'll do the same thing with Act Two."

It was a long day. Including this morning's Equity call, we worked for eight hours and forty-five minutes.

7:30 p.m.

Tube to Finchley Road tube station. Shopped at Waitrose. Staggered home down Goldhurst Terrace with my laden bags and finally...

8 p.m.

... at "ada clark" (so called in the US), I tucked into my wholemeal toasted buns, Earl Grey tea, yoghurt and fruit dip, banana, pear and apple.

Before rehearsals tomorrow morning, we have an early 9:45 a.m. company call. An important meeting with our Equity people.

THURSDAY 20th MAY 1993

9:45 a.m. Riverside Studios. Studio 2. Equity Meeting

"Do we have a quorum?" I cried, trying to seem super business-like.

"You're really getting into it," Rachel Carter teased.

Rachel and Hilary Strange (from Equity) were sitting side by side with Nigel Wright (stage manager spokesperson) and me. Facing us were only sixteen cast members, also seated. The missing twelve were either late or not coming. We waited a few minutes and then began to discuss the proposed TV documentary deal.

I had earlier passed on to Rachel all the company's comments made at yesterday's meeting. She now clarified them and we voted to accept RUG's offered deal. We have to tolerate unlimited use of TV extracts screened overseas (except USA) because there's no alternative now. The big problem here is that the old standard agreement was modified to accommodate small independent production companies, who (unlike the BBC) do not have the facilities to handle royalties. For example, in the past I've received many repeat fee cheques for BBC TV dramas shown in Australia. But these days, the BBC is buying in TV films from small outside companies. Confusingly, they are often formed to produce only one single movie or one TV series. That company could have stopped trading but somewhere a producer is still pocketing repeat fees for the showing of those programmes. It's a fairly wretched situation being looked into by Equity.

The five percent which Equity takes off royalties from the record sales every six months has a ceiling of up to £100 per artist in each distribution pay. This £100 is Equity's fee for auditing the royalties. Overall, the deal on the *Sunset Boulevard* recording is the best so far for all such show recordings made in London. I'm just hoping the summary of the offered deal that I typed out, photocopied and distributed to the company is acceptably comprehensive and accurate. Fingers crossed.

Now our task is to find out if the three American principals (Patti, Kevin and Daniel) have a separate LP record royalties auditing fee deal with RUG. If they have, will they *also* expect to receive a percentage of the 7.5% (effectively 7.1%) paid to all Equity cast members in the show? Until this is clarified, we can't vote on what sort of "share-out of the points" system we will adopt. The musicians have their own separate union agreement.

Patti arrived as the meeting closed, saying, "Where's Peter?"

I was puzzled that she appeared just after Hilary had left.

"Peter, my record deal with RUG is not agreed yet." She seemed to feel it was important I should understand this. She then mysteriously added, "My agent in New York said that we will never know what proportion of the shares will come out with Equity."

This was totally incomprehensible to me and I begged her to discuss the matter with Hilary but she adamantly refused. Does Patti think we are prying into details of her private financial arrangements? All we want to know is if she has a separate LP royalties deal with RUG, or if her agent is taking a percentage of the royalties allotted to the company. Oh brother!

If Patti regards me as her British Equity spokesperson, why didn't she attend today's meeting? Is it because she is on an American Equity contract?

Patti said the other day, "I'd be happy to do an even split of the points as long as my own separate fee isn't affected." But that was an off-the-record conversational remark. However, when the LP deal was mentioned at today's company meeting (perhaps a bit previously), some of the leading actors were a bit unsettled. They probably suspect this particular framework of points distribution is being pushed to the front prematurely – before everyone has had a chance to vote on it properly. Sounds like a proportional "Who's got the most solo lines on the record" system will be adopted.

Later, as someone queried a detail, Rachel Carter leant sideways and muttered to me, "People get so greedy the moment money comes into the discussion. Pound signs pop up in their eyes."

Her comment puzzled me. What else are we talking about? Money is absolutely central in Equity's job of protecting actors' rights.

I felt I had to reply. "Well, it is our livelihood we're fighting for here, Rachel. And the bottom line is that huge profits could be involved, as on previous show recordings, like *Phantom* and *Cats*. We don't want to lose out on what is fairly ours."

Oh well. Back to the coal face.

10:40 a.m. Riverside Studios, Studio 2

We started rehearsing without Kevin – he was having a costume fitting.

"While Kevin's not here," Trevor said, "I'd like to run the scene when Norma visits Paramount in Act Two."

Trevor watched us perform it several times, trying out different positions for everyone and varying our movements around Patti to see how they looked.

Act Two

We prepared to start our first full run of Act Two. I like to use a substitute prop when rehearsing the role of Jonesy, the Paramount Studios security guard. I shall be wearing his dark blue uniform in the show, plus a peaked cap, much like a New York policeman's cap. Today, I wore my baseball cap with the *Empire of the Sun* logo on it. It was in a goodies bag Warner Brothers gave me when I finished work on that film. Also, it reminds everyone what a big movie star I am. But even internationally famous actors like wot I am make mistakes.

Today, when I mimed picking up the wall phone to call Stage 18 with a message for Mr DeMille, I forgot Joan Washington's dialect coaching instructions. I mispronounced the word "eighteen" and wrongly used a hard d instead of t. I then added, "Oh fuck. Eigh-*teen*."

After that, I couldn't continue because the entire company were roaring with laughter, particularly Patti.

I apologised to everyone. "I'm sorry. It's the heat."

Trevor replied, "It's the hat!"

Another big company laugh.

Trevor seemed in good spirits, clearly pleased with his re-adjusted positioning of the scene.

"But just one word of warning," he said. "I have to insist that you cannot treat Mr DeMille as if he was just anyone. You never brush past Mr DeMille. Me? Yes. But not him."

More laughter.

2:45 p.m. Act Two. A Full Run

Kevin arrived back from his costume fitting and we began an Act Two run. This was the first time we've heard Kevin sing the song "Sunset Boulevard" that opens the second half of the show.

Kevin is giving a strong performance which well matches up to Patti's Norma, considering that Joe Gillis is arguably a more passive, reflective, less demonstrative character. Kevin is what I call a theatre beast. Some fine actors internalise their work, which is wonderful for camera close-ups but it doesn't always get across in a big theatre. Projecting the interior world of such an introspective person as Joe Gillis can be tricky. Kevin isn't afraid to "cheat front" – to face the audience and engage with them during a song and make it look natural.

Okay, no one wants phony but this theatre seats 1,500 people, on three different levels. What we do and say must carry – travel away from us beyond whoever it is we are addressing on the stage.

This is easier for Patti. Her character is as big as she wants to paint her. Well, maybe not exactly easier but Norma's style is extravagant, demonstrative, hence more theatrical.

This morning, we ran the scene when Norma Desmond phones Betty Schaeffer after finding out Joe has formed a close friendship with Betty in the world outside, away from Norma's control of Joe (Kevin) in her prison-like mansion. When Norma rings Betty and makes jealous comments to her, Joe snatches the phone from Norma's hand.

Today, as Kevin grabbed the phone and pulled it away from her, its cord also yanked the heavy dialling base off the desk. It swung free and bashed poor Patti's knee like an anvil. She yelled out and doubled up in pain on the sofa. Soon afterwards, Kevin slammed the phone down on its cradle, which sliced his hand open. He proceeded to lick the bleeding cut during the following scenes.

1:40 p.m. Lunch. Riverside Studios Canteen

I sat with Nigel Planer, the brilliant forty-year-old actor and writer. Nigel rents an office in Riverside Studios and was keen to hear how our *Sunset* rehearsals are going.

Back in 1978, when Nigel was twenty-five, he worked with Andrew Lloyd Webber. He understudied David Essex as Che Guevara in the original production of *Evita* which Andrew produced and also co-wrote with Tim Rice.

Nigel said, "Our *Evita* set was complicated as well. And dangerous. Joss Ackland played President Juan Peron and he was hit on the head by a cinema screen that descended at a wrong angle."

My co-ensemble actor Alisa Endsley joined us. I introduced her briefly to Nigel but he had to dash off, so they just shared a hello-goodbye.

"Please tell me about Nigel," she said. "I've only been in Britain two months and I don't know who anyone is."

I mentioned Nigel's connection with Andrew through *Evita*.

"He's very clever. He's also written and starred in some satirical TV shows, especially the BBC comedy series *The Young Ones*, about a daft collection of would-be anarchic young men, the complete opposite of Cliff Richard's nice, squeaky-clean image in his 1961 film musical of the same title. Their TV series had hilarious slapstick comedy between Rick Mayall and Alexei Sayle, sometimes alarmingly violent, bashing and thumping each other with all manner of objects. And in another TV series, *The Nicholas Craig Masterclass*, Nigel played a fictitious actor (Mr Craig) who has published a ridiculously pretentious book called I, An Actor

– about the art of acting. In fact, Nigel was ridiculing a real actor, Simon Callow, who wrote a book called *Being an Actor.* Simon didn't take him to court for that. Bizarrely, however, an actress did try to sue Nigel. She told a lawyer, 'Nigel Planer implied that I deliberately adopted a silly professional name in order to be ridiculed in his book!' She didn't even get the case heard."

2:45 p.m.

We spent the afternoon running company numbers.

5:45 p.m.

As the rehearsal finished, Trevor commented favourably. "However, I've one query about the final scene. Why were eight people missing?"

It seems Richard Tate, Peter Rutherford and Michael Bauer were having fittings. No one knew where the other five had gone.

Trevor added, "I have to leave now for an important production meeting. We *won't* be rehearsing in the theatre on Monday, as I hoped, because we're behind schedule with both the set and the costumes."

6 p.m.

Walking to the tube station, I said to Peter Rutherford, "Shows that have delayed openings like this are nothing new. Huge productions are often forced to cancel previews. *Phantom of the Opera* did."

"True. But poor Antony Powell, our costume designer, is getting in a state. He's complaining that he wasn't given anywhere near enough preparation time. He's got to design 250 costumes, and have them made and ready in three weeks. It all seems surprisingly chaotic. Wardrobe are way behind and complaining bitterly at the impossible amount of work they're expected to complete by the dress rehearsal. It's been the same for me. I wasn't offered the role of Sheldrake until four days before rehearsals began. Mark my words. The balloon is about to go up."

"By the way," I said. "I wanted to ask you. What happened to your first line to Kevin after the opening number? It used to be, 'Joe! What the fuck brings you here?' Now it's, 'What the hell brings you here?'"

"I think Andrew decided 'What the fuck' was too strong."

FRIDAY 21st May 1993

10 a.m. Riverside Studios, Studio 2

Company call. Vocal warm-up.

10:15 a.m.

Trevor gave us notes on yesterday's Act Two run. He spoke for two and three-quarter hours. We were told to grab tea or coffee on the hoof as best we could.

"To begin, I would like to establish a new mode of conduct during our rehearsals. My request is based on something which I have a slight cavil and would prefer to discourage. I mean, it's very nice that you show how much you appreciate your colleagues' work, and feel the need to express your enjoyment with applause at the end of every scene or song. The only problem is this. The time will come when, for one reason or another, you *won't* applaud, and whoever's been performing will think, 'What did I do wrong? Was I no good today? How can I get the applause back?' And that's not the aim of these rehearsals."

I was glad Trevor mentioned this because our younger company members are mega generous with their clapping. They clap after every vocal warm-up, physical warm-up, note session and rehearsal. Even at the end of an Equity meeting! – maybe from sheer relief that it's over.

The next general note Trevor gave was about the sound levels of spoken dialogue. "Having thoroughly explored the acting possibilities of the piece, we should now apply a quality of *sharing* the choices you've made while you perform. And I assure you I'm not using the word 'sharing' in the modern psychology sense of intimate confessions. I mean sharing your work with the audience in a more openly expressive manner."

His comment comes as no surprise to many of us who have watched the principals' scenes. Some exchanges of dialogue and sung lyrics have been far too quiet, some totally inaudible to anyone more than five feet away. Similarly, many performers' intentions are only visible to people sitting in the actors' immediate eye-line.

Trevor then said something that puzzled me. "The story needs to be spelt out more clearly in the second act."

Was this comment made for all of us? Just the leads? Himself? Did I even understand him correctly? Like the original 1950 film, our show mainly involves only four characters: Norma, Joe, Max and Betty. Adapting that screen drama into a stage play and clarifying its plot is surely the scriptwriter's job.

Trevor then embarked on a long description of the second act, stressing the fact that Norma holds onto her impossible dreams of a screen comeback until her final shattering confrontation with Joe, his painful home truths and unbearable walk-out. Trev next turned to a small but important detail. During Norma's visit to Paramount Studios, Hog-eye (Richard Tate) the electrician up in the gantry turns his spotlight onto Norma seated below. It has to hit her bang on a musical cue.

In our rehearsal room, Richard uses a practical lamp to help clarify this moment. Trevor queried what he thought was a delay in the light reaching Norma.

"I thought I'd try something new," Richard replied.

Uproarious laughter from the company, perhaps because this phrase is often said by actors exploring complex, subtle acting moments. Trevor also took his remark with equally good humour, especially when Richard added, "You said nothing's set in concrete yet".

There was more to come. As Hog-eye slowly pulls his spotlight's beam across the empty studio floor, Leslie Hayes, on the piano, is playing a dramatic orchestral build-up. The melodic crescendo increases till the light hits Norma, sitting alone in her chair. Leslie then plays the almighty crashing chord – *Fortissimo!* To describe this musical climax as "grandiose" barely does it justice.

Richard's comment was, "It's a hard one to hear."

Another loud outburst of hilarity from the company.

Trevor's next note was for me when I play Jonesy, the Paramount security guard. As Norma arrives to see Mr DeMille, I warmly welcome her and permit her chauffeur Max to drive Norma straight through the gates. I then use the studio phone on the proscenium wall: "Put me through to Studio 18. I have a message for Mr DeMille."

Trevor said, "I advise you to take your time as you cross over to the phone simply because a big set change will be taking place upstage. It's unseen by the audience because huge black runners slide on to hide it. So, to pad the moment out, I suggest you pick your teeth, stick chewing gum under the phone, and so on."

Various other helpful suggestions came from the cast, some of a rather personal nature. I might use them.

"I have a final plea to make to you all this morning," Trevor added. "Simply this, to have as quiet a background as possible in the room during rehearsals. For example, when you all stand up together and prepare to perform an ensemble number. Also, when the stage management set out the props and furniture for the next scene. What else? Oh yes, just one other thing. As I said yesterday, we will *not* be working on the set next Monday because it isn't ready. It now looks as if we'll probably get into the Adelphi next Wednesday 26th or on Thursday 27th. Does anyone have further questions?"

Kevin said, "In 'Let's Have Lunch', can I possibly change my line from, 'Hello Artie' to 'Hi Artie'?"

Trevor considered this carefully and then muttered, "On your own head be it. I believe 'Hello' was a form of greeting in California in the 1940s. Okay, everyone," he continued, "I must now emphasise this important point. Remember, this afternoon's run will still be for *you*, however much it might feel like a semi-public performance in front of unfamiliar faces."

12:15 p.m. Tea Break

We had been told that our first run-through of the show this afternoon, due to start at 2 p.m., would be watched by Sir Andrew and his production team, plus other "specially invited people."

I asked around, "Who are these mysterious honoured guests watching us later?"

No one in the cast seemed to have a clue.

The rest of the morning was a forensic examination and clean-up of the sections Trevor mentioned during his notes.

12:30 p.m. "Let's Have Lunch"

Something very unfortunate happened as we ran this opening number for Trevor and Sir Andrew.

A hollow polystyrene tube, some twelve feet tall, has been leaning in a corner of the rehearsal room. It is a stand-in prop Mark Inscoe uses for the Indian totem pole he will carry across the set playing a studio props man. The tube suddenly toppled over and hit Leslie Hayes, our rehearsal accompanist, and bashed her shoulder as she was seated at the piano. Poor Leslie was horribly shaken. She is of slight built and had to be assisted out of the room to recover from the pain and shock. Leslie wasn't, thank heavens, seriously hurt but the Musicians' Union will need to be informed.

That sobered everyone up a bit. Bob Avian finally told Nadia to stop flinging herself about all over the place. Not before time too. She had been prancing about with the prop lampshade on her head. But who's perfect? Not me.

I have a confession. While holding my position as we rehearsed Norma's arrival at Paramount, I did a soft-shoe shuffle and unknowingly trod on a wee winged insect.

Richard Anthony, a fellow ensemblighter, said, "You got it."

And me attending Sunday Buddhist meetings! Bad karma, man. Mea culpa. No. Just a minute. It was Richard Antony's fault. He was watching. He could have warned me. Phew! I will still return to Earth in my next reincarnation – a transcendental entity in freshly-laundered white sheets.

David Caddick (musical supervisor) was playing the piano for us while Leslie was away. I asked him about a line I sing in the New Year party cabaret as I mimic Cecil B. DeMille: "Meeting me must be quite a thrill."

"My cue to sing this is just one chord, David. It sounds a bit abrupt. How about a corny octave glissando on the piano instead?"

"Sir Andrew hates glissandos," David replied.

"But isn't this supposed to be a cheesy skit?"

He gave me an icy stare.

Oh dear. I forgot. We are here to obey instructions. Must buy a packet of Shut-Up-and-Do-As-They-Say pills at Boots.

We then checked over "The Lady's Paying", the number in which Norma's salesmen strip Joe to his underwear and bedeck him in posh evening tails.

Andrew simply cut a couple of beats before our final lyric, "And why not have it all?"

During the New Year's party number in Artie's apartment, Andrew removed the bash of the dinner gong that heralds my entrance as Sammy impersonating DeMille in our jokey *Samson and Delilah* cabaret, and Trev trimmed my improvised comments during that routine.

Andrew left us.

Bob Avian (our choreographer) returned to the show's big opening production number. "Several things I must have a look at and check during all your interweaving moves. I'm going to ask you, Peter, to slightly delay your cross downstage to greet Joe."

1:20 p.m. Lunch Break. Riverside Studios' Entrance

There's trouble afoot. I heard Patti speaking on the phone at the reception desk.

"That's how I *feel!* We're talking about my *feelings* here!"

Was she speaking to her agent in New York? She sounded exasperated. Furiously indignant.

2:20 p.m. The First Run-through of Sunset Boulevard

A pretty largish audience watched us. We were scheduled to perform in front of Sir Andrew and the whole production team but others were also quickly invited – including Don Black and Christopher Hampton (the book's authors) and John Napier (set designer). But not Anthony Powell (costume designer). Anthony is still desperately assembling the 250+ costumes.

No major mishaps, just one tiny one which caused us lot in the chorus much amusement during the post mortem afterwards. (Oh, shame on me! I used the c word: chorus.) David Caddick, our musical supervisor, has been bellyaching at inordinate lengths about the way the ensemble sing one particular phrase at the end of the first act when we express our shared hopes one day to become movie stars, to win Academy Awards and to enjoy a "yellow brick road career".

We've sung those four wretched words for David countless times to his constant yells of "No! Wrong again!" It's too fast, or too slow, or too loud, or too quiet. Having finally nailed the infernal bugger down, when we reached that phrase this afternoon one of the male ensemble jumped the gun and belted it out one beat too early!

It could have easily been me but not in this case, thank goodness, and nothing will induce me to name names. No threats, bribes, even holiday vouchers. My lips are sealed. There's a kind of poetic justice about it, over which I shall draw one of Salome's veils.

Oh, all right then. It was Richard Tate. The irony is that Richard repeatedly asks how we should sing words or harmonies, showing his eager attention to detail.

Having said that (sorry, Richard), now it's my turn. I did even worse in the opening number. By slightly delaying my move downstage, I bumped slam-bang into poor Meredith (Betty). We stared into each other's eyes with mutual astonishment. I was told the shock registered 1.2 on the Richter scale. We then exchanged phone numbers for insurance claims. Actually, the real villain was all the tinkering and fiddling about with the choreography. It messed up the timing of several other people's moves, too. You can over-rehearse a thing.

And that ends, your Honour, the accused's plea of innocence. I hereby rest my case.

3:30 p.m. Interval/Tea Break

Sitting amongst our audience was Jan (pronounced Yan) – Andrew Lloyd Webber's driver.

During the break, I asked Jan's honest opinion. "Oh terrific. No question. It's going to be a big success. Sir Andrew knows what he's doing. The only person he's up against is himself. He's his own worst critic because he is a perfectionist. Every detail has to be exactly right."

As we spoke, I remembered a remark someone made. "You can always tell what kind of mood Sir Andrew is in by the colour of Jan's tie. If it's a sombre colour, Andrew is worried or bad-tempered about something."

This afternoon, I noticed Jan's tie was a very dark blue…

3:45 p.m. Act Two

The pace of this show feels slow. Our pianist Leslie Hayes hasn't yet returned and David Caddick is accompanying us. His tempi are disconcertingly unfamiliar.

4:40 p.m.

When we reached the last moment of the whole run, there was a brief, chilly silence. However, that was followed by a warm burst of applause from our audience. We were astonished because they had watched us respectfully but without making any response at all. Not even one laugh.

4:50 p.m.

Trevor gathered us together for a final word. "During the first complete run-through of a show one of two things can happen. Either it can collapse and fall apart, or it can come together. This performance came together. I hope you all felt that. Next week, we will continue rehearsing here at Riverside. A few days later, we will put the show on the Adelphi stage and the same principle will apply. It could either deteriorate or benefit from yet another leg-up."

Patti had a few questions for Trevor about Norma Desmond's stuffed pet monkey. She asked for precise directions. When should she pick it up? How should she hold it? And when should she show its face?

Trevor said details like that would be left open until we get into the theatre. Personally, I feel strongly that Patti shouldn't touch the beloved corpse, maybe just lift the blanket to reveal it, otherwise it might trigger the wrong kind of nervous laughter. The way preview audiences respond often solves a tricky problem like this.

I inwardly queried another point – how the show ends. When Joe walks out on Norma, he tries to follow Betty using the front door, but Norma bars his way on the staircase. So, Joe turns round and, as he walks down the stairs, Norma shoots him in the back. Is he going to leave her house through the rear garden? It's fuzzy.

Here is how I would direct Joe's attempt to leave Norma. She becomes like a character in one of her silent movies. She pitifully clings onto Joe, begs him to stay and he has to tear himself from her grasp. When that's no good, she switches into the grand gothic style, like in a silent movie! She angrily bars his exit by the front door with her arms outstretched. Joe laughs at her and Norma feels humiliated. She seems to give up, turns and mounts the stairs as if going to her bedroom. Joe watches her for a few seconds and then opens the front door. He looks up at Norma. She stops, faces Joe, produces her gun and shoots him. He staggers and stumbles down the stairs. Norma follows him to the landing. She shoots him again. He lurches forwards into her garden and falls into the pool. Blackout.

During this blackout, Norma exits through the front door to do her quick change offstage. She then goes to the top of the stairs for her Crazy Lady re-appearance later.

Nobody listens.

5:15 p.m.

As Trev released us for the weekend, he called for a round of applause for the stage management, "who have done such a great job of setting up each scene in this rehearsal room without a single stop in the action."

A well-deserved thanks. The cast clapped and loudly cheered them.

Still no sign of a camera crew to film our rehearsals. And after all that hoo-ha! Will they appear on Monday?

7:30 p.m.

As I got off my train at West Hampstead tube station, happy Arsenal football fans were yelling incoherently on the platform. They wore red and white woolly hats and had red and white painted stripes on their faces.

Turns out they were celebrating yesterday's match against Southampton in London. Arsenal won, 4 – 3.

I didn't stop to discuss offside position rules.

SATURDAY 22nd May 1993

Went for a run round the streets. Exercised. Photocopied my comedy *Warm to the Touch* at a shop in Store Street off the Tottenham Court Road. Three pence per page. Six copies of the play for £16.60.

SUNDAY 23rd May 1993

Lovely lazy morning. Cooked, ate and then sun-bathed nude in my little front garden.

Washed shirts, underpants, sheets and pillows.

I typed three letters to Patti, Kevin and Daniel. Here's the condensed nitty-gritty:

Would you come in and have lunch with me and Hilary Strange at Riverside Studios one day this week? Hilary is our Equity West End Theatre organiser. She has offered to join us and privately explain the royalties points and how they could be shared out. As the company's elected Equity deputy, I am trying to help everyone reach an agreement over this… blah-blah-blah. Please be assured that I respect all artists' privacy and discussing your salaries is not a part of my job. That's none of my business. Basically, I am simply the messenger.

Yes, I typed out three copies of this tricky letter. On Sunday. My day of rest. Aaagh!

MONDAY 24th May 1993

5 a.m.

Woke to ghastly news on the radio. The IRA have exploded a fourth bomb. That's one a day since Friday.

10 a.m. Riverside Studios, Studio 2

A call for notes on last week's run.

It was delightful to see Leslie Hayes, our excellent and pretty pianist, has returned and feels well enough to accompany us.

Trevor spoke for two hours. Solid. He gave very detailed notes to actors playing named roles but none to the ensemble.

Thank heaven something made me buy The Independent at Hammersmith tube station. I'm reluctant to read a newspaper while others work on scenes that don't involve me; it can make the place look like a doctor's waiting room. But the air in our rehearsal room these days is dangerously warm and soporific – the stuff nice naps are made of. If you stare at the opposite wall, you might nod off till your snores wake you.

Watching the director mumble inaudibly with actors grows boring after the first five seconds. To make comments about the leads' performances is always highly appreciated, but if you gossip and share loud guffaws – that's frowned on by actors exploring the inner recesses of their character's psychology. So, my Independent newspaper was a lifesaver.

I'm in good company here. My partner Paulie worked with Sir John Gielgud at the Theatre Royal RSC Company at Stratford.

Paulie said, "I noticed that Johnny G, like me, was doing The Times crossword puzzle while waiting to rehearse. One day, he left his copy behind on a chair so I took a peek at it. Completely finished! All the squares filled in! I looked closer. Every word was total gibberish."

This morning, the company seemed a bit weary after the weekend break. Daniel Benzali (Max) particularly; he sat alone, away from us, occasionally emitting deep, soulful sighs. No funnies from Trevor and a distinct feeling of treading water.

The next logical step for us is to move into the Adelphi Theatre and work with the actual scenery. Many staging problems are better solved in situ. Tinkering and fiddling with them in a big empty room begins to feel irrelevant. So much gets changed when the cast begin to use the actual sets, furniture and props. Also, perfectly sound work in rehearsals can be damaged or lost by sheer over-examination or boring repetition.

Trevor pointed out that, "The original showcase performance of *Sunset Boulevard* at the Sydmonton Festival last year was eighteen minutes shorter than last Friday's run. We haven't added a note of music, but what we have added is this huge space."

That recital version for backers starring Patti was presented in a converted – and deconsecrated! – sixteenth century chapel situated in the grounds of Andrew Lloyd Webber's home, Sydmonton Court in Hampshire, about eighty miles from London.

"I must stress, by the way," Trevor continued, "That there is no ideal running time for a musical. Some people insist that it's two hours, although how they arrive at that precise, optimum estimate is a mystery. We were heavily criticised when *Les Miserables* opened because it ran for three hours. I was told that no musical which ran that long could be a success. Well, I'm sure its critics would say it's still too long. However, many people often emerge from a show which they've enjoyed enormously saying it was very good but should've been shorter.

"What we need to do now is to add momentum to the play. This simply means finding where the tempi are too slow or where there are unnecessary pauses. For example, when people are held up waiting for a musical cue to start singing. This happened last Friday partly because David Caddick played the piano for Leslie, who wasn't well. David's tempi weren't what you were used to, which affected a lot of the action. But today Leslie is back with us – and fully recovered, I'm glad to see.

"Aside from that, we must check, for example, where the underscoring needs to move along faster so that the arias can occur directly out of the dialogue without any sense of a hold up. A prime example is the song DeMille sings about Norma after her exit. We had a stage full of characters obediently watching him with that look of 'I have a feeling that any minute now Mr

DeMille is going to burst into song'."

Patti said, "Trevor, I have a slow musical section like that which bothers me. It's when I first describe my film project to Joe. I tell him the story of Salome while Max gets the champagne for us. I seem to have to wait forever to place those lines. Can't the music come in a bit quicker over that?"

"Yes, I do understand, but at that point Max needs sufficient time to pour the champagne. He can't do it on the run. I've a feeling it's slightly a case of you both waiting for each other there. We'll have a look at it. What else? I shall want another run-through as late this afternoon as possible to spend maximum time beforehand on sorting out these and other problems."

12 p.m.

Coffee Break

12:15 p.m.

We rehearsed all the sections Trevor pin-pointed.

1:15 p.m. Lunch Break

Richard Tate said, "I watched the film again over the weekend to touch base and noticed several marked differences between the two versions, especially how much nicer and softer Norma is in our version. In the film, she's a domineering, egotistical monster who orders Joe about like a servant; makes him walk her dogs and even empty ashtrays at her bridge party."

It's years since I saw the film and I'd forgotten those razor-sharp details. When a book or film is transformed into a West End stage musical, harsh or subtle edges are sometimes smoothed over by the adaptor.

I gave Patti, Kevin and Daniel the letters I typed out for them last night, telling them that Hilary Strange, our Equity contact, could join us for lunch one day this week in order to clarify the recording points system and to help the company agree on the royalties share-out.

Later in the day, however, Patti came to me and said, "To be honest, Peter, I'm reluctant to discuss this subject with Hilary."

"As a matter of fact, I've just spoken to Hilary on the phone. She's offered to come in tomorrow, Tuesday, to meet us during our lunch break before the run-through. Daniel and Kevin have agreed to come in."

"I can't," Patti replied. "I'm busy tomorrow. And also, I'm not in a position to discuss my record deal because it hasn't been agreed yet."

"Yes, of course. I appreciate that. The meeting is only for Hilary to clarify the situation – nothing else."

But Patti was intransigent. All her defence barriers were up. I greatly admire her as an artist and a colleague. She's passionate, direct, totally committed and very good-humoured. The last thing I want to do is add to her workload by making further demands on her time and attention – unless those demands are absolutely necessary. But how can I find out if they are? Well, if I can't, I can't. Okay. That's it. From now on, I am going to relax and hand over this entire recording royalties business to Hilary Strange to sort out. It's been a logistical and diplomatic minefield for me, not to mention an exhausting pain in the neck. I'm sure Hilary will produce her royalties wand, weave a magic Mary Poppins spell over this messy pile of poo and turn it into a nice, neatly folded pile of poo.

2:30 p.m.

Before the run-through, Bob cut all the cute bits of dancing he gave us at the beginning of Schwab's Drug Store. We enter simply walking in time with the music, chatting to each other. The result is I now don't perform a single dance step in the whole show.

And then what else did we check? *Yet again* the last four words of "This Time Next Year", the company song at Artie's New Year party. For the billionth time, we drunken revellers polished our favourite phrase "yellow brick road career" till it sparkled like Liz Taylor's Krupp Diamond. But I bet those bars will always cause foul ups because they are musically shambolic, containing several time signature changes, broken triplets *and* an inconsistently conducted rallentando (slow-up). There's one in every show…

3:40 p.m. Our First Full Run-Through

Unbelievable. In the complicated opening number "Let's Have Lunch", I listen out for an important sung line: "This is the greatest film ever made." I need to hear this because it's my cue to reply, "They're talking nominations." But no one sang my cue. It completely disappeared! So, I didn't sing my reply. Wonderful. After all that polishing.

Turned out I was just one victim amongst several in the domino effect of errors that were kicked off earlier by unsung bars. It just shows how fragile the structure of this intricate number becomes. Let's wait and see what the orchestral arrangement throws at us, then we'll *really* get to grips with this awkward little critter and sort it out once and for all.

6:15 p.m.

At the end of our first full run-through, Trevor expressed his approval.

Not only that! Sir Andrew delighted us with this announcement: "Tomorrow is our final day here at Riverside Studios. To mark it, we will have a drinks party – but not in this rehearsal room. It isn't exactly the best place for a jolly get-together. So, to show my appreciation for your splendid and very hard work, I thought it would be nice if you all came back to my house in Eton Square for a party at about six o'clock when we finish. We'll lay on transport for those without cars."

His surprise invitation was very warmly received by the company.

Still no camera crew… Maybe tomorrow?

TUESDAY 25th May 1993

5 a.m.

Up to write.

7:30 a.m.

A run and a workout. The full company call is at 12 p.m.

10:30 a.m.

At West Hampstead, the tube train driver made an announcement from his cabin: "This train will not be stopping at Green Park due to a security check."

Thank goodness I left home early. Not a day for an Equity deputy to be late.

At Baker Street, I changed onto the Hammersmith and City line. It opened in 1863 – the world's very first underground railway service! How do I know? A charming notice on the wall says, "Its original gas-lit wooden carriages were hauled by steam locomotives which filled the tunnels with smoke."

130 years ago! Feels to me like only yesterday.

11:40 a.m. Riverside Studios

Something odd caught my eye outside the entrance. Lying on the road were glittering fragments of blue glass. I wondered whose car window had been broken into. Nick Colicos was also inspecting it and told me it was none other than Sir Andrew's limousine.

"His Mercedes Benz," Nick said. "Imagine the surprise of the would-be thief to discover a *second* layer of bulletproof glass underneath, preventing them from getting at all the lovely high-tech goodies inside."

12 p.m. Riverside Studios, Studio 2. A Full Company Call

As I entered the room, Richard Oriel handed me a faxed copy of a formal letter of agreement between Equity and RUG which allowed our afternoon run-through to be filmed – purely for reference purposes and to be used only by understudies. It clearly states that the film tape will not be sold or broadcast afterwards, so no fees will be paid to the artists and the tape will be destroyed at the end of the show's run. Officially.

I'm pretty dubious about what really happens to such sound or video recordings but I saw no reason to object so I stuck the letter up on the board.

1:50 p.m. Riverside Studios Canteen

After lunching with Peter Rutherford, he said, "We're not needed for forty minutes. Let's go for a stroll."

Peter was smartly dressed for this evening's party at Andrew's house, sporting a splendid cream and white striped jacket, a pale pink shirt and dark blue tie. We sauntered along the path that runs by the River Thames and under Hammersmith Bridge. I asked him what he thought of the production's merits and shortcomings.

"The costumes will add a great deal but I feel a real sense of the period is missing. Kevin is giving an excellent performance, but he's far too modern and loose-limbed – exactly as a young man in L.A. would behave today. And for me, Patti is not enough of a regal, charismatic star. Also, she's too young, only forty-three. Gloria Swanson was fifty-one when she made the film and really had been a hugely popular leading lady in silent movies. You accept that her Norma is a monster, an egotist poised on the brink of mental derangement. But looking at Patti, I just don't believe she was ever a huge star. She's too common and too plain."

In her defence, I said, "Well, for me Patti does evoke the likes of Theda Bara and Polla Negri in their silent films, such as I've glimpsed on TV. Norma Desmond's enemy is the truth – that her days of being a young glamourpuss goddess are over. She could find a good supporting role – a comedic mother-in-law or a ruthless businesswoman; they sometimes steal the picture! But Norma won't. Like all tragic people in fiction, she has a fatal flaw. Macbeth's is ambition and Othello's is jealousy. Norma's is blind vanity. As far as I can tell, Patti is generating that 'I'm still a big star' egomania."

2:30 p.m. Studio 2

Before the 3 p.m. run-through, Nadia was given a new line, "I'm writing for Betty Hutton" to rhyme with "Should you undo a button?"

I think it's cute.

Here's an example of the tortuous crafting one single word can undergo in our script's dialogue. Today it's a four-letter word, boys and girls. No, not that one. Concentrate. The preposition or conjunction "till".

During the chit-chat at Artie's New Year party, Joe talks to Betty, who is a script reader at Paramount Studios. Joe claims that DeMille's 1949 film *Samson and Delilah* is the most expensive movie ever made. To which Betty used to respond, "Till his next project." She is referring to his forthcoming 1952 spectacular circus movie *The Greatest Show on Earth* which will be even more costly.

But Joe's line was cut and Betty's reply was then transferred to another party guest, a heavily disguised Peter Rutherford playing a Latin American film star. This didn't work either, so Betty's line was handed to me, playing Sammy, the actor at Paramount.

But wait a minute! Without keeping Joe's remark which prompted Betty's reply in the first place, the word "till" sounded illogical coming from Sammy. So, out came the editor's scissors and "till" was snipped. Now instead of singing, "Till my next project", I simply warble, "My next big project". And that's how side-splitting theatrical anecdotes are born.

There then followed a discussion between Trevor and Don Black. Don is one of the writers of the book and the lyrics (with Christopher Hampton). Trev and Don debated whether my line "My next big project" should be "My next *huge* project", which seemed of no great consequence in the scheme of things. Don preferred "big" so Trevor agreed to keep it.

As we rehearsed these minutiae, Patti came and sat next to me.

"Peter," she whispered, "Do you know if anyone has a needle and thread? I'm going out to see a play this evening and I have to sew on a button that's come loose on my shirt top."

I found something mildly puzzling about Patti's little request, but I said, "Okay. Sure. Happy to oblige. There are costume fittings going on in the dressing rooms. I'll nip out and ask our wardrobe people if they're packing haberdashery heat."

I tracked them down but with no luck.

They said, "Sorry, Peter. Tell Patti we're only taking measurements today and we haven't got any of our usual bits and pieces with us."

I explained this to Patti with a jokey apology. "Just to let you know that I attend to your every need."

But wait. Patti's theatre-going plan had set off a faint alarm bell in my head; something was distinctly odd about it. What play was Patti seeing tonight? Why was it so important? And then two thoughts suddenly struck me.

First, Patti should switch her theatre booking to another day. She is this evening's star guest at Andrew's company party in his home. Is she deliberately snubbing his hospitality and goodwill? Hmm. The more I thought about it, the more unfriendly it seemed. But if so, why? What has Andrew done to mortally offend her?

And then a second thought hit me. I recalled Patti's furious words on the phone last week, almost shouting, "That's how I *feel!* We're talking about my *feelings* here!" Were those impassioned words linked to her no-show at Sir Andrew's tonight?

3 p.m. A Full Run-Through of Sunset Boulevard

5:10 p.m.

I'm pretty well pissed off. After I spent hours discussing a financial deal for filming videotape extracts for a TV documentary, no film camera crew of any kind turned up this afternoon to shoot the run-through, for reference purposes, TV extracts, porn movies, nothing. What on earth was all that argy-bargy about? It wasted acres of my time and put me to tedious trouble sorting out salary terms agreeable to both RUG and the company. And I'm willing to bet there's a lot more of this kind of crap to come.

"Very good," Trevor announced at the end of the run. "*Very* good. Okay, listen up everyone. The show is in a really fine state to leave it, I'm pleased to say. Try to hold it together like that, because what we'll be doing now – coping with huge technical problems in the Adelphi Theatre – could easily cause that wonderful solid company feeling you've created to fall apart in fragments if we're not careful. So, please retain it. And also, don't forget that the next ten days or so are going to be a great test of everyone's patience. It's a bit like fishing. You wait hours for that moment when the float suddenly goes, and, the second it does, you've got to be right there, ready for it, poised for action. Please have patience everyone and be prepared to stand by. Including Nadia," he added, smiling.

"Why am I being specially singled out?" Nadia complained.

"You're always doing dance steps and leaping about, Nadia," Trevor explained lightly. "That's all I meant."

Buggering about and not concentrating I would have said. To be fair Nadia is a talented actress/dancer – a tall, elegant, stunning beautiful young woman with gorgeous ice-blue eyes. If she focused on the work in hand, she could really go places, but her silly attention-seeking behaviour is distracting. Basically, I suspect she's bored with having nothing interesting to do. But hey! Join the club, Nadia! That goes for all of us in the ensemble.

Today's final run-through at Riverside Studios was watched by an audience comprising the Adelphi's technical backstage staff and the Really Useful Group's office personnel. Their applause afterwards was terrifically enthusiastic.

As everyone was preparing to leave, I had a quick word with Sue Strother, the wig mistress on this production.

"If you don't mind, Sue, I'd really love to hear your absolutely honest opinion of the show. No holds barred."

Sue and I worked together during the 80s on several Gilbert and Sullivan operas for Robert Meadmore's London Savoyard's Company. I knew she'd give me an honest reply.

"Do you think it's okay, Sue? Just between ourselves."

"Oh yes! I thoroughly enjoyed it. I really did. It's extremely good; very moving. And exciting! I'm sure it'll be a big hit." Her gold seal of approval came as a tremendously encouraging thumbs up.

A luxury tourist bus was outside, waiting to drive us to the party.

6:30 p.m. Eaton Square, Belgravia

As we entered Sir Andrew's beautiful terraced house, caterers in black jackets offered us a choice of drinks – champagne, orange juice, a non-alcoholic strawberry cordial, Perrier water and white Burgundy wine. I chose the wine as my tipple.

Leila, a Filipino maid, moved amongst the guests serving trays of taramasalata, chicken drumsticks, small pitta bread envelopes with humus inside, and big green and white asparagus tips wrapped in slices of smoked salmon. Being a vegetarian, I gladly took the humus and some asparagus tips. Dear Leila noticed and soon found me a plate and popped on more humus and asparagus tips, stripped of their fishy overcoats.

What an elegant house Andrew has! What a classy collection of paintings!

Chatting to Mark Inscoe, I said, "There's a Landseer oil painting of a horse on the landing and a pre-Raphaelite annunciation in the reception room. It's amazing. And upstairs there's a Millais, and a huge Canaletto depicting what looks like St James' Park in the 1700s."

"Yes, I know. I was told it's authentic," Mark murmured. "Worth ten million."

Copies of the *Sunset Boulevard* poster were on a chair. One of the ensemble was discussing it with a woman whose face seemed familiar but I couldn't quite place her. I introduced myself and asked if she had designed the poster.

"No!" she retorted, somewhat indignantly. "Dewynters."

A few minutes later, I asked Mark who she was.

"She's Andrew's wife, Madeleine Gurdon. His third."

"Oh crumbs. I had no idea. She seems a bit young to be his wife."

"Andrew is forty-five and she's thirty-one. A keen horsewoman. Takes part in big riding competitions. Her friends call her Gurtie."

I then met Sarah, Sir Andrew's charming P.A. "Forgive me, Sarah, but I have to ask you the big question on all our minds. Why hasn't a film crew come in to shoot our rehearsals for the BBC TV documentary?"

"Because of Patti," she answered, and then instantly looked as if she'd spoken indiscreetly.

"You mean Patti refused permission for the filming to take place?"

Sarah forced a smile. "Yes." She gazed into the middle distance and then evasively added, "Apparently."

"But why?"

"I don't know. Excuse me for a second." Sarah went. End of discussion.

What's going on? If Patti has blocked any filming, she must have given Andrew a reason for doing so; and Sarah, being Andrew's P.A., would know all about it. Why is the *Sunset* company being denied an explanation?

This comes as a real body-blow. Most of us ensemble are on the lowest salaries, and if a documentary film is made *without* using shots of us, we might lose more than £500 – nothing to feel overjoyed about. I wanted to ask Sarah if Sir Andrew made this clear to Patti. I feel I'm owed an explanation after all the discussions I conducted on the vexed subject. *And* the letters I sent to Equity. *And* the company statements I typed out. *And* the phone calls to Equity I made about it during my coffee breaks. *And* the company meetings I had to organise and oversee – which

Patti refused to attend.

I looked for Sarah. She had mysteriously vanished.

My mind raced. Why would Patti trash the TV documentary? Is she angry with Andrew because of the photographic display in the Adelphi foyer advertising Barbra Streisand's recording of "With One Look"? That makes perfect commercial sense because Streisand has a big fan base and it might generate excellent publicity for our show. Whatever Patti's grievance, she could share it with either Nadia or me, her Equity representatives.

The documentary deal must be sorted out amicably or it will create bad feeling in the company. I love Patti to bits but that's the last time this underpaid fifty-one-year-old chorus boy goes hunting after a needle and thread for a leading lady.

Today, I discovered that our company manager (Richard Oriel) has put me in a dressing room way up on the top floor of the Adelphi Theatre, eighty-four steps up from stage level. I counted them. Curiously, it's the same number of steps going down. This is my home-from-home for the next ten months, till my contract ends, on the 12th March next year. There is only one lift that runs between the stage and my dressing room's landing. It carries six people maximum; it's often full and sometimes out of order.

Okay. I'm just a small cog in *Sunset Boulevard*'s huge wheel. I serve a function as part of the frame surrounding the interesting action. It's my choice; I'm lucky to be earning a weekly wage packet and working with such a classy production team. I shall give it my best shot and remember the wise Buddhist principle: turn poison into medicine. In other words, transform your suffering into wisdom; learn from your mistakes and convert a negative approach into a "think positive" one. Walk-on and understudy are certainly not poison; but it is a professional status comedown for me on acting's wobbly ladder. Just do it.

This suddenly reminds me of a line in Shakespeare's comedy *The Merry Wives of Windsor*. Master Fenton, on the lookout for a rich, gorgeous girl to wed and bed, says, "What cannot be eschewed, must be embraced." Eschew is an interesting archaic word, nothing to do with eating. It means to avoid, escape or prevent. In other words, what cannot be avoided should be faced and dealt with. Summarises my situation neatly.

So, heads up, Adelphi Theatre! You've had your multimillion pound makeover. Now get ready for an actor who has eschewed the living daylights out of his negative thoughts and transformed them into a welcoming embrace. Here comes positive thinking Pete, hitching a spectacularly staged ride along *Sunset Boulevard*!

PART 2

Break a Leg
The Adelphi Theatre

Chapter 5

MAY 1993

WEDNESDAY 26th May 1993

1:30 p.m. Adelphi Theatre

Today began with an unexpectedly nasty shock. A bracing contrast to yesterday's encouraging run-through and Sir Andrew's jolly party.

Trevor's company call for notes was at 2:30 p.m., so for lunch I grabbed an early takeaway veggie pizza in the Strand to eat in the dressing room.

The Adelphi's frontage is being repainted black and white, and, although partly obscured by scaffolding, it already looks classy.

The stage door keeper gave me the key for my dressing room on the fourth floor. I'm sharing it with Bernie Sharpe and Mark Inscoe.

Here is my estate agent's report:

This reasonably sized residence seats three persons, is newly carpeted and adequately appointed throughout. It boasts two double sash windows, spacious mirrors, two washbasins and also benefits from being freshly redecorated. Occupants must provide own towels.

One thing puzzled me. There's no star on my dressing room door. Our theatre manager should fix that.

Then came the nasty shock.

As I munched my takeaway lunch, a message sounded over the Tannoy, "Would Peter Gale please go to the company manager's office."

I wondered if Richard Oriel had fresh info for me about the proposed TV documentary as I trotted down the stone stairs to his office. Is RUG offering the cast a better financial deal? Hang on! Has the BBC dumped the whole video doc idea?

Richard's office surprised me. Far from grand, it's a modestly small, windowless room. Having just moved in, it looked austerely bare – one big desk, two chairs and a bulky cardboard packing case. Nothing else.

Richard had company. Sitting next to him was Alastair Smith, also waiting to see me. Alistair is our production manager and one of Andrew Lloyd Webber's top four production team. They both looked oddly sheepish.

Without a third chair to offer, we all stood.

I grinned and said, "Cosy place you've got here, Richard."

Neither smiled. Oh dear.

Alistair began. "This is… um… very awkward, Peter. We have some rather serious news for you. About something that's happened during the last forty-eight hours."

What on earth's the problem, I wondered, devouring my veggie pizza in its takeaway box. Must be important if it needs both of them to discuss it. Then paranoia kicked in. Have I done something wrong? Is the problem *me?* Is this a reprimand? I froze in mid-munch. Am I getting the sack?

"It's about Peter Rutherford. A very difficult decision has been reached which has absolutely nothing at all to do with his ability as an actor or his performance. Peter is being replaced. The problem, basically, is this. The show starts with an important interview between Kevin Anderson, playing an American writer, and Peter, a Hollywood film producer. Kevin is a real American, and Peter is a very good English actor *pretending* to be American. And it simply wasn't working."

I breathed again. "I see. Well… What can I say? I'm really sorry to hear this. I like Peter a lot. We acted together at the Overground Theatre in Kingston in a play I wrote. He was a joy to work with and extremely good in it. I shall miss him very much. Oh, poor man."

"Of course, we appreciate how difficult this is for Peter himself and for the whole company, but sometimes unpleasant decisions like this have to be faced and dealt with before they create worse problems later." As Alistair elaborated on this theme, I felt slightly puzzled.

"Yes, I do see your point, Alistair. Could I ask you something? Why am I being told about this? To help Peter in some way?" An awful thought hit me. "Does Peter know yet? Have you spoken to him about this? Oh my God. Are you telling me because I'm the Equity deputy? I'm not the one who has to break this awful news to him, am I?"

"No, no. Don't worry. He's already been told. But we thought we should explain to you what's happened, because, being as you say the company's union representative, you might be receiving a call about it from Peter himself, or his agent. So, if you don't mind, for the moment we would greatly appreciate it if you could keep all this to yourself. At 2:30, there's a full company meeting in the dress circle for a ten-minute talk with Trevor. He will explain about Peter and why it's happened. Then you're all going over to the Royalty Theatre to do some work there, because the Adelphi stage isn't quite ready yet."

I kind of reeled out of that office. Peter is an immensely experienced and likeable actor. I shall miss him greatly, both as a colleague and a friend – particularly his beguiling sense of humour.

And then my mind lurched from one question to another. Where is Peter right now? At home with his wife in Brighton? How is the poor man feeling? Should I phone him? I'd like to talk to him about this but will he want to discuss it? Is he feeling too hurt? Too upset? Too angry? Oh brother!

2:30 p.m. Adelphi Dress Circle

Trevor Nunn gathered all the workforce together – the entire cast and stage management staff; everyone except Patti and, of course, Peter. We sat in the dress circle front rows. Trevor stood in front of us, with his back to the stage.

He expressed his admiration for the auditorium's newly painted décor, beautifully restored to its original 1930s Art Deco design. The front cloth was in, painted with the *Sunset Boulevard* poster design, splendidly enlarged to fill the entire proscenium arch.

Trevor said, "I shall ask for the front cloth to be flown out for you to see what's behind it."

Just as this was being dealt with, Sir Andrew arrived.

"Good afternoon everyone. Welcome to the newly redecorated Adelphi Theatre. I feel I should explain to you why we've been prevented from rehearsing here on the stage till today. While our workmen were stripping clean the interior of this theatre, they revealed the auditorium's original panelling which they soon realised was genuine teak – now an endangered species of timber.

Great care has been taken to match up those parts that needed to be replaced with convincing look-alike wood."

Just then Andrew was upstaged by the pros arch front cloth. It began to rise – very slowly... inch... by... inch...

Andrew noticed the company's altered focus of attention and he turned to watch it. Some of us voiced quiet words of encouragement. "Keep going... Go on... Go on..." However, only a few feet up, it playfully stopped, like a striptease dancer in a nearby Soho nightclub.

With more egging on, it rose a few feet higher and halted again which only prompted louder urging. Shamed into behaving properly, the sulky front cloth reluctantly complied. But exactly halfway up, it froze dead again. Bursts of loud laughter, yells and whistles from everyone really got the darn thing's mojo going and the front cloth resumed its rise... and rise... until finally *there it was!*

Revealed in all its opulent glory was the main set – the interior of Norma Desmond's house, with its spectacular staircase and twisty black and gold pillars, a lavish feast for the eye. The whole company cheered and applauded John Napier's beautiful design. He smiled appreciatively.

Trevor said, "I'm sure you'll agree that this superb set alone would be sufficient for an entire play."

Strong murmurs of agreement. And to think, when all other bits of scenery slide off or fly away, this splendid vision will descend like a huge spaceship and gently land on the Adelphi stage! That will be some theatrical moment.

"And now for not such good news," Trevor said.

About Peter Rutherford's absence, I wondered?

"We aren't able to start the technical from the top of the show because under the stage there is a computer. Now this computer contains special valves which move the scenery, and it's these valves that operate hydraulic lifts that do all the scenery shifting – lowering, raising and sending heavy units on and offstage. The valves are provided by Vickers, a perfectly reputable multinational industrial company. However, we have found that the valves are so sensitive they are also picking up signals coming from vehicles passing in the road outside. Their mobile phone signals activate the computer's valves which start our scenery moving when it shouldn't. So this, of course, must be rectified before we can safely work with the sets."

The mind boggles. It sounds like something out of a Stephen King horror story...

"That evening, during a performance at the Adelphi Theatre, a nearby van was delivering kinky underwear to a sex shop in Soho. The driver, Skip, made a mobile phone call to the shopkeeper.

'Are you still open? I've got a box of fifty Bona Strapping Stripper jock straps to deliver.'

Unknown to Skip, his phone signal was also picked up by a computer in the Adelphi Theatre during a public show. The wood in the scenery stiffened. Doors, stairs, windows and flats shuddered and suddenly lurched into action, roaming unpredictably about the stage and down into the orchestra pit, trapping and mangling helpless actors, stagehands and musicians, cutting off their arms and legs and crushing their heads flat.

The audience thought the horrific injuries were all part of the production and loudly applauded what appeared to be clever special effects..."

"The construction team," Trevor said, "Are working day and night to fix the computer. Until that problem is dealt with, we shall rehearse over at the Royalty Theatre, as much as we're able to, and then come back here later to the Adelphi, and concentrate on scenes which are acted on this set. No great hardship, since seventy-five percent of the play is located inside Norma's house. Okay. So, let's all make our way over to the Royalty."

No word yet about Peter's absence.

As we were leaving, Michael Bauer turned to me, looking puzzled.

"Where's Peter Rutherford?" he asked.

I shrugged a blank response.

2:30 p.m. Royalty Theatre

The company sat in the stalls and Trevor talked to us entertainingly about the history of the Royalty Theatre. "This relatively new theatre was built on the site where the old Stoll Theatre once stood. That's now an ugly little underground venue which developers are planning to convert into a car park for an office block. But you never know with theatres. What was a white elephant yesterday might be the home of a long-running hit tomorrow. Everyone complained about the New London Theatre until we put a show in there called *Cats*. People gave us two warnings. First, that a musical about dancing moggies will never work. And second, definitely not in a new theatre nobody can find. Well, twelve years later, *Cats* is still playing to packed audiences."

The phrase Trevor used, "white elephant", intrigued me so I've looked it up. In 543 B.C., King Bimbisara of Siam (now Thailand) gave valuable and rare albino elephants to courtiers he disliked, knowing the huge cost of feeding and protecting the animals would financially ruin the owners.

Today, it means any item that is expensive to maintain and of little use. Not the fate of the New London Theatre, fortunately.

3 p.m.

We took chairs up onto the stage and sat round the piano to brush up the company numbers with Trevor.

"Before we begin," he said, "Some very sad news for you about Peter Rutherford. You must have noticed that he hasn't been with us all afternoon. Since the party at Sir Andrew's yesterday, a very difficult decision has been discussed and finally decided on." Trevor broke the news to the company. "Another actor will take over the role of Sheldrake for an interim period – an American actor who lives in London. I'll be speaking to Peter later this evening myself. It's a horrid, nasty, messy business. I take part of the responsibility, for which I apologise, but it's better it should happen now than later."

The cast sat in a state of speechless shock. Grim looks were exchanged. We were like characters in an Agathe Christie murder mystery. Will more victims follow? Who will disappear next?

Kevin was sitting in front of me. He turned round, looked at me, smiled, pointed a finger at himself and whispered, "I'll be next."

3:15 p.m.

We spent the afternoon vocally polishing four big company numbers, "This Time Next Year", "The Lady's Paying", "Let's Have Lunch" and the beauticians number.

At one point, David White examined a melodically tricky phrase. To check our intonation, he threw over his shoulder, "Give me a D," to our rehearsal pianist. He little realised Andrew Lloyd Webber had arrived and was seated at the piano, quietly absorbed in copying out new bars of music for us.

Without so much as a blink, Andrew played a D on the piano and continued working, totally locked into his task. Cool multitasking.

4 p.m. Tea Break

Peter Rutherford's disappearance, coming at the same time as hearing that the documentary is probably being scrapped because of Patti's greedy agent, has somewhat deflated the company's confidence and expectations.

A group of us left the Royalty Theatre. As we walked up Holburn to buy takeaway meals, they asked me if I knew more details about Peter's removal from the show.

"All Peter said to me was that he was cast only four days before rehearsals began, and that he'd been working on his American accent with Joan Washington, and she seemed very happy with what he was doing. I'm sure that if he'd had a worrying problem, he would have mentioned it to me yesterday at Andrew's party. I'll ring him tonight to ask what happened and let you know tomorrow."

9:30 p.m. Home

I rang Peter.

The dear man sounded philosophical. "I'm fine, thanks. Except that it came completely out of the blue."

"Oh Peter, it's hard to believe that Trevor and Andrew could be so cold-blooded. Didn't they make any comment earlier that roused your suspicions? Or give you some kind of hint that it was on the cards?"

"No. That is what's so odd. Nobody said anything like that to me at all, including the voice coach, Joan Washington. None of the production team expressed any criticism of my performance or American accent. If I'd suspected that they were considering getting rid of me, I would've mentioned it to you, as one does. But there wasn't the least inkling of a warning. In fact, the last thing

Trevor said to me was how happy he felt about the way the first scene was working. He said, 'I like the new gruff quality you've introduced.'"

A slight note of cynicism entered his voice. "What's really extraordinary is that I only happened to hear about this because at around eleven o'clock this morning, and completely by chance, I decided to visit my agent. *She* broke the news to me. I then phoned the theatre and spoke to Debbie Cronshaw, your assistant stage manager, who was in a hysterical state. And no. So far Trevor hasn't rung me."

THURSDAY 27th May 1993

11 a.m. Palace Theatre, Stage Door. Costume Call

Backstage at the Palace, I had my first actual costume fitting. This was where my measurements were taken five and a half weeks ago. The lady who made my "shape" arrived at the same time and we shared the lift up to the fourth floor. She was delightfully droll.

"The last show I made costumes for in this theatre was the original *Sound of Music*, some thirty years ago." She raised her eyes wearily to heaven. "I did twenty nuns. There's nothing worse than stitching endless yards of black material together with reels of black cotton. After a time, you go cross-eyed. I could barely see what I was doing!"

The lift door opened and we were greeted by the associate costume supervisor, Christopher Porter. He said, "I have to apologise. I'm afraid these rooms are very small and full of boxes."

My "shape-maker" lady replied, "Yes, they warned me about lack of space. They said, 'You might have to do the fittings in a dimly lit corridor.'"

Christopher smiled at me. "Exactly. I really do apologise. Is this corridor narrow enough for you?"

I leant forwards. "Shouldn't it be a bit darker?" I asked, pretending to peer at him through the shadows.

Christopher smiled and beckoned us to follow him. "Kindly walk this way. No one else has arrived yet so we should be fine in here. I've got a few bits and pieces ready for you."

In fact, he led us into a surprisingly bright orange room, decorated with fancy orange wallpaper and tasselled silk curtains. On the wall were framed ballet paintings by Leon Bakst, the Russian painter and theatrical designer.

Christopher pointed to costumes hanging on a clothes' rail. "These were worn in previous shows. I thought some bits and pieces might be useful."

On a desk, Christopher had laid out glamorous studio publicity photos of Greta Garbo, Gloria Swanson, Myrna Loy and other Hollywood movie stars, all coiffured in "exotic" hairdos. I guess they will help when styling the hats and wigs for the female ensemble who play film extras at Paramount Studios.

I said, "This is a surprisingly pretty little room. Very chic."

"Lloyd Webber bought this theatre. When he and Sarah Brightman were married, they had the whole floor of the Palace refurbished. Basically, it's a completely self-contained flat, with a living room, kitchen, dining room and bedroom, all en suite. I hear they called it their love nest."

Antony Powell, our costume designer, and Christopher Porter, hats and wigs, arrived. They showed me the gold breastplate Jason Donovan wore two years ago in *Joseph and the Amazing Technicolor Dreamcoat*.

I put it on and stood there for an hour as a massively long piece of material was hung and pinned onto me. They referred to this first layer, an off-white calico robe, as my "shape", another word for a template. It helps when cutting out the real material to make the costume. Then came further drapery, and on top of all that a long cloak was added.

The costumier has done a wonderful job working from Antony's pen drawing, and Christopher (hats and wigs) has created for me a splendidly tall golden crown and a beard of ringlets on elastic, both easy to take off and carry under my arm when I play Sammy chatting to Joe Gillis (Kevin).

I need to look impressive; Sammy is a Hollywood actor playing a high priest in DeMille's *Samson and Delilah* at Paramount Studios. My personal nickname for this elaborate high priest costume is the Mighty Beast. The entire outfit has to go on me in a matter of seconds, immediately after I leave the stage as Jonesy, the security guard at Paramount Studios gates.

Anthony reassured me. "Peter, this whole costume will be made in one piece and then cut straight down the back and fastened with a Velcro opening to make your change easy. Did you know the Americans have invented a *silent* Velcro? Specially for army soldiers, apparently, so they can have a pee in secret hideouts without giving their positions away."

Christopher gave me a saucy smile, "What a shame. I love the noise Velcro makes when you rip it open."

Talking of zips and hooks reminded Antony of working with the Hollywood star Lauren Bacall. "She came over to play the lead in the musical *Applause* at Her Majesty's Theatre in 1972. Not an easy lady to deal with. She gave the poor girl who looked after her wigs a nervous breakdown. Bacall also insisted on having two identical copies of a dress made. It was just in case, during a quick change, the zip on one became stuck. And at Pinewood Studios, Marilyn Monroe was sewn into her figure-hugging costume for every shot in *The Prince and the Showgirl* to show off her curves. Vivienne Leigh was in the original stage play version, *The Sleeping Prince*, and although she wore the same dress during the play, for every performance Vivienne actually put on a completely different but identical dress for each of her twelve entrances, so that she always looked absolutely fresh. And when the Bolshoi Ballet came over to London in the 1950s, they were sewn into their costumes, to avoid the risk of a zip getting stuck or a hook snapping."

Stories about the 1971 film *Nicholas and Alexandra* followed.

"The Tsarina's costume jewellery was specially made to be worn by the actress in the movie. It was only coloured glass but looked gorgeous. They sold it afterwards and the money they got for it paid to redecorate a Spanish restaurant. The film's wonderful ballroom floor ended up in its dining room. The film's director, Franklin J. Schaffner, was rumoured to have bedded all the Tsar's daughters. He also, allegedly, promised a juicy leading part to a glamorous French model as a reward for services rendered in the boudoir. In the event, only one small role was available for her. She ended up amongst a crowd of extras playing a factory drudge in filthy rags."

12:30 p.m. Adelphi Theatre. Onstage

When I arrived, the male ensemble were going through "The Lady's Paying". I was miked up and joined Manfred's salesmen.

Oh, the changes I've seen. Actors in stage shows wear mikes now. Even in plays at the National Theatre! Twenty years ago, in 1973 I played Tom Trainer, the young male lead in *No No Nanette* at the Theatre Royal Drury Lane. That theatre seats 2,162 people. I sang "Tea for Two" with no throat mike and accompanied by a full orchestra. We ran thirty-three weeks and I warbled that romantic lyrical ballad 227 times without any vocal amplification system whatsoever.

In West End musicals today, you use a completely different vocal technique because you sing into a little radio mike attached to your face. Sometimes it looks like a skinny pinkish millipede crawling out of your hair and down your forehead or nestling by your ear. The sound of your voice comes out of speakers on the proscenium walls on the left and right, and your vocal volume is controlled by a sound operator working on a big sound desk at the back of the stalls.

Before each performance of *Sunset Boulevard*, a sound operator knocks on my dressing room door. She or he puts a skin-coloured elastic loop around my head, like a coronet, with a tiny mike fixed to its front. A wire from Tiny Mike runs to the nape of my neck and then down my back and plugs into a battery inside a bag hanging round my waist on a belt. Unlike the old days, projecting your voice to be heard by people up in the gods is unnecessary. The sound operator will adjust Tiny Mike's volume level. This means a more relaxed, intimate style of singing style sounds infinitely better.

But nothing is infallible in life or show business. Tiny Mike is so essential in today's musicals, some leading actors often wear two mikes in case one fails. Anthony Powell, our costume designer talked to me about this. He said, "I suggested the idea to Patti of wearing two mikes. 'No,' she said to me. 'You only wear one, and if yours doesn't work, what you do is you reblock the scene and move close to someone wearing a mike and share it with them.' And if she's singing a solo, she said she goes downstage and works to one of the mikes along the front of the stage. The sound people can then adjust the level of the one she's using."

I said to Anthony, "That's excellent advice. But what if your character is alone, unable to walk and lying on a bed upstage?"

"Pass. You'll have to ask Patti yourself."

1 p.m. Lunch. Luigi's Cafe in Covent Garden

Bernard Sharpe and Nigel Wright (our stage management spokesperson) said to me, "Would you ring Peter Rutherford and find out how he's feeling? The whole company is shocked at the unkind way he's been dismissed."

"Yes, of course; I was going to anyway. But I will. I promise."

"There's something else people are wondering. Is Kevin on drugs?"

"What?" I responded, surprised. "Why on earth do you ask me?"

"Because he's sort of floating through everything."

2 p.m. Company Manager's Office

I needed Richard Oriel's help. "Is Madeleine Gurdon the full name of Andrew Lloyd Webber's wife? I must write her a thank you card."

"Yes. That is her correct name."

"At the party someone said her friends call her Gertie, but we haven't got onto nickname terms with each other yet. That'll come later."

Just then Kevin Anderson joined us. He appeared very badly under the weather.

"Are you all right, Kevin?" Richard asked. "You look awfully tired today."

I said to Richard, "Kevin's just moved house. You were up till 5 a.m. yesterday, weren't you? Packing."

He gave me us roguish grin. "Amongst other things."

What a dog.

2:30 p.m. Onstage

We rehearsed "The Lady's Paying" again and this time Kevin was definitely not operating on the button. Maybe he was just tired. His five o'clock shadow and the dark rings under his puffy eyes didn't help.

4 p.m.

We were released.

At Charing Cross tube station, I saw the Evening Standard's headline: Clarke is Now Chancellor as Lamont Quits. Both Kenneth Clarke and Norman Lamont are Conservative ministers but I bought a copy on the principle of "know thine enemy".

I've been a staunch Labour party supporter all my life. It's entirely thanks to them I'm sitting here today writing this diary. My adult acting career began when my local Slough Labour Council awarded me a grant to train at Central School of Speech and Drama. I was nineteen years old and the fees would have been way beyond my parents' pockets. The plot thickens…

A recent opinion poll showed seventy-three percent of us think the National Health Service isn't safe in Conservative hands. They seem hell bent on destroying it but why? It's one of the glories of our democracy. Simple. Most of them are rich. They can afford private medical insurance. Kenneth Clarke is our new Chancellor of the Exchequer. How he helps the NHS remains to be seen.

4:50 p.m. Home

I rang Hilary at Equity. "Thanks for faxing me the suggested royalties split. Your list doesn't include everyone. Three people want their names added: Maggie Goodwin, our assistant choreographer; Andrew McBean, our assistant director, and Lee Fowler, an assistant stage manager."

"You might like to put this idea to a company vote, Peter.

Specifically ask everyone if they think the first two names should be included."

Another blessed vote? More work for me. My heart sank.

"I should explain," Hilary continued. "It's not normally done to give points to assistant choreographers or assistant directors for several reasons. I know they're members of Equity but they receive other perks which you aren't given. For example, they don't have to audition for their jobs. Also, they're on 'run of the show' contracts and *Sunset* might keep going for years. And when the show closes, it entitles them to redundancy pay. The rest of you don't receive that. The other thing is, if the Really Useful Group dismisses you *before* you've been in it for two years, you get nothing. This is what recently happened on *Joseph*. Lloyd Webber's Really Useful Group replaced all the actors just before they'd completed two years in the musical and engaged an entirely new cast. It saved them a fortune in redundancy pay."

"Do you have any more news about us making the show record?"

"No. There's no rush to settle an LP agreement for the company because Patti's agent, Mathew Oberstein, hasn't yet sorted out a deal on her behalf with RUG. I was told he's demanding such a ridiculously high sum it makes a recording financially unviable for Sir Andrew. The same applies to filming a TV documentary, although RUG are still struggling to sort that out."

"I must tell you, Hilary, I was given a word of warning about Patti's agent. He's reputed to be one of the toughest in New York. Us lower paid artists in *Sunset* won't be pleased if the recording is scrapped because Patti's agent refuses to compromise on her fucking fees. Excuse my language, Hilary, but that's how we all feel."

"No need to apologise, Peter. I hear a lot worse, believe me."

"Anyhow, thanks for your suggestion. I shall tell the company about Maggie and Andrew having run of the show contracts but also wanting shares in our royalties split. I'll see what everyone's reaction is to that idea. And, Hilary, could I possibly ask you to type out and fax me a simple statement clearly showing the adjusted royalties points that Patti's agent wants? I'll make photocopies for the cast – a bit of light reading over the weekend."

FRIDAY 28th May 1993

5 a.m.

Got up to write this. Went for a run.

7:50 a.m.

Caught the train to Swanley to record a voiceover tape for Proactive Marketing, a company run by Peter Middleton. He often books me for these and I'm very grateful.

9 a.m.

A three-hour session. £180. Peter makes audio cassette commercials that help companies sell products to customers. The fee I'm paid is a fraction compared to actors doing big TV commercials but it's still good money and excellent practice for me in the mysterious art of the voiceover. Successful v.o. artists make it sound easy. It's not.

12:42 p.m.

Caught the train back to London.

2:30 p.m. Riverside Studios, Studio 2

We are back at Riverside today because the computer that moves the scenery at the Adelphi Theatre is still undergoing open-heart surgery.

Canteen

I lunched with the actor Robert Swann. In 1981, we were in the BBC TV series based on Jane Austen's *Sense and Sensibility*.

I said to Robert, "You have the kind of looks which my friend Jean Marsh calls patrician."

He laughed and said, "I don't know Jean but I enjoy her work. She was lovely playing Rose in *Upstairs, Downstairs*. Won an Emmy for it. What is Jean is like as a person?"

"Excellent company. Enjoys cooking; a real *bon viveur*. Jean was in Alfred Hitchcock's 1972 film *Frenzy*. She said to me, 'Hitch is absolutely obsessed with food and wine.' He barely gave her any acting directions. All they discussed was menus, cooking recipes and fine vintage wines. After her last day of filming, when Jean got home, she found an expensive Fortnum and Mason hamper on her front door! She said it was from Hitch. She was highly delighted with that but not impressed by *Frenzy*. She didn't think it worked on any level. Nowhere near as good as *Psycho*, she thought. I agreed with her."

Robert was sitting in the canteen next to the delightful, attractive operatic soprano Kate Flowers.

I said to Robert, "What a small world! Kate and I played the leads in *Ruddigore* at Sadler's Wells Theatre a while ago. So, tell me, Kate, what are you two working on at Riverside today?"

She said, "A very ambitious, interesting project. Robert and I are hoping to present a series of operas at Riverside Studios under the umbrella title, *The Garden Venture* – that's *if* we can raise enough money."

The money thing rang a bell. I've often been told that the job of a theatre producer is weirdly difficult. Successful producers call financial backers their "angels". They often keep their angels secretly hidden to prevent other people stealing them.

I wanted to hear from Kate and Robert what operas featured in their Garden Venture but they were avid, like most people, for news about *Sunset*.

"We were shocked," Robert said, "To hear about Peter Rutherford's brutal treatment by RUG last Wednesday."

Just shows how quickly the word gets round in this business.

The usual questions followed: "How are rehearsals going?" (Very well, fingers crossed), "What's Andrew Lloyd Webber like?" (Very reserved), "How does Trevor Nunn direct rehearsals?" (Terrific attention to detail), "Is the show going to be good?" (With luck, marvellous).

3 p.m. Studio 2

Our last rehearsal at Riverside. After a vocal warm-up, we listened to the orchestral recording of the first number, "Let's Have Lunch". We'll probably sing to it as backing when we record the album. David Cullen has written a 1940s Big Band sound arrangement, reminiscent of Stan Kenton. Not as heavy on the bongo drums as before.

Our choreographer Bob Avian and his assistant Maggie Goodwin were there to check how Bob's staging worked with the orchestration. Maggie greeted me surprisingly warmly with a kiss and a squeeze.

"Hello, possum. I just wanted to let you know that I attended all the recording sessions with Bob. We fought hard to make sure they didn't let the tempos drag. You remember how we said it's got to have that upbeat feeling, otherwise it's so dreary for all of you to work to."

Why was Maggie telling me this? She had never discussed the subject with me before. Then it struck me that I was being addressed as the company's Equity representative. She was highlighting her creative role in the recording process – maybe to justify the extra royalties she will be receiving (which the cast won't, as Hilary pointed out yesterday).

This first hearing of David Cullen's orchestration of "Let's Have Lunch" received enthusiastic clapping and whooping from the company. David said to me, "It's been *very* difficult to arrange."

"Well, please allow me to congratulate you on a terrific job," I replied. "It's fractured and jagged like something out of a modern opera but has a gorgeous melodic texture which Andrew's devoted fan base will love."

"They won't have heard anything like this in his shows before," David said with an impish grin. "I think it'll surprise quite a few people."

"I think you're right."

Nadia Strahan arrived, half an hour late.

"We saw you, Nadia!" Maggie called.

As we moved the number, I readjusted my whole physical attitude down to a slower and smoother style, allowing for the weight and length of the Mighty Beast, my nickname for that elaborate temple priest costume. Gone are all my subtle "ka-chings"! They are now, alas, a ka-ching of the past.

My three dancing temple virgins were being choreographed to fling their heads back in their dance, so I said to Bob, "Anthony Powell has designed gorgeously elaborate coiled wigs for them, like Marlene Dietrich in the movie *Kismet*. It might modify their mobility."

"Thanks for the warning. I would have kept that factor in mind if I'd been given the costume designs to look at."

Don Black called me over. "Peter, I was wondering if you'd

let me change one of your lines. After you sing to Joe, 'How do you like my harem?' Joe looks at your gyrating temple virgins and he replies, 'How do you get such lousy breaks?' – to which you respond, 'One learns to grin and bear 'em'. Instead of that, could you sing, 'How would you like to share 'em?' I think it's a better rhyme than 'bear 'em'."

I was surprised by the question. I wanted to say, "I think your original line is better," but at that moment Sir Andrew appeared.

Don asked him for his opinion about this but Andrew ignored both me and Don's question and completely changed the subject. He said to Don, "I'm still waiting for a rhyme for 'agent' in that number."

As they wrestled with this pressing problem, I retreated. Sir Andrew can only concentrate on what is directly in front of him and of prime concern to him at that moment. Anyone or anything else is beyond his mental vision. It's not rudeness; simply the path he is on. Other activity is a distraction, as irrelevant as small talk. My line is just one of a thousand components in this intricate musical box he's assembling.

4:45 p.m.

A last run of this opening number, "Let's Have Lunch".

5 p.m.

We broke.

Our next call is tonight at 7:30 p.m. over at the Adelphi Theatre. Finish at 10:30.

The stage management started to pull up the ground plan we've been working on for the past five weeks at Riverside – multicoloured sticky tapes stuck to the floor outlining a map of the sets. We all helped by pulling up a red, yellow or blue strip to keep for good luck.

"It's a crime to destroy such a work of art," I exclaimed. "It looks like a huge Mondrian painting. Did anyone take a photograph of it?"

No. Gone forever.

5:10 p.m.

Sandy, our dance captain in the ensemble, kindly gave five of us a lift back to the Adelphi Theatre in his "Vulva" – the nickname he uses for his smart Volvo.

Gardening fans were leaving the Chelsea Flower Show in the brilliant sunshine. They strolled past us along the King's Road carrying glorious armfuls of towering pink and white lupins.

5:45 p.m. Adelphi Theatre

I caught a quick nap in our newly repainted dressing room on the top floor. For some odd reason, the decorators had left the windows shut and the smell of fresh paint was overpowering. One of the lads has named our room "Anne Frank's attic". I can only apologise to the memory of that wonderful girl.

6:15 p.m. Company Manager's Office

Richard Oriel said that Hilary Strange had sent me a new fax from Equity. It details the recording royalties share-out. I collected her fax from Richard and made photocopies of it in his office to distribute amongst the cast and the stage management later.

I rejoined everyone in the theatre. Walking into the stalls this evening delivered quite a weird surprise – almost surreal. The first twelve front row seats have completely gone, leaving empty space all the way back from the orchestra pit to row K! The missing seats are stacked against the walls in the side isles. Taking their place are tables and chairs, arranged for the production team and the technical staff. They will operate the electronic hardware gubbins required to present a spectacular show like this. I counted fifteen computer screens, plus many keyboards which control the sound levels, the sliding panels, the lighting and goodness knows what else.

The full company were watching Patti and Kevin go through the scene just before the end, when pistol-packing Norma shoots Joe dead.

I sat in the middle of the stalls. From my angle, I noticed for the first time that when Patti stands at the top of the staircase only her head is visible. The ornate banister rail is so high it completely masks her from the neck down. Her position there is important for Norma because, in the very final moments of the show, that is where she appears unexpectedly and sings her crazy lady song to the policemen and press reporters gathered below.

Sitting in the stalls closer to the stage in row A, you can barely see Patti at all. I'd say people watching from the front of the dress circle enjoy the best overall view of the show.

Someone whispered, "Patti is supposed to be imperious and dramatic in this scene but the set is so big and ornate it overpowers her. She looks like a munchkin."

The full company were waiting to rehearse the show's very final scene.

Before we began, Trevor gathered our attention. "A word of warning. You'll find it's extremely dark in the wings, very cramped and boxed in, so be especially careful as you get on and off the set. You'll notice there's a narrow gap on the floor between the mobile set and the top of the stairs which you use to walk on or off. You'll also see that strips of white gaffer tape have been put down along the edges of those steps, marking the place where the stairs finish and the mobile set takes over." Trevor then added, "'Mind the gap' is the password."

While we were waiting, I handed round copies of Equity's

proposed recording royalties share-out for the cast to peruse over the weekend.

"And, right now, that's all it is," I pointed out. "Only their *proposed* deal for us to consider and discuss."

A few people reacted strongly.

Daniel Benzali was angry and contemptuous. "This offer is ridiculous! It's got to be a joke!"

"These terms," I tried to explain, "Are only a suggested starting point, Daniel, to set the ball rolling. Please don't complain to me. I'm not in a position to deal with your objections right now. I'm simply passing on information to everyone as I receive it from Equity."

"Whose suggestion is this then?" he demanded indignantly.

"Hilary Strange at Equity. As soon as everyone's had a chance to look at it, I shall organise a company meeting to discuss the proposed deal and take a vote on it. Meanwhile, I shall convey people's reactions back to her. And by all means, Daniel, do feel free to ring Hilary yourself and say you're unhappy with the terms."

"I'll tell my agent to call her."

The general feeling amongst the ensemble is basically this. We are being offered far too low a share of the recording royalties compared to the supporting role actors.

And here's my personal opinion, to which I'm as entitled as anyone.

The whole company – the leads, the supporting role artists, the ensemble and stage management, all of us – should share the points equally, because – and here comes the crunch – the principals will be negotiating their own *separate* salaries *in addition* to the royalties share. But even the equal shares idea won't happen because the pecking order is a very prickly area, albeit discreetly hidden below the surface at the moment. More of this later. *Much more no doubt.*

Trevor began to fine tune our positions on the set for Norma's final, dramatic appearance at the top of the stairs, making sure the whole audience have a clear view of her. We ran it again.

Daniel Benzali descended the stairs and looked down at his feet to make sure he wouldn't trip on the steps. He loudly yelled, "Lights! Camera!". His mike was attached to his shirt, right underneath his chin, and his amplified words exploded like thunder through the entire auditorium. Nearly deafened the lot of us.

Finally, Trevor asked the ensemble to sing the final chorus of "This Time Next Year" at Artie's party to hear how we sounded wearing our mikes.

"Extremely encouraging," was Trevor's verdict. "Wonderful clarity. Very good everyone!"

10:30 p.m.

We were released.

On the way home, I bought a bottle of wine and drank the lot.

SATURDAY 29th May 1993

9:30 a.m.

Went for a run round the streets. Did a workout, then lunch.

Sun-bathed. Well, someone has to do it. My butler's on holiday.

5:45 p.m. Chelsea Arts Centre

Went to see John Webster's gore-fest, *The Duchess of Malfi*. Introduced myself to a twenty-five-year-old play director and writer, Phil Willmott. He said, "I'm here to see this production as one of the judges for a fringe venue award." A serious, intelligent, good-looking, bespectacled face.

I called Peter Rutherford again. "Did Trevor ring you on Wednesday as he said he would."

"No," Peter said. "I was hoping he might but Trevor hasn't phoned me at all. He's probably too busy."

I only hope that Peter receives a generous golden handshake from RUG. Something tells me he won't.

Author's note: I wish to add a few words here. After leaving Sunset Boulevard, Peter Rutherford played Denny Ponance in the 1994 TV series Highlander. Very sadly, the following year, Peter died of a brain tumour on Sunday 21st May 1995 at his home in West Sussex, aged fifty-eight.

SUNDAY 30th May 1993

Gusty wind and showers.

Rang Julia McKenzie. She is rehearsing *Sweeney Todd* at the National Theatre. Her voice sounds croaky.

"It's going very well, thanks, Pete. But I'd completely underestimated Mrs Lovett. It's a huge role, incredibly demanding. We're working without mikes and it's a long show. We've been doing ten hours every day and we're still rehearsing. Dennis Quilley is playing the judge and we are the only two actors in named roles who've done a musical before. It's held us up a bit, as you can imagine."

11:30 a.m. Theatre Museum, Covent Garden

I drove my sixty-one-year-old next-door neighbour Jill Beck into London to hear a lecture about the operatic soprano Maria Callas, with projected slides and recordings of her appearances at the Royal Opera House.

The only time I saw Callas perform there was in June 1959 when she played the title role in Cherubini's *Medea* – its only revival at the Royal Opera House since 1870. Not altogether surprising; very static. I was only seventeen years old, and at grammar school. To bag first night tickets, I queued overnight on the pavement till the box office opened, but we were a jolly, chatty crowd. Every performance sold out within three hours. All I could afford were seats miles up in the amphitheatre. From that distance, the singers' faces below were almost featureless blobs.

1:15 p.m. Food for Thought

Jill and I lunched at this veggie restaurant, then off to the Adelphi Theatre. A security guard kindly allowed me to take Jill onto the stage to see some of *Sunset*'s scenery. She was particularly impressed by the enormous golden gates of Paramount Studios.

Jill was a humble typist for well-known names back in the days before people had their own laptops and printers. Her customers included Laurence Olivier, Joan Collins, composer/author Leslie Bricusse, Barbara Taylor Bradford, Shirley Conran, and playwrights John Osborne, Tom Stoppard, Anthony Shaffer and Peter Shaffer.

"In those days," Jill said, "They all needed me to give their scripts a professional look. I could type sixty words a minute. But if my client was under pressure and wanted their work finished yesterday, which was nearly always the case, I could type a hundred words a minute."

A good friend of Jill's was a proofreader called Jean Penfold.

"Penfold used to proofread for all kinds of interesting people, especially Molly Parkin who founded Nova magazine. Do you remember it, Peter? It was a real ground-breaker."

I do remember it well. Nova was a 1970s glossy, breakthrough women's magazine that featured all kinds of taboo subjects, like abortion, homosexuality, contraception and royal affairs.

"Molly Parkin became a successful novelist and the fashion editor of Harpers & Queen and The Sunday Times." Jill smiled. "Penfold said Molly Parkin's favourite trick at a smart dinner party was to take out her false teeth to shock guests." And if that isn't enough to put you off your grilled parsnips, I don't know what is.

3:30 p.m.

Jill returned home.

I sped to the Barbican Centre, grabbed a coffee and buttered scones, then went to the concert hall to see Cole Porter's *Du Barry Was a Lady*, presented in a series called The Lost Musicals. They are script-held performances devised, directed and presented by Ian Marshall Fischer. I've appeared in several over the years. The scenery and any complex action is described by a narrator. The cast wear evening clothes and mime any props, but the shows really come over. This one was no exception.

Great show! Great perfs!

In the foyer afterwards, I met my wonderfully witty friend Dick Vosburgh. He is a sixty-four-year-old American writer and actor, born in New Jersey and now living in Islington with his wife Beryl. Dick has written comedy material for Ronnie Corbett, Ronnie Barker, Frankie Howerd, David Frost and Tommy Cooper amongst many others. He also wrote the lyrics for the hit show *A Day in Hollywood/A Night in the Ukraine*.

Dick deplores lazy rhymes in a lot of today's lyric writing. He said, "I can't stand their awful *rhynes.*"

This afternoon, Dick was escorting his friend, none other than the marvellous American actress Kim Hunter. For a moment, I was tongue-tied. Miss Hunter could be described as American theatre royalty. She notably played the original Stella in Tennessee Williams' 1947 stage play *A Streetcar Named Desire* on Broadway;

also in the Warner Brothers film adaptation.

I had to ask, "What was it like to be involved in such a seismic event that launched Marlon Brando's major movie career?"

"It's funny. When I discuss it with people, they sometimes can't believe me but this is true. We thought it was just another interesting new play by a good writer and simply did our best, as usual. Marlon was good-looking but a bit young for the role of Stanley and, like the rest of us, an almost completely unknown actor. We were absolutely astonished by the huge public reaction. No one dreamt it would have such a major impact."

The *Du Barry* cast went to have supper in Kettners restaurant in Soho. But I was bushed. Headed home.

10:30 p.m.

In bed.

We have completed five and a half weeks of rehearsals for *Sunset Boulevard*. Previews begin in exactly five weeks' time. That's if the actors/crew/costumes/scenery/rostrums are ready. And if the crazy computer, its weird valves and the moody hydraulic lifts agree to play nice. A big *if.*

Lights out, Pete. *Zzzzzzzzz…*

MONDAY 31st May 1993 – Bank Holiday

5 a.m.

Woke early to write. Woke is an interesting word! As well as being the past sense of wake, since the 1960s it's meant "well-informed" in Black English. You dig? Hey, cool, man. Give me a high-five.

7:30 a.m.

Went for a run round the streets. Did a workout.

Our afternoon rehearsal call is at 1:30 p.m.

11:30 a.m.

I drove over to Tom Conti's house in Reddington Road in Hampstead. I know Tom (the famous award-winning actor) and his wife Kara through my chum Gay Hamilton. Tom and Kara are away for the bank holiday weekend and Gay is house-sitting for them. She first met them in 1960 at the Royal Scottish Academy of Music and Drama in Glasgow and the three have been close pals ever since.

Like me, Gay loves classical music so I gave her two CDs: a Chopin compilation and a Maria Callas selection of live 1957 recordings, including "I Puritani".

This morning, Gay was playing the lady of the house – looking a vision of elegance in a white silk dressing gown.

"It's wonderful," she said, "To be surrounded by so many beautiful paintings and ornaments. As I walk about, each object I look at costs a fortune – according to my standards. I love it!"

I followed her gaze. "Yes... And they have that lovely little secluded back garden, as well as this spacious living room with its big kitchen." I was silently thinking, *And it's all spotlessly clean!*

We took our cups of coffee onto the back garden veranda to sit and chat, but the wind was too buffety. After ten minutes, we thought it best to withdraw into the conservatory. As one does. Ooh, la-di-da!

12:15 p.m.

Drove home. Cooked a quick lunch.

Phone rang. Our company manager Richard Oriel. "Peter, the call has been put back to 3 p.m. and we'll be rehearsing at the Royalty Theatre."

My heart plummeted. Merciful maggots! Not *more* sitting round the piano bellowing "Let's Have Lunch" and "This Time Next Year". For hours each day, we park our bums on chairs and grind out these festering chorus numbers! How much longer?

1 p.m.

On the tube train going in, I sat next to Gareth Snook.

He expressed the same dread. "Exactly. And just when we thought we could say to David Caddick, 'You can leave us alone! The numbers belong to *us* now.' We proved that on the stage last week. We all know we can sing them and that they sound good when we're miked."

We discussed Trev's style of directing. I said, "Admittedly, I'm not playing a leading role but I'm a bit disappointed. I find him cold and very guarded. He spends most of his time flirting with the girls when he's not actually directing the show."

"I've worked with him before," Gareth replied. "His crowning ability is to get up in front of the cast and talk. He understands the value of bullshit and has absolute command of the language. You've heard the phrase, 'being Trevved'? Well, you know when he's doing it to you, but you don't care. He seduces us and we love it. His arm goes affectionately round your shoulder, as if you were the most important person in the world, and he talks to you in his soft, confidential voice and you feel great. You've been Trevved!"

"That's true," I said. "I've watched him doing it to people, but so far, he hasn't Trevved me. I'm beginning to wonder if there's a reason. Maybe he's more wary of the older ones."

Gareth very kindly suggested the company should write a letter to Peter Rutherford.

"Good idea," I said. "Maybe we could all sign him a card."

Talking of bullshit, I went into the stalls to take a leak in the gents' toilet and discovered that someone had defaecated in the urinal bowl attached to the wall. Of all places! Three bulky logs languished in the white porcelain basin – the bizarre calling card of what mysterious visitor? We'll never know. The plot of a new horror movie? The Phantom of the Crapper.

1:45 p.m. Royalty Theatre. Stalls Bar

The cast gathered downstairs to chew over weekend activities.

Kevin said, "On Sunday evening, I invited Nadia, Anita and Adam over to the house I'm renting in Hampstead. We had a lot of fun."

I bet.

Mark Inscoe surprised us. "I went to see *Sweeney Todd* at the National Theatre. I thought it was well-directed by Declan Donnellan but not as well acted. The exception, Peter, was your friend. Julia McKenzie. Her Nellie Lovett was particularly splendid." Then he added, "And last night Patti was on TV. She sang 'With One Look' on Michael Aspel's show, *Aspel and Company*. Did you see her?"

"No. I had no idea Patti was guesting – otherwise I would've watched."

By chance, several others in the cast caught Patti's appearance. I just wish management could have alerted us that our leading lady was in Michael Aspel's star line-up.

I first met Michael twenty years ago when he was dating Elizabeth Power. She was a knockout good-looker and he used to visit her backstage when Lizzie and I were appearing in *Cole* at the Mermaid Theatre – a very successful Cole Porter revue. Lizzie sang "I Get a Kick Out of You" in it and my solo was "I'm a Gigolo", with the line, *"I'm a flower that blooms in the winter, Sinkin' deeper and deeper in snow"* (cocaine).

3 p.m.

We were ushered into the stalls. I noticed that on the stage chairs had been set out in elegantly curved rows round the piano. Yet more sitting down hammering away at the infernal dots! It's like the new film that opened in February, *Groundhog Day*. What weird life lessons must we learn to end these infernal day-after-day-after-day repetitions?

We then went onto the stage and sat on chairs. Trevor stood facing us and spoke in hushed tones, gently pulling at his beard.

"I have to explain to you all why we are here at the Royalty this afternoon."

Kevin Anderson, seated in front of me, turned round, gave me a wicked grin. "Who's being fired now?" he said, and pointed at himself. "Me!"

Trevor ignored Kevin's remark. "The faulty valves in the computer at the Adelphi Theatre are still being worked on. They must be properly fixed, of course, otherwise the hydraulics that operate the scenery could be activated by random signals received from passing car phones – even mobile radios."

Did he mean the computers might hear pop records played on Ken Bruce's Radio 2 show and start the scenery dancing around? The idea sent shudders through the company. Patti spoke for us all.

"That is scary!" she exclaimed.

"So, until that's corrected and made absolutely fail-safe," Trevor continued, "We aren't able to begin our technical, which should be the next stage of our progress. Meanwhile, in order not to lose that wonderfully cohesive grasp of the play which you all achieved at the final run-through last week, I felt it would be a good idea for you to do a vocal run-through here at the Royalty this afternoon, including all the sung, spoken and underscored text, to keep the spirit of the piece alive. This evening we might be able to go into the Adelphi Theatre and start work there. But we might not.

"I don't wish to sound unnecessarily negative about the prospects of using the stage, but on the other hand, I see no point in painting an overly optimistic one either, which I could easily. So, let's hope for the best and start with a warm-up! Then I want to hear you sing through the tricky ensemble sections. While we're doing that, upstairs Patti, Kevin and Daniel will sort out a few adjustments and changes. And then we'll run Act One."

And so, we did.

It was clearly a case of Trev trying to motivate a large company to keep repeating themselves, knowing that, as we do, most of us will spend ninety percent of our time sitting on these chairs listening to the three leads going on and on for hours. I sympathised, inwardly, with his problem, and am only too happy to cooperate to the best of my ability, but I imagine it's a real concentration test for those with even less to do than me.

As Trevor talked to us, Patti's three-year-old little boy, Josh, wandered about the theatre auditorium, staring at everything and everyone with his large, dark eyes. Patti took flash photos of us singing the brisk vocal warm-up.

Trevor gave us an important note before we embarked on a thorough brush-up of the ensemble numbers. "Make sure that each solo line you sing sounds different," he commented. "They tend to lack attitude and lose a sense of individuality."

With this in mind, we sang through "The Lady's Paying".

Trevor then said, "I'd like to hear that again. And this time, Peter, I want you to pronounce the g more clearly at the beginning of the phrase, 'Glen plaid trousers'." It's my only solo line in that number.

He applied the same note to the first consonants of other people's lyrics, such as the b in Richard Tate's phrase, "In black". They are his only two solo words in the song: "chalk stripe suits *in black* or blue." I remember this well because Richard was sitting next to me. When it came to that point in the score, he sort of exploded. He screamed the word, "black!" then fell sideways across my lap, as if he'd been shot through the head.

When the laughter died down, he confessed to being as baffled

as everyone else how "black" suddenly burst from his face like a bullet out of a gun. "I was trying to make it different," was all he could offer.

Trevor didn't appear convinced or amused. "It's called blurting."

I wonder if Trevor felt that he was being sent up. It's obvious that the last thing he wants to do is lose control of these rehearsals and allow them to disintegrate into fun and games and giggles, but this afternoon there was definitely a spirit of playfulness bubbling in the air.

Patti, Kevin and Daniel rejoined us. Remaining seated, we did a purely vocal run-through of Act One, speaking and singing the entire show like a radio performance – a good one, except for a single moment.

At the end of a scene, Kevin's character (Joe Gillis) picks up a musical phrase and he continues whistling it before his next chunk of narration. At this point, Kevin changed the whistle into a completely extraneous tune. It was unfamiliar to me but he got a big laugh from the company. I soon discovered why…

During the tea break, I went into the gents for a pee. Soon after, Kevin and Trevor followed.

As the three of us stood side by side in a solemn row, Trevor said to Kevin, "The run's going very well, but for goodness' sake don't you whistle anything in that scene except what you're *supposed* to whistle or you'll get us all lynched. Didn't you see Andrew wandering in and out of the stalls, and conferring with me?"

Kevin's response was a quiet chuckle.

"What was Kevin whistling?" I asked Trevor.

"'Love Changes Everything'," he replied.

That song's title meant nothing to me, so I later asked Nick Colicos to put me wise. "Can you explain why Kevin whistling that particular melody riled Trevor so much?"

"Trevor was making a very serious point. Kevin might have thought it was just a light-hearted joke, but that tune he whistled, 'Love Changes Everything', is from Andrew's musical, *Aspects of Love*. Andrew is hyper-sensitive to the accusation that he copies melodies not only from other composers' shows but even from his own!"

Today, a newcomer joined the cast: Harry Ditson. He has replaced Peter Rutherford in the role of Sheldrake. Harry is a well-established Canadian actor who has lived and worked here for some time. He recently sold his house here and bought another in Toronto, intending to move back to Canada. He exchanges contracts in July but he has agreed to stay in Britain and appear in *Sunset Boulevard* till September.

Harry has worked with Trevor before, in *Once in a Lifetime* and *Porgy and Bess*. He explained the reason for Trevor's closed rehearsals.

"He likes to work very privately with actors, very closely and intimately, which would be no good in a crowded rehearsal room. That's why actors love working with Trevor, because it's so personal. He's great."

Those hardly involved in Act Two till the show's final scene were now released. After our appearance in Paramount Studios, Richard Tate and I crept off the stage and left.

Tomorrow's call is 1:30 p.m. at the Adelphi Theatre. Fingers crossed it won't be changed to an earlier time.

Chapter 6

JUNE 1993

TUESDAY 1st JUNE 1993

5 a.m.

Up to write.

12 p.m. Lunch

Shopped at Sainsbury's, then cooked and ate.

Richard Oriel rang. "Just to tell you, Peter, the 1:30 p.m. call has been put back. We'll start at 3 p.m. and finish tonight at 9 p.m."

2:15 p.m.

Forgot to take my travel card, didn't I? Dang nab-it!

3 p.m. Adelphi Theatre

After being miked up, we were taken on a guided tour of the backstage area. Walking into the wings is like entering a sinister labyrinth of murky stairways and tunnels. It's as dark as midnight. For health and safety reasons, strips of white reflective tape have been stuck to the edges of low, wooden, jet-black, head-bashing beams. These white strips also run along the hard-to-see corners of steps on black ladders we use to climb to reach higher stage entrances. These ladders are on wheels so that they can be moved about, as and when needed.

There are big square openings in the stage floor. Through them steel cables stretch upwards like ski-lift pulleys and hydraulic pistons hiss in the dark as if they were snake pits. The steel cables pull palettes on and off the stage.

Palettes are low platforms, about six inches high, on which pieces of scenery, furniture and people can be placed and then slid on and off the stage. Also in the wings, fixed to the black beams, there are emergency stop buttons. Beneath each one is a glowing red light. I guess the buttons are there to press in case the palettes need to be suddenly halted for safety reasons.

In the wings, furniture is stacked in piles against the walls, waiting to be placed on these palettes. Black masking curtains hang everywhere.

Trevor gathered us into the stalls. "As you've all now seen, the offstage wing space is a confusing, frightening, bewildering labyrinth, but I promise you that it will – after familiarisation – become comprehensible and easy to traverse."

A fascinating word of warning came from Pippa Shaw, our stage

manager. "You see those tall black panels hanging up in the flies? Each one can be lowered separately to mask the upstage area. They can also be used to create a variety of different gaps for various entrances and exits. Please remember: do not touch those panels. They are *very sensitive*," she added with disturbing emphasis.

"Also," Trevor explained, "The valves in the computers that move those panels are still being fixed. This means we can only continue with the technical rehearsal today *without* using the panels, proceeding carefully, bit by bit. After we run one section, we will stop, then manually move the scenery before we carry on into the following scene."

But no one has explained to us what these valves actually do and where they are hiding. I later learnt these fascinating facts from one of the lighting operators – or "programmers".

He said, "The valves are underneath the stage, inside the computers. They are manufactured by Vickers. Valves like these are inside the engines of planes, that's why no passengers are allowed to switch on mobile radios during a flight, or use portable telephones in case they inadvertently operate the valves."

A seriously alarming prospect. I guess if a taxi passing by in the Strand received a mobile phone message on a certain wavelength, one of our computers might also receive that call and Norma Desmond's house could start twisting and lurching about the stage, trying to leave the theatre and collect the passengers who rang for the cab at Waterloo Station and take the blighters home. And all of us will then be trapped inside a huge 3D timber maze that's heaving and swerving around like a fairground ride.

Leslie Hayes played the piano as we rehearsed the opening scene.

As the show starts, the first thing the audience sees is a huge gauze with blue and green ripples playing across, filling the proscenium arch. It is the view from the bottom of a swimming pool looking up at the surface. A dummy made with Kevin Anderson's proportions, wearing his clothes and his face mask, hangs in the centre of the gauze. Mr Dummy is pretending to be the dead body of Joe Gillis, floating on the surface of the pool. Well, that's the idea. It looks dangerously like a dummy dangling in front of a blue gauze.

In these opening moments, a group of reporters and L.A. cops are briefly glimpsed at the edge of the stage. The cops are dragging

Joe's body out of the pool (from the orchestra pit) with poles. At the same time, they are being watched by another group of police cops standing on the top level of the upstage rostrum, looking down. The police cops are played by Harry Ditson, Richard Antony, Nick Colicos, Gareth Snook and me.

This is a striking shot that opens the original Paramount film.

"To help create this image," Trevor explained, "I'd like you men on the top of the slope looking down into the pool (my group) to lean back. Then the lights on you will fade and you walk up the slope to the top level and exit while the identical action is being performed down at the edge of the stage."

As we waited to start, we discovered Trevor's warning about this set is all too real. It's very dark on that upstage rostrum. It's also dangerously high. No hand rails. Step over that level's edge and you fall some twenty feet.

Connected to the top of this rostrum is a large adjustable flap. When raised, it can create space underneath it for the garage, for example, or, as now, it can be slightly lowered and raked, making a steep downwards slope towards the audience. Its surface can be made either smooth or a flight of steps.

We managed to run the opening scene in short-winded bursts. We waited as panels, pallets and towers were pushed manually on and off and positioned by the stage crew because no scenery can be operated automatically yet but everyone's keeping patient and good-humoured about it.

The set, designed by John Napier, looks glorious – basically a sun-drenched, golden box with atmospheric shadows of palm trees, scenery towers and telegraph poles. Above, a pale blue and yellow sky. Very hot. Very California.

As the show begins, after doing my US cop standing by the pool bit, I exit offstage right, climb down the stairs and change into Jonesy's security guard outfit. I quickly glue on a moustache, and then re-enter in front of the huge Paramount Studios double gates. They are made of elaborately curled and gold-painted wrought-steel.

Weeks ago, when we first set this scene, I said to a stage manager that John Napier's model didn't include a small side door in one of the two huge golden Paramount gates for studio workers to enter or leave.

"Will one of the gates be open?" I asked.

"No. Both those main gates stay shut. A small door will be cut into the stage right gate. As you enter playing Jonesy, you will open the door and then close it when the scene ends. This is important. Be sure you've shut it securely before that huge golden gates' flat flies out. If you don't, it could cause a problem."

No trouble. But today – no small side door.

"This will be attended to," I was told. Till then, one huge stage right Paramount gate is set ajar for studio personnel to walk through.

6:15 p.m. Tea Break. Covent Garden Piazza

I sat outside in the courtyard with a pot of Earl Grey tea and a carrot cake, enjoying the bright evening sunshine and people-watching.

7:15 p.m. Adelphi Theatre. Onstage

We continued to go over the opening number in stop-start fragments. After my exchange as Jonesy (security guard) with Joe (script writer) in front of the Paramount Studios gates, I go off and change into the high priest costume that I wear playing Sammy, a Hollywood actor working on the set of Cecil B. DeMille's film, *Samson and Delilah*. It includes a full-length elaborate robe and long trailing cloak. Then, in the wings, I climb the steps.

Now, as Sammy, I re-enter on the high upstage rostrum, this time followed by Anita Louise Combe, Sasha Millard and Dawn Spence, all dressed as my high priest's dancing temple virgins. The girls are very scared of the narrow platform on which they perform their Hollywood-style oriental dance, with spins and backbends. And I don't blame them one bit. I only walk on, mercifully.

We actually reached the end of the number – when the movie tycoon Mr Sheldrake slides into view from stage right on a low mobile rostrum. He is seated at his office desk speaking into the phone as Joe Gillis enters to discuss the script he sent him.

Our new Sheldrake, played by Harry Ditson, is smoking a cigar and singing, "Get me that shithead, Nolan," into one phone and then, "It won't work," into another.

9:15 p.m.

We broke.

WEDNESDAY 2nd June 1993

12 p.m. Adelphi Theatre. Jessie Matthews Suite

I had costume fittings for two walk-on roles: an outfitter in "The Lady's Paying" number and a newspaper reporter in the final scene.

As I chatted to our costume designer Anthony Powell, he recalled the first time he worked with the actor Sir Ralph Richardson. "He was very eccentric. He asked me to insert an extra deep and wide pocket in his coat because he liked to carry his pet ferret Eddie onto the stage. He even held Eddie in his hand during scenes. Sir Ralph washed Eddie each week in Lux soap flake suds."

I said to Anthony, "A friend of mine, the actress Sheila Ballantine, worked with him. She told me they were in a play at St Albans and Sir Ralph used to drive up there from London on his motorbike with a parrot called Jose tucked inside his leather jacket!"

1:15 p.m.

Tanya Franks and I met for lunch at Cafe Sante.

"If you'd like me to, Tanya, I'll write a letter to Ian McKellen on your behalf to see if he'll play Sartorius in the reading of Shaw's *Heartbreak House* you're producing in early October. I've never acted with Ian but in 1969 my partner Paulie was in *Edward II* and *Richard II* with him at the Piccadilly Theatre and they got on extremely well."

Just as Tanya and I were about to leave the cafe, the heavens opened. We waited a short moment while the rain hammered down, then picked our way between puddles, huddling under my little red umbrella. I love its cute wooden handle – shaped and painted like a duck's head.

3 p.m. Adelphi Theatre

Talk about a dry tech! Back at the theatre, I found a fast-flowing stream of rain water was pouring from the stage door all the way down the concrete steps and onto the stage! Even in the theatre auditorium the carpets had puddles in various places. We continued to rehearse without sound coming from the actors' mikes because backstage flooding had knocked out the amplifiers or generators or hydraulics or speakers or something.

We did a run of all the scenes from the end of the opening number, "Let's Have Lunch", and stopped at the beginning of Schwab's Drug Store. The car chase section was skipped over because its scenery is still being made at the Cambridge Theatre.

This afternoon, Patti found out for the first time how it felt to work on the set. As she tried out her moves on the superb interior of Norma Desmond's magnificent house, she asked, "Has anyone noticed that this set is taller than I am?" She then declared, "I feel like a munchkin on it."

Turns out we weren't the only ones to notice this last week. But, with all their other problems, the production team needs Patti's complaints like they need a hole in the head (to quote the old 1960s phrase). One of the wardrobe ladies told me that Patti has also insisted that her wigs be made in America, and that her own wig dressers be flown over to take care of them. Is this another crack in the rift between Patti and Sir Andrew's RUG management?

Andrew Lloyd Webber's wife Madeleine was seated in the stalls with her thirteen-year-old step-son, Nicholas. I joined them for a few moments' chat.

"Underneath the floor of this huge house set," I explained, "There is a complete lighting rig. This means that when the house is raised up into the flies, it can light a scene that takes place below it. Every inch under the floor is utilised to hold lamps. Those two big sofas are completely hollow. Inside them, there are lamps pointing downwards. Must make the sofa very warm to sit on!"

Andrew joined his wife and said, "That set is wrong."

He was referring to the guest bedroom above Norma's garage where she lodges Joe and where he types the *Salome* screenplay for her. It is a tall section that slides on from stage left on a pallet – a ramshackle room with a slanting windowed roof and an old bed. Steps lead up to it from stage level.

Madeleine was puzzled. "What's wrong about the set, Andrew?"

"The room should be lowered at least half way down."

"Why?"

"Because Max can't sing on it."

"Why not?"

"Because he's far too high up. He can't relate to the audience."

Andrew clearly has an eye and an ear for what works and what doesn't, but perhaps constantly making such fault-finding comments, however astute, might explain why, when Andrew appears at rehearsals, people tend to gaze up at the ceiling and sigh, "Oh God. Here he comes."

6 p.m. Tea Break. Fatboy's Diner

I went for a veggie burger in the American style cafe that looks like the exterior of a US train railcar. It's right next to the stage door of the Adelphi Theatre in Maiden Lane, Covent Garden.

Eating in this area is absurdly expensive. I must remember to bring in my own food sometimes to lighten expenses. £7 for a meat-free burger with chips and a coffee!

7 p.m.

We continued the technical till we reached the first scene in Schwab's Drug Store.

9 p.m.

We broke. Tomorrow's call is 3 p.m. for a tech.

THURSDAY 3rd June 1993

10:30 a.m. Home

Hilary Strange rang me from Equity.

"Not good news, Peter. We can't proceed yet with a company vote on the recording royalties share-out because Patti's agent is demanding thirty percent even before Kevin, Daniel and Meredith take their chunks. That would leave precious little for the rest of the company. I was hoping to apportion forty percent to the four principals, sixty percent to the rest of the cast, maybe settle for a fifty-fifty split. It now looks as if it'll swing in the opposite direction against the company. On Lloyd Webber's 1991 recording of *Joseph and the Technicolor Dream Coat*, Jason Donovan took thirty-two points, but there were only two other sizeable roles; one took eight points and the other, six. The remaining fifty-four points were shared amongst the company."

I typed the letter to Ian McKellen on behalf of Tanya Franks, and also scribbled a quick airmail letter to Jacqueline Parker in New York. She's an avid theatre-goer, hoping to come over to London in August to see *Sunset* and *Sweeney Todd*, amongst other shows. She worked at the top of the World Trade Centre, one of the Twin Towers – the tallest buildings in the world with ninety-four floors. Five months ago, Al-Qaeda terrorists exploded a bomb in an underground garage beneath it, killing six people. By sheer chance, Jacquie was at home when it occurred. It took survivors up to two hours to walk down the smoke-filled, darkened stairwell to safety.

12 p.m. Lunch at Home

I had a quick cottage cheese and spinach salad, then off to the Royal Academy Summer Exhibition preview. I forgot that today was the private view for members and should have taken a chum. I tried to ring Jill Beck, my neighbour, but she was out.

As I've said, Jill works for a company called Scripts. It was set up by the actor Victor Maddern and Jill's job was to take a poorly handwritten film, play or novel and produce a clean, neatly-typed professional-looking copy. Jill said, "I typed several versions of *Lawrence of Arabia* over fourteen years for different directors, until it was directed by David Lean in 1962. It won seven Academy Awards! And I also typed *A Flowering Cherry* for Robert Bolt. That was in 1957; he was only a schoolteacher then. And Tom Stoppard often came into our office with his plays. Best of all was typing Laurence Olivier's autobiography. He rang me at Scripts one day and quoted some funny anecdotes from it, so I suggested he should bring it into the office with all his newspaper cuttings for me to photocopy everything. He was so charming. Great fun to work for. He said, 'There are several details that need to be checked. Could you ring the Dorking Water Board and find out what the water rates were in 1927?' For some odd reason he wanted to be accurate about the bills he'd paid. A real stickler for detail."

"Just like his acting," I said.

1:15 p.m. Royal Academy of Arts

I went to the RA's Summer Exhibition for this year's Liquorice Allsorts eyeball pick and mix of delicious, delightful and daring. Not to mention the dainty, the dopey and the daunting.

3 p.m. Adelphi Theatre. Technical Rehearsal

As the ensemble arrived, a top fight arranger was advising Patti how to slap Kevin's face during their alone together at midnight New Year scene. Patti has been making the sound by hitting her own hand. The arranger suggested Kevin should make the noise, which does look better.

We then continued checking the scene in Schwab's Drug Store, this time using the flat that houses the double doors. They are made of thick Perspex pretending to be glass. One of them is wildly warped, like a crazy piece of modern art. On the shop counter, there are milkshakes and hot dogs on plates made of plastic that look amazingly real. The positions of the stools round the counter were clearly marked on the floor and, happily, I had a stool to sit on – not always the case in rehearsals at Riverside Studios.

I was determined to keep my spirits up, but working with some of the younger ensemble is a trial. Added to this, Bob Avian (our American choreographer) orders me around as if I was a low-grade chorus boy. Not good for the self-esteem. Bob is only four years older than me. It seems my status in this show doesn't entitle me to polite treatment.

"And Peter Gale, let me see your gestures like I asked you. Make it big, so you pull focus". I thought technical rehearsals were for checking lighting, scenery and sound, without giving a fabulous full-out performance.

Choreographers are infamous for treating ensemble members as if they were lazy, bloody-minded children. Some notoriously choose a whipping boy and focus their cruel bile on the unfortunate soul – painfully demeaning for the person and horribly embarrassing for everyone else. In contrast, such choreographers are often bum lickers to the show's stars and leading actors, handling them with kid gloves, like a superior form of life.

I passed on Equity's news about Patti's "greedy agent" to the ensemble. It provoked a few aggrieved and angry responses. We watched Patti in her scene with Kevin, slinking up and down the staircase doing her Salome gestures. Patti was using a practice costume to work out her physical business but also still wearing her thick-framed spectacles. I've never yet seen Patti rehearse without them. Maybe she'll wear contact lenses for the show, unless the glasses a part of her characterisation.

6 p.m.

We broke.

Mark Inscoe and I walked over to the Strand Theatre stage door to deliver first night cards to our chums. My dear old friend David Alder is in a new musical opening there called *Leonardo*, based on the Mona Lisa, a painting by the great Italian Renaissance painter, inventor and architect. Surely, such a grandiose subject would need the vocal dimensions of an opera?

When David and I were seventeen, we played two Shakespearean heroines. I was feisty Viola to his vainly beautiful Olivia in Slough

Grammar School's production of Shakespeare's *Twelfth Night*. David is the most consistently cheerful and friendly soul I've ever known. The half-hour call had gone but the stage door keeper phoned a message through to him and David popped down for a quick chat and a good luck hug.

The corridor was swamped with an avalanche of evening-clothed people, flowers, greeting cards, wrapped gifts and showbiz fun – an exhilarating buzz. Rob Bettinson has directed *Leonardo* and it stars Paul Colis, Jane Arden, James Barron and Lisa Hollander. However, the word on the show is not too good…

Dear David said, "The show opened in Oxford and had rave reviews. I joined it when it came to London but it's been chaos. The management decided to change all the songs and rewrite the original script. Yesterday evening, we had last minute cuts put in the show, but for some stupid reason they weren't passed on to everyone in the cast. It caused some very eggy pauses."

I later discovered that, bizarrely, the show was financed by a government official in the republic of Nauru, a tiny island in the middle of the Pacific Ocean which had made more than two billion dollars in phosphate trade.

Sadly, *Leonardo* was a disaster. The first night lasted almost four hours. By the end, most of the audience had walked out. In spite of the good luck card I gave to David, the show closed five weeks later – one of the biggest disasters in the history of London theatre.

6:30 p.m. Joe Allen's Brasserie

Feeling in a "Oh what the hell. Love it or hate it, I'm in this terrific crappy profession right up to the top of my bald head!" kinda mood, I treated myself to a Caesar salad and a coffee. Alone.

7:30 p.m.

We ran "The Lady's Paying", not my favourite number in the show but over quickly.

I'm an outfitter who dresses Joe in his evening togs. At the end of the scene, I carry the heavy clothes rack up the stairs and then exit. I am the last person to leave the stage. And late. Not a pleasant sensation.

Patti and Kevin rehearsed "The Perfect Year". It's a slow waltz as Norma and Joe welcome in the New Year. She wore a long red practice skirt.

During this number, Norma's house rises ten feet. Underneath it, pallets slide on from the wings carrying Artie's flat where Artie and his friends are celebrating the New Year. From upstage centre, another truck brings on a piano. Today, this truck caused a major problem. It stuck. The computer wasn't feeling in the mood to move it.

During the break, Nigel Wright (stage management's spokesperson) said to me, "We held a production meeting with Trevor earlier and we explained to him it's not us being slow or uncooperative or bloody-minded. It's the set's mechanics not responding to orders from the computer. If those complex pieces of machinery refuse to do what they're told, shifting these sets manually is a really slow and awkward business for us."

I sighed, nostalgically. "Ah, for the good old days of ropes and hooks."

8:30 p.m.

Managing to grab a moment with Alistair Smith, our production manager, I asked him, "Any news on the proposed TV documentary?"

"Yes," Alistair said. "I'm sorry to tell you Patti has refused to allow the film to be made because she isn't being offered enough money."

"Alistair, I hugely admire Patti as an artist, but here's my problem. I'm the company's Equity representative. On their behalf, could I ask you to explain to Patti that if she stops the filming, she would be depriving us lower paid actors of much needed extra dough. It was a major inducement for us to accept this job."

Alistair promised he would try to help. "I'll look into the maths for you. But, to be honest, we're dealing with a very starry, selfish lady who gives the impression that she's unlikely to give a toss."

His words surprised me. Patti is a likeable and professional colleague to work with. Let's hope Alistair will be proved wrong. Fortunately, there's a plan for extracts from the show to be filmed using just the ensemble in full costume as preview material for News Access TV. If that happens, us lower salary lot might bag some welcome financial perks. There must be very strong ill-feeling between Patti and Andrew Lloyd Webber if Alastair, one of his closest production associates, speaks in such a surprisingly hostile way about her. Oh well. Another day, another dust-up.

9:30 p.m.

With various components of the set now usable, we did a couple of runs of the rowdy party number, "This Time Next Year".

We are at stage level. Directly above us, Norma Desmond is alone, prowling about in her enormous mansion. This takes "upstaging" to a hugely higher level. Trevor responded with enthusiastic praise, both for the performances and the effect of the two dramatically contrasting scenes.

Today, Kevin pinned a message on the company noticeboard inviting everyone to a barbecue this Sunday at 2 p.m. in the back garden of his flat in Hampstead where he's staying.

Incidentally, three days ago, Kevin kindly gave me his lawyer's name and phone number so that Hilary Strange at Equity can call him about the LP royalties share-out. His name is Ira Schreck; in German "schreck" means "terror"!

Kevin is an extremely engaging, good-natured, hardworking and likeable guy. During pauses in rehearsals, he holds impressive stretching yoga positions. Kevin fancies the ensemble girls strongly. And vice versa. Especially Dawn Spence.

Tomorrow's call is 3:30 p.m.

10:50 p.m. Home

I found six messages on my answerphone.

One was from Hilary Strange at Equity. "Hello Peter. I suggest Nadia, Nigel, you and I should have a meeting next week. By then, I will have spoken to the three American artists' agents. I was given the show's score and I counted everyone's solo bars as a guide to establish the royalty points share-out but it was no help at all. Could you call me about this tomorrow?"

FRIDAY 4th June 1993

5:30 a.m.

Up early to write.

10:30 a.m.

I rang Hilary Strange at Equity. She suggested that Nadia, Nigel from stage management and I should have a meeting with her next week about the royalties points share-out.

Then I called Margaret Fenn at the Theatre Museum to see if Tanya Franks could use the Gallery Room for a reading of a Shaw play in October.

Margaret said, "Yes, Peter. Tanya may use it indeed. She only has to pay for the staff. I suggest that we three should have lunch next Wednesday to discuss this. And maybe also a series of readings of Shaw's plays on a regular Sunday afternoon basis."

I rang Tanya who was overjoyed. "Oh Peter, that's wonderful! It's the perfect venue. Thank you. I'll ring Margaret to clinch it."

The weather is still warm. I cooked myself a veggie lunch, spaghetti with soya mince, and sat in the front garden on my park bench. My neighbour Jill joined me for a coffee.

She said, "I've made these six photocopies of your play *All My Love* and had them bound, so you can start sending them out."

"Oh, thanks, Jill! They look great!"

3:30 p.m. Adelphi Theatre. Full Company Call. Act Two

We rehearsed the opening when Kevin sings his big solo number, the title song *Sunset Boulevard*. He performed it twice, using the huge flight of steps which the centre stage rostrums can create. It's a driving, jagged song and Kevin gives it a restless, loose-limbed cynicism. His Joe Gillis is a weirdly self-destructive character but not a passive observer of his own fate. In this number, Kevin can externalise the angry animal inside him, one of his few opportunities to give full rein to that.

People are bound, of course, to compare his performance with William Holden's in the film. Holden was thirty-two when the film was made. Kevin is thirty-three, but Holden appears a more mature man who has the smell of failure already clinging to him. Kevin's boyish looks convey the impression of a talented but reckless young man, wilfully allowing his chances of having a fine writing career and a loving relationship with Betty to be destroyed by an inner demon of self-hate.

I thought, *All the best people have inner demons. Celebrities agonise about them in newspapers. I must try to get one. Perhaps Boots the chemist shop sells them.*

We skipped over Norma's arrival at Paramount Studios in her luxury 1930 Isotta Fraschini convertible. The cut-out section of the limo is still being worked on at the Cambridge Theatre. We picked it up from the moment when, as the security guard Jonesy, I cross to the telephone box on the stage left proscenium, open it and call the switchboard: "Gimme Stage 18. I have a message for Mr DeMille".

DeMille then enters with a group of assistants. His secretary (played by Alisa Endsley) informs DeMille of Norma Desmond's presence on the lot. The sliders fly away revealing Stage 18 in all its movie-making confusion.

However, we couldn't run the sequence because those parts of the set are still being operated manually.

We slowly progressed into Norma Desmond's meeting with DeMille and her big number, "As If We Never Said Goodbye". Patti did the scene twice, crying tears both times as she sang. Trevor expressed his admiration.

6:15 p.m. Bella Pasta

Had an avocado salad supper with Leslie Hayes, our rehearsal pianist. On our way back to the theatre poor, Leslie said, "I was told by my doctor I've got the beginnings of multiple sclerosis, Peter."

I don't know Leslie very well, but she lives not far from me in West Hampstead, so I said I would do my best to be supportive. What shattering news. It's a horrible, paralysing disease.

Two weeks ago, Leslie suffered that nasty shock at Riverside Studios. As she was playing the piano, the prop totem pole fell over and struck her shoulder. Could the two be linked?

7:30 p.m.

We continued with Norma saying goodbye to DeMille and leaving Paramount Studios.

Trevor adjusted our positions on the set. And this is what rehearsals mainly consist of – standing around while some invisible soul somewhere tries to work out why a slider or a panel or a flyer or a pallet isn't responding to the press of a button. Or why, when the thing finally *does* move, it decides for no fathomable reason to stop halfway and contemplate the origin of the universe. But at least we're all standing in the right position when it does.

Everyone is good-humoured. Heaven knows the crew and stage management are having the most knackering time. On average, they work from 8:30 a.m. till 10:30 p.m., including weekends, but they are coping brilliantly well and, let's hope, pocketing good overtime pay.

The big problem seems to be the sheer volume of scenery, its complexity and the limited space to contain it. This is compounded by the sulky disobedient "hydraulics", whatever they are. I looked the word up. It means using water under pressure to operate machinery, from the Greek words *hydro* (water) and *aulos* (pipe).

The actors have said they want me to organise a meeting to air their feelings about the recording royalties share-out. And also, specifically, the alleged demand by Patti's agent for thirty percent of the points.

9:15 p.m.

Rehearsal ended.

After we were dismissed, the company gathered in a dressing room; all except Patti, Kevin, Daniel and Meredith. We had earlier agreed to meet in the Jessie Matthews Bar but in the confusion, it all got changed.

Certain people are very angry at what they see as our star's lack of cooperation and her agent's greedy recording royalties demands, trying to grab more than her share. I tried to explain the situation.

"Until Hilary has had a chance to discuss the situation with all the principals' agents, we can't really take a clear or firm stand."

However, Nick Colicos forcefully proposed that we should challenge not only those agents but also our Equity representative, Hilary Strange.

"We've had enough of this treatment. As a company, we want to split the whole seven and a half percent evenly. And anyone who isn't happy with that can negotiate their own separate deal."

I was confused. If an equal split was accepted by all the agents, how could separate deals be negotiated?

We didn't take a vote but there was general agreement on the "even split" idea. The meeting was thrown together in haste, so without writing materials, I couldn't take minutes. A lot of angry things were said which were more soreness than sense. I tried to get a vote on whether the actors wanted to exclude the assistant director and assistant choreographer in the royalties share-out but it was decided that we should think about that over the weekend.

Nadia chaired the meeting. If she agrees with anything, she calls it "cool". I feel very old and out of place.

9:45 p.m.

I left and just missed seeing Tanya Franks. She had been waiting at the stage door to meet one of the crew, Melanie, who is staying at Tanya's place.

She left me a message with the stage door keeper, so I said to him, "Thanks. I'll phone Tanya tomorrow morning."

Got home and guess what? Drank a whole bottle of red wine, and for a perfectly logical reason. Because I'm stupid.

SATURDAY 5th June 1993

A sweltering hot day. Feel washed out. No wonder, after all that wine last night. Gormless goofus! Typed a letter to Peter Rutherford saying I miss him.

10:30 a.m.

Rang Tanya.

She said, "The most extraordinary thing happened last night, Peter. I went to see *On the Ledge* at the National, a play about people standing on a window ledge. Amazingly, a man had been actually standing on a window ledge above Cafe de Mario near the Adelphi Theatre. He'd cut his wrists and was threatening to jump."

I asked her if it was Andrew Lloyd Webber.

11 a.m.

Rang Julia McKenzie and she kindly fixed me a ticket for *Sweeney Todd* at the National this afternoon. I hear her Mrs Lovett is splendid.

Since working with Julia in *Cowardy Custard*, the 1972 Noel Coward hit revue at the Mermaid Theatre, I've been sending her a constant flow of good luck first night cards. How I wish my career had made a comparable journey. But, my God, how she deserves her success.

2:30 p.m. Cottesloe Theatre in the National Theatre

Julia's Mrs Lovett in Stephen Sondheim's *Sweeney Todd* is a superb piece of acting/singing, a complete creation. Every facet is beautifully integrated – from farce and light comedy to the darker side of melodrama and Grand Guignol; all of it truthful. Excellently directed by Declan Donnellan.

Chelsea Physic Garden

Drove over to attend a posh wedding. I don't know the groom, Adam Bennett, but his dad Rodney Bennett (the TV director) and his lovely mum Jill (the illustrator) are both dear friends of mine.

Rodney directed me in six successful TV productions – including *Hamlet* in 1980 in which I played Osric to Derek Jacobi's zany Dane, and the following year, I was nice but dim Robert Dashwood in Rodney's production of *Sense and Sensibility*.

Jill and Rodney both sat at the top table in a marquee. Rodders (as Jill calls him) was dressed in black tails, and Jill wore an elegant white suit and hat.

Antonia – sister of the bride and one of the bridesmaids – caused comment. Charmingly (I thought) she chose to dress in a pink tutu, pink tights and pink ballet shoes. Oh dear, oh dear. It caused tut-tutting comments from a few pursed lips. Not traditional enough for members of the Strict Marriage Protocol Observance Society.

So, I made a point of grabbing a quick word with Antonia. "I must tell you, I think you look absolutely delightful!"

SUNDAY 6th June 1993

Hot morning! Feel ghastly. Is it the air pressure? Am I ill? Forced myself to go for a run and do a work-out. An arduous battle. Recovering a bit but can't write another word now. Maybe try later.

1:30 p.m.

After lunch, I felt better so I rang Gay Hamilton, a friend and neighbour.

"Our leading man Kevin Anderson is having a barbecue party this afternoon. The company's putting him up in a flat in Heath

Drive, near Hampstead Heath. Would you like to come as my guest?"

Gay was only too happy. We've known each other for thirty-one years! In 1962, we did our first professional acting job together in a season of plays at the Byre Theatre, St. Andrews, Fife. The summer attraction was *Billy Liar* (two shows daily), a comedy written by Keith Waterhouse and Willis Hall. I played Billy who tells lies to cheer up his boring life in provincial Yorkshire. Gay doubled as both my girlfriend Liz, a free-spirited swinger, *and* my elderly grandmother Florence Boothroyd! Gay was only nineteen years old and it was during her summer holiday between terms at drama college!

Her big break came thirteen years later when she landed the major role of Nora Brady, in Stanley Kubrik's handsome historical 1975 film, *Barry Lyndon*, based on William Makepeace Thackeray's 1844 novel. It was showered with Academy Awards and nominations. Gay's handsome leading man was Ryan O'Neal.

"He did his best to have his wicked way with me in our Irish location hotel, but that wasn't acceptable to me, a well brought up girl from Uddingston in Lanarkshire. Ryan's twelve-year-old daughter, Tatum O'Neal, was very sweet. She used to tie up the laces on my corsets – sometimes, in her enthusiasm, a bit too tight!"

4:30 p.m. Flat 1, Number 11, Heath Drive, Hampstead

When Gay and I arrived at Kevin's big, handsome garden flat, No. 1 Heath Drive, the front door was opened by the breathtakingly beautiful Brooke Shields. She very warmly and graciously welcomed us. I told Brooke Shields that I didn't want any wine, so she kindly made a cup of tea, especially for me!

She's visiting her loved one, Kevin. "But not for long," she said. "I fly home to America tomorrow to make two films back-to-back."

About half the *Sunset Boulevard* company turned up and we sat on the sunny lawn in the back garden. Gay looked extremely pretty and summery in a white linen dress, with narrow blue stripes edging her short sleeves and the hem of her skirt. She had a long chat with Daniel Benzali – clearly a smitten kitten. He asked Gay for her phone number. Patti was relaxing, lying on the lawn as her little boy Joshua had fun scampering around, picking handfuls of grass and sprinkling them on her.

John Napier, our set designer, was there, and the actress Zoe Wanamaker and also Andrew McBean, our assistant director, looking cute in his tennis shorts. Zoe is the daughter of the American actor/director Sam Wanamaker whose brilliant, single-minded project to build Shakespeare's Globe Theatre on London's Bankside at Southwark is at last being realised.

6:45 p.m.

I drove Gay home so that she could prepare herself for work the next day. When not acting, she earns a bit of dough by teaching English as a foreign language to overseas students.

7:15 p.m.

Arrived home feeling horribly sluggish. No phone calls. No alcohol. Just wanted to lie down. Dear diary, is this old age? Bed by ten.

MONDAY 7th June 1993

7:30 a.m.

Woke up. Can't do the 5 a.m. wake-up to write anymore.

Richard our production manager rang. "Peter, today's call has been changed to 3 p.m."

Huge cheque arrived from the Alliance and Leicester TV commercial I filmed on June 8th last year. £5,019 and *37* pence! Banked it, which helped to make me feel slightly better but not completely. Think it's the heat.

Rang Julia McKenzie and congratulated her. She's off for a couple of days holiday on Wednesday, driving around France with her hubby, Jerry Hjert, an actor and a very charming guy.

He said, "I was born in Seattle to Swedish parents and I'm thinking of changing my surname to Harte. Hjert means heart in Swedish but no one can pronounce the damn word."

3 p.m. Adelphi Theatre. Stalls

Trevor called the company into the auditorium to watch the crew do a technical run of the opening scenes. We all sat near the stage, spoke the dialogue and sang the numbers. Almost immediately, one of the sliders stuck.

The opening image of Joe's body floating in the swimming pool looks a bit strange to me. As I wrote last Tuesday, the first thing the audience sees is a huge, blue-lit gauze. It fills the whole proscenium, surrounded by a black frame. In the middle of the gauze hangs a dummy, dangling on a wire, pretending to be the dead body of Joe Gillis floating in the bathing pool. A dappled water effect plays over the gauze. Well, for a start, the blue gauze doesn't look like a pool, and the dummy just looks like a dummy. It is too solid and sharp compared to the flickering water effect. Maybe a shadowy silhouette of a body would be more effective.

The stage management had several "dry runs" of the opening (using just the scenery – without actors). As the cast watched from the stalls, we applauded each run. The whole crew have been working incredibly hard to solve countless technical problems and they deserved our warmest praise and encouragement.

The sets look just fabulous, especially the Paramount gates – a golden vision, like the gates of paradise. They cost £22,000. The smaller version, which was built for Act Two, has been scrapped. They cost a mere £12,000.

We've not yet seen the car chase sequence. Stage management refer to it as the "box of tricks". That has cost £200,000 to make.

We were then allowed to work the stage, but all through the afternoon and evening, the fliers jammed, or the panels froze, or the pallets or the trucks or the sliders stuck. Here's an example…

Trevor sits in the stalls. When he murmurs into his microphone, we can hear his voice over the speakers. "Pippa, Sheldrake's office didn't come on as a single unit. One of the upstage pallets hasn't moved at all."

Pippa Shaw (our production stage manager) walked onstage from prompt-side wearing her headphones. "Yes, we know, Trevor. It hasn't happened before."

"Did it move all right this morning?"

"Yes, it worked perfectly. We'll try to find out what's wrong. It *will* work," she insisted, smiling brightly.

These sorts of holdups make it all but impossible for Trevor to work out the order in which items of scenery assemble or disappear because all the sequences need to be run many times to judge how they looks.

10:15 p.m.

By now, we'd reached no further than the end of the opening number leading into the scene in Sheldrake's office. Most of our time was spent chit-chatting and joking, and – in Nadia's case – doing gymnastics in the middle of the stage for Trevor's benefit. Today, she wore a dark one-piece bathing suit with tan briefs over them, her legs completely bare.

Trevor concluded today's rehearsals by adding, "And thank you for the entertainment."

I overheard the younger ensemble girls making jokes about being "eager beavers". I think Anita Louise Combe was responsible for the popularity of that one. This features in their parody of Peggy Lee's hit number, "Fever". Their version is "You give me beaver." Hence the nickname for a penis – a beaver basher. Similar terms of endearments I've heard are: John Thomas, the bald-headed butler, the custard launcher, the trouser snake and the yoghurt gun. Well, it passes the time.

Technicals are notorious for being wearisome and even horrendously exhausting if they drag into all day and all night affairs. So far these have quite a calm, leisurely atmosphere.

I caught this quote about us on the TV news last night: "It has been rumoured that the first night of *Sunset Boulevard* might be put back because the theatre is still being redecorated and refurbished."

I wonder who cooked that one up. No. The show itself is being redecorated and refurbished.

Tomorrow's call is 3:45 p.m. at the Adelphi to continue the tech.

TUESDAY 8th June 1993

12 p.m. Home

Richard Oriel, our company manager, rang me.

"Hello Peter. About today's 3:45 p.m. call. Just to let you know that the stage crew are having major problems with the set so we probably won't need you this afternoon. But could you stay near your phone in case you're called later? Thanks."

I rang Hilary Strange at Equity for any updates regarding claims made by our American stars' agents on the recording points split. To my horror, Hilary *denied* telling me that Patti's agent had asked for thirty percent. I couldn't believe my ears.

"No," she said, "He hasn't asked for anything yet."

"But last Thursday, you told me he'd asked for thirty percent."

"No, the thirty percent was the proportion of song bars which the Really Useful Group mentioned as being Patti's contribution to the recording."

"You told me that RUG was sending the score to you so that you could count the number of her sung bars for you to work out the points proportionately on that basis but got nowhere with it because the ensemble has so little to sing in the way of solo lines. Then you said Patti's agent is demanding thirty percent even before the supporting leads get their share. This is terribly embarrassing for me. I told the company what you said about Patti's agent wanting thirty percent. Now I'll have to tell them it's not true."

"No, Peter. You don't have to tell them. Don't say anything."

"But I've got to. It's caused a lot of ill-feeling and resentment. Oh my giddy aunt."

"Leave it for the moment, Peter."

This has really upset me. It means one of two things. Either I am an incompetent old fool and have misinformed the company with a false rumour about the allegedly greedy demands of our star's agent, or Hilary has been giving me confused or incorrect facts.

I felt I should type out a statement for the company noticeboard saying that: "due to a misunderstanding, for which I apologise, these are the facts of the situation. Patti's agent has made no request for any number of points. Hilary is going to ring American Equity and get their views on the situation and also their experience of comparable recording agreements. On Thursday at 12:30 p.m.,

Nadia, Nigel and I will go to Equity, get an update from Hilary, and then report back to you and organise a company meeting to decide about the share-out."

This is a wearisomely complex, time-consuming, thankless job and I wish to heaven and all its jitterbugging saints I'd never volunteered to do it.

6:45 p.m.

Having received no word from Richard Oriel, I rang him at his theatre office.

He said, "Sorry, Peter. I meant to call you. No, you won't be needed this evening."

I rang my chum Gay. We met in our local Washeteria, had a coffee then went for a delightful walk on Primrose Hill. A large area of grass has been left to go to seed – ooh! Looking all lovely and meadowy!

WEDNESDAY 9th June 1993

Heat! The M4 motorway has *buckled*, causing "traffic chaos".

12:30 p.m. Adelphi Theatre. My Dressing Room

The company call was at 1:30 p.m., so I went in an hour earlier and re-recorded for Peter Middleton one sentence in the voiceover we taped last week. He runs a video company called Proactive Marketing. He fixed up the mike and we recorded a few takes between loud passing cars and Tannoy announcements. I've heard that technology is so advanced now that voiceover artists can record commercials using their home phones to call a studio anywhere in the world.

After that, I went to Richard Oriel's office with the company statement that I typed yesterday explaining the confusion over Patti's agent's percentage demand and made photocopies of it.

Completely out of the blue, Richard said, "I have to tell you, Peter, that one of the ensemble, Kate Normington, has been arrested for working here as an illegal alien."

"What? Arrested? Poor girl, that's terrible. But, I must admit I'm not altogether surprised. Several times Kate expressed her anxiety about her precarious situation here. She was applying for a work permit when she was offered this job and only accepted *Sunset* because she thought it was far too good an opportunity to turn down, knowing it put her in a desperate position. She was even planning to marry a gay chum of hers next Tuesday!"

When Kate first told me about all this, I wasn't sure I approved. British actors face a ghastly unemployment problem in our overcrowded profession. The weirdest thing is that Kate told me her mother is British! Born in Scotland but not married to Kate's father. That's what invalidates Kate's citizenship claim. Why don't her parents just get married?

I said to Richard, "When you say arrested, do you mean she's in jail? Isn't it possible for me to speak to her?"

"She's in custody. She's being held for questioning."

"Oh, my heavens. Poor girl."

"It could get the Really Useful Group in trouble too. As if they didn't have enough problems!"

"How could it?"

"For employing somebody who's an alien."

I was hoping Richard was also going to elaborate on RUG's other "problems" but no.

I said, "Can we contact Kate somewhere? Help her at all?"

"I shall tell the company if we receive any more information."

Speaking personally, I shall really miss Kate. She is an attractive, intelligent, obviously talented girl, with a charmingly mature, self-possessed quality, a delightful smile and a sweetly teasing, ironic sense of humour.

1:30 p.m. Onstage

We embarked yet again on running the opening scenes, beginning with Paramount gates, but we had to stop almost immediately because the panels that slide on from the wings refused to perform properly. One of them is always too slow, or else it simply freezes.

The stage management and crew used torches to peer down black gaps in the floor while the company stood around passing the time of day.

And so, it went on… and on… the whole afternoon and evening.

To beguile the idle hours, some of us swapped tap steps. I said to them, "I once worked with a dancer who appeared in a film directed by Gene Kelly. It was shot in France, called *The Young Girls of Rochefort*. Mr Kelly taught this hoofer a very useful tap break and the hoofer taught it to me."

I demonstrated the step to the ensemble who picked it up and it suddenly turned into a little show.

"I think Peter is unquestionably the best," Trevor announced over his microphone from his table in the stalls, which made me look a right show-off. What the hell. I raised my clenched fists like a boxer in mock triumph.

Having made photocopies of my statement in Richard Oriel's office, saying that Hilary Strange is going to ring American Equity for their advice on the situation and their experience of comparable recording deal agreements, I distributed them to everyone's dressing rooms, except the principals'.

During the day, I answered questions about it, and several actors asked me to organise a vote on the method of points distribution.

6:35 p.m. A Company Meeting

This took a big bite out of our evening dinner break, but at last we finally and definitely voted to accept an even, across-the-board split share of the points – assuming that Patti and Kevin have their own separate recording deal. We also agreed to make a concession of extra points (to be decided on later) for Daniel and Meredith, being the two other leading principals who do *not*, so far, have a separate recording deal.

We did not, however, take a vote on whether the assistant director, assistant choreographer or the musical director should also be included in the seven and a half percent company share of points. People have very mixed feelings on that.

For instance, Debbie, our stage manager, said, "Where is this going to stop, Peter? Our sound designer, Drew, has a case for being included as a creative contributor to the recording."

7:40 p.m.

We continued to rehearse.

So far, when Norma Desmond's huge house interior rises or descends, travels forwards or back, it moves… very… slowly, like a huge… ocean liner… docking… Sometimes you have to look closely to see if it's actually moving at all!

We eventually reached the scene in Schwab's Drug Store. The upstage glass double doors section (made of Perspex) was flown in and as it landed it tore a big chunk of wood off the drinks bar section. *That* woke everyone up.

9 p.m. Tea Break

I stood with John Napier (our set designer) on the pavement outside the stage door, feeling the New York style humidity. He seemed so downhearted I wanted to say something to cheer him up.

"The Paramount gates look wonderful. Your beautiful designs remind me of Gordon Craig's drawings."

"I can't understand it," he said. "I've designed far more complicated things than this. I did a huge dragon for a spectacular in Las Vegas – seventy foot high! It contained fifty separate computer-operated parts and had to work perfectly to within a fraction of a millimetre, two shows a day. No problem!"

9:20 p.m.

Patti has a cold with a chesty cough but is still singing superbly. I feel a hundred percent better now, thank heavens, though the heat is enervating.

And so is the endless standing, sitting and lying around on the stage making daft conversation. Some of the cast knit, solve crossword puzzles, massage each other's shoulders, stretch out on the stalls carpet, or make yet another cup of Earl Grey tea, camomile tea, blackcurrant tea, builder's tea or an instant coffee, using hot water from the steaming urn in the Vivian Ellis Bar.

11:15 p.m.

We stopped, having got as far as Schwab's Drug Store in Act One.

THURSDAY 10th June 1993

12:50 p.m. Adelphi Theatre. Jessie Mathews Bar

Shoes and costumes fittings. Mine all good!

The front of house bars now have new showbiz names. In this bar, there are framed photos of the British star Jessie Mathews, and in the dress circle's Billy Wilder Bar, there is a terrific big close-up of the great man himself, plus some stills from his movies.

1:30 p.m. Rehearsal Call

Nothing. We waited in our dressing rooms to begin.

1:45 p.m.

A message over the Tannoy: "Would the company and all the heads of the technical staff please go to the dress circle."

Dress Circle

Trevor and Sir Andrew were waiting.

After we were all seated, Andrew began. "What has long been suspected will now happen. It's become obvious to everyone over the past couple of weeks that, due to problems beyond our control, we are facing an impossible deadline. We are two weeks behind schedule and therefore, after careful deliberation, we realise it would not be possible to open a week next Monday."

Sir Andrew read out a press statement that he will release announcing these new opening dates.

Previews begin: 28th June. First night: 12th July.

"I'm in a very difficult position," Andrew explained, "As the composer and producer, being both inside the show and outside it, I think it's the best score I've ever been involved with and I have absolute faith in the show. I believe it's terribly important that we don't lose heart at this point just because of technical problems."

Trevor then enlarged on the subject. "People tend to forget that it's a common occurrence for the first night of a show to be postponed for technical reasons. Both *Cats* and *Phantom of the Opera* were delayed. So, we would ask you to be on your guard against snooping reporters, who really will be hanging around looking for dirt. Remember, careless talk does cost lives. They'll be trying to prove, for example, that the reason we've given for the postponement is just a cover, and the truth is we've had problems with the script, the show itself doesn't work and it's all falling apart. We all know that's not the case. Computers and hydraulics and machinery are not the show. You are the show, and it works wonderfully. So, we appeal to you to bear with us and keep the impetus going."

Patti, sitting next to me, suddenly made me jump. She cried out, "How can the first night be on the 12th, Trevor? My mother flies back to New York on the 12th!"

This got a pretty good laugh from everyone.

We spent the rest of this rehearsal running the latter half of the first act, (missing out "The Lady's Paying").

For the first time, we tried the New Year's party scene with all of us entering on the trucks. Trevor distributed the body weight load on the three "pallets". It was colourfully explained to me why they are so called. "They are used to paint pictures on a stage, like an artist's palette." But no. That is *not* the correct reason.

A pallet is a low platform on wheels upon which goods can be stacked and then moved around and stored. They are used in large warehouses to shift goods, where gangsters persuade business associates to cooperate – or else.

Today, our damn trucks acted like stubborn, bolshy teenagers. As I walked from the bathroom area pallet stage left across to the piano area pallet centre stage, I failed to notice a twelve-inch gap between the two. The moment I stepped down into it, the wretched pallets decided to close. I pulled my foot out just before the two sections slammed together.

Later... much later... we rehearsed the end of the scene when we all travel offstage on the three pallets. The first time this was attempted, the stage right pallet refused to move at all, but the centre one abruptly shot upstage. It then stopped dead with such a jolt Nadia Strahan and Richard Purro were hurtled full-length on the floor. The table carrying the plastic punch bowl and glasses was flung off, hitting the stage completely upside down with a spectacular crash, sending the bowl and glasses flying and bouncing around everywhere.

And throughout this number, the huge set of Norma Desmond's living room hovers only a few feet above us. And… it's… still… ever… so… slow... moving… into… its… various… positions.

9:45 p.m. Female Ensemble's Dressing Room

Kate Normington, who left the show because she had no work permit, came to watch the final run of the last scene. She came backstage to tell us what happened.

"They released me on bail. It's been awful. At first, the authorities questioned me really aggressively; now they're treating me a bit more considerately, but I'm definitely being sent home to South Africa."

"I'm sorry to hear that, Kate," I said. "I shall miss you very much."

11 p.m.

We finished the Act One tech.

As we were leaving, it was announced over the Tannoy that Michael Bauer won't be rehearsing tomorrow. He has to be at the hospital because his wife is having a baby.

FRIDAY 11th June 1993

1 p.m. Cranks Restaurant, Carnaby Street

I'm so stupid. Halfway through my lunch at Cranks, it hit me! I would be playing DeMille at today's 1:30 rehearsal in his scene with Norma Desmond at the start of Act Two. I tore the hell over there.

1:15 p.m. Adelphi Theatre

Went through the dialogue and music, had a quick revision with Carol Duffy (first understudy to Norma), was given Michael's microphone and I was on!

1:30 p.m. Technical Rehearsal

Today, Bernie Sharpe played Jonesy, the security guard at Paramount Studios.

I was never allowed to forget that I once said, "Gimme stage eigh*dean*", instead of "eigh*teen*" in my early exploration of that huge, emotionally complex role. My nasal delivery was compared to many famous American icons – from Mr Magoo to W. C. Fields, and I humbly acknowledge the colossal debt of gratitude I owe those great performers.

Bernie Sharpe kicked off the day's technical rehearsal with his walk (my walk!) from stage centre over to stage left. He then mimed taking the telephone from the proscenium wall.

As he opened his mouth to speak, all my beloved colleagues gave a vocal impersonation of Peter Gale's deathless line. The words echoed in stereophonic ripples from every corner.

"Gimme stage eigh-*dean*!"

I very much enjoyed playing DeMille, even though I'd never had an onstage rehearsal. Everyone told me when to enter, where to go and when to exit. We worked through the second act but the crew are still unable to fly Norma Desmond's house in and out properly due to technical problems.

Today's Evening Standard have printed a baleful statement forecasting doom for *Sunset Boulevard*, as if they hope it will be a disaster.

"Technical difficulties are plaguing" our show. A delayed opening is "threatening millions of pounds in advance ticket sales, sending a shudder through the West End today", as fears are growing that "other productions may be at risk from similar faults."

They quoted Sir Andrew (correctly) saying: "I made a call on my mobile phone and the set moved. I made a second call and it moved again. The machinery that moves the sets is being affected by radio transmissions from passing taxis, motorcycle couriers, or anybody. I cannot adequately say how disappointed and frustrated I am that a production I have been working on for several years should be given this sort of set-back due to something quite outside of my control. My cast and colleagues feel like athletes at the peak of fitness whose race is suddenly postponed."

According to the article, more than 10,000 tickets will have to be exchanged or refunded. It then added that the manufacturers of the set (Vickers Systems of Havant, Hants) have expressed no wish to comment on the defect.

Kevin asked for earplugs to rehearse the scene in which Norma shoots Joe. While he was waiting for them to arrive, Kevin decided to slide down the banister of Norma's staircase. Finding it good fun, he repeated the sitting slalom seven or eight times.

I said to Kevin, "You should do that in the show."

We worked through the last scene with the set in its final position.

11 p.m.

Rehearsal ended.

SATURDAY 12th June 1993

11:30 a.m. Royalty Theatre. Band Call

But everyone calls it a sitzprobe. The German word literally means "seated test". It's simply a run-through of the entire score and script but with the musicians and cast sitting on chairs. Essentially, a sitzprobe is for the composer, the arranger and the musical director. It allows them to listen to the show and judge how it sounds.

Our orchestra (they've been rehearsing for five days) were already seated on the stage. In front of them, two rows of chairs were lined up for the cast. We sat facing the conductor and members of the production team. A row of five mikes were positioned downstage right. Artists with solo songs, duets or even an isolated line during a number, had to move forwards and work with a mike.

Downstage centre, Sir Andrew and Trevor sat at a table, side by side, facing us. Andrew followed the music with his score.

Today, Michael Bauer (Cecil B. DeMille) was absent again, so I sang DeMille, which was quite a thrill.

Nadia Strahan arrived over an hour late. She said, "Sorry. My alarm clock didn't go off."

The orchestral arrangements by David Cullen and Sir Andrew sound fantastic. I was thinking, *If the set behaves properly, and that's a mighty big if right now, this show is going to be absolutely marvellous.*

Patti's (Norma's) song at Paramount Studios, "As If We Never Said Goodbye", really took off. It soared like a glorious bird so beautifully some of the ensemble girls were moved to tears. As it ended, the entire cast stood up and cheered as we applauded Patti, Kevin, Sir Andrew, David Cullen (his orchestrator) and the orchestra.

1:30 p.m.

Ah! If only Equity were as strong and efficient as the Musicians' Union! Here's a small example.

We broke for lunch at 1:30 p.m. *on the dot.* None of your "let's continue to the end of the act" nonsense. Working with musicians, you stop at the exact scheduled moment, and then you pick up again precisely at the time planned.

I recognised a violinist in the orchestra, a delightful grey-haired lady who played in a trio during a party in Tom Conti's house one evening. She was extremely complimentary about the show and the score.

"It's a joy to play; the violin parts have been so beautifully written. And David Caddick is lovely to play for. So relaxed and easy to work with."

A very different person from the intense, impatient, often red-faced driver who confronts us ensemble. If he could lighten up with us, we might also warm to him.

2:30 p.m.

The sound coming from the speakers is well balanced by the guys on the mixing console, although it must be very difficult for them to achieve. Standing in front of a row of mikes, several people, including Patti, sing with their mouths almost wrapped round the damn things which made the fold-back speakers distort and pop hideously.

I still find certain lyrics and dialogue tricky to understand. However, today the sound engineers did a very nice job. I'm sure Martin Levan (our sound designer) and his excellent team will produce terrific results in the theatre.

5 p.m.

Rehearsal ended.

It was as if Trevor personally gave me this curiously fulsome speech for my diary.

"You can write in your autobiographies and memoirs – On today's date, June 12th 1993, you heard the full score of *Sunset*

Boulevard played and sung for the first time. We have all witnessed a moment of theatrical history, and I'm sure you join me in saying that Sir Andrew has written the most exciting musical score of this century."

I imagine that in America this speech would trigger yelps and whoops of support, but we sober Brits only clapped politely.

Trev next led applause for Chris Hampton and Don Black, our book and lyrics writers. Then for David Caddick the musical supervisor and for the orchestra. Then for an American gentleman who had done work on the synthesiser. And then for David Cullen, the orchestrator.

Yes, I know a director's job is to unite and lead a company and generate an atmosphere of positive energy but, as our rounds of applause grew more half-hearted, Trev's speech teetered on the edge of becoming a joke.

And Trev has no fear of pointing out the fairly obvious. He concluded by saying, "This is the last we will hear all actors and musicians performing as one assembled unit. When we get into the theatre, the orchestra will be tucked away below the stage in the pit."

Actually, the sound balance wasn't that wonderful. We stood in front of a mike and a lot of people, including Patti, worked with their mouths almost wrapped around the damn things, causing the sound to distort and pop hideously. Certain lyrics and dialogue I still have yet to comprehend, particularly from Kevin, Patti and Meredith. I think Martin Levan, our sound designer, will be able to achieve a better balance from the sound desk as we perform in the Adelphi Theatre.

My Monday call is at 11:30 a.m. An understudy rehearsal in the Billy Wilder Bar. No prob.

SUNDAY 13th June 1993

1 p.m.

Slept in this late! Didn't mean to. Shocking.

2:30 p.m. Boulevard Cafe at Fortune Green

I had delicious crepes with spinach for lunch then went for a walk over Primrose Hill.

4 p.m.

My jolly next-door neighbour Jill invited me to sit in her back garden with two of her old chums, the actress Anne Wakefield and Jean Penfold, a journalist.

Jill met them years ago when she was a professional typist. For Annie, she typed a children's story and for Jean, she typed newspaper articles published in Nova magazine.

They asked me to sing them bits of the show, especially, "As If We Never Said Goodbye", so I did.

"That's a very beautiful song," they said.

"Thanks. I just wish I had a number as good as that to sing in the show."

In 1953, Annie enjoyed a terrific success playing the comedic Mad-cap Maisie in *The Boy Friend*, the original London production of Sandy Wilson's musical starring Anne Rogers as Polly Brown. Annie went with the show to Broadway where Julie Andrews played Polly.

In the US, Annie married the American film, TV and stage actor, John Crawford. Sadly, their little boy Mark died from cancer aged only two and their marriage broke apart. Annie is now hoping to find work back here in London.

8 p.m.

I watched the very final episode of *Cheers*. Wonderful. The multi award-winning US sitcom has run since September 1982. 275 episodes!

MONDAY 14th June 1993

11:30 a.m. Billy Wilder Bar, Adelphi Theatre. Understudy Call

We were called to rehearse DeMille's scene in Act Two.

12:30 p.m.

Lunched at Cranks.

1:30 p.m. Adelphi Theatre

Another agonisingly slow day.

First, it was the dummy. It seriously delayed rehearsals. As I said two weeks ago, when the show begins, the front cloth flies out and the first image seen by the audience is a huge frame containing a blue rippling water effect. A dummy dangles in the middle of it on a wire. Mr Dummy is playing Joe's dead body floating in Norma Desmond's swimming pool. But it looks dangerously like a stuffed dummy dangling on a wire, etc.

Nick, Gareth and I play cops who have to drag Joe's dead body (Mr Dummy) to the edge of the pool (to the edge of the frame) and then we pull Joe's body out of the water (we detach it from the wires). Well, whad'ya know? The dummy doesn't look like a person's body floating on water. It looks like a – yes, a dummy! Its splayed arms and legs buckle in all directions, as if every bone in its body is broken.

We tried it upside down. The dummy, I mean. Not us.

"Okay," Trevor calmly announced. "Obviously this problem

has to be given further consideration. We'll continue."

2:15 p.m.

Trevor made a calm announcement over his auditorium mike.

"It is now 2:15 and we have not yet begun the technical rehearsal. I should remind everyone that this is our final week of technical rehearsals. Let's make a start."

We continued, but now it was the computer's turn. A sliding panel refused to slide. Here's the problem. If any piece of scenery, like this sliding panel which moves along a groove in the stage, doesn't receive a correct instruction from the computer, it is either late to slide on or off from the wings, or it stops halfway. And sometimes the computer folds its arms and flatly refuses to move anything at all!

And then there are flying panels which should descend from the grid or rise up. But if a motor that operates a flying panel seizes up, that panel is left stuck on the stage. And when this happens, no other scenery can be persuaded to glide in any direction. The motor responsible for operating these sections is situated somewhere up behind the proscenium arch.

Today, it was finally decided that we would continue rehearsing without the benefit of a sliding panel and other bits of scenery which the motor had also immobilised.

Pippa Shaw is our stage manager. She known as "the caller" because she calls the cues over her headphone. Pippa sits in a specially built prompt corner. It's like a mysteriously invisible bird's nest, perched on a shelf craftily hidden halfway up the stage left proscenium arch.

Safely seated inside this eerie eyrie, Pippa speaks to Trevor and to the company in a gentle, calm voice over the intercom, sounding a bit like Hal in Stanley Kubrick's *2001: A Space Odyssey*.

Trevor sits at his table in the stalls and replies to Pippa or gives his instructions through his handheld mike. The theatre is filled with their softly modulated, well-tempered exchanges, as the cast and crew wait patiently for the next problem to be identified, tackled or left for later.

Meredith Braun does a crossword. Kevin Anderson lies on his back downstage and does yoga stretches. Nadia Strahan, wearing her leotard and black, thick-soled boots, bursts into a noisily thumping tap dance. Sandy Strallen juggles – with a pair of gloves! Daphne Peña Pardy goes over a tricky bit of movement in the first number, one of many involved in her duties as Swing Girl. Richard Oriel passes amongst us as we sit in the stalls, giving us details about our next wig, shoe or costume fittings. I gently massage Leslie Hayes' shoulders who is seated at the piano. Gerard Casey perches on the edge of the stage and takes off Judy Garland singing, "I Was Born in a Trunk", or else a shrill voiced Jean Hagen in "Singin' in the Rain", exclaiming, "Oh Pierre, you shouldn't have come."

And so, it goes on. Or doesn't.

"Okay, Pippa, what's the hold up now?" Trevor asks through his mike.

"I'm programming the new cue into the computer, Trevor. It'll only take a few more minutes".

3 p.m.

I have a wig and moustache fitting.

3:30 p.m.

Another hour goes by We run the opening sequence again.

"Okay, Pippa, there was a long gap before the flyers went out in the ripple formation."

"That's because there is an inertia period between my giving the instruction to the computer and the flyers moving. I have to anticipate the delay."

Trevor softly replies, "I see."

Before we ran the show's first number again, Trevor smoothly exhorted us to curb any elements of ridicule in our repeat performances.

"Okay. Let's set back to the top of the show…"

"Okay. We'll set back to the top of the contrapuntal…"

"Okay. That's working a lot better. We'll set back to Sheldrake's office…"

"Okay. We'll stop there for just a moment. Pippa, what happened to the towers?"

"Okay. So, what we'll do now, of course, is set back to the Paramount Studios gates…"

4:30 p.m.

"Okay. We'll set back to the top as soon as we can, and run that whole sequence again incorporating all those changes."

A couple of actors asked me, "What happened to our tea break, Peter?"

"I'll find out."

I went over to Debbie Cronshaw, seated in the stalls. Debbie is Pippa's second in command assistant stage manager. There was no need to explain.

As I was about to speak to her, Debbie looked up at me, nodded and murmured, "He knows."

5:35 p.m.

We had now worked without an official tea break for over four hours – from 1:30 to 5:35 p.m. And, as Equity representative, I was being asked, "What is the situation regarding a tea break and overtime pay, etc.?" And, "Exactly what are you going to do about it?"

I spoke again to Debbie. Debbie had a word with Richard Oriel (company manager), who was also sitting in the stalls.

He looked at me and nodded back, meaning, "Yes, I know. I've already told Trevor."

5:40 p.m.

Trevor said, "Thank you, everyone; that's working much better. We'll break there. Thank you for working the extra time. We'll come back in one hour and ten minutes."

I tore upstairs to the stage door. Tanya Franks was waiting to see me.

"Thanks for being so patient, Tanya. Let's go and have a bite to eat at Cranks."

Over a quick meal, we discussed plans for her idea – a series of one-hour readings of extracts from Shaw's plays at the Theatre Museum over Christmas.

I said, "I did contact Ian McKellen about your idea and I've had a really charming letter from him." I showed it to her.

"Dear Peter, it was lovely to hear from you and have your news. I think a full-scale revival of Shaw is well overdue. I'm sorry that I can't at this point be involved as I intend to be out of the country in October. Very good luck to you and to Tanya Franks. Every possible luck for *Sunset Boulevard*."

Below this, he added a nice drawing of Shaw's bearded face. Ian's a good man. We shall have to look elsewhere.

6:50 p.m.

We rehearsed the show's opening number "Let's Have Lunch" and continued into the car chase without using the complex scenery still being built for that sequence. We stopped when Joe Gillis fatefully parks his car in Norma Desmond's garage. This triggers the whole story.

A rare accident occurred. Poor Liz Greenaway, a member of the crew, somehow got her foot caught between the edge of a step and a heavy piece of furniture as it was sliding along. It squeezed the bridge of her foot sideways. She promised me that she'll go to her GP as soon as possible.

10:35 p.m.

We broke.

10:50 p.m. On the Tube

As I stood in the crowded carriage, for the very first time in my life someone offered me their seat. I must be looking as old as I feel. The kind gesture came from a young and pretty Japanese lady.

After a moment's hesitation, I gratefully accepted and thanked her. At first, I had thought, *Oh no*, but as I sat down it thought, *Oh yes…*

I smiled at the woman next to me, about my age. She was from outside London and seemed pleased to have a friendly chat with a stranger in the metrollops.

She smiled sympathetically. "I know how you feel," she said. "I was warned by a friend that this would happen to me one day. And sure enough, it did. It's a shock to your pride, but my goodness it's worth it. You almost say, 'No, thanks, I'm fine,' but you don't, and your vanity evaporates surprisingly quickly the moment you've sat down."

How right she was.

Two young British lads were sitting opposite. They stared at us blankly, perhaps unfamiliar with old-fashioned good manners.

TUESDAY 15th June 1993

A bright, sunny, fresh morning. Ironed shirts, then a lovely walk in Golders Hill Park, its flowerbeds aflame with colours.

Cooked lunch, and, because the sun was so warm and inviting, I went for a further walk to Regent's Park along the Outer Circle. Watched the elephants across the canal in London Zoo having buckets of water thrown over them. And loving it, the rascals.

6:30 p.m. Adelphi Theatre. Act One. Schwab's Drug Store

This scene begins with the ensemble's reprise of "Let's Have Lunch". Still a problem, how to blend vocally. Each one of us is in our own world, an individual character in the coffee shop, either serving customers or arriving and queuing up to buy drinks, or sitting and waiting to be served or leaving.

For some reason, the stage left pallet that carries the bar and stools into the wings is sluggish. To lighten its weary load, Trevor directed several people to step off the pallet earlier in the action. I'm sitting on a stool and have to swivel sideways, otherwise my knees hit a downstage flat.

Talking of knees, Steve Deveraux is still absent with his twisted knee. He plays one of the two car repo men chasing after Joe at the opening of the show.

7:40 p.m.

A long time was spent lighting the interior of Norma Desmond's house when Joe and Norma relax on the sofa to watch her old movies.

They sit centre stage facing the audience in semi-darkness, lit only by her film screen's flickering light. Later, it was realised that the house set needed to be moved six feet further downstage for this particular sequence to work. With that done, the entire scene had to be re-lit.

9:15 p.m.

We went into "The Lady's Paying" number.

We did this number two weeks ago but it felt more like a month; we were all over the place. Ran it again.

Someone said, "This isn't a technical rehearsal. It's a way of life."

11:20 p.m.

Two hours and five minutes later, we broke.

The whole process is as slow and boring as watching a film being made. But without the film being made.

WEDNESDAY 16th June 1993

1:30 p.m. Adelphi Theatre. Act One

We picked it up from the moment the salesmen leave after dressing Joe Gillis in his evening clothes in "The Lady's Paying".

At the end of that number, Norma's tailors are arranged on the staircase. Blackout. All the men exit onto the halfway landing and then down a narrow set of steps. I am the last actor to leave the stage, carrying a big wooden clothes rack. Very awkward.

We continued running into the next two scenes until the curtain comes down on Act One. Kevin tripped on the stairs carrying Patti up to the bedroom but he didn't drop her. My back was aching and so, during their scene, I thought I'd lie on the carpet in the stalls for ten minutes. When I stood up, three pieces of chewing gum were stuck to my shirt.

"Okay, that's all beginning to look extremely good," Trevor said softly. "What we'll do now is set back to the top and try for a complete run of Act One."

Patti called out to him from the stage, "Do you think we'll be sick of this show by the time we actually perform it?"

Even Trevor, for a moment, was lost for words.

"Sorry, Trevor. Forgive me," she added. "It was a joke." Patti ran down the temporary wooden steps and into the stalls. "I must apologise to Trevor."

They embraced and laughed as the crew changed the set back to the opening.

Today, everyone (except Patti, presumably) has received a letter from Allan Benson. He is head of Andrew's Really Useful Picture Company.

In his letter, Allan explains that the Really Useful Group has "encountered some problems regarding the documentary film" he was hoping to make. He said that he sadly had to abandon his plan to shoot it as the problems proved to be "insurmountable" but stressed that the negotiations with Equity on our behalf were painless, good-natured and were resolved very satisfactorily. He felt particularly sad about this state of affairs because he thought we were all "part of a very impressive and unusual piece of work."

So, the documentary film is off and we've been given no clear reason why.

Alastair Smith, our production manager, joined some of us ensemble artists sitting in the stalls. As the Equity deputy, I said to him, "Would it be indiscreet to ask on behalf of the company what this insurmountable barrier to making the documentary was exactly?"

"Yes, it would be indiscreet," he answered.

"Would you describe this insurmountable barrier as being of a financial nature?"

"No," he answered.

We all exchanged meaningful looks. The company, especially

the lower paid members (like me) are extremely disgruntled at losing £500 for the documentary and the News Access day's shoot. Why did the two have to go? Because the same film crew would have filmed both the documentary and News Access. The Really Useful Group Picture Company is now unlikely to engage a camera crew just for News Access.

Gerard Casey did a funny Bette Davis imitation, quoting her line in the 1949 movie, *Beyond the Forest*: "What a dump!"

5 p.m.

Come five o'clock and we still weren't ready to run the first act. The bald-headed dummy won't hang convincingly on the gauze. We wondered why they're bothered about that; we were told it's being rethought.

Just as it seemed finally ready, Mr Dummy suddenly suffered a very nasty turn and slid down his wires, tearing a fourteen-inch long hole slap-bang in the centre of the huge gauze. Even so, we embarked on our first go at a non-stop run of Act One of *Sunset Boulevard*. Without Mr Dummy.

Yes, we did begin, but before we even got through the opening number, someone yelled out. No one seemed to know who it was. Or why. But we stopped. It was soon discovered that the new cladding on the stage left tower had caused a jamming problem.

Trevor said through his mike, "That shows you that you should never add anything to a set without first having a technical rehearsal with it." Trevor added then, "It was obviously hubris on our part to attempt a run of Act One at this stage. We'll break there and start on Act Two at 6:30."

5:30 p.m. Cafe Sante

As I ate my dinner, I composed a letter to the Writers' Union about *Gatsby*, the play I directed at the King's Head Theatre last

March. I joined the Writers' Union and still feel hacked off at their lack of support when I received no co-adaptor credit on the posters or programmes.

6:30 p.m. Adelphi Theatre

Kevin sang his Act Two opening number. We had to stop to solve this tricky problem – how to get the timing right when the swimming pool section is raised downstage.

Patti had trouble pitching her vocal entrance after Kevin's song. Trevor asked us to do that section of dialogue again.

Patti joked, "Of course, we will, Trevor. We'll do it twice for you if you like. We'll do it as many times as you want. That's why we're here."

"Okay. After those few supportive words from our sponsor, let's continue."

How can we call this a "technical rehearsal"? We don't have the sets to tech with!

In Act One, we still haven't incorporated the "car chase" scenery. Also, a member of the crew told me that Norma's Act Two arrival in her Isotta Fraschini at the gates of Paramount Studios is still being mulled over. The staging is supposed to feature a cut-out section of the front of her car, behind which Norma and Max are seated facing the audience. So far, this vehicle is a thing of the imagination.

I play Jonesy, the guard who greets Norma at the gates. I've never had the luxury of actually rehearsing this scene (with or without Norma's cut-out car section) so I asked Trevor if I could enter earlier, mainly because offstage it's hard to hear an entrance cue. He said I could.

The tall black sliding panels are between me and Patti and they muffle all dialogue spoken by her, Daniel and Gerard (who is playing the younger studio guard). But how the hell does Jonesy know that Norma has arrived at Paramount specifically to see DeMille? It isn't explained. I guess he assumes she's visiting the director of her great silent movies.

A crew member said, "Act One's 'Paramount gates' are being used for this scene." But Norma is sitting (offstage) in her car, waiting to be *driven* through those gates. Max wouldn't park Norma's limo and then expect her to *walk* through the gates. A long wait ensued.

Onstage, Patti sat on the floor with her back against the proscenium arch, swigging water from a plastic bottle.

"Gin?" I asked.

"Vodka." She splayed her legs and stuck out a drunkard's thick tongue.

At Paramount Studios, Patti sang "As If We Never Said Goodbye" twice, crying both times.

Someone said to me, "This is a *technical* rehearsal. Why are we having to give full-out performances of all the scenes? We should cut from cue to cue, rehearse the technical stuff, getting *that* right."

I agreed. "This has to be the slowest, most time-wasting technical rehearsal of any show in the entire history of technicals."

As I was sitting in the stalls, Bob Avian, our choreographer, came over and sat beside me. "I wish Patti would throw a wobbly and wake everyone's ideas up."

The next thing we knew, Patti was doing exactly that. She marched to the back of the stalls and began shouting, "I want to go home to New York! I am *completely* fed up with being kept *hanging around* like this! From now on, I'll only work from 1:30 to 10:30 and *that's it!* I'm not being paid overtime! Who the *hell* do they think they are? I'm going to pack my bags and my trunks and I'm flying home!"

This was shouted at our company manager, Richard Oriel. At the same time, Trevor carried on trying to direct the rehearsal, speaking softly into his handheld microphone.

Vivian Ellis Bar

As John Napier made himself a coffee, he told me that Trevor was taking him out to dinner after rehearsals.

"To Joe Allen's. Ooh, I'm scared," he joked, biting his knuckles. "He's going to shout at me and hit me and tell me off because my camera tower is too noisy when it's being set up. Don't say anything but I won't be here on Saturday. I'll be at Lords, for the Ashes." John is crazy about cricket.

9:50 p.m.

The girls began to work on the beauticians scene.

Richard released the rest of us. Tomorrow, my calls are:

At 12:10 p.m., I've a costume fitting in the Jessie Matthews Bar.

At 2 p.m., we will rehearse.

"And at 2:45 p.m.," I was told, "You have a fitting at BMA."

I said, "You mean the British Medical Association?"

No. They got it wrong. It's MBA. Monty Berman Associates, the costumiers, established in the early 1950s by Mr Max Berman.

I hate acronyms. Why don't people just say, "You have a fitting at Berman's," like they used to?

THURSDAY 17th June 1993

12:10 p.m. Jessie Matthews Bar, Adelphi Theatre

Harry Ditson and I waited half an hour here for the costumier to arrive. It has a stylish collection of framed posters on the walls – part of the makeover Sir Andrew's company RUG have given the Adelphi. There are jolly magazine front pages and stills of Jessie Matthews, a vivacious British stage and screen star, a hugely popular pre-war actress/singer/dancer.

12:40 p.m.

The costumier arrived. "Sorry I'm late! The traffic was terrible coming from Ilford. Okay. Now! Let's see… Peter, all I've got here for you to try on today is this jacket. It's the white seersucker with fine grey stripes that you wear as Sammy for the scene in Schwab's."

It fitted me just fine.

12:50 p.m. Wig Room

Jeanette said, "I wanted to give you a trim, Peter. Just a quick short, back and sides." And as we chatted, she added, "There are seventy plus wigs in this show. It's going to keep us quite busy in here."

2:45 p.m. Berman's

Oh, sorry. MBA.

Up to Osnaburgh Street near Regent's Park for my fitting of Sammy's high priest costume – I call it the Mighty Beast. Penny has made it using very thick blue, purple and orange upholstery material. It's the heaviest and hottest garment that has ever been hung on my poor shoulders.

I said to Antony Powell, our costume designer, "It's just as well I'm a strapping lad of twenty-one."

Penny said, "Yes, I made this with great difficulty. It's not easy pushing this amount of fabric through a sewing machine! But don't worry. To help you do quick changes, the whole garment will be cut up the back and an industrial zip will be sewn in. Then you'll finally wear the cloak on top of it all."

I walked up and down the smart premises.

Penny said, "You're doing very well, Peter. How does the costume feel as you move?"

"As if I'm dragging all the furniture in this room around with me as well."

Sasha Millard appeared, wearing her costume as Hedy Lamarr filming *Samson and Delilah* at Paramount. She looked a stunningly beautiful vision.

4:15 p.m. Adelphi Theatre

Nothing seemed to be happening. Heaps of it.

5:20 p.m.

Dismissed after hanging about for over an hour.

Bliss. I went to the Body Shop to buy some fragrances. A feast of smells!

And then I had a meal in Cranks, in Covent Garden Piazza. A feast of tastes!

7 p.m.

Company call. We rehearsed the final scene.

10 p.m.

A complete run of Act One.

At the last minute, Bob added more complex movement during the opening number which caused awkward snarl-ups and traffic jams. Take away or change or delay just one move and this whole 3D human jigsaw puzzle collapses.

The car chase scenery has arrived. It's hanging up in the flies but hasn't so far been incorporated into a tech run of Act One.

In Artie's party, the stage right truck – sorry, pallet – didn't make an entrance but we carried on regardless. At the end of the scene, the centre pallet smashed into the rostrum as it travelled off upstage. Why? Because it could.

Trevor made a congratulatory speech over his microphone, pausing first for us to applaud: 1) the crew, then 2) our stage manager, then 3) Pippa and then 4) our pianist. But not the cast. Surely to goodness 1, 2, 3 and 4 could've applauded us actors just to be polite. *So* unfair.

The stage crew have been working for about two months now on a seven-day week, fourteen hours a day. That's a ninety-eight-hour week. They are all in extremely good spirits but have that pale, hollow-eyed look of the walking dead. Accidents are waiting to happen but we've had surprisingly few. Phew! It's a great tribute to the crew's patience, skill and tireless concentration.

This evening, I spoke to Liz, the crew member who hurt her foot last Monday, accidentally getting her foot caught between a rostrum and a heavy piece of furniture, squeezing her instep sideways. It still gives her pain, worse if anything. Her GP told her to rest it for three days but RUG warned her that if she was absent that long, she'd be dismissed.

I begged her to go to casualty and have her foot X-rayed and bound up properly; also, to make inquiries about insurance cover, which the Really Useful Group might have. If she is laid up, I'm sure RUG could work out a civilised solution with her union without this brutal threat of sacking.

FRIDAY 18th June 1993

2 p.m. Adelphi Theatre. Costume and Technical Dress Rehearsal

We worked with whatever costumes and wigs had arrived.

Michael Bauer, dressed as DeMille, looks splendid in his £900 riding boots. He said, "They pinch the top of my calves."

"You have to suffer to be beautiful," I replied. Best I could do.

Nine weeks of rehearsal and no time for a costume parade, one of the most important elements of mounting a show. We all wore what we had in our dressing rooms and the rehearsal began.

Working with some of these very young, inexperienced performers is a tedious pain. Anita Louise Combe and Nadia Strahan literally screamed and yelled with laughter when they saw Adam Matalon in his wig and costume. God knows why. It's a very sensitive moment for actors when they appear for the first time in front of their colleagues fully dressed as their character – which may be to the actor's liking, maybe not. It's a time to offer moral support, behave with tact and sympathy and mind your own business.

Talking of which, my partner Paulie worked with a friend of ours, the actress Zena Walker, in 1972 in the TV mini-series *The Man at the Top*.

Zena used to do a very funny take-off as two actors at a costume parade. The first walks onto the stage, clearly pleased with a perfect outfit, spot on for her character and highly becoming. She greets the director and designer, both seated in the stalls, and says, "Just what I wanted. No problems at all. Fits perfectly. Shoes are lovely. Beautifully comfortable." She moves around, smiles sweetly, blows them both a special "thank you" kiss, a quick wave and dances off into the wings, a happy bunny.

Zena then impersonated the next actor. She stomps onto the stage like a grumpy thundercloud. Halts. Faces front. Stares coldly at the director and designer. Turns round in a circle. Shrugs and says with a fed-up, tight-lipped air, "Well, it wasn't what I expected, but there you are. If you think it's right, I suppose that's it. What can I say?" She glances down at the garb with a baffled frown, a brief sigh, then off she stomps.

In 1968, Zena won a Tony Award on Broadway for her role in *A Day in the Death of Joe Egg* by Peter Nichols.

3:15 p.m.

We did a stopping run, going back to repeat fast costume changes or tricky ones. And also ones that are fast *and* tricky. The Mighty Beast hasn't arrived for me to work with yet; that's my nickname for the costume I wear playing Sammy, the actor appearing as the high priest in the film *Samson and Delilah* at Paramount Studios. Patti wears an entirely different outfit (dress, wig, hat and shoes) for every scene, some involving *super* quick costume changes, helped by more than one dresser in a very confined space – only a couple of feet out of the audience's eye-line!

Patti is obviously worried about this and often warns Trevor of her fast costume change problem. And Trev always counters her concern with the argument that practice will render them easy and quick. However, they remain at this point a source of anxiety and exhaustion for Patti.

We muddled through the tailoring salesmen's number, again lacking the correct set of evening clothes to put on Kevin. This is crazy. Several offstage costume changes we rehearse, but the one we carry out in full view of the audience we just keep marking, without using even stand-in garments. Us male ensemble lot have to undress Joe down to his underwear during the number, divest him of his own casual clothes and then don him in immaculately elegant white tie and tails – shoes and all! – *in a matter of seconds*. He then performs a long scene wearing this outfit – even dancing a tango – which means the shoes have to be laced correctly and the tie on straight. That can't be faked with Velcro otherwise it would be *seen* to be fake, and also it might undo during the following action.

This was a *costume* tech rehearsal, exactly when things like this should be rehearsed, but we muddled through Kevin's change, leaving him at the end wearing only his undervest, tails jacket and trousers. No shirt and no tie. And his shoes undone.

5 p.m.

After the break, we continued up to the entrance of the three pallets which slide on carrying the New Year's festive crowd. The centre pallet has a table with party drinks on it. It sped onstage then suddenly stopped dead, flinging the table upside down and scattering the plastic cups and punch bowl all over the stage with a spectacular crash.

Will these benighted pallets *ever* behave themselves? Yes, we know they only take orders from a certain computer, and if that Fiend-That-Must-Be-Obeyed decides a pallet is going too fast, as it did in this case, it brings it to an abrupt permanent halt, just like a stubborn nine-year-old who won't eat its spinach. Is this due to a built-in safety device? You'd think there would be an over-riding cancel button somewhere to change the computer's mind. But no, there isn't. No bribe, no offer of a free "Holiday for Two" in the Lake District. *Nothing* will move it.

Half an hour later, the computer had second thoughts and allowed us to carry on. But even at the best of times, that particular pallet always arrives several inches short of its mark. It stops dead, making it difficult for us to move from the bathroom section on the stage left pallet, and through to the living room. It also tends to stop short of its mark when it goes *off*. That means the pallet is not properly housed when the sloping top section of the upstage rostrum descends on it, and we hear a blood-curdling sound of wood crashing and crunching.

The costumes feel bulky and make working in the confined set of Artie's flat not difficult but tricky. Richard Antony's wig came off in the jolly melee when he found himself lying flat on his back on the floor with Anita Louise Combe on top of him – yes, authentic wild Hollywood party behaviour but not what we'd rehearsed. His excellent wig was then used as an object of fun, thrown from hand to hand and stuffed up the girls' skirts.

I retrieved it and handed it to Chris, our master carpenter, who happened to be standing offstage quite near me. He very kindly agreed to put it safely into the hands of a dresser. I hate to sound like a goody-goody but these wigs cost a fortune and are the result of hours of hard, painstaking work and artistry by the ladies in the wig room. Two moustaches have also disappeared and will probably never be found.

10:30 p.m.

We finished.

Trevor's final soft-spoken message over his microphone from the stalls. "Okay, listen up everyone. Tomorrow is Saturday. We'll start at 1:30 from the top of Act Two. After which, we shall try to keep going without any stops. We must achieve a complete run-through of the whole show soon."

SATURDAY 19th June 1993

10:30 a.m.

I went to my local optician's.

In the first scene, I wear glasses as the police cop so I had to get a lenses prescription for them. None of your plain glass tat for this show, otherwise I might not see a rogue pallet trundling straight at me with malicious intent.

The tube train was full of young men with crew cuts on their way to attend the Gay Pride March. The police expect a serial killer will be amongst the crowd. He recently murdered five gay men.

To whoever it may concern, I have worn a different coloured tie to rehearsal each day this week. It has caused comment. Today, was no exception…

Male: "Seriously, Peter. Do you have a day job?"

Female: "Sexy."

1:30 p.m. Adelphi Theatre. Act Two Dress Rehearsal

The Act Two dress was scheduled to begin but a dry tech was still going on. It's when the stage crew run all the set changes without using actors.

3:30 p.m.

Even while the dry tech was proceeding, it was decided we should start rehearsing Act Two with the cast wearing costumes and wigs.

As I walked through the wings, the huge house set was descending. It made such a deep, penetrating hum, it felt as if the whole building was vibrating.

"Why is the set making that noise?" I asked one of the crew.

"I don't know," he said. "It's never done it before."

My high priest costume (the Mighty Beast) hasn't arrived yet, so I couldn't rehearse changing into it or moving about in it.

No telephone has yet been fixed onto the stage left proscenium wall, and so as Jonesy I must still mime talking into it. And we don't have the cut-out car for Norma and Max to sit in when they arrive at Paramount Studios gates. We rehearsed without that too. And this is supposed to be a technical rehearsal.

Trevor most often remains calm and even-tempered, but at rare times, the pressure under the surface does makes its presence known.

Alison was slightly late for a cue by just one second, which was easy to do in the stop-start-go-back confusion of a tech.

Trevor's response was terse. "Okay, we'll start the scene again and this time please concentrate everyone. It's unfair of me to remind you that we should have been doing our second preview today."

Was he implying it was *our* fault that we weren't?

Technical rehearsals (techs) are usually conducted cutting from cue to cue. To save time, you leave out stretches of dialogue or music which don't involve technical detail, like lighting or set changes. But in these techs, we are running all the scenes and songs every time.

Patti sang "As If We Never Said Goodbye", her heartfelt reaction when Norma returns to Paramount Studios. She sang it twice, beautifully. The second time, even as she began, tears poured down her cheeks.

Afterwards, Patti sits in the canvas chair and the company (film studio crew and actors) warmly gather around her (Norma). Patti dabbed her eyes with a tissue offered to her by a make-up girl.

She laughed and said to us, "I look so fat in my end of Act One costume. You girls are all beautifully slim. I can't bear it."

6:15 p.m.

We broke for supper. The run-through starts at 7:30.

7:45 p.m. Run-Through

It began fifteen minutes late.

8:30 p.m.

A complete halt! The set suffered terrible damage.

I was standing in the wings stage right with Emily, our assistant stage manager, waiting to go on for Schwab's Drug Store. Emily handed me one of the "practical" magazines, one that you can take hold of and read – not attached to the set.

"This magazine wasn't pre-set, Peter. Could you carry it on with you?"

"Sure, no problem."

And at that moment, from immediately above us, we heard an almighty crack and a terrifying splintering and ripping sound. It seemed to go on for several seconds. I was convinced Norma Desmond's entire house was collapsing on us. Oddly enough, no one ran for their lives.

It happened as the huge house was rising into the flies. Six panels hanging up there had somehow shifted by only a couple of inches. The panel at one end became romantically attached to the house, allowing itself to be torn out of its steel groove.

A full damage inspection ensued for fifty minutes.

9:20 p.m.

We carried on.

11:05 p.m.

At the end of the beauticians scene, Trevor decided to stop the rehearsal for the night.

"Don't be downhearted," he added softly into his mike. "We are making progress. It is getting there. So, keep your chins up. We'll begin again on Monday at 1:30. Have a nice day off everyone."

As long as I live, I shall never forget the noise that panel made being wrenched out of its metal housing directly above my head. It sounded louder than the clap of doom.

SUNDAY 20th June 1993

My chum, the jazz singer Elaine Delmar, rang. "Is it true you're having trouble with the pool leaking all over the stage?" Which only goes to show.

"No, my love," I said. "It isn't leaking anywhere because there is no pool, just the chrome handrail and steps going down into one. But I guess that doesn't sell newspapers. When Kevin is shot by Patti, he staggers towards the audience and collapses, flat. Then he rolls over the edge of the stage into a sort of canvas cradle."

Elaine laughed. "Rather him than me."

"I agree. There's a sound effect of a splash and the cradle Kevin falls into is pulled under the stage and out of view – to the surprise of punters seated in the front row just a few feet away from him."

"Today's Sunday Times has glamorous photos of your leads.

"Good publicity. But I gather the Sunday Mirror has quoted complaints from customers who've had to change the dates of their first night tickets."

"Well, darling, to quote Oscar Wilde, 'there's only one thing in the world worse than being talked about, and that's *not* being talked about.'"

MONDAY 21st June 1993

Adelphi Theatre Backstage

There are eighty-four steps from the stage up to my dressing room. I counted them. It's on the top floor. And the lift is out of action till Wednesday.

Whenever I check my G pigeonhole for mail at the stage door, I notice there's an odd message waiting for "Gavin – Unusual Rigging". Turns out "Unusual Rigging" is the name of Gavin Snelling's company, not a description of his physical endowments. He is its production manager.

1:30 p.m. Notes in Stalls

Trevor's call was to give us notes and run a couple of things, but the stage was a seething mass of activity. It didn't clear for an hour.

Fire Inspection

To carry out this important investigation, a few rows of seats in the stalls were briefly replaced.

During our rehearsals, they are stacked against an aisle wall to leave enough space for Trevor and the production team's table. The fire inspection now over, the tip-up seats are again uprooted and leaning against the aisle wall, looking like lost refugees.

As the company waited to hear Trevor's notes, I sat on one of these refugee seats. Only a few minutes later, the hinge snapped and the seat collapsed under me, dropping me to the floor. I staggered to my feet and picked up the seat – its metal hinge had completely sheared. I looked at Trevor. He raised his eyes to heaven.

The orchestra had now assembled for the music rehearsal and, like us, were still waiting. Trevor remained calm, but during the next hour he sporadically said he needed the stage to work on with the ensemble.

2:30 p.m.

Trevor finally made this announcement over his microphone in a controlled voice: "I just want to register my protest that the crew and the stage management have kept me waiting to rehearse for one hour. I have notes to give but the orchestra is now here and we'll have to proceed with the rehearsal." Proceed?

First Full Technical and Musical Run-Through

We began, without using costumes but wearing any wigs or hats that our microphones are attached to. Patti wisely did *all* her changes.

As usual, we began with the body in the pool. Yes, the dangling, bald dummy is still with us. The last we heard he was being rethought.

Only minutes into the show and one of the six flying panels became jammed on the downstage raised pool section. After fixing that, the next thing that went wrong were the six flying panels. They didn't come in at all. One of them is still missing anyhow because of the broken steel groove accident on Saturday.

Trevor's tone was exasperated but calm. "Okay, we'll have to carry on working without the panels. We won't use them. We must get on".

At the end of the first number, "Let's Have Lunch", a pallet slides on carrying Sheldrake's office with the film producer Mr Sheldrake (Harry Ditson) seated at his office desk.

Caught in the middle of a phone call, he sees Joe.

"Joe!" Sheldrake exclaims. "What the hell brings *you* here?"

Fine. Except the pallet in the wings Harry was seated on refused to move one single inch. However, courtesy of his throat mike we heard him saying offstage, "Joe, what the hell brings *me* here?"

4:30 p.m.

We broke for a fifteen-minute tea break. Or rather, the musicians did, so we *all* did. Bless their little bongos.

5:30 p.m.

We had only got as far as "The Lady's Paying" when the musicians stopped for their supper break, so we *all* did. Bless their little banjos.

The male ensemble are still miming Kevin's change into his evening clothes. He now finally protested (pretty late in the day, I feel) that the actual clothes must be used the next time we do the number because, to date, how we physically redress him in less than half a minute has been deferred every time.

"We'll rehearse the change later," Kevin was told yet again.

When, for Pete's sake?

6:30 p.m.

Back to do a run. Without the orchestra?

7:30 p.m. A Run of Act One

The musicians returned. We started from the top of the show again and continued to the moment when Joe drives his car into Norma Desmond's garage and parks it there.

At this point, we heard the sound of splintering wood and all the sections hanging from the flies stopped moving.

"Okay, Pippa, what is it?"

"We've got a problem, Trevor. The vignette has been caught by the panels. We'll have to stop."

"Indeed. What exactly is the problem?"

"The trouble is that everything hanging in the flies is so tightly packed together. That's what causing it to jam."

The rehearsal came to an expensive halt with the full orchestra sitting in the pit, silent. As the snagged panels were cautiously flown in, bits of wood cascaded onto the stage. These were fragments of the so-called vignette, the huge trellis-like gateway entrance to Norma's drive. It's attached to a framed gauze which was gently lowered. It looked a sorry sight, lop-sided, its wooden tracery partly crushed and broken, and the gauze holding all the pieces together badly ripped.

Every time we try to run this show something different goes wrong, or doesn't work, or is damaged. I was told there is such a huge weight of scenery hanging up in the grid, the walls of the stage area had to be reinforced with thick steel girders to stop the building collapsing inwards.

The black panels downstage were lowered so we could rehearse with the orchestra, not using the scenery. We went through the numbers to the end of Act One.

We then went back and picked up the tech from where we left off but we still don't have the car to rehearse Norma's arrival at Paramount. To rub this in, at the point when the car horn should have sounded there was... silence.

Someone shouted, "Honk!" after which the computer made up for its mistake by blaring the sound of a US bell telephone ringing stridently.

Some good news! Liz, our crew member told me her foot is mending after the injury she suffered last Thursday. The swelling has disappeared and so has the pain. And so has the threat of losing her job through absence.

I was late getting onto the house set for the final scene. In the wings, there is a tall mobile wooden tower. It's painted black and has a staircase for actors to make a higher entrance onto the set. At the top of this staircase is a gate which is closed after the house lands in its final position. I had to creep onto the set from the stage level instead. When overnight towers have stopped running and you've missed the last tower, you have to walk all the way home and use the side floor entrance onto the set.

Someone whispered to me, "At the end of the show, when Norma and Joe have their last exchange of dialogue before she shoots Joe dead, Sir Andrew was sobbing uncontrollably at the back of the stalls. He kept crying out, 'It's crap! It's absolute crap!'"

I've yet to discover exactly what he was referring to.

Sir Andrew then tore into John Napier, allegedly. John is our production designer. I hope by adding "allegedly" I'm absolved from any risk of libel. Tempers are bound to fray.

Tomorrow's call is 1:30 p.m. Someone said the production team are holding a meeting tonight at midnight.

TUESDAY 22nd June 1993

1:30 p.m. Technical Dress Rehearsal

Apparently, yesterday's midnight production meeting at Sir Andrew's house went on till 2 a.m. It seems that his cry of, "It's crap!" did not refer to the actors. It was a comment on the scene design (John Napier) and lighting design (Andrew Bridge) but no one knew the exact reason for it.

At today's call, Trevor announced that the delicate vignette tracery flat hanging above the stage has been removed to give the other scenery more space in the flies. The plan for this afternoon was to do a technical dress rehearsal with the orchestra, cutting out the dialogue scenes, and then to do a full run of the show in the evening.

We only got as far as the beginning of Paramount gates, not even into the first company number, when the pool gauze frame became jammed against the proscenium arch and wasn't able to fly out. All it needs is to swing a couple of inches and it gets caught. We started again.

As we reached Schwab's Drug Store, the panels descended too early. They are meant to be flown in *after* the pallet carrying the coffee bar has moved into position. The stage left pallet that travels downstage (carrying scenery on it) almost hit Richard Tate who was standing on the pallet behind the coffee bar set. People shouted "Stop!" as the truck dragged the huge panels downstage with it.

What baffles everyone is that the computerised hydraulics are intended to render all this mechanical set-changing superefficient. And yet so much of it still depends on human judgment and suffers from unpredictable human error. The two cues for the truck and for the panels are obviously not synchronised on one computer. They are two separate cues given by a stage manager. During today's run, they were misjudged.

People keep saying, "It's never happened before." This is the mantra oft-repeated every time something fouls up.

The three temple virgins' costumes arrived, minus a drape or two. And so did my high priest – the Mighty Beast. No one had believed me when I told them how weighty it was.

"It *is* heavy!" the dressers exclaimed.

The long cloak that goes on top of the whole damn outfit still hasn't appeared, but one thing at a time.

Dawn Spence tripped on her chiffon veil and very nearly fell down the high central flight of steps. It gave her a nasty shock and it's left her feeling considerably nervous about it happening again, even with the veils pinned just above floor length.

5:30 p.m.

We broke.

7 p.m.

Called back early for the men to rehearse "The Lady's Paying", and to work out how to dress Kevin (Joe) in his evening tails outfit in full view of the audience. After nine weeks of rehearsal!

7:40 p.m. Dress Rehearsal

We got through the show without any major hold ups.

Having never done my quick change into the Mighty Beast in Act Two with Patrick (my other dresser), I was a bit late on, but it didn't greatly matter. The fact that the Mighty Beast was undone down the back was a secret hidden by the cloak. The crucial thing is that the Beast stayed on long enough for the scene.

For the first time, Patti didn't cry tears at the end of "As If We Never Said Goodbye".

10:10 p.m.

At the end of this run, Trevor made a soft-voiced speech over his theatre microphone, congratulating "the stage management and crew."

The cast applauded.

"And Pippa Shaw, our lovely stage manager."

The cast applauded.

"I see infinite possibilities for improvements; however, we have finally achieved a non-stopping run of the whole show. It is a ledge on which we have at last attained a foothold. We can now proceed further."

But where was my applause? Trev must have forgotten. So much on his mind.

WEDNESDAY 23rd June 1993

1:30 p.m. Adelphi Theatre

A call for the whole company, minus Patti.

Today's rehearsal turned out to be one of the slowest, most excruciatingly tedious yet.

Trevor announced to the assembled cast, "It's now clear that this opening number must be completely restaged. It lacks flavour. We have to understand why Joe complains that no one in this town has treated him well. We need to see his vision of Hollywood life, the hard sell, the phony friendliness, the self-serving, ingratiating behaviour."

So, at last Bob Avian was let loose on "Let's Have Lunch". He added manic movement, exaggerated gestures, a heightened physical picture to match the brash, brassy music.

The scenery is now simplified. The sliders stay on, keeping all the criss-crossing of characters in the early section downstage. Then, on the loud, musical section, the sliders open revealing the complete interior of the Paramount Studios soundstage milling with people.

The three temple virgins are given an extra dance to perform downstage, after their routine on top of the unit. The girls are still unhappy about the veils they wear and the steps they have to do. Dawn's veil was ripped when it was caught by Sasha's shoe. Also, DeMille's walk across the stage is put in a different place – *much* better. More eye-catching.

The contrapuntal section now becomes a nightmarish, echoing vision, lurid and surreal, confused and confusing, as if seen from inside Joe's head – a bigger, more imaginative way of staging it. Never too late, but I do think this might have been tried out earlier.

Trevor is afraid of losing "the reality", but a musical is a larger-than-life statement. We can't just meander about when that big band sound is letting rip.

"After ten weeks of suppression," Bob mutters to me, "I set the number in one hour!"

The improvement is enormous. Trevor expressed his approval to Bob Avian (musical staging), who was standing next to Trevor. Bob put his arm round Trev and kissed his be-shirted shoulder as a thanks.

When I asked Patti what she thought, she was very enthusiastic.

"It looks *great*, Peter! *Now*, it looks like a Broadway show!"

Sir Andrew was extremely pleased. He was even heard to announce, "It's the best opening to any of my shows."

New dialogue for Harry Ditson was rehearsed in the Sheldrake's office scene. Much better.

We proceeded through to Schwab's Drug Store. There is still no scenery during the "on the road" car chase sequence. Everyone is avid to see this "box of tricks" (as it's called) in action. Why the modesty?

11:30 p.m.

Come thirty minutes to midnight and everyone felt very tired and fed up. Just to get this far, it has taken hours of resetting computers and relighting.

Trevor is now regrouping people in Schwab's Drug Store. What has he been looking at for the past nine weeks?

11:35 p.m.

Trevor released us.

I reached Charing Cross station before I realised I was still wearing my microphone, battery pack and all.

Doubled back to the theatre to hand it over to Jane like a good person.

12:20 a.m.

Arrived home, worn to a frazzle.

THURSDAY 24th June 1993

12:15 p.m. Pineapple Studios. Understudy Call

This morning, Andrew McBean, Trevor's young assistant director, managed to upset Michael Bauer.

Michael, playing the film director Cecil B. DeMille in the

show, is also understudying the leading role of Max. He was rehearsing the scene when Max stands silently upstage, dressed in his chauffeur's uniform, watching Norma visit DeMille at Paramount Studios where DeMille is directing his epic film *Samson and Delilah*. In the plot, Norma first worked with DeMille when she was an ambitious seventeen-year-old actress, going on to become a huge star in silent movies. As their scene ends, they share a final duet – their touching farewell.

"No one in the audience," Andrew McBean explained to Michael, "Is looking at you and Norma Desmond when you sing your last goodbye to each other. Everyone is looking at Max, her chauffeur, standing upstage – this motionless figure in black."

Andrew is a young, likeable Canadian, and clearly very bright; however, tact is not his middle name, and he has much to learn about dealing with performers. Heaven knows, "honesty is the best policy," doesn't always hack it.

Michael Bauer was less than pleased by Andrew's comment. He later grumbled to me in his growly bass baritone register, "That scene is all about Norma and DeMille. That's the *whole point* of it! If the audience aren't looking at us, something's very wrong!"

Michael was simply fighting his corner, as all actors must, but his indignation amused me a little. Whether we like it or not, audiences will look at all manner of things during a play at the most unlikely moments. It is part of the director's job to focus the audience's attention where necessary. Also, to be honest, an aloof character clad in black, standing upstage centre, completely motionless, watching and listening to an exchange going on downstage, cuts an oddly compelling figure.

I remember taking Ingrid Bergman to see Bernard Shaw's play *On the Rocks* at Chichester. During one scene, an actress brought garden flowers into a drawing room, plonked them straight into a vase and then carried on with the scene. Was it mean to be an innocuous, charming piece of business?

Well, Ingrid and I looked at each other. Ingrid whispered, "She hasn't put any water in the vase."

Precisely what I was thinking, and I bet we weren't the only ones. It looked unconvincing and diverted our attention from the following dialogue.

1 p.m. Neal's Yard, Covent Garden

I grabbed a humus sandwich and a tub of frozen yoghurt with mixed berries, then ate them in the secluded cobbled courtyard sitting in the warm sunlight. Delish!

1:30 p.m. Adelphi Theatre. Billy Wilder Bar

"Let's Have Lunch". A company music call with our rehearsal pianist, Andrew Friesner; he is also our assistant musical director.

So many Andrews in this production!

1) Andrew Friesner: assistant musical director
2) Andrew Lloyd Webber: composer
3) Andrew McBean: resident director
4) Andrew Bridge: lighting designer

Never mind Andrews, we have five Davids!

1) David Caddick: production musical supervisor
2) David Cullen: co-orchestrator
3) David Grindrod: production coordinator
4) David White: musical director
5) David Donoghue: chief electrician

David Caddick gave us ensemble some new music and lyrics, and Trev redirected Kevin to be a silent observer at the end of the opening number physically. Joe's holding back vocally makes sense. He's dead, after all.

I was given extra lines, "Hi there, Lisa!" and a "Gotta run!"

3 p.m.

We worked on the stage. *Finally,* a decision was made about Norma's momentous arrival at the gates of Paramount Studios in her beautiful Isotta Fraschini limousine. She doesn't.

Max now walks on from the wings downstage, having honked the horn and presumably parked the car some place. He meets two Paramount Studios security guards. Gerard Casey plays the younger one, and I play the older, named Jonesy (wearing my hastily stuck on grey moustache).

Max (Daniel) first talks to the unhelpful younger guard in the middle of the stage. I am on duty, standing nearby, stage right.

From offstage, Norma shouts "Jonesy!". I hear this and cross below Daniel and Gerard to face Norma as she enters downstage right.

I exclaim, "Why, if it isn't Miss Desmond!" recalling our old times.

Hmm... It is a very awkward, compromised piece of staging.

The glaring mistake is that Norma Desmond would never set foot out of that car. The moment the whole story has been building up to – Norma Desmond's triumphant re-entry into Paramount Studios after a twenty-year absence – and the great star has to leave her limo outside the studio gates in a public carpark? Then get out and walk? No.

The terrible irony of Norma's return to Paramount, sweeping through those gates, seated majestically in her luxurious Italian made Isotta Fraschini, is that she is of no interest to the studio bosses or film directors. It isn't Norma they want to use. It's her car, then worth $50,000, today half a million.

After the dialogue, Patti, Daniel, Gerard and I walk off into the wings.

The only big improvement today is that we have the glorious Paramount Studios gates instead of the sliders. But – the gates are not practical, i.e. they can't be opened or shut. So, we couldn't show Norma driving through them even if we had her magnificent car.

The writers have given me an extra line! After I say, "Why, if it isn't Miss Desmond!", I now add, "How have you been, Miss Desmond?"

DeMille also has a fresh piece of dialogue. His secretary (played by Alisa Endsley) tells him that Miss Desmond has arrived. To save his embarrassment in an awkward situation, Alisa now adds, "I could give her the brush." To which his response is, "Thirty million fans have given her the brush. I'll be back in a minute."

We continue with these alterations. Like yesterday, the orchestra has been called but is not playing most of the time; just sitting there. The expense must be colossal.

The atmosphere in the theatre is enervating and boring. Scene changes are repeatedly run. The lighting is readjusted again and again.

During one of many tedious moments, as Patti and all the female ensemble were hanging around onstage rehearsing the beauticians scene, and waiting for someone to decided something about something, Patti called out jokingly to Trevor, "Do you think we could postpone the opening, Trevor, baby? Could we?" As if she was trying to wheedle money out of her sugar daddy. "Could we, honey? Maybe we could just keep on and on rehearsing the show? Maybe it could be like *The Twilight Zone*."

"What do you mean, *like The Twilight Zone?*" Trevor answered. "This *is The Twilight Zone!*"

Our rehearsals bear a striking resemblance to making a movie. That often involves hours of just hanging around waiting while nothing seems to be happening. Of course, it's happening somewhere, often invisibly inside people's heads. A prop is changed, a lamp is fixed, dialogue is discussed, altered and tried, then cut, or left as is.

To an observer not privy to the alteration, the process is as fascinating to watch as a tea towel drying on a radiator. But when shooting a film, you've at least got several minutes in the can by the end of the day. Let's hope something terrific comes out of these acres of boredom.

We ran "The Lady's Paying" with a new orchestration. I guess it sounds less strident and more sparkly but not vastly different. We all hate the festering number so much we don't care if it sounds like "Land of Hope and Glory". And anyhow, what interest we might have had in hearing that was nothing compared to our gob smacked astonishment at Kevin's behaviour during his costume change. He staged a one-man rebellion!

We tailors partially undress Kevin – remove his shirt, jeans and shoes, down to his socks, underpants and vest. We then deck him out in spiffing full evening tails attire. Yes! A complete sartorial transformation before the audience's very eyes! And that's what Kevin doesn't like. Having nursed this grievance for nine weeks, today he acted on it, grabbed the evening shirt, jacket, shoes and trousers, walked upstage with them and disappeared behind the clothes rack, where he changed his pants, etc. Alone. We looked at each other, bewildered. Were we expected to follow him there?

Personally, I find Kevin a terrific guy – talented, intelligent, an engaging sense of humour, etc. But I wish he had warned us tailors about this mutiny. Of course, it was entirely his concern and he has every right to protest in whatever way he chooses. However, his restaging involved other actors who deserved a prior word of a warning.

The band played on as we seven jolly tailors stood downstage centre, like tits in a trance, still singing the lyrics of the number and with egg all over our faces. For something to do, we covered our surprise and awkwardness with a jokey front (sorry, Trev).

Mark Inscoe danced a time-step. I smiled stupidly and fanned myself with a wooden coat hanger. Down in the stalls, meanwhile, our choreographer Bob Avian was boiling over with anger. Since rehearsals began it's been a generally frustrating nine weeks for him, and, like us, Kevin had given Bob no prior warning about this restaging.

The number ended like a jelly tipped from its mould before it has set – a runny shapeless mess. As Bob was clawing the walls in the stalls, Trevor hopped up the stairs and onto the stage to confront Kevin, imploring, demanding and chiding all at the same time. Remonstrating with him, he insisted Kevin should to do what we had rehearsed, waving aside all his grievances. Finally, he held Kevin by the shoulders and spoke very closely into his face, in the most discreet but insistent manner possible, obviously controlling the urge to explode like an incendiary bomb in front of the entire company.

"No, Kevin. You can't *do this* to Bob. You simply can't."

"Yes, but I don't want the audience to see me—"

"No, please, Kevin. Don't give me that. Trust me…" And so on.

Someone whispered to me, "What about, 'You can't do this to your fellow actors?'"

Well, Kevin was fighting his corner like any actor – pleading his case with the director. "I don't want my vest with the padded shoulders seen by the audience."

"But the vest *isn't* seen, Kevin. I *promise* you. It happens so fast."

No, Kevin insisted. He hated the idea of several hundred people watching him being visibly stripped down to his underwear during every performance. Personally, I felt he had a point; it wasn't dignified, and anyhow, such a quick change makes no conceivable sense in realistic terms. Finally, it was decided. No, he would *not* hide behind the rack. The problem would be sorted out later. Not now. Later.

On top of all this, I was half deaf. After the dinner break and just before rehearsing this number, I seized the chance of a quick catnap. I stretched out on the floor of our dressing room, and – because the stage door keeper's Tannoy announcements kept loudly interrupting my chance of forty winks, I shoved some tissue paper in my ears. It certainly did the trick, and I slumbered sweetly for ten minutes.

So, what was wrong with that? This. After the snooze, I couldn't get the damn paper out of my right ear. I tried every means of hooking it out but to no effect. Rendered me half deaf.

10:40 p.m. Home

I tried again. Probably pushed it further inside. It's still in there. Feel so stupid.

Oh well. I'll have to go to the doctor tomorrow morning.

FRIDAY 25th June 1993

9 a.m.

Rang early for an appointment at the doctor's emergency surgery.

10 a.m. Surgery

I saw Dr Mendel and he sent me with a letter over to Mr Grant at the Royal Free Hospital in Hampstead.

12:30 p.m. Royal Free Hospital, Ear Nose and Throat Ward

After waiting an hour and a half, Mr Grant saw me.

He peered inside my right ear and said, "Hmmm."

Further inspection followed. At one point, he turned to the nurse and said, "Could you get me the hoover?"

This sounded majorly drastic. Suddenly I was Homer in *The Simpsons*, about to have my brains sucked out with a household vacuum cleaner and then hastily crammed back inside again upside down.

Finally, Mr Grant decided the hoover wasn't necessary after all.

"Try not to move your head. I'm going to use an extremely fine pair of tweezers."

I held my breath and sat as rigid as a cast iron door stop.

Mr Grant's pincers plucked at the pesky paper and out it popped! A practically perfect procedure, and Pete was properly pleased.

1:30 p.m. Billy Wilder Bar, Adelphi Theatre

I got back to work bang on time, then hung around while Bob Avian added more movement for some of us who play actors and staff outside Paramount Studios in the opening number, "Let's have Lunch".

3 p.m.

Why were we in this small bar room?

Stage management explained. "Sorry everyone, but you have to rehearse with Bob in here just for now because Trevor is onstage teching the car chase sequence. He's using the new 'box of tricks'. It's good fun, but complicated."

4 p.m.

Only a few worked on the first number, so the rest of us went and sat in the dress circle to watched the new "box of tricks" scene being run.

The front sections of two cars face the audience. On the right, Kevin sits alone in his car (playing Joe), gripping the steering wheel. He is being chased by Richard Purro and Steve Devereaux, (the two repo men). They are on the other side of the stage, sitting behind their car's steering wheel and also facing the audience. Steve is the driver. They are determined to reclaim Joe's hired car. Behind this action, a screen has descended from the flies. Onto this is projected the actual car chase footage in the Billy Wilder film, showing the road fast receding in the background.

The two cars slide across the stage, from side to side. Above them are big speedometers showing each car's speed. All of this is accompanied by fast and furious chase music. Hanging above the repo men's vehicle is a car tyre. It suddenly bursts and as it goes flat their speedometer loses speed and slows down to a halt. Likewise, the music grows calm and ends.

This box of tricks is a source of great curiosity to the company; we've heard it's fun but never seen it.

Before arriving this afternoon, someone had told me that Trevor was sitting at his table in the stalls giving vent to his anger and frustration, screaming blue murder at the stage management.

"For goodness' sake, this is unbelievable. Why in hell's name can't you get this right?"

This is in stark contrast to Trev's even-tempered manner with the cast – to maintain company morale, I guess.

It reminded me what Sarah, Sir Andrew's charming assistant, said to me the other day, "It's a stressful time for everyone."

One of the cast remarked, "Trevor's self-control with us is extraordinary. After spending the whole day struggling to maintain his calm, he probably goes home and beats the hell out of his beautiful wife."

Soon the car chase box of tricks sequence was sorted out, and yes, it worked excellently! We all applauded. Trevor was happy.

"There now!" he declared. "Is that fun or is it fun?"

Yes, it certainly is!

I went to the wig room and they fitted me with a ringleted beard to wear with my high priest costume as the actor Sammy filming at Paramount.

4:30 p.m.

We were called onto the stage to rehearse a couple of new moves in the opening number, but a faulty sprinkler in the proscenium arch had sprung a leak and water was dripping all over the table, downstage left. Unbelievable. Every day something different.

Steve, the assistant stage manager, was fixing paper towels to the floor with gaffer tape.

We also rehearsed "The Lady's Paying", altering it so Kevin will *not* be seen by the audience when we undress him. We now stand in front of him.

Bob Avian confided to me, "I'm very unhappy with all these last-minute mutilations of my staging."

The same thing has happened to the beauticians number. Norma Desmond is massaged on a portable masseur's table. Except that it *isn't* portable. It's built of solid wood and steel, and it's a fiend for the girls to carry onto the stage, to unfold, set up, then later fold up, close shut and carry off, keeping in time with the orchestra and the choreographed moves.

Brainwave! Two female members of the stage management were commandeered *to take part* in the scene – to their agonising embarrassment. The end of the number now consists of them struggling to tip it on its side, collapse its legs flat, then cart the weighty thing up the stairs and offstage in full view of the audience.

So much for Bob's cutely crafted exit of the beauticians in time to the music. Bob said to me, "I'm getting so desperate I will personally pay thousands of dollars, whatever it costs, for a special, purpose-made *lightweight* table to be built for this number."

6:40 p.m.

My dark blue policeman's shirt at last arrived for tonight's run-through. How can I describe it? Huge is the word.

I consulted the ladies in wardrobe. "This must be a mistake. The cuffs come down to my fingernails. I have a fifteen-inch neck. This one has an eighteen-inch neck."

"No, it's not a mistake, Peter. These shirts were specially made."

"Yes, I'm sure it was, but who for? Certainly not for me."

Of course, wardrobe have heaps of more important things to attend to right now and don't want to be bothered by an actor bellyaching about a shirt.

As they pointed out. "To be frank, Peter, you're lucky to have a shirt at all."

Now that is a reply I might have expected in a cash-strapped provincial rep theatre thirty years ago. Not in a multimillion-pound Andrew Lloyd Webber premier production in London's West End. But, after being soundly put down, I beat a humble retreat – my shirt-tail between my legs.

7:25 p.m. Company Call. A Full Run

We assembled and waited, standing behind the front screen.

The show began with bald-headed Mr Dummy floating in the swimming pool.

Richard Purro glanced up at him. "Look," he whispered to me in amazement. "It's got hair!"

"Yes," I said. "But, is it his own hair? I think it's just a wig."

For the first time in the opening number, I did my quick change into the high priest costume – a hugely tall golden crown, a ringleted beard, a colourful full-length robe and a long resplendent cloak. Worked okay.

When I came off, I glanced at myself in the quick change room mirror. From inside a mass of psychedelic curtain fabric, two tiny eyes peeped back. I looked like a tiny sparrow perched in a huge tree blazing with autumn-coloured leaves.

At the end of Artie Green's party, six of us merry-making guests sit on the sofa and sing "This Time Next Year". The sofa is on a pallet and when it travels offstage, I'm perched on the arm of the sofa; Sasha sits on my knee. To fast-anchor both of us, my right hand grips the back of the sofa and my other hand tightly clasps Sasha's waist. Tonight, the pallet suddenly stopped dead. If I wasn't firmly holding on, we would've both been thrown headlong onto the floor.

Never mind the floor, I heard Patti hit the roof! During her first scene with Kevin, he came out with a new line of dialogue he'd been given. Patti had never heard it before. It came just after her first big song "With One Look". She ends on a loud top note, the orchestra thundering away.

Patti: "I'll be meeeeeee!" End of song. Big applause.

Patti: (turning to face Joe/Kevin) "Now go."

Kevin: (New line) "Shush. You'll wake the chimp."

Not much of a laugh from the audience.

Later, Patti said to me, "I think he could've warned me about it."

Author's note: *Kevin's new line was cut the next day.*

This evening's run-through was beset by *four* scenery problems – one potentially dangerous. The tall black panels were lowered from the flies before Norma Desmond's house had risen out. The panels crashed loudly onto the floor of the house. If Patti had been standing underneath them...

In the wings, Patti said, "What's going on, Peter? It's never right. Every time we run the show the set fouls up. We seem to be jinxed."

After the run, Trevor spoke to us through his desk microphone in the stalls, exhorting us to be encouraged. "Don't hang your heads. It's going to be *terrific.* It *will* be, I *promise* you. We *are* getting there. *Really.*"

Sir Andrew also said, "We are in the hands of a great director who is making it work time after time after time. He is a star."

Only a smattering of applause. We're all too tired to keep clapping each other's wonderful efforts.

"I'd also like to add," Andrew continued, "That for the first time in my career (What was coming?) I decided that in the second act, I would have the orchestra in the pit play without any amplification whatsoever. The acoustic is so incredibly good in this lovely theatre with all its wood – it doesn't need any mikes."

SATURDAY 26th June 1993

Today, a Greenpeace march was held in London; it caused traffic problems and they have my complete blessings. I have been a member of Greenpeace for many years.

Author's note: *And, dear reader, twenty-eight years later, aged seventy-nine, I still am!*

1:30 p.m. Adelphi Theatre. Notes in the Stalls

Trevor's main comment, aside from four scenery foul ups, is audibility. He is discretion itself but, obviously, those with most to say (Patti, Kevin, Daniel and Meredith) need to pay closest attention to this problem. Trevor's concern comes as no surprise. Even in the rehearsal room, I couldn't make out certain lines and lyrics because they were muttered too intimately.

Trev said that my shouted lines in Artie's party are completely unintelligible. I'm well aware of the fact. The orchestra is blaring away, a stage full of actors are screaming and laughing and a saxophone is letting rip up my backside. Actually, I reduced my volume to show the solution is not for me to shout louder but the background noise to be lowered and the sound operators to boost my mike level. All this constant singing and yelling is making me hoarse which really pisses me off. I was dreading Trevor wanting to rehearse that scene but there was no time. Thank heavens!

We did some work on the show's opening number; Bob put in additional choreography. Next was Schwab's Drug Store with new lighting, and then the show's final tragic climax. Oh boy, what more could possibly be added? This…

Norma Desmond appears on the stairs resembling a mad prisoner who has escaped from a locked attic. Till today, at this traumatic moment, Patti has worn her fuzzy bald wig, no make-up and Norma's everyday clothes. The real Norma Desmond finally reveals herself. No gloss, no glamour. It is the end of her story and, like Salome, stripped of all her veils! She slowly descends the stairs in front of the lights and the cameras – believing her great wish has come true; she is at last playing Salome in DeMille's movie. Yes? No. This is no longer the idea.

Today, Patti came onto the stage wearing a costume that immediately puzzled everyone. What scene was it for, we wondered? It comprised a sparkly tiara topped with a row of hugely tall white feathers. Her black full-length dress was smothered in glittering diamond frosting and dripping with ropes of pearls.

Someone asked me, "Will Patti be wearing this in an earlier scene?"

"Beats me," I replied. "What scene would it be right for?"

I asked Andrew McBean.

He explained, "This is a costume that Norma Desmond has paid a professional costumier to make for her, according to her own design, to wear in her *Salome* film."

Maybe Norma should point this out somewhere in her dialogue.

We proceeded.

The moment Patti made her sensational entrance, looking like a showgirl at the Paris Lido, most of the younger cast screamed with raucous laughter. The noisier female ensemble loudly screeched their hysterical hilarity. It certainly was "the shock of the new", as Trevor later delicately pointed out, seated at his desk.

Attached to the base of her elaborately tall white-feathered headdress was a snood – a vast net bag full of hair hanging down her back. The entire pouch was larger than a rucksack.

"It's Grumpy the dwarf," some wag observed.

"More like a dung beetle," another joker added.

I had to admit it did resemble a North American Indian ceremonial headdress, but taller and more feathered than anything Hiawatha's wife Minnehaha could have pictured in her wildest dreams.

Nick Colicos solemnly commented, "I have always had great respect for your people."

Patti took it all extremely sportingly. When she got to her line, "I'm ready for my close-up, Mr DeMille," Harry Ditson declared, "I don't think my lens is big enough."

Patti's response was snappy. "You're just saying that, Harry, because *you* want to wear it."

She went through her moves in this exotic finery. It can't be easy to descend those stairs at the best of times but she coped wonderfully. My only feeling is that Norma Desmond's mental health isn't exactly robust at this point, and overseeing the creation of such an elaborate garment and putting on all its bits and pieces without professional help would surely be beyond her. But I thought, *Listen Pete, if it works, it works.*

I later asked Jodie (Bob's American assistant choreographer) for her general opinion about the whole production. Jodie will be helping Bob stage the show in L.A. and she hadn't seen any rehearsals till yesterday's first full run.

After a moment's reflection she said, "The first act is... okay. You think, 'Yes, I see now why they decided to do it like that and it's all right.' The house set is impressive but you're not overwhelmed. But after the interval, you really get into it, and by the end, you think it's absolutely wonderful."

In the dressing room, Mark Inscoe was listening to classical music on the radio.

"What is it?" I asked.

He said, "Verdi's opera based on the Scottish play." Talk about tempting fate.

I didn't complain because I'm not superstitious but according to an old showbiz tradition, it's inviting bad luck even paraphrasing the title of Shakespeare's Caledonian tragedy anywhere backstage. I've a theory that's probably more to do with dangerously under-rehearsed savage fights using lethal heavy swords.

7:45 p.m. Run-Through, Full Costume and Make-Up

This was the schedule. Half an hour later, there had been no beginners' call over the Tannoy.

8:15 p.m.

Out of curiosity, I wandered downstairs to see what was happening.

Underneath the stage were two of the crew. They looked like miners, stripped to the waist, making metal repairs to the left palette with oxyacetylene cutting torches. Similar flashes of blue-white light crackled in the dark further upstage. I returned to my dressing room.

In the old days, there would've been sounds of hammering. Now it's last-minute welding, like a ship builders dockyard.

8:20 p.m.

Pippa announced over the company Tannoy, "Ladies and gentlemen, the section of floor under the pallet in the stage left Bay One is being manically worked on. We'll be starting as soon as possible…"

I asked a crew member what was wrong.

"Two things happened," he said. "First, it was the pallet carrying the furniture and doors. It should slide off safely into the wings before the downstage 'poolside' section is raised from the pit, with its chrome handrail and vertical steps. The problem was that the 'poolside' section was lifted up before the stage right pallet had moved off, so the pallet was completely ripped from its groove in the stage. You should've heard the noise it made being torn out of its steel track. Louder than the crack of doom."

There was more to come.

"And the second thing was the upstage right unit." This pallet is a huge block, one of three. It moves up and down the stage, guided by a keel in a metal groove. "The keel snapped, so the unit became inoperable. Hence all the welding. None of us can work out why that keel snapped."

Andrew was furious. "I want to see the whole show this evening with everything working *properly!*" he insisted. "Fix that pallet *now*! I want to watch it all working *exactly as it should!*"

But it was not to be. The crew couldn't mend it before the run so we were warned that we'd have to perform the show without the pallet. This meant the stage management team had to carry all the furniture and props on and off manually.

Ironically, people who watched the run said it was an improvement! This puzzled me. "Oh yes," they explained. "Far less distracting and much quicker. And more effective."

8:40 p.m.

During the opening, we reporters and policemen stand on the rostrum behind the pool effect. A machine inside Mr Dummy makes Joe's dead body undulate, as if floating on the water.

But tonight, it caused Mr Dummy to grind his hips as if he was engaged in a very different activity. We could barely suppress our mirth. What with that *and* the squeaky violin noise Mr Dummy makes as he slides down the supporting wires – sorry, I mean… as the police pull Joe's dead body to the edge of the pool. well… The word "bizarre" is barely adequate.

11 p.m.

After the show, Trevor congratulated us over his microphone in the stalls. "If we'd had a paying audience in this evening, it would have been a privilege for them to have seen this performance. You were all terrific. Contrary to a rumour going round, I'm not calling the actors in tomorrow. I want you all to get a good rest this Sunday. The call for Monday is 1:30 p.m. for notes. Have a nice day off."

Sunday or not, for our stage management and crew tomorrow is "business as usual".

SUNDAY 27th June 1993

BBC Radio News

America has bombed Iraq Intelligence Service Head Quarters in Baghdad.

President Clinton called the offensive "a firm and commensurate response" to a plan devised by Iraq's officials to assassinate former President George Bush in mid-April. In January, the US carried out airstrikes against Iraqi missile and radar sites, but aiming for and destroying the Iraqi Head Quarters also involved killing civilians, of course.

3:45 p.m. Cinema 1, the Barbican

Ian Marshall Fisher invited me to see the script-held musical he is presenting in his script-held *Forgotten Musicals* series. This afternoon's was *Music in the Air*, a 1932 Broadway show-within-a-show, featuring Oscar Hammerstein's melodies and Jerome Kern's lyrics.

Ian began presenting his *Forgotten Musicals* series in 1989 at the Theatre Museum. He asked me to be in his first one, *The Golden Apple*, a sung-through musical (music by Jerome Morros and lyrics by John Treville Latouche).

I later played leads in several others, including Jupiter in *By Jupiter* (Richard Rogers and Lorenz Hart) and also Whitelaw Savory in *One Touch of Venus* (Kurt Weill and Ogden Nash).

MONDAY 28th June 1993

OUR FIRST *SUNSET* PREVIEW

1:30 p.m. Adelphi Theatre Stalls. Call for Notes

Trevor's main concern was still audibility. But surely he means intelligibility. It's not a question of volume – the microphones provide that. Trevor is discretion itself but Patti and Kevin have most to say and sing so their diction must need more clarity. Weird stresses on words don't help. It seems to be a feature of modern musicals.

The confusion starts in Norma's very first number.

Friends have said to me, "I got lost at the beginning of the show. I couldn't understand what was going on. She's singing a lullaby to her dead monkey as if it was an army veteran of all things and deserves a military grave."

I said, "Yes, that is strange, I have to admit. It's a household pet, not a war hero. And later Joe sings to Betty that *they* might have *had* fun. It should be they *might* have had *fun.*"

Trevor then focused on verbal text. "This is the first musical Sir Andrew has written in ten years containing spoken dialogue instead of being sung-through. One must retain reality but the presence of music adds a heightened emotion that has to be matched by the style of acting."

Trevor is a subtle, persuasive and diplomatic man. Basically, he was saying to our leads: please bring it up and enunciate clearly. Don't get quiet, slow and under-energised.

"Imagine," Trev went on, "That your aunt, who you haven't met for years, has flown in all the way from Australia specially to see you in the show. And she's sitting right at the very back of the upper circle. Think how disappointed she'd be if she couldn't understand what you are saying."

"Oy-yoy!" Patti cried, in her best Brooklynese accent. "So, make us *noy*-vous, why don't ya!"

Everyone laughed, including Trevor. "I'm simply encouraging you…"

"You're talking about an *audience!*"

"I'm trying to *warn* you…"

And that immediately triggered another laugh. We don't need to be reminded, let alone *warned,* that tonight is our premiere show in front of ticket-buying customers.

Kevin appeared to be on edge. Was he simply nervous about our first public preview, or worried that Trevor implied that his delivery is incoherent and slow? He sounds fine to me.

"Now," Trevor continued, "I would like to rehearse the beginning of the final scene, when the house rises halfway up, allowing the stairs unit to slide forwards underneath it."

This was tried twice. Both times the house rose too slowly.

Kevin said, "Couldn't we keep it as it was? Anyhow, I don't think the house should move before I do, otherwise we're signalling to the audience what's going to happen. Can't it wait till after I've crossed in front of Norma? It's fucking dangerous, Trevor. I'm standing here, right on the edge of the set, and as the house moves it's rocking from side to side."

"Okay," Trevor said. "Pippa. Don't start the house moving till Kevin has crossed Norma."

"That'll give us even less time to get the house into its next position."

A slight pause.

"Yes," Trevor said.

"Okay," Pippa answered.

They ran it again. It still didn't work.

Kevin grew more insistent. "I tell you it's dangerous, Trevor. Why can't we keep it as it was?" he pleaded.

"Yes, Kevin. I hear what you're saying. Look, I'm honour-bound to do this, so please, Kevin, I ask you to bear with me."

2:30 p.m. Run of Act One

We ran the first act without using costumes, except for "The Lady's Paying", during which we outfitters arrive at Norma Desmond's request and change Joe Gillis' clothes from his casual attire into a full evening suit.

Kevin had specially requested this but he again wore his own personal jeans and sneakers – a nightmare to get the damn things off him, and so the change was inevitably messy and ended late.

"This sucks!" Kevin snapped as the number finished.

4 p.m.

We worked on Kevin's change. Then we ran it, twice.

5:40 p.m.

We broke. There was no time left even to look at Act Two!

Preparing for the first public preview, I discovered a policeman's shirt *in my correct size* had materialised in my dressing room. Jonesy was a happy bunny, boys and girls.

7:30 p.m.

As we police officers waited on the upstage units for the overture to begin, we heard Pippa made an announcement to the audience through the auditorium speakers...

"Ladies and gentlemen, welcome to the first public preview of *Sunset Boulevard*." There was an audible frisson from the packed audience. "May I remind you that the use of cameras or tape recorders is forbidden."

And away we went!

I didn't see the show so I can't say how it looked. All I know is that I fouled up my entrance in the first number wearing Sammy's high priest costume. I mistook the music cue to enter. Sasha, Anita and Dawn were standing behind me in the wings, shouting, "Go on! Go on!", but I was stupidly convinced it was a whole musical section too early.

As a result, they were late on for their dance as the temple virgins at the top of the unit. When they came down the stairs for the second half of the dance, Anita snagged her foot in one of her veils and fell over. She was one angry temple virgin. In fact, temple virgins don't come more hacked off.

As I followed her upstairs to the dressing rooms, she was spitting tin-tacks, badmouthing the whole production, her presence in it and me too, no doubt. I don't blame her.

However, that aside, the show proceeded with no technical mishaps and the audience response was very good. Not great, but positive.

During the curtain calls, I stood next to dear Nicola Jane Filshie. Nicky is a pretty girl from the Scottish Highlands, as I guess from her bonny accent, and the youngest member of our company. This was her West End debut! She is one of the swings – no easy job, understudying all the female ensemble. But tonight, Nicola was put into a couple of scenes in the second act to pack out the staging and also to give Nicola her very first appearance in a London West End show.

When the curtain calls finished, we all exchanged hugs and congratulations from sheer relief. I turned to Nicola – she was standing rooted to the spot, weeping tears of emotional overdrive.

We shared a celebratory hug, and then she exclaimed in her beautiful Scots accent, "Oh Peter, I can hardly speak. It's so wonderful!"

"Yes, it is. You're right. It may drive you crazy sometimes but there's nothing else like it." I smiled at her. "For better or worse, my darling, from now on you will always feel that this is where you belong."

Trevor congratulated the whole company over the Tannoy.

Then Andrew added a short speech, something along the lines of, "Gosh! What can I say? You were all terrific. Every *one* of you. Well done, *everybody!*"

9:55 p.m.

As we left the theatre, I said to Gareth Snook how much I admired Trevor Nunn as a director.

Trevor reminds me slightly of Steven Spielberg. Steven is forty-five years old and Trevor is fifty-three. Both are phenomenally successful but not in great physical shape. Steven's eyes are always hidden behind protective tinted spectacles. No wonder. His sight is his life! And Trev has shifty, sleepy-lidded eyes, but don't be fooled; he is wide awake and watching. He also has the weirdest combined moustache and beard. It looks like a droopy chinstrap. He strokes it now and then while contemplating a problem, as if it was a false beard, glued on and still needing to be gently pressed onto his face. And he traces an occasional delicate finger across his brow along the fringe line, as if he'd received an interesting marriage proposal that deserved careful consideration.

I once acted with Sharon Lee Hill, the Australian born actress/dancer. Sharon was married to Trevor for five years after he had directed her in Andrew's musical, *Cats.*

I remember her laughing as she said, "Trevor thinks he is very attractive."

I replied, "I know what you mean but I do think he is. Maybe not conventionally handsome or in fine physical shape, but he has the magnetism of a highly charismatic, powerful, confident, talented and successful man."

One of the *Sunset* cast said to me, "These days, Trevor's currently romantically involved with the actress Imogen Stubbs. He directed her a couple of years ago when she played Desdemona in *Othello* on TV. Very pretty."

Talking of romantic involvements, I'm wondering when I shall see Dave. We haven't enjoyed a get-together for weeks. The situation is tricky. But that only makes it all the more exciting.

As a friend of mine said, "You'll have to make do with Mrs Thumb and her four daughters."

I said, "You're right. Only in my case, it'll be Mr Thumb and his four sons, all over twenty-one, of course."

Dave said the sweetest thing to me a while ago. "Peter, your kisses are wonderful."

I'd better calm down and make myself something to eat.

Our opening press night is two weeks away.

TUESDAY 29th June 1993

2 p.m. Adelphi Theatre

Trevor rehearsed a new musical lead-in to DeMille's walk across the stage during "Let's Have Lunch", the opening scene. Then, he cleaned up the so-called "contrapuntal section" (or "cuntrapontal" as vulgar persons call it). It was ragged last night because a few words had been recently altered. The "echo effect" added by the sound crew hardly helps. It's supposed to create a surreal atmosphere but it doesn't. Just sounds messy.

2:45 p.m.

Trevor repeated the "vocal clarity" note he gave yesterday. "There is a definite audibility problem in some of the spoken text. Also, I find the delivery is often slow and undynamic."

Well, the fact is this criticism applies only to our four principals: Patti, Kevin, Daniel and Meredith. The rest of us have very little spoken dialogue, if any at all.

3:10 p.m.

We rehearsed Artie's party for the millionth time, with new groupings and thought processes. I get the impression some of the younger ensemble aren't pulling their weight in this scene, even walking through it looking bored. Or else they play silly buggers. What the hell is their problem? Do they think being amongst the ensemble is beneath them? At their age, I would have considered myself massively lucky to be involved in such a major West End premier production. Where is Trevor's assistant, Andrew McBean? Why isn't he keeping a beady eye on the offenders and tearing them off a strip?

Trevor also rehearsed sections of music to be played quieter during the part in Artie's flat, so that I can be heard shouting, "Coming attraction!" and "In glorious Technicolor!" and suchlike during the DeMille sketch I perform to entertain our movie studio chums. My voice is sounding husky with all the bashing it's getting.

Patti spoke up. "Trevor, I have two major problems. One is that we can't hear the orchestra clearly enough, and the other is that the temperature backstage is too hot. My clothes stick to my skin in my quick changes."

Trevor said, "I'm afraid I must firmly resist your request to have electric fans in the wings to blow the air around. My main concern is that they would make the gauzes billow and then become snagged on other flown pieces of scenery." Trev also admitted that, "although the show didn't grind to a halt, there were four near-mishaps last night."

He said one of them was noticed early on by Pippa, our stage manager. She discovered that the black masking that hangs from the flies had trapped itself under one of the gauzes. The masking resisted all attempts to fly it out, and so Patti, waiting to deliver her first piece of dialogue, found herself trapped upstage of it, hidden from the audience behind the black masking, not knowing what on earth to do. It eventually somehow unhitched itself and flew out just in time to reveal Patti as she spoke her very first line, calling to Kevin from her window, "Hey, you down there."

7:30 p.m.

This evening's Royal Gala Charity was in aid of two organisations. Birthright was founded to help women facing unplanned pregnancies, and the other, Tommy, fundraises for medical research into miscarriage, still-birth and premature birth, and it provides information on having a healthy pregnancy.

Sarah Ferguson was the nominal royal but the national anthem wasn't played before show because Fergie is no longer a fully paid-up royal princess. She is still the Duchess of York, even though last year she formally separated from Prince Andrew. Allegedly, the Queen has refused to pay her ex-daughter-in-law's debts, and so Fergie is struggling to cope on a divorce settlement lump sum of £3 million, plus a £15,000 a year pension.

Celebs watching tonight included Joan Collins, David Frost, Tony Bennett and Margaret Thatcher.

Patrick, one of our dressers, said, "Peter, your moustache is missing from the prop table."

I explained to him that I have to slap it on quickly in the wings with toupee tape during the first scene when I do my quick change out of Sammy and then re-enter as Jonesy. "That 'tache needs to be taken great care of, Patrick. It's complete mayhem in the wings."

But what could Patrick do? The little hairy one is easily knocked on the floor during the chaos and kerfuffle. And in the second act, I again have to remove said 'tache and hastily place it somewhere safe when Patrick gets me *out* of Jonesy's security guard uniform and *into* Sammy's Mighty Beast.

So tonight, I went to Jeanette in wigs who gave me a spare 'tache. Guess what? During the interval, when I went to collect it from my box on the prop table, that had also dematerialised. Obviously half inched. So poor old Jonesy was clean shaven in the second act. I *knew* it would happen. It's Naff-on-Sea rep. My obscenely denuded upper lip caused Patti to shoot me a sharply quizzical frown during our brief exchange outside Paramount gates.

Earlier, David Caddick, our orchestrator, said, "Peter, during your sung line in Artie's party, 'By this time next year' and so on, your throat mike is also picking up the music coming from the saxophone player standing behind you. Could I ask you to keep your mike away from the sax's bell?"

I said, "Okay, I'll try." But what I wanted to say was: David, how the hell can I possibly do that when I'm stuck in the middle of that chaotic crowd? Please tell your saxophonist to point his splendid instrument somewhere else. Over the years he must have aimed his bell-end in all kinds of unusual directions. But that would have been suggestive. So, I didn't. I just yelled my lines, with no detectable quieter playing from the band or the sax.

At the end of Artie's party, the pallet on which we noisily celebrate the New Year carries us discreetly offstage. But tonight, it sighed, "Sorry, everyone. I'm too exhausted; lost the will to live. Please make other arrangements."

So, we all shambled off into the wings, shouting stuff like, "Hey! C'mon, everybody! Let's all go on somewhere else! How about a night club? Great idea! Ha-ha-ha!"

10:15 p.m. After Curtain Calls

The cast lined up on the stage in pecking order, from the lowest to highest paid (saving the best till last). I shook hands with Fergie. She leant forwards and murmured, "Peter. Your quick changes in the first scene were the highlights of the whole show. Well done."

Author's note: Correction. That will feature in the erotic movie version. Fergie smiled at me, briefly. No pleasant chit-chat.

10:40 p.m. Dressing Room Tannoy

Trevor made this jolly announcement: "Dear company, this is your friendly local radio station again, just to say very well done, and do get an early night. Resist the temptation to go out and party-party. I beg you, save your voices. It was the second performance and, true to form, energy levels were lower, which was a good thing in many ways. You couldn't possibly stay at that high emotional pitch you worked on yesterday. So, go straight home and get lots of rest and I'll see you tomorrow afternoon to look at some scenes."

He then gave us the calls, which included this: "I need to work with the male ensemble at 4 p.m."

Tube train to West Hampstead.

11:40 p.m.

At home, I wound back the video tape. I'd recorded a TV documentary, *By Satan Possessed*, about Devil worship, made by a friend of mine, Antony Thomas.

Quite by chance, I'd also taped the end of the evening news. And what d'ya know? There was the Adelphi Theatre and all the celebs and household names arriving, togged up in their fancy finery and packing into the foyer to see a musical called *Sunset Boulevard*.

David Frost was interviewing Joan Collins. "I hear it's fabulous," she enthused. "I'm looking forward to seeing it enormously."

Cut to a lady reporter. "It seems that rehearsals were held up due to faulty hydraulics operating the complex scenery."

I couldn't relate this glossy glamour to our sweaty backstage quick changes, panicky hunts in the dark for stolen moustaches, pallets refusing to perform their trundling duties, me running up and down eighty-four steps between my dressing room and the stage, new music cues sounding wrong, and so on.

On the TV was Fergie, whose hand I'd just shaken, smiling silently in response to an indiscreet question about her separation from Prince Andrew after only seven years of marriage. Details of their divorce arrangements were then given. Surreal.

I rang Peter Middleton. "Can we put back tomorrow's 10 a.m. voiceover session by a couple of hours?"

"Sorry, Peter. No. I've booked the studio."

"That pisses me off," I ungraciously snapped. "I could've had the whole morning to relax. It means that afterwards I shall have to kill time in London before the four o'clock rehearsal call."

It was unkind of me to gripe but I feel bone tired and out of sorts. I stupidly forgot to ring railway enquiries for the train times. It's way too late to do that now, so I'm going to bed with no idea what train I'll catch tomorrow.

12:50 p.m.

Hit the sack.

WEDNESDAY 30th June 1993

7:30 a.m.

When I woke up, my throat felt like sandpaper.

Shot out of bed, belted to West Hampstead station and managed to catch the 8:59 a.m. train to Swanley.

This voiceover fee is £175; it'll come in mighty handy. Peter Middleton runs a company called Proactive Marketing. They produce advertising audio tapes and videos.

Peter kindly said he'd pick me up at Swanley railway station at 10 a.m. but I began to panic when suddenly I noticed the Thameslink timetable said my train wouldn't arrive till 9:58 a.m.

And then the guy in the ticket office said, "I'm new to this job," and was thrown into complete confusion struggling to issue me a ticket. I couldn't wait. To avoid any risk of being late, I caught the train *without one*. Shock-horror!

My voice was as husky as hell. As I sat in the compartment, I tried to nudge my upper register gently back into some kind of shape, thinking, *How can I keep this up for nine more months? Bashing out all that loud singing and shouting in Artie's party is going to wreck my vocal cords.*

As we recorded, I cheated my rough vocal deliver by softening the higher inflections. Peter Middleton and his studio technician seemed pleased and, like today's sunny sky, the grey clouds inside my head cleared to a happy blue.

Peter Middleton found this delightful little studio in the Yellow Pages! It's inside a converted oast house, a tall conical building, which is attached to a Norman barn on farmland near the River Derwent, now a conservation area.

After we recorded, Peter and I went outside and relaxed on a bench with mugs of tea. Paradise greeted us. A goose and a gander relaxed in the long grass as a pony called Cindy and some horses grazed in the farmer's field. Wild flowers, peace and sunshine…

I'm beginning to wonder what I'm doing, knocking my guts out in London day after day? What for? Yes, regular dough, but I just hope the pressure calms down a bit when we settle into the run.

4 p.m. Adelphi Theatre. Company Call

The ensemble waited over an hour for a few notes. This was mine.

"Peter," Trevor said, "You miscued your lines in the cabaret."

"Yes, I know. I was waiting to hear the orchestra dropping its volume."

"It did," Trevor answered.

"Didn't sound like it to me."

In that instant, I knew Trevor would never employ me again.

Author's note: Dear reader, I was right.

5:30 p.m.

I popped into the wig department to consult Jeanette about my missing moustache. She was busy. Sue faced me, fag in her mouth, hands on her hips, overwhelmed by piles of problems, all needing far more urgent attention than my titchy tash.

"Sorry, Peter," Sue said. "We haven't got any spares. If you could do me a big favour and go out and manage to buy one, I'd be really grateful. And I promise, I shall reimburse you."

Being a wonderful, warm human being, I nipped over to Charles Fox's in Covent Garden, purchased the necessary facial addition, trimmed the little rascal and wore him in tonight's show.

Tomorrow, I shall ring The Times, Guardian, Mirror and Daily Mail and get them to carry front page headlines and shock-horror photos of me pointing to my scandalously naked upper lip.

7:30 p.m.

Another Gala Charity, this one for the Samaritans. It was attended by the Duchess of Kent. The Samaritans provide wonderful practical help and advice for people with all kinds of problems and often considering suicide.

As the Duchess is not a full-blown sovereign, the band played only half the national anthem. I am told that she is privately known as Katharine Kent. Kitty Kent! An enthusiastic football and tennis fan, Kitty has presented more trophies at FA cup finals and Wimbledon Lawn Tennis Championships than any other member of the royal family.

During the show, I was called downstage to the quick change room in the wings to have a word with Patti. She was having problems…

"Peter, I can't hear the orchestra. And this heat is unbearable. In all the quick changes, my costumes are literally sticking to me. It's impossible to get them off! Can you find out if Equity has any ruling about air temperatures backstage? Aren't there limits to the heat that actors can be made to work in? Equity should tell our theatre manager to provide us with electric fans."

"Of course, Patti. I will do so as soon as I can."

The shameful fact is that on the stage we have no air conditioning. Consequently, we are boiling our backsides off while the audience feel as if they are sitting in a refrigerator going full-blast. In fact, the air is so chilly for the public, some men are taking off their coats and putting them round the shoulders of their female partners to keep them warm. In other words, actors don't matter; they can roast alive as long as the audience is cool.

At one point, the scenery became stuck. Richard Bullimore, our production manager, was consulting with the stage crew in the wings, trying to get it to work. Richard finally said, "Okay. I don't see any other option. We'll have to stop the show."

His words acted like Dorothy's magical mantra, "There's no business like show business. There's no business like show business…"

The set suddenly felt a stirring in its loins and forced its levers, wheels and pulleys into action. The show was on again!

Before doing "The Lady's Paying" number, Patti does a ten-second costume change on the tiny offstage landing halfway up the stairs in Norma's house. She is only hidden from the audience by a curtain. Tonight, in the middle of it, Patti called down to a stage manager in the wings.

"Someone's head mike is coming out of the speakers onstage!"

"We know, Patti. We're working on it."

It turned out to be one of the crew's headsets.

10:15 p.m.

After the curtain calls, we lined up on the stage to be presented to the royals. I shook hands with the sixty-year-old Duchess of Kent. Seemed nice, but they never speak to me. According to protocol, you shouldn't initiate chit-chat.

No rain for ages, and yet this has been the wettest June on record. How does that work? The big news is the Royal Observatory authorities at Greenwich have engineered today's twenty-four hours to last one second longer than normal. This is to bring atomic clocks into alignment with our planet's irregular movement.

Chapter 7

JULY 1993

THURSDAY 1st July 1993

It's true! Yesterday, the final minute of June before midnight was sixty-one seconds long. Oh boy! Thank heavens for that extra time in bed. It felt great!

No rehearsal this morning because of our 3 p.m. matinee.

3 p.m. Adelphi Theatre

Sunset's first matinee performance.

The dress circle was about one third empty.

During the scene in Sheldrake's office in Act One, his phone rings so he picks it up and talks to his caller. Today, he picked it up and began to speak. The phone continued to ring. A titter ran round the audience.

4:50 p.m.

During the final scene, the huge house set descended to the stage level as the flute was playing its quiet solo. There was a loud sound of ripping wood. The huge house was slowly and remorselessly crushing one of the flats (or travellers) which had unwisely got in its way. You don't mess with Norma Desmond's mobile mansion and get away with it, kid.

5:50 p.m.

Before the matinee, I left a complementary ticket at the box office for the actress Vivienne Martin. Now someone in our dressing room mentioned that she was at the stage door asking to see me. There had been no message for me over the Tannoy.

By the time I sped downstairs, Vivienne had gone but she very kindly left me a written message. "I shall ring you tomorrow."

8:45 p.m.

This evening during Act Two, Paramount Studios Patti sang her number, "As If We Never Said Goodbye", and, as always, shed tears. She then sat in Hedy Lamarr's canvas-backed chair and we studio workers crowded round her.

Trevor has given us strict orders. "At this point, it's vitally important that you all remain in character."

But, it has to be admitted, our private chat with Patti is not always kosher. She shared a joke which I didn't hear, and then dried her eyes with tissues given to her by the make-up girl, played by Nicola Jane Filshie.

After smiling at her, Patti suddenly turned to me and, as Norma Desmond, said, "That's a splendid costume you're wearing. Tell me, what part do you play in Mr DeMille's *Samson and Delilah*?"

As the actor Sammy, I am dressed in an elaborate, floor-length ancient Egyptian high priest robe made of heavily layered multicoloured material, with a long train, a breastplate and golden gauntlets. I am also wearing a tall gold crown.

I said to Patti, "I play the cleaning lady."

Patti disguised a snigger, then gave a knowing nod.

"You look like my cleaning lady."

Sorry, Trevor.

9:15 p.m.

Tonight, in the final scene, Patti appeared at the top of the staircase *without* the huge Hiawatha headdress. Instead, she wore a bald wig with fuzzy hairs on it. She was dressed in long black negligee edged with marabou feathers and a long necklace of white sparkly beads. She looked horrific. People's verdict later was: "Electrifying!" Patti received a standing ovation at the curtain calls.

As we walked off the stage, several of us stopped to congratulate Patti, including me.

Trevor's message over the Tannoy was full of praise.

"But," he pointed out, "We are still climbing the mountain. We've managed to achieve Camp Six. We still have to reach Camp Ten."

Trev's tone is avuncular, charming and good-humoured, but some of the younger company members receive his comments with cynicism and derision, especially when he exhorts us to get early nights and save our voices. The fact is actors can be hard to please and quick to complain. I've worked with directors who were cold, aloof, and slow to offer words of praise or encouragement. Not so Trev.

FRIDAY 2nd July 1993

Still no rain and hotter than ever.

I rang Vivienne Martin who saw last night's show.

"Your front of house people aren't very gracious or welcoming," she said. "There was a mix up with my complementary ticket. And when you arrive, they search everyone's bags. An usher in the foyer said, 'Check your bag in,' meaning I should *leave* it with him! So,

I said, 'No, I don't want to do that or need to.' He said, 'Have you got a Walkman?' I said, 'Yes, I have,' and he said, 'You'll have to check that in.' I said, 'No, I won't because I'm not going to record this show. I used it today when I was rehearsing.'"

"I'm sorry to hear that, Viv. But did you enjoy the show?"

"Oh yes. I *loved* it! And they gave me free coffee and ice cream in the interval – a courtesy of the management for the ticket foul up."

Years ago, I greatly admired Vivienne's performance as the lead in the 1966 musical *The Matchgirls* at the Piccadilly Theatre. And in 1978, I had the amazing luck of being flown with her to Hong Kong to appear in an American musical called *Something's Afoot*, a funny spoof of Agathe Christie's whodunnit novel, *Ten Little Indians*.

We performed the show at the Hilton Hotel, no less, where they built a theatre stage at one end of the ballroom specially for us. We were accompanied by a Chinese band and conductor – all of them a joy to work with.

On my arrival at the airport, I discovered by chance that the native Chinese really do have trouble distinguishing between r and l sounds in English pronunciation, as mimicked by the politically-incorrect comedian Benny Hill. The driver of my taxi asked me about my plane journey. I told him that it was a twenty-hour flight.

"Twenny hour fright?" he exclaimed. "Somethin' long with engine?"

Spoiler alert. If you plan to see *Something's Afoot*, the following paragraph gives away the plot. Vivienne played the amateur sleuth, Miss Tweed (like Christie's Miss Marple). Miss Tweed is strangled when her scarf is entangled with an old-fangled spear on a wall. Fiona Fullerton was Hope, a pretty houseguest, and I played Geoffrey, her love interest, a college student and a dashing cross-country runner, popping in to escape the rain. They instantly fall in love.

George Cole played Flint, the caretaker – killed by an exploding gas stove. Angela Douglas was Lottie, a maid, who gets chopped up in bits when she falls inside a booby-trapped Ming vase – a large one! Virginia McKenna (still a good friend of mine) played Lady Grace, fatally electrified by a deliberately booby-trapped light switch.

Finally, Hope and Geoffrey both drop dead after drinking poisoned wine. Yes, every character in the musical winds up horribly murdered, and a hilarious time is had by all.

2:30 p.m. Adelphi Theatre. A Full Company Call

A boring afternoon. The ensemble had to sit in the stalls as leading and supporting actors were given dialogue cuts and new lines to try out.

Much later, we ran the opening, but instead of using sex-mad Mr Dummy as drowned Joe Gillis, we rehearsed with our young assistant stage manager, Nigel Wright. He wore a harness and dangled from a wire behind the gauze. I didn't envy him. Those harnesses can be a pain in the family jewels area.

6:45 p.m.

When I went upstairs to change, I discovered that one of our dressers, Colin, had written this amusing message for me in which he refers to a magazine called Boyz. I had left it open on my dressing table showing the centrefold pin-up photo of a handsome naked young guy.

Colin wrote, "Please be aware that innocent dressers, raised in the home counties, have to pass through this room with your costumes. Such literature could leave emotional scars on the impressionable."

7:30 p.m.

This evening the swimming pool steps section became jammed as it was lowered.

8:40 p.m.

The opening of the second act was held up because the computer that runs the entire show suddenly lost the will to live and had to phone a psychiatrist.

10:40 p.m.

A Tannoy message from Trevor saying we would be rehearsing Monday afternoon. There are now only two more shows before we open to the critics.

My dear friends Julia McKenzie and Jerry Hjert (her hubby) watched the evening show.

SATURDAY 3rd July 1993

Stiflingly hot.

11:15 a.m.

Jules rang. "To be honest, Pete, I wasn't that keen on it." She has been a chum since we were in two hit revues at the Mermaid Theatre. *Cowardy Custard* in 1972 was about Noel Coward, and *Cole* in 1974 was about Cole Porter.

I greatly admire Jules as an artist but this morning, I simply needed a few encouraging words of friendly support. Of course, everyone is free to dislike a production, but old pals should be generous when an actor has to crank out the blessed show eight times a week after said pal has deposited their lofty judgements and swept off to greater things.

Please, everyone, make an effort to sound positive when you conduct your post mortem. Save perceptive gripes till the damn thing has closed or the actor has moved on to a job more worthy of your wise and refined consideration. Then you can kick the unholy crap out of it.

5:50 p.m.

After today's matinee, I bumped into David Toguri in Covent Garden. He brilliantly staged the aforementioned *Cole* at the Mermaid Theatre and he choreographed the 1975 movie, *Rocky Horror Picture Show*. David is sixty but still has the sparkle and energy of a twenty-year-old.

He's currently working on Kenneth Branagh's new film, *Peter's Friends*, and on *Maggie May* with the National Youth Theatre.

10:20 p.m.

John Napier, our set designer, threw a company party tonight after the show. I hadn't spotted his invitation on the noticeboard and only heard about his bash at the very last minute, literally leaving the stage door. Felt too bushed to go. John impresses me as a warm-hearted, generous and hospitable guy.

SUNDAY 4th July 1993

11 a.m.

Drove in terrible traffic to my brother's little house down in Ripley, Surrey, but well worth the journey. We went for a stroll in the bright sunshine through the Surrey countryside along the lovely banks of the River Wey, greeted by dragonflies, ducks, caddis flies and swans.

I stripped to my waist in Bob's little back garden and used his watering can to pour deliciously cold tap water over my head.

12:30 p.m.

Took Bob to a jolly lunch in the local pub.

MONDAY 5th July 1993

Start of our second week.

1:30 p.m. Adelphi Theatre

A call onstage to rehearse "The Lady's Paying". I now sing facing front and standing in a row with Steve, Simon and Mark so that Kevin, behind us, is less visible being changed into his evening togs.

We also tried Paramount gates with Norma Desmond standing onstage (as if still seated in her car) talking to us studio guards (Gerard Casey, Simon Hayden and me). We all face the audience, looking at the "exit" sign at the back of the stalls. It feels really odd but if it works, it works.

Rehearsed cuntrapontal section. *Again.*

One of the ensemble said, "Andrew Lloyd Webber's American 'right-hand man' Tyler Gatchell has died. He was aged only forty. Andrew's flying over to New York."

The air is cooler now, praise be! Also, a face level circular hole about one foot across has been sawn in the door next to the stage level lift gates. I couldn't find anyone to tell me exactly why, but ah! It provides a welcome breeze!

However, there is still no airflow backstage and that hole is going to be filled in with glass to conform with fire regulations. So, what in tarnation is the point of it? Another illogical Kafkaesque event.

5:50 p.m. Stage Door

As I arrived, Patti was marching up and down the corridor, shouting for her dressing room key.

"Have they changed the fucking lock on my door *again?*"

She stormed upstairs with the stage door keeper's master key and then re-appeared in a boiling rage, yelling her head off.

"I want to see the manager of this *fucking* theatre!"

I can't understand what Patti is so furious about these days. Apart from her huge salary, I noticed in the show's programme she has been well booted and suited by the management. It lists individual credits of the top-class makers of her costumes, wigs, hair, make-up, gloves, millinery, jewellery and shoes. What is fuelling her anger?

7:30 p.m.

Our nineth preview performance.

At the beginning of Schwab's Drug Store, the enormous flat which carried the double doors and the newspaper and magazine shelves came in very fast and late. It landed with a thunderous thump as I began to move upstage. The flat would've hit me if somebody hadn't grabbed my shoulders and pulled me back just in time. It very nearly caught Kevin as he was waiting to enter.

10:30 p.m.

An announcement came over the Tannoy while we were changing to go home.

"Tomorrow's photo call is 1 p.m. for the ensemble."

This really isn't on. RUG must have planned these company calls earlier today or even yesterday. They should keep us better informed. We also have a few things to organise. Like our lives.

As we left, this was Trevor's message over the Tannoy: "We've now seen, after a day's rest, how all the numbers are badly affected by a lower energy level. The first night is next Monday, exactly a week away. That'll be after a gap of one day, Sunday." I guess it had to be said.

TUESDAY 6th July 1993

1 p.m. Adelphi Theatre. Press Call

The male ensemble were called for the press to photograph us dressing Kevin in "The Lady's Paying".

It began over an hour late.

2:15 p.m.

We sat in the stalls and watched Patti and Kevin posing for press photos of their tango dance routine.

3 p.m.

We then watched Patti and Kevin being videoed performing their tango for use in a TV commercial.

3:45 p.m. Circle Bar. Company Meeting

Feelings and opinions were aired about a possible video commercial deal. I tried to make notes.

At the end, I said to the company, "As your union representatives, Nadia Strahan and I will present your reactions at our 12:30 p.m. meeting tomorrow at Equity with Alistair Smith, one of RUG's five company directors, and David Grindrod, our production coordinator."

4:30 p.m.

A notes session with Trevor.

WEDNESDAY 7th July 1993

12:30 p.m. British Actors' Equity, Guild House, Tower Street

12:50 p.m.

The meeting began twenty minutes late. It was held between Alistair Smith, David Grindrod, Nadia Strahan and myself.

Before reading out the company's statement, I said to Alistair and David, "Please keep in mind that Nadia and I are not the entire cast. We are only a *part* of the ensemble. I must stress this point. Some feelings expressed at yesterday's company meeting might conflict with Nadia's own personal opinions or with mine."

A summary of what I read out:

"We, the ensemble, wish to be treated with more respect and consideration by the management. We accepted very low salaries on the clear understanding that three extra financial perks were to be negotiated through Equity and would be forthcoming. These inducements should not have been mentioned because it now seems they will not, in fact, form a significant part of the agreement.

"We have lost £580 for these two possible payments:

1) for a TV documentary.
2) for a News Access video.

Both failed to materialise through no fault of the ensemble, but because the management were unable to negotiate a deal with one of the principals. News Video extracts were shot but the ensemble were not informed and were excluded from the filming.

"We are requesting £580 be paid to each ensemble member as compensation for loss of that agreed sum for the projected TV documentary and the News Access video.

"The ensemble feel that their contribution to the success of this production is every bit as important as complex machinery, spectacular costumes and a lavish first night party (which they are considering boycotting as the only feasible and reasonable form of protest available to them). The ensemble hope to carry out their contractual duties in a spirit of goodwill and cooperation, and therefore respectfully ask the management to give this statement the most serious consideration."

2 p.m.

Meeting closed.

3 p.m. Adelphi Theatre

A rehearsal of the final scene.

"Let's strike while the iron is hot," Trevor suggested with a crafty smile. I guess this means while Andrew Lloyd Webber is away.

"We need to look at several things. As you know, I wasn't previously allowed to have any spoken dialogue in the final scene, so I'd like to try out some new, improvised exchanges there. Also, the new curtain calls don't work. I'd rather not expose the house set to full lighting. It spoils the mystery. Talking of which, the house is still too slow going out. What else? We need to rehearse 'The Lady's Paying' with the extra line of dialogue. And after that, I shall keep the girls to rehearse the beauticians scene.

"I understand your feelings and problems. Remember, I am not one of 'them'. I do not have a contract with the Really Useful Group. I am nurturing and sympathetic. I see what you do onstage – both when you are improvising in character and when you are sharing a private joke."

Trev did his best to rally the troops and we proceeded to rehearse. However, there is now a distinct feeling amongst the cast that all is not well. We aren't playing to packed houses and the word is our producers (The Really Useful Theatre Company Limited and Paramount Pictures Corporation) are making huge financial losses – "haemorrhaging money", as they say in America.

THURSDAY 8th July 1993

11 a.m.

Ran. Exercised with weights. Made phone calls. Typed out a noticeboard statement detailing the responses expressed at Tuesday's company meeting about a TV commercial deal. Missed lunch.

3 p.m. Adelphi Theatre

Matinee.

4:45 p.m.

Someone said to me, "Patti's last scene is getting hammy."

"Well, yes, that may be true, but it's a tricky one. Overacting is in Norma Desmond's blood. Some stars' performances in those old silent films look really corny to us today but that was how they were directed to act in their movies. And it's been Norma's life. She says so herself, sharing her emotions with the camera and the cinema audiences who loved her."

4:50 p.m.

Trevor's messages over the Tannoy are becoming a joke.

He gave another one after today's matinee. "That was a smashing performance but I must exhort you to conserve our energies for the evening show."

"Yes, we know," one of us ensemble sighed.

My dear friend Angela Morant came to see today's matinee. Angie and I studied acting at Central School of Speech and Drama. When we left in 1962, we shared the Gold Medal. Angie married Ben Kinsley in 1966 and they had two children. In 1976, she played the role of Octavia Minor in BBC TV's *I, Claudius*, and she recently played Barbara Harrison in *Brookside* on ITV. Since we renewed contact, I've kept in touch with Angie and today she watched the matinee with her cousin Susan Travers.

Susie, as Angie calls her, notably played the wife of the Dutch detective in *Van Der Valk*, the successful 1972-73 Thames Television crime drama series starring Barry Foster. Susie retired from acting and has been married for thirty-three years to Cornel Lucas, a well-known photographer of popular film stars, including Joan Collins, Marlene Dietrich and Gregory Peck. Corny, as Angie calls him, famously photographed Diana Dors in Venice sitting in a gondola wearing a mink bikini. Miss Dors, not Corny.

5:55 p.m.

I met up with Angie and Susie after the matinee and we went to Cranks. They only had tea as I scoffed my dinner.

"Okay," I said. "Let's hear it. What's the verdict?"

Angie considered. "So-so. It has its moments. It doesn't help that, just before the curtain falls on Act One, while Joe Gillis is carrying the suicidal Norma up the stairs in his arms, ice cream sellers are marching along the aisles – ruining the dramatic atmosphere."

Susie said, "We spotted Maggie Smith sitting in the audience, and someone told us that the *Spiderman* company was there."

They made no further mention of the show and I got the impression Angie and Susie were underwhelmed.

8:50 p.m. Act Two

A potentially dangerous evening.

At the beginning of the second scene outside Paramount, a big hunk of metal fell from the flies and landed on the stage with an almighty *thud*.

Fortunately, nobody was hit. It would certainly have injured, possibly even killed anyone standing underneath it. I asked a crew member why it happened.

"It was the big steel bracket that protects Schwab's Drug Store's neon sign transformer. As the Paramount gates flat was raised into the flies, it bashed the Schwab's flat and ripped out the bracket, screws and all."

As I stood in the wings waiting to enter, a stage manager warned me. "Don't go onstage just yet, Peter. Wait till the Paramount gates have flown in and stopped moving."

"Why?"

"In case any more pieces of metal fall off the electrical fitting."

Lethal. Plenty of witnesses. Something for the show report.

At the end of the Act Two during the Paramount Studios scene, there was another terrific crashing noise. It was a prop studio lamp falling off DeMille's movie camera tower.

During the final scene in Norma Desmond's house, when Patti appears dramatically on the staircase, she holds in her hand the red silk tape she uses to bind Norma's precious *Salome* film script. As she sings, Patti weaves this tape through her fingers. A nice idea.

But tonight, at that point, as Patti descended the stairs, her elaborate string of dangly necklace beads became caught in the banister rail; I suspected they might one day. This meant she first had to unweave the red tape from her fingers in order to release the necklace from the banister.

9:50 p.m.

As we were leaving, Nadia had a quick word with me. "Peter, I rang Equity this morning and spoke to Hilary Strange. She said that Patti's agent wants a large percentage of the LP recording sales points."

This doesn't bode well for the ensemble's record deal.

Watching tonight's show were friends of a New Yorker chum of mine, Jacqueline Parker. I've never met them but they kindly left a note at the stage door, saying, "Fabulous! Brilliant!"

Jacquie is a keen theatre-goer and has gathered an impressive collection of original autographs of famous showbiz names, including a few of Cole Porter's, of whom she's a crazy fan. I gave Jacquie a card sent to me by Ingrid Bergman to add to her collection.

Also tonight another Trevor message over the Tannoy. "I realise my name is mud, but it is necessary to improve the curtain calls, and Friday is the day for it."

We were given a 2:30 p.m. call for tomorrow. Trevor is a genius and we love him but we just hope he won't keep us hanging around all afternoon while he faffs about with the principals. I mean, while he works with them.

We ensemble were given first night ticket allocations. Awful for us pond life. Very high in the upper circle, the top level – way above all the good seats below in the stalls and the dress circle.

FRIDAY 9th July 1993

2:30 p.m. Adelphi Theatre. Full Company Call

Well, surprise-surprise. For over two hours, the ensemble sat in the stalls and were kept waiting while Trevor rehearsed with the principals, giving them a few dialogue cuts and new lines.

At one point, Gerard Casey was sitting and chatting to Patti in row two when Sir Andrew approached them.

"When did you fly in?" he said to Gerard.

Patti said, "He isn't not one of my American friends, Andrew.

This is Gerard. He's a member of the company."

4:40 p.m.

We finally reworked the beginning of Schwab's Drug Store.

5:40 p.m.

After that, the very opening moment of the show was changed. The first thing the audience sees is a huge gauze screen showing the rippling surface of Norma Desmond's swimming pool as viewed from below. Joe's body is floating on the surface. So far, a stuffed dummy dangling on a wire has been performing the role of shot and drowned Joe Gillis.

But, Mr Dummy has been sacked! I shall discuss the matter with Equity. Will he be eligible for holiday pay?

Today, Nigel Wright, one of our young stage managers, nobly stood-in for Mr Dummy and played the floating dead Joe. I say it was noble of Nigel because when you fly you wear a body harness hooked onto a wire, and your tender crotch takes your entire dangling weight. A sensible guy makes careful private arrangements beforehand.

At one point during a general note session, Trevor confused Gerard. Trevor used his favourite word for damaging or harmful.

"What you did, Gerard, was *deleterious*."

Gerard had to ask him what it meant. He wasn't the only one puzzled. I've never heard the word before. However, I've looked up "deleterious" in my Oxford English Dictionary and it is right there! It means harmful or damaging. Go, Trev, baby!

Lastly, we rehearsed Trevor's promised new curtain calls. The moment the show's final scene ends, the stage management have to leap into action. They quickly remove the newsreel movie camera and its tripod and then completely clear the stage for the entire company to take their bows. Several crew members were very nearly hit by the huge sliding panels while working out how to carry off the camera and tripod.

7:30 p.m. Act One

At the start of tonight's show, the raised poolside section became stuck. It should descend into tactful oblivion. It refused.

8:50 p.m. Act Two

The beginning was held up because the jammed poolside was still causing a problem. And during the second scene at Paramount Studios, a serious accident almost happened.

Sandy Strallen was standing on the upstage right rostrum. At that point, it appears to be the top of a broad flight of stairs. The steps then flatten into a plain slope. Tonight, the steps were abruptly flattened too early, transforming the whole unit into a smooth, sloping ramp. Without receiving a word of warning or given time to move off the unit, Sandy lost his footing, tumbled over and slid all the way down to stage level. He wasn't hurt, thank goodness.

The word going round is that our show has one big crucial problem – the way it ends. No one likes it.

Most people say to me, "I enjoyed the show very much but the last scene is a let-down."

I suppose they expect something to happen, a big finish of some kind. But what exactly? A ticker-tape parade? A Californian earthquake? Norma Desmond conducting a heart-warming singalong in a psychiatric hospital?

Apparently, there's been only one notable positive opinion about the end. "Sarah Brightman likes it," is the much-repeated phrase. So that's that.

Even though she and Sir Andrew divorced two years ago, he seems reluctant to question or ignore Sarah's opinion. Allegedly.

But now it seems enough people have told Andrew, "Audiences just think the end is an anti-climax. A damp squid."

So tomorrow, it is going to be changed. Tomorrow is Saturday. We open to the press on Monday.

9:50 p.m.

After the show another message over the Tannoy from Trevor. "We are at the south column. It only needs another surge of effort to get us to the summit." Serious voice. "I implore you, please do not go out tonight and party and drink and wreck your voices."

Oh Trevor, *trust* us! We wouldn't dream of doing such a thing. We are professional artistes. Evil chuckle: "He-he-he…"

Everyone is frazzled. Even Sir Andrew's driver, Jan, the Italian version of our name John. "I've had enough," Jan said to me. "At the end of next week, I'm going away – off home to Palermo. That's all I'm telling him. Andrew said to me, 'I've cancelled the helicopter. I'll need you here this weekend.' He hasn't given me a day off for weeks. I've been up at eight each morning and working till two o'clock every night. I can't stand any more. I'm near breaking point."

Still no rain. Backstage, the whole building is hotter than ever.

Only two more shows before we open.

SATURDAY 10th July 1993
OUR LAST TWO PREVIEWS

3 p.m. Adelphi Theatre

This is our final matinee before the first night on Monday.

Someone at last has managed to get the message through to Andrew and warn him, "The punters don't like the way the show ends."

Better late than never, I guess, but this is mega late.

The result is that Patti has been given new dialogue for the last scene, but hasn't been able to rehearse it with the company. She has written out her altered words and music on pages and sellotaped them by the door leading onto the stage.

My chum, the actress Louise Gold, watched today's matinee. After the show, she left me a message. "I'll phone you next Monday."

Louise and I have appeared in several of Ian Marshall Fisher's script-held *Lost Musicals* at the Theatre Museum in Covent Garden. Last year, we were together in an interesting show called *One Touch of Venus*, a classy piece of Broadway writing, with songs by Kurt Weill and Ogden Nash. Louise was the gorgeous Venus, a marble statue of the Greek goddess which amazingly comes to life and causes delightful mischief. I played Whitelaw Savory, the surprised and extremely pleased millionaire owner of the statue.

10:20 p.m.

Coming to you, live, backstage, from the Adelphi Theatre in London, another message over the Tannoy from Trevor. "A *fabulous* last preview performance, everyone... bla-bla-bla... *Do*, I *beg* of you, get an early night and save yourselves... bla-bla-bla... We are on the final ice column, but we still have to make it to the top camp... bla-bla-bla..."

Enough with the camps, Trevor. In any case, we kinda stop listening after the first few words.

And then Andrew added his tuppence worth over the Tannoy: "Thank you. I hate to strike a gloomy note, but please don't celebrate yet. Get lots of rest over the weekend.

I thought, *It's only twenty-four hours, Andy. Not a weekend. I've planned to stay in bed, let my housekeeper and butler do a week's shop, see to the chores, cook breakfast, lunch and supper, put the bins out, hoover, dust and weed the garden. If anyone rings, my secretary can answer. I shall loll on the sofa, file my nails and then pack my staff off to wild shindigs that celebs have invited me to; let them whoop it up till 3 a.m.*

To be fair, I guess Trevor and Andrew must say something to rally the troops, but a touch of humour or warmth wouldn't go amiss.

SUNDAY 11th July 1993

Managed to get an afternoon nap watching awful tv programmes. Knackeroonied, man.

MONDAY 12th July 1993

10 a.m. Morning of the First Night

Something incredible happened. Last week, I was just browsing through books at Samuel French and came across a play script. It was Terence McNally's 1982 off-Broadway comedy called *It's Only a Play*. It sort of jumped at me, so I ordered a copy.

The fictional plot is about the major opening night of a new Broadway play and it paints a vivid portrait of the cast sharing all the excitement, mishaps, angst and reviews.

And it arrived today! It dropped through my letterbox just now – the morning of our *Sunset Boulevard* first night! Oh brother.

I made a cup of coffee and sat in bed reading it. As the play begins, some of the actors gather in the producer's house, waiting for the early morning papers, wondering what the critics' reviews will be like. Downstairs a party is going on with Trevor Nunn and Patti LuPone amongst the celebrity guests! The morning papers arrive and the reviews are stinkers. It is *very* funny, but by page twenty I was a gibbering bag of nerves. Heaven knows I'm not playing an important role in *Sunset* but it's a seriously busy show for me and I don't want to screw up.

11:15 a.m.

I rang my agent. "Roberta, could you tell Pippa Ailion, the casting director I've invited to the show with you tonight, that I shall leave her guest ticket with yours in the box office to be collected."

12:30 p.m.

Feel ill. Had to force-feed myself some lunch.

Rang Louise Gold who saw our Saturday matinee. "Are you enjoying it?" she asked. "I think it's really mean of them not to put your character's names in the cast list."

"What do you mean?"

"The roles you play. Sammy, for example. You aren't credited in the programme as playing him. The four leads get top billing, then the cast is listed in alphabetical order, only naming the roles performed by eight actors. Then it just says, 'Other parts played by members of the ensemble.'"

My stomach turned over. "I didn't know that."

"Oh God. I'm sorry. Have I depressed you?"

"No. It's all par for the course. Typical of this management."

I put the phone down. My first night nerves had evaporated. All I feel now is a mild annoyance. And I'm pretty glad I had the guts to shoot my mouth off at that Equity meeting last Wednesday with Alistair Smith and David Grindrod. What on earth am I paying my agent for? She put me up for a walk-on and understudy job, negotiated a lousy salary for me and didn't even get me a decent mention in the programme.

I said to myself, "Listen, Pete. This is your own stupid fault. It's called paid work. Get a grip. And count your blessings."

So, I did. And I did.

1:30 p.m.

Left home and took the tube into London to save money on a cab.

Now, spot the deliberate mistake… I put my black socks and patent leather shoes in my backpack and carried my evening jacket and trousers over my arm on a wire coat hanger, protected by the dry cleaners' cellophane cover.

Heading to West Hampstead tube, I called into NatWest and placed a cheque into my account. Then I went to the station. The train arrived. The doors opened and I stepped inside the carriage feeling a bit puzzled.

Something was wrong but I couldn't put a finger on it… Then it came to me. I wasn't carrying my evening suit! I'd left it in the bank, hanging on a display for "reduced loans".

Just as the tube train doors began to close, I darted out onto the platform, tore up the station steps and raced back to NatWest. My evening suit was still hanging there, exactly where I'd left it, thank goodness, patiently waiting for me to return and be collected. It looked like something in a charity shop.

2:15 p.m. Adelphi Theatre. Stage Door

Inside the entrance, visitors packed the narrow corridor delivering wrapped gifts, bouquets, potted plants, stacks of liquor, and a blizzard of good luck cards and telegrams.

I did a round of the dressing rooms delivering "break a leg" cards for everyone in the show and the stage management team.

Bernard Sharpe approached me in the corridor. "Have you been into wardrobe? It's like a brewery. You've never seen so many bottles of champagne, wines and spirits. They could open an off-license."

I was intrigued and peeped into wardrobe. Bernie wasn't exaggerating.

Meredith Braun told me she received a beautifully wrapped bouquet of flowers sent to her by Nancy Olson. Miss Olsen was twenty-two when she played Betty Schaeffer in the original 1950 film of *Sunset Boulevard.*

Newspapers listed these celebs seeing tonight's show:

Jenny Seagrove, the theatre and TV actress.

Angela Rippon, the TV newsreader, presenter, journalist, writer.

David Emanuel, who styled the actors' clothes for the Sydmonton Festival performance of *Sunset Boulevard.* In 1981, he also designed the wedding dress Princess Diana wore when she married Prince Charles.

Michael Ball, the actor and singer, and star of *Les Miserables, Phantom of the Opera* and *Aspects of Love.*

Cathy McGowan, his partner. She is a broadcaster and journalist. In the swinging sixties, she presented *Ready Steady Go!,* a very popular British rock/pop music TV programme and she became a role model for young female admirers of her groovy clothes and lifestyle.

David Frost, the ubiquitous writer, journalist and TV host.

Shirley Bassey, the multi award-winning singer.

Judi Dench, one of Britain's greatest and most loved actresses. I have admired her since I was nineteen and saw her play Juliet in Franco Zeffirelli's breathtakingly passionate production of *Romeo and Juliet* at the Old Vic in 1960.

Gloria Hunniford, the TV and radio presenter.

Roger Moore, the film actor and star of eight James Bond films.

Nicola Formby, the model, accompanied by…

Jason Donovan, the actor/singer.

Twiggy, a world famous model in the 1960s and now a fairly successful actress/singer, accompanied by…

Leigh Lawson, her hubby, a handsome stage and film actor and also a director. He starred in *Madame Sousatzka* with Shirley MacLaine in 1988.

Roger Rees. In 1983, he enjoyed a massive and well-deserved success playing Nicholas Nickleby in the Royal Shakespeare Company's terrifically successful adaptation of Charles Dickens' novel for which he won an Olivier Award and a Tony Award. After repeating the role on Broadway, he has since worked extensively in America. He is now starring as the Sheriff of Rottingham in a new film comedy, *Robin Hood: Men in Tights*, directed by Mel Brooks.

Rowan Atkinson, the comic actor and writer, famous for his extremely funny *Blackadder* TV series and his droll character Mr Bean.

Sunetra Sarker, his wife, accompanied him. The beautiful twenty-year-old actress plays Nisha Batra in the long-running TV series *Brookside*.

Joan Collins, the film and stage actress. She is also an author and an eloquent and beguiling TV interviewee.

Richard Eyre, the distinguished theatre, opera, TV and film award-winning director and the artistic director of the National Theatre.

Bruce Forsyth, the multitalented and award-winning actor, tap dancer and comedian on TV, stage and film.

Emily Lloyd, a young actress who played Jessie Burns in *A River Runs Through It*, an award-winning film directed by Robert Redford.

Bob Monkhouse, the comedian and host of many TV game shows.

Terry Wogan, a popular Irish radio and television broadcaster.

Cliff Richard, a pop singer and actor.

Des O'Connor, comedian, singer and TV presenter.

John Gummer, the Environmental Minister. My kinda guy. He was awarded the Royal Society for the Protection of Birds Medal, and is also praised by Friends of the Earth.

Betty Boothroyd, a politician and Speaker of the House of Commons.

Glenys Kinnock, politician.

Lord Lew Grade, the legendary theatre agent who represents the most prestigious British stars in show business, including both Sir Laurence Olivier and Sir Ralph Richardson, and also the classical cellist Julian Lloyd Webber (Andrew's brother).

Frank Rich, New York Times theatre critic.

Nancy Olson, who played Betty in the 1950 Paramount film of *Sunset Boulevard*. Now aged sixty-five, she is about to watch our first night, escorted by none other than…

Billy Wilder, the director and co-writer of the original, flawlessly terrific Paramount film, *Sunset Boulevard*. My one hope and prayer is to meet the great man and ask him to sign my souvenir programme.

3 p.m. Adelphi Theatre. Onstage

A call for a company warm-up and a run of bits.

Patti arrived wearing a curious red and green pixie's outfit, complete with cap and hood. As my mum used to say, "Bless her cotton socks."

We ran Act One up to the end of Norma's first scene in the

house. I was worried because the massive Paramount gates flat was late to fly in.

"We're being careful with it," one of the stage management confided. "We're still worried about it hitting the Schwab's flat."

"You're not the only one who's worried," I replied. "While it's being lowered, I am standing bang underneath the bloody thing. Just looking up at it is scary."

Perhaps "bang underneath" isn't the best way to put it.

4:10 p.m. Adelphi Foyer

I took my agent's comps to the box office but they said, "Sorry, Peter. No first night tickets for guests will be held here to pick up. Audience members who don't already have tickets won't even be allowed to enter the foyer from the street."

"What shall I do?" I asked.

"Leave your guests' tickets at the stage door. Then just ring your guests and tell them to pick up the ticket there."

So, I did. And they did.

Patti's first night gift to everyone in the cast was a black and white T-shirt. On the front, there is a photo of herself as Norma Desmond with dark glasses and a turban. On the back, in gold letters, are the words, "I will not have it butchered" – that's Norma Desmond's warning to Joe Gillis about her beloved *Salome* film script. I guess Patti's T-shirt quote is aimed at our show's critics. Kevin Anderson gave me a beautiful little bookmark made of hallmarked silver.

A member of the stage management said, "RUG forgot to get first night gifts for the ensemble, so we were instructed to rush out and buy catalogue-order powder compacts for the girls and spectacle cases for the men."

That was nice, but, wouldn't you know? The girls don't use make-up and the boys don't wear spectacles.

4:30 p.m. Onstage

We sang through Artie's party and rehearsed a couple of changes to the curtain call.

Then Trevor Nunn and David Caddick, our musical supervisor, told us how wonderful we were. "But please," Trevor exhorted us, "Don't be all eyes and teeth, just because it's a first night."

And that was it. Curtain up at 7 p.m.

5:15 p.m. Cranks

For a quick savoury snack and salad.

5:40 p.m. The Canadian Muffin Shop

Nipped over to King's Street for afters – a delish takeaway frozen yogurt with raspberries. A treat for Pete.

6 p.m. Adelphi Theatre

Back to my dressing room to sort out the pile of good luck cards and prezzies I received.

7 p.m. First Night

As we waited onstage to start the show, we heard Pippa make this special announcement to the audience:

"Welcome, ladies and gentlemen, to the world premiere of *Sunset Boulevard*."

A few isolated, self-conscious whoops, but no clapping.

The curtain rose on the opening image of Joe Gillis' body floating in the swimming pool. It was greeted with a round of applause.

9:10 p.m.

The show had gone well, as far as I could judge. No mishaps. Patti was clearly nervous singing her first number, "With One Look" – hardly surprising – but she was rewarded with very enthusiastic applause, and she quickly settled down. Her second number in Paramount Studios, "As If We Never Said Goodbye", sounded really beautiful.

I did okay, thank heaven. After the final curtain call, I heaved a massive sigh of relief, having obeyed the time-honoured theatre dictum: "Remember your lines and don't bump into the furniture." But in this show, it's equally important not to let the furniture bump into *me*. Heaven knows, our hyperactive sets gallivant around the stage as much as we do.

On top of that, I had to get right all my fiddly bits of business, my choreography, my changes of costume, wigs, hats and harmonies, and my cues when to enter, speak, sing and exit.

9:15 p.m.

After the curtain calls came a terrific message from Trevor over the Tannoy: "We made it to the summit. Congrats."

Champagne in the dressing room with invited guests. All us fellas sporting our dashing evening attire. Dead posh.

Roberta, my agent, daunted by the huge crowd, didn't come round.

10:15 p.m. The Savoy Hotel. First Night Party

The Savoy is a classy five-star luxury hotel but, oh dear, I have to say it. Sir Andrew's opening night bash was a ghastly disappointment. Why? Because the Really Useful Group sliced the company into two unequal halves.

The leading actors were seated with the top brass producers in one room, while the supporting ensemble/understudy actors and the technical and stage management team were seated in a room one floor below.

The Abraham Lincoln Room

Only eight actors playing named roles were allowed to dine here with personal guests, the show's producers, the director, the choreographer and a host of celebrities.

The Riverside Room

The ensemble, understudies and stage management were seated a floor below in Riverside. It is equally as beautiful as the Lincoln but we felt separated from the specially invited glitterati upstairs.

Here we sat with our more humble guests in baffled isolation, wondering where the hell Sir Andrew, Trevor, Patti and Kevin were, plus all the household names who had just seen us perform, especially the original film's director and co-writer, Billy Wilder, no less. I was dearly hoping he would autograph my *Sunset Boulevard* programme but I didn't even catch a fleeting glimpse of Mr Wilder.

None of the Really Useful Group management team nor their star guests came near us – with one delightful exception. The forty-eight-year-old actor Roger Rees took the trouble to find us. He very charmingly came to my table, introduced himself and offered his congratulations; an extremely friendly gesture on his part because I'd never had the pleasure of working with Roger or had even met him before. I knew he is a much-loved actor, enjoying a wonderfully distinguished stage, film and television career. He was nominated for an Emmy for the TV series *The Life and Adventures of Nicholas Nickleby*. He has also won Tony and Olivier Awards, and makes special guest appearances in US TV series like *Cheers*.

The casting director I invited as my personal guest, Pippa Ailion, was obviously disappointed. She wanted to be where the action was and to mingle with the celebs. I could see Pippa was bored. Her polite smile said it all.

"Peter, I would really love to meet and congratulate your stars, Patti and Kevin." She sighed. "They were wonderful."

"I'm sorry, Pippa, but I haven't the faintest idea where Patti or Kevin are dining." If I'd had an ounce of initiative, I should've asked a waiter where they were seated, blagged my way into their dining room with Pippa and paraded her about. But I didn't because I felt tired, humiliated and exasperated.

11:45 p.m.

Pippa made her excuses. "Sorry, Peter, but I've got to go. I'm starting work early tomorrow." And she left.

12:15 a.m.

Half an hour later, I decided to say my goodbyes and hit the road.

Bumped into Trevor briefly on my way out, but it wasn't convenient to speak. In fact, since rehearsals began, Trevor and I have barely exchanged a single word privately, apart from that odd encounter in the gents' toilet six weeks ago at the Royalty Theatre. Not as scandalous as it sounds.

It was during a rehearsal tea break when I was taking a pee, standing alongside Trevor as he berated Kevin who had whistled the tune of "Love Changes Everything" during his exit at the end of a scene, a song from Andrew's show, *Aspects of Love*.

As I left the Savoy, Michael Bauer passed me in the corridor. He had, of course, been sitting upstairs in the Lincoln Room with the VIPs. I asked him if he had seen Billy Wilder.

"Oh yes, Billy Wilder was at a table near us. He came and sat with me and we had a long talk about Cecil B. DeMille."

My guts twisted with envy; but his next remark made them

somersault.

"Wilder said to me, 'You looked more like DeMille than *DeMille* did.'"

Not only is Michael playing a tasty cameo role but he had wined and dined with the director and co-writer of the highly acclaimed film on whose script our musical is based! And then the living Hollywood legend paid Michael a charmingly witty compliment.

Bitterly disappointed, I felt pangs of jealousy. After all those Sunday Buddhist meetings I attended after Paulie died, vainly seeking inner calm and peace of mind, and I failed this very minor test. And the yoga classes! Oh, how I struggled to hold downward facing dog and achieve a mystical union with the unknowable. And here I was, allowing my transcendental non-attachment to be sullied by worldly envy. Yes, the proverbial iron entered my soul in the Savoy's plush dining room.

Yoga… That reminds me. During a class one day, we were being shown how to do the above-mentioned position. For short, our instructor called it downward dog. We had the palms of our hands and feet flat on the floor and our bums in the air, creating a perfect upside down v shape. Did I say perfect? Not quite. As we gasped and grunted with various levels of competence, a woman's voice exclaimed to our teacher, "Oh! Is this position called downward dog? I completely misheard you. I thought you called it Darren the dog."

In my heart, from now on, it will always be Darren the dog.

During this *Sunset* first night bash, I wanted to feel like a classy hotel guest.

"Come on, Pete. Find a partner, take her to the ballroom and polish the parquet. You'll be rubbing shoulders with the Savoy's starry ghostly guests of yesteryear: George Gershwin,

Noel Coward, Gertrude Lawrence, Charlie Chaplin, Cary Grant, Marlon Brando, Marilyn Monroe and Audrey Hepburn."

Many elegant photos of these celebrities are framed on the walls. However, I could hear sounds of a blaring disco coming from downstairs, and valuing my precious eardrums, I left the kids to it.

2:30 a.m.

Splashed out on a cab home, wondering what happened to Andrew Lloyd Webber's amazing idea for this party.

Nick Colicos mentioned it nine weeks ago – a grandiose piece of showmanship to rival *Miss Saigon*'s first night bash in 1989 when Cameron Mackintosh hired a boat to ferry the *Saigon* company to a Thames-side restaurant. Sir Andrew's mine's-better-than-yours plan was to transform the Strand into a palm tree lined Californian boulevard, like parts of Sunset in Los Angeles. A red carpet would be laid down outside the Adelphi Theatre and all the way along the Strand to the Savoy, exclusively for the company and our first night audience celebrities to strut their stuff to a swanky bun-fight.

Maybe the LCC refused to close the public highway for such a frivolous reason. For authenticity, Sir Andrew could have paid a few tramps to push their junk-filled prams along the pavements outside the Adelphi. That's what I saw there in Los Angeles way back in 1968 when I spoke to some hobos.

I was in a tour of two English comedies by Bernard Shaw and Noel Coward presented by the Theatre Royal Windsor. Those poor down-and-out souls were a glimpse of America's poverty-stricken underbelly, largely invisible to the outside world, and only depicted in American feature films as loveable comedic characters.

Author's note: *Talking of underbellies, one early Sunday evening in 2016, I came out of an art exhibition at Somerset House and saw a group of men queuing up for hot meals being served to them from the back of a food van run by a charity.*

I chatted with one of them, a well-spoken, personable young man, who said he would be sleeping rough underneath Waterloo Bridge that night. He said, "You can't get a job if you have no address. And you can't get an address if you have no job. You'd be surprised how many people in this country today are only two weeks' salary away from where I'm standing now."

THURSDAY 15th July 1993

1:40 p.m. Adelphi Theatre, Stage Door

I signed in and, by chance, met Trevor's secretary in the corridor, Mary-Lee McNulty. She greeted me warmly. "Hello. I've been hearing nice things about you from someone you know."

I said, "That's a change from all the filth. Who was this person?"

The name Mary-Lee mentioned meant nothing to me. Didn't ring the faintest bell, for a very good reason. It turned out it wasn't a friend of mine but of Michael Bauer. Michael and I have little in common except we are of a similar age and both bald. Which makes us practically identical, of course.

Richard Tate is ill. The poor man has shingles and will stay home for at least two weeks. Maybe some kind of reaction to the stress of our opening night three days ago? Bernard Sharpe is playing Richard's ensemble roles.

There was no voice message from Trevor over the Tannoy today.

Two new films have opened, *Grease* and Spielberg's *Jurassic Park*.

FRIDAY 16th July 1993

2 p.m. Adelphi Theatre. An Understudy Call

Hilary Strange at Equity sent me a letter containing information for the cast. I made photocopies and distributed them.

5 p.m.

A vocal warm-up with David White (musical director). Patti came!

The company then discussed with David the proposed LP recording deal. A vote of no confidence in Hilary was mooted but then suspended until we can take advice from a lawyer via Equity.

Patti said, "Sorry, but I have to leave."

After Patti went, Nick Colicos offered to help solve the problem. "If you like, I'll ask Patti if she would still agree, as originally, to take an equal split of the LP recording royalties. She told me she doesn't know anything about her agent's demands but will send him a copy of Hilary's letter."

I feel very depressed that I've let the company down. I should've gone to Patti and discussed this with her myself.

TUESDAY 20th July 1993

5:30 p.m. Adelphi Theatre. Circle Bar. An Equity Meeting

The company voted for a three tier system of points. I didn't contribute to the discussion because I was afraid I might say something I'd regret.

The four sub-principals are holding us over precisely the same greedy barrel as the two stars, insisting that it's a hierarchical production, and therefore they want commensurately more royalties. In other words, they are adopting the same attitude for their own gain which they profess to despise in others.

They even said, "We will refuse to make the record if the company vote for an even split."

So, we've no choice but to accept a three tier deal.

We then voted *not* to include David White (our conductor), Maggie Goodwin (the assistant choreographer), and Andrew McBean (the assistant director) in the company's share of the points.

We also passed a resolution to complain to the head of Equity about Hilary Strange's lack of robustness in her negotiation with RUG on our behalf, and also to demand that Equity should only take five percent instead of the twenty-nine percent which she recommended we should accept.

Author's note: It was just as well we did because, in the event, we pushed for only five percent and we got it.

Nick Colicos wanted the stage management's share to come out of our two stars' share of the points as well, or something, but he was told to give it a rest by everyone.

After the meeting, I shared the lift with Meredith Braun, who plays Betty Schaefer and is the wife of our conductor, David White.

"Peter, we must hold another Equity meeting to take a second vote. At least ten people were absent today. Also, the stage management should have voted." She listed three people to be considered for inclusion: her husband David White, who is our conductor; the assistant choreographer Maggie Goodwin, and the assistant director, Andrew McBean.

I felt Meredith was being tiresome, so I said, "I disagree."

Even if I'd thought Meredith was right, I would probably still have disagreed.

"Of course, they should be included," she remonstrated.

"They're members of Equity."

I felt like replying, "So is Maggie Smith but she doesn't have a vote because she's not in the cast." But I said, "David is working in this show as a conductor, a member of the Musicians' Union, and not as an Equity member actor."

I hear Meredith's charmless behaviour has made her rather unpopular with some of the company. Steve, an assistant stage manager, told me Meredith had a big row with her leading man, Kevin Anderson.

Steve asked me if I knew what their clash was about.

I said, "No, I haven't the faintest idea."

Later, a company actor explained. "Meredith gave Kevin a note – not to upstage her. Her command was not gratefully received by Kevin with open arms. She's got a lot to learn, that little madam."

Later, Carol Woods, one of our rehearsal pianists, said, "As I spoke to David White, your show's conductor, I received the full blast of his anger at the company's decision to exclude him from your share-out of the LP points. David said to me, 'I'm not going to be Mr Nice anymore. I'm furious at the company's lack of respect, after all my hard work. From now on, I'm going to work strictly by the book and make no special allowances for anyone!'"

During the show's interval, by coincidence, I again shared the lift down to the stage with Meredith. There was an awkward silence. It spoke volumes.

Meredith said, "I think everyone has been very, very mean." And as she walked out of the lift, she called over her shoulder, "I don't mean you personally, Peter." Which made me feel much better.

FRIDAY 23rd July 1993

3:30 p.m. Adelphi Theatre.

An Understudy Rehearsal

4:30 p.m.

A full company call for a special rehearsal with Alisa Endsley who covers Patti as Norma. Alisa really knows her stuff. And, boy oh boy, there's an awful lot of it to know.

THURSDAY 29th July 1993

8:55 p.m. Adelphi Theatre

The set continues to behave like an intractable child. The secret villain is the computer under the stage that moves the scenery. Or doesn't.

For the second time this week, tonight's show came to a complete stop just before the duet in Act Two. The pallet carrying Schwab's Drug Store serenely slowed to a restful halt and expressed no desire to move another inch. None of the technical team could even work out *why*.

Debbie made the all-too familiar announcement to the waiting audience over the public address system. "Ladies and gentlemen, due to a technical fault, the show is unable to continue, but if you remain seated, I am sure we will be able to sort the problem out very soon. Thank you."

Debbie then explained the problem to the company over the Tannoy. "The computer has crashed. This means that the stage left machinery and also the flying panels have seized up, leaving the panels permanently stuck halfway down."

And as usual, nothing would shift the mutinous tykes. After waiting fifteen minutes for the panels to play ball, it was decided the performance should continue without their kind offices. However, this meant that in the final scene, when Norma dramatically walks halfway down the stairs to the landing, she was only visible to people sitting in the two front rows of the stalls. Maybe a few sitting further back caught a peek of her feet but nothing else.

Crucially, in that final scene, punters who were sitting above the stalls had no idea Norma was packing heat. When she produced her gun and shot Joe dead, the loud bang made them leap out of their skins and a few women screamed loudly with shock.

FRIDAY 30th July 1993

1:30 p.m. Adelphi Theatre

Cuts! Sir Andrew Lloyd Webber himself called a rehearsal to put in several edits. He hadn't long begun before we were treated to a peevish, crimson-faced outburst from Andrew.

"We're going to start stopping standing on ceremony *right now!* These are cuts that *I want,* and they're *going in!* So, let's get on with it! And I want your *full* cooperation and no more *farting about,* because, if this show is to run beyond December, it's got to be got right! These cuts could make a *huge* difference! *Come on,* everyone! We must *pull together* and make it work!"

Andrew is clearly exasperated beyond measure. However, his problem is simple but tricky. To command respect and inspire obedience in your troops, you need the charisma of a compelling field marshal. So far, Andrew has seemed to be a very self-protective, shy, diffident soul. Today, he blustered like a petulant Sunday school choirmaster act demanding our obedience. It only looked unconvincing and was merely a bit embarrassing. And this was when his credibility hit rock bottom.

"It's been a difficult time for everyone, but *especially me!* I even had to cut my holiday *short* to come back here to do this!"

Our hearts bled for him. Didn't Ryanair give him a refund on his last-minute cheap deal offer? Andrew spoke as if the show's problems and faults are entirely due to the ensemble being an idle, bloody-minded lot, and that everything would be fine and dandy if only us lazy riff-raff pulled up our jolly-old socks.

Okay, here's the thing. Since the opening night, we have been battling with indisposed actors, a temperamental computer, scenery that keeps jamming, constantly altered moves, endless understudy rehearsals, tiresome Equity meetings and, worst of all, no director. And all this, while Sir Andrew has been relaxing in a luxurious first-class hotel somewhere on a sunny beach.

"Where is Trevor?" I asked one of the company. "We need him to oversee these changes that Andrew's made."

"After we opened, Trevor went off to Cornwall for a ten-day holiday, returned very briefly to London, then flew straight over to the States to cast the L.A. production of *Sunset Boulevard*."

And this comment has been voiced more than once by the cast: "It's called take the money and run."

To my knowledge, Trevor hasn't seen one performance since the first night three weeks ago, and nor has Bob Avian, our choreographer, who also fled the country.

Andrew's testy short, back and sides trim in Artie's party removed half my cabaret material, including yelling, "See this amazing motion picture! Coming soon to a screen near you!" And good riddance to the lot.

Likewise, Patti was delighted when Andrew axed her take-off of Charlie Chaplin in "The Lady's Paying". In the original movie, Gloria Swanson's routine had the luxury of quickly edited shots, but for Patti it's exhausting, and for the audience as hilarious as an ingrowing toenail.

Andrew also trimmed "Boy Meets Girl", the romantic slow duet Kevin and Meredith perform in Schwab's Drug Store. They sang it very beautifully but it seemed to drag on longer than *Tristan and Isolde.*

5:35 p.m.

As I left the stage door, I bumped into Anthony Powell, our costume designer. He said, "Your choreographer, Bob Avian, rang me from California. He's busy with Trevor holding auditions for the L.A. production. Bob's verdict is, 'They're all dogs.'"

"That surprises me," I said. "The word 'dog' is American slang for an unattractive woman, isn't it?"

"Exactly."

"But I thought California was supposed to be the land of glamorous Hollywood peaches."

"Apparently not, according to Bob. How is the show going?"

"To be honest, Anthony, we need Trevor's vigilant eye on this production. There's so much buggering about and sharing of private jokes amongst the young ensemble, you wouldn't believe it. Some of them behave as if working in a major West End production is beneath their dignity. People sitting in the front stalls can clearly see them exchanging silly smirks and comments and giggling. Trevor's assistant, Andrew McBean, seems completely unaware of it. Trevor should secretly come in, watch the ensemble numbers, then crack the whip and give detailed notes."

Chapter 8

AUGUST 1993

MONDAY 2nd August 1993

7:20 p.m. Adelphi Theatre

Trevor spoke to the company over the Tannoy just before the show began. It made me wonder if Anthony Powell had relayed to Trevor my comments last Friday about some of the ensemble's ill-disciplined behaviour.

Trevor: "Hello company. This is Trevor speaking. I have—"

Pippa: "Ladies and gentlemen, this is your beginners' call for Act One, your beginners' call for Act One."

Having been absent for two weeks, Trev was cut off in mid "hello". But he wasn't going to let a little thing like a beginners' call stop him. He soldiered on, but most of us were running down the stairs, checking our bits and pieces on the prop tables, hanging up costumes in the wings for quick changes and getting to our opening positions.

"As I was trying to say, I have been informed that a number of cuts have been inserted which I was not here to organise personally. I've never been in this situation before. I shall be seeing the cuts tonight and will decide how best to deal with them."

We were astonished that Sir Andrew hadn't given Trevor a list of his cuts he put in the show on Friday. Hence, one of the jokes doing the rounds…

"Why is working for this company like being a mushroom?"

"Because they keep you in the dark and throw shit at you."

9:40 p.m.

After the show, another message from Trevor over the Tannoy as we were all changing and leaving. He referred to Sir Andrew's cuts as "amputations, some of which are bleeding." He then added, "I might call a rehearsal later in the week to adjust these cuts."

"Oh, for crying out loud!" was the collective reaction from the dressing rooms, the stairs and the corridors.

TUESDAY 10th August 1993

2:30 p.m. Adelphi Theatre

Cuts with Trevor. What in the name of hell is going on?

Okay. Last Friday, Andrew put in his cuts. Today, Monday, Trevor has *altered them* and put in *other* cuts. But he didn't stay to watch the show this evening. Where does Trev go? And what's the point of making changes if he doesn't watch them in performance to be sure they work?

SATURDAY 14th August 1993

Tonight, Harry Ditson sprayed shaving foam inside the three harem girls' brassieres. Anita, Sasha and Dawn were not amused. They have to put on these bras super fast in their quick change during the opening scene.

Saturday nights are hell.

MONDAY 16th August 1993

4:30 p.m. Adelphi Theatre

As I hoped, Trevor called us in to re-rehearse scenes and to make other alterations. He has restyled the curtain call, made it about fifteen seconds shorter – an improvement.

He also restored the original company sweep downstage. This means that the show ends, the curtain falls and the audience applauds. When the tabs rise again, all the scenery has gone. The actors are standing upstage in a long line facing the audience. We then hold hands and march down in one sweep to the footlights, à la the Royal Shakespeare Company. It has terrific élan and panache! However…

9:45 p.m.

… This evening's curtain calls were buggered up by the computer which left Norma Desmond's house stuck onstage, so we resorted to the *original* curtain calls with the cast standing on the staircase, etc. Lorks love a duck! What a shambolic carry on.

TUESDAY 17th August 1993

7:40 p.m. Adelphi Theatre

Tonight, we were ten minutes late going up because Patti was in a state. She gets Variety, the American showbiz paper. It quoted Sir Andrew saying that he is "looking for a star" to play Norma Desmond next year in the Broadway production of *Sunset Boulevard*.

Patti hit the roof and called David White our conductor to her dressing room to tell him how upset and angry she feels. I suspect there will be more of this to come. A whole lot more.

THURSDAY 19th August 1993

6:40 p.m. Adelphi Theatre

After the matinee, we were warned by stage management over the Tannoy that an intruder was roaming around backstage. I think I saw him walk down the aisle in the stalls and then use the pass door. I assumed he was an electrician.

When Patti and I talked about this, she said, "He tried to kiss me!"

I went to all the dressing rooms delivering copies of Equity's information sheet. As I approached Anita Louise Combe's room, I was about to tap on her door when I noticed it was ajar.

I said, "Hello?" and peeped inside.

Anita was sitting at her dressing table, but facing me. She was smiling, naked from the waist down. Her knees were wide apart and she was plucking her pubes with tweezers. Removing grey ones? Hoping to shock me? I guess it pays to advertise but it wasn't anything I hadn't seen before.

For customers who like that job done professionally, I'm told there's an upstairs shop in Soho called "Pluck My Snatch" if they don't mind a few rats scuttling about. Anita's private(s) exhibition was definitely for my benefit. People often say my erotic allure drives them insane.

FRIDAY 20th August 1993

9:45 p.m. Adelphi Theatre

After tonight's performance, there was no water at all in our dressing rooms – for showering, washing or even *flushing the toilets!* Who said showbiz isn't glamorous?

SATURDAY 21st August 1993

8:30 p.m. Adelphi Theatre

This evening, some of the younger ensemble playing gentlemen's outfitters in "The Lady's Paying" went onstage with the front of their wigs pulled into kiss curls and quiffs. They thought it was funny.

SUNDAY 29th August 1993

Drove down to Kingston Vale to have lunch with Margaret Johnstone.

Maggie became a dear friend of mine in 1978 when my partner Paul Hardwick was in a play with Ingrid Bergman at the Haymarket Theatre, London. Ingrid loved giving dinner parties and Maggie was Ingrid's caterer.

Ingrid died in 1982 on her sixty-seventh birthday, exactly eleven years ago today. After lunch, Maggie and I toasted Ingrid with a loving cup of coffee.

Later, I took flowers to the Swedish Church to celebrate her cherished memory.

I shall never forget the first time I drove Ingrid in my little white Mini. Paulie and I had invited her to lunch.

Afterwards, Paul said, "You don't need to order a cab. Petey will drive you back to your hotel."

If my car insurance company knew my passenger was a winner of three Oscars, a Tony Award, two Emmy Awards, four Golden Globe Awards and a Bafta Award, they would have raised their eyebrows – as well as my insurance policy premium. Was I tense? I gripped the steering wheel as if I were dangling from a skyscraper's top floor window ledge.

As I drove along Abbey Road, Ingrid laughed. "That's how I like my driving!" she declared. "Straight through a red light on the wrong side of the road!"

TUESDAY 31st August 1993

5:50 p.m. Adelphi Theatre

At exactly one hour and forty minutes before curtain-up, Alisa was rung at home by Richard Oriel (company manager).

"Sorry it's so late, Alisa, but Patti isn't well. She's seen the doctor and he said she has tonsillitis and won't be able to perform tonight. I know you're Patti's second cover but the problem is her first cover, Carol Duffy, left the country two days ago on a pre-booked holiday. And so, Alisa – you're playing Norma Desmond tonight!"

Alisa's preparatory work and professionalism paid off magnificently. She was word and note perfect throughout the entire massive leading role. And costume perfect! At her insistence, all her hats, shoes, wigs and immaculately tailored clothes were completely organised. Equally important, she had rehearsed each one of her warp-speed quick changes; they all went without a hitch.

She is about twenty years too young for the role of Norma Desmond but her performance transcended that factor triumphantly. Although the pre-show announcement about Patti's absence triggered groans of disappointment from the audience, when Elisa took her curtain calls, she received a richly-deserved loud standing ovation. Brava, Elisa!

THURSDAY 2nd September 1993

3 p.m. Adelphi Theatre

Patti is still off with tonsillitis. Again, Alisa was excellent.

5:15 p.m.

Tea with Alisa. She is great company, very funny and cute as a button. Although she is playing this huge lead and barely off the stage for two and a half hours, she carries the responsibility very lightly on her young shoulders.

"Patti has very kindly allowed me to use her dressing room. She also arranged for Murray Lane, her dresser, to move all Patti's make-up and personal stuff on her dressing table to one side for me."

7:45 p.m.

During tonight's show, the scenery broke down. Our computer that takes no prisoners decided it would be fun to shove Sheldrake's office set straight downstage underneath Norma Desmond's flight of stairs. It didn't quite fit. The show stopped.

There was the usual apology spoken to the audience over the loudspeakers, followed by a fifteen-minute wait…

We restarted the show from Norma's call from her window.

"Hey! You down there! Why are you so late?" Alisa's line was rewarded with terrific laughter and applause from the audience.

FRIDAY 3rd September 1993

Adelphi Theatre

Patti has returned – in great voice.

FRIDAY 17th September 1993

Adelphi Theatre

Now Kevin's voice is going…

SATURDAY 18th September 1993

Adelphi Theatre

Kevin was off both shows with a throat infection. Gerard Casey played Joe Gillis and he did splendidly well.

TUESDAY 28th September 1993

9:50 p.m.

A call over the Tannoy: "Message for Peter Gale. Please go to Kevin Anderson's dressing room to meet a guest."

It was David Warbeck, the fifty-one-year-old New Zealand born actor. David generously hosts great parties at his beautiful turreted house near Primrose Hill; its local name is the Convent.

David once said to me, "Twenty years ago, I was reasonably handsome and made a pile of money starring in awful Italian horror movies. They paid for this house!"

Those films included *The Razor Blade Smile* and *Twins of Evil*, in which he played a vampire killer called Anton who stabs a Satan worshipper through the heart with a spear. Another film he was in was *Trog*.

David said, "We made *Trog* in Britain. It starred the Hollywood actress Joan Crawford. She was drinking neat vodka all day. The plot was about a very unhappy cave dweller, a missing link troglodyte with dreadful teeth. Not played by Joan. One film reviewer film said, 'So cheap and silly, it is the stuff of legend.' I cried all the way to the bank. It was impossible to turn down those rotten films. They paid for this house! Not many people can claim that they've appeared in a movie described as 'One of the Best 23 Zombie Films of All Time'. Another film guide placed *Trog* amongst 'The 100 Most Enjoyably Bad Movies Ever Made'."

When David was a dashing thirty-one-year-old, he was short-listed for the 1973 James Bond film *Live and Let Die*; it went to Roger Moore.

Tonight, as I talked to David, I was shocked to see how ill he looked. My first thought was AIDS. Several actor friends of mine died of that dreadful disease, including Gary Bond, a fellow drama student, and Geoffrey Burridge, who was Alec McCowan's spouse. Dear Geoffrey appeared with me in the Noel Coward revue, *Cowardy Custard* at the Mermaid Theatre.

I later asked Kevin, "Is David Warbeck all right? He looks awful, poor guy."

Kevin replied, "He's ill. He's having treatment for cancer."

Author's note: Very sadly, David died four years later, aged fifty-six.

THURSDAY 30th September 1993

9:20 a.m. Local Doctor's Surgery

An appointment with Dr Mendel. My throat feels rough.

5:30 p.m.

And then a double treat for Pete! A delicious supper with Sarah Whiting, my favourite assistant stage manager, in my favourite vegetarian restaurant, Cranks in Carnaby Street.

We met working together on a 1977 musical called *Maggie* at the Shaftesbury Theatre. I was the show's leading man. Sarah is very good for my ego.

"You are *still* a star!" she insists, in spite of my humble status in *Sunset.*

FRIDAY 1st October 1993

1:30 p.m. Adelphi Theatre, Photo Call

I am going stir crazy. I'm never out of this frigging building: doing eight shows a week, holding Equity meetings, attending understudy rehearsals and this afternoon we've a company photo call then two shows.

4:50 p.m. Royal Academy of Arts

After the matinee, I bathed in the consolation of art.

I took Sandy Strallen (a fellow ensemble and our dance captain) to see "American Art in the 20th Century" at the R.A. It was full of wonderful paintings, photos and sculptures from 1913 to 1993 – de Kooning, Pollock and Calder. My fave rave is Edward Hopper, who is to painting what Chekhov is to theatre – a champion of obscure, uncelebrated souls.

In *Automat,* a young woman sits alone at a cafe table with a cup of coffee. It appears innocuous but could be a disturbing moment from a Hitchcock film. Why is she alone? Who is she waiting for? Something's afoot!

Meanwhile, back at the Adelphi more excitement…

9:50 p.m.

Today is Harry Ditson's birthday – or buffday!

Seven weeks ago, as a practical joke, Harry put shaving foam in the three harem girls' bras which they quickly put on during the opening scene.

After tonight's show, some of the wilder ensemble gals took

their revenge on Harry's prank. They grabbed him in the corridor, took off his trousers, tied him up and left him dangling from a coat hook on the wall. Oh Harry. Hoist by your own bra strap. You mess with an ensemble gal's lifts-and-separates at your peril.

SATURDAY 16th October 1993

Adelphi Theatre

Richard Oriel, our company manager, gave me a copy of an alarming fax he sent to Harry Dagnall, who is the Adelphi Theatre company administrator.   Richard's fax says: "The recent thefts from the dressing rooms show no sign of abating."

The stolen items included the following:

From Patti's room: bottles of Coke, brandy and a fan heater.

From Adam Matalon's dressing table: whisky drunk from a bottle.

From Harry Ditson's dressing room cupboard: sizeable amounts of bourbon.

From Daniel Benzali's dressing room: almost a whole bottle of Courvoisier has been drunk.

From Liz Greenaway's room: cigarettes have been stolen and a bottle of lavender oil knocked over.

His fax adds that numerous other items "have disappeared in the past: Adam Matalon's watch, items of make-up, fresh fruit and show fruit from the stage management office."

The poor cleaners are the chief suspects but it's more likely to be the same mysterious stranger I saw two months ago roaming about backstage. I wrongly assumed he was an electrician.

SUNDAY 17th October 1993

11 a.m. Theatre Museum

I directed a script-held reading of Bernard Shaw's 1892 play *Widowers' Houses* for Tanya Frank's company, Stock-pot Productions.

5:30 p.m.

It went well. Shaw's first play is a marvellous attack on the exploitation of poor people by ruthless slum landlords. It also shows how some high-minded idealists choose to turn a conveniently blind eye. The play deserves to be revived.

Les Dennis played Lickcheese, the rent collector, Frederick Pyne played Sartorius and Tanya played Blanche. What a joy to work on such a marvellous piece of writing!

Les is thirty-nine years old and his background has been mainly as a comedian on TV. He was extremely agreeable to work with and he proved himself a highly accomplished actor.

FRIDAY 22nd October 1993

My Paulie died exactly ten years ago. Each day a happy memory of him sooner or later pops into my head. Yes, I'm sure he's watching from above, divinely bored with my grief and wanting me to do what Joan Rivers the tough-talking American comic advised in her gravelly tones, "Get over it. Get on with it." Easier said than done.

Chapter 9

NOVEMBER 1993

SUNDAY 21st November 1993

Feel lousy. Flu symptoms – I'm hot, headachy, weak and sporting a cold sore on my upper lip. Attractive. Maybe just a bit under the weather?

WEDNESDAY 24th November 1993

10:15 a.m. Royal Free Hospital

I am off the show.

After three days running a temperature, I bit the bullet. Hauled myself into A&E at the Royal Free in Hampstead. Just getting there this morning was a major achievement.

Doctors always say the same thing to actors: "Take aspirin, drink plenty of water and rest for the next two days." Very sensible advice but they've no idea how we are expected to soldier on.

I can barely stand, let alone climb up and down those eighty-four steps to our top floor dressing room. And as for sharing the stage with so much hyperactive scenery trundling about! It's like being inside a crazy robot's brain while it hallucinates on drugs.

1:30 p.m.

Arriving home from the doctor, I rang Richard, our company manager. I explained that I can't work tonight. He was kind and sympathetic.

"I do hope you feel better very soon, Peter."

Collapsed on the sofa all day – feverish and washed out.

THURSDAY 25th November 1993

10:45 a.m.

Well, surprise-surprise. After missing just one show last night, guess who phones? Yes, Richard.

"I know you're not well, Peter, but we have a very difficult situation here. I'd greatly appreciate it if you could possibly come in today and do the matinee and evening performances."

"Oh Richard. Please. I'm in a shocking state. Honestly. I'm so weak and dizzy I can barely stand, never mind do two shows. I'm not swinging the lead. You know me; I'm never off."

Coughing and wheezing, I pleaded my pitiful case but as Shakespeare would say: 'twas fruitless. Nay, bootless! Alack the day, my masters.

"I'm really sorry to do this to you, Peter, but here's my problem. I promised Sandy Strallen ages ago that he could be released today to drive up to Birmingham and direct his industrial show. It's a crucially important commitment for him; a big deal."

"Yes, I see, but… Why me? Can't you ask someone else?"

"That's the snag. Several other members of the ensemble are off as well. They've gone abroad on their official holidays. In fact, today's date was written into their contracts. They've pre-booked their flights. So, if you are absent as well, Peter, I won't be able to let Sandy go, otherwise there'll be hardly any male ensemble in the company scenes at all! Only about five!"

Sandy runs an outfit that puts on "industrials". They resemble a TV commercial but each one is like an hour-long musical, often performed in the big dining room of a posh hotel where a temporary stage is built for the actors, singers and dancers to put over specially composed production numbers. The star of the show is often a celebrity who is paid serious dosh. The invited audience might be managers of shops that sell household goods, or clothes, or foreign holidays, etc.

After a slap-up meal, the audience stay at their tables and watch the show which praises the virtues of a specific company's terrific product. This could be gardening equipment, floor carpets – even domestic lavatory cleaners, for all I know.

"Okay," I said to Richard, "I'll come in and do the show tonight."

Then Sandy rang me. I could hardly get off the sofa to answer.

"Thanks, Petey. I promise you on my word of honour that I shall donate my director's fee to a charity of your choice."

"No, Sandy. You mustn't. I wouldn't dream of such a thing. You have a family to support." His three lovely daughters, Scarlett, Summer and Zizi Strallen, all hope to carve showbiz careers, so Sandy needs every extra penny he can get. Besides that, his intelligence, professionalism and sense of humour are a blessing and a daily tonic to my jaded spirits. He helps me to keep sane inside *Sunset's* mind-mangling loony bin and some of its undisciplined, unprofessional, egotistical, selfish, greedy, grumbling, giggling, moaning, moustache-thieving and farting inmates.

SUNDAY 28th November 1993

12:30 p.m. A Lunch Party

I am a scientific miracle. Woke up this morning feeling chirpy enough to attend a buffet lunch in Putney! Actors talk of Doctor Theatre. It echoes an Ancient Roman proverb, "By walking you shall be cured." In other words, as long as you aren't gravely ill, it can be more therapeutic to get up and do the best you can rather than languish on a sickbed. I suffered no serious damage after Thursday's two shows.

The lunch party was given by two dear friends of mine: Rodney Bennett, the TV and film director, and his wife Jill, the children's book illustrator. She was the first artist to work with the author Roald Dahl. Jill drew delightful pictures for his book *Fantastic Mr Fox*. I've bought a splendid print of rascally Mr Fox smiling wickedly as he bursts into a hen house, raising a flurry of frenzied feathers.

Rodders (as Jill calls Rodney) has directed me in six film and TV productions, including BBC's 1980 TV *Hamlet* starring Derek Jacobi. I played Osric, and in 1991, I was Mr Shell, a petty official tax inspector, in Yorkshire TV's series *The Darling Buds of May*, based on H. E. Bates' novel, starring Catherine Zeta Jones as the irresistibly lovely Marietta Larkin.

A while ago, Rodney asked me how rehearsals were going for some play.

"Well, fine," I said. "But there's a problem."

Rodney smiled sympathetically. "Peter, there's always a problem."

I thought, *There speaks the voice of experience.*

Chapter 10

DECEMBER 1993

WEDNESDAY 22nd December 1993

4:50 p.m. Doctor's Surgery

Three days of cough-cough-cough. My local doctor has diagnosed asthma and given me a squirty inhaler thingy. I am now an officially registered asthmatic. What a lovely Christmas present!

As a child, I had bronchitis and I dread it's making a ghastly comeback. Could the cause be working at the Adelphi Theatre? As you look at the audience, you see countless dust particles swirling in the air.

FRIDAY 31st December 1993 – New Year's Eve

Alisa Endsley and I have become good chums. She slept with me last night. Dear reader, don't get excited. Alisa is doing ensemble and understudy in *Sunset* like wot I am.

Yesterday, I galloped to her rescue. She is distraught, poor soul. Her husband, thirty-seven-year-old Mark McKerracher, is playing the title role in *Phantom of the Opera* in Manchester.

Last night, Alisa said, "I've just discovered he's having an affair with one of the chorus girls."

Apparently, it often happens to the actor who plays Phantom. More than one marriage has hit the buffers because a cute little ballet dancer in the haunted Paris Opera bewitched and bedded its Phantom.

"Alisa, you can't be alone on New Year's Eve," I said. "I insist you come home with me and we'll welcome the damn thing in together! You can have my double bed. I'll sleep downstairs in the kitchen on the new Japanese futon I've bought!"

Sleep? I didn't get a wink of shut-eye. I might as well have been lying on a slab of concrete. That was the first time I used it and definitely the last. Why are futons so trendy? The deep, relaxing pleasure will come in the Oxfam shop as I wave it a fond farewell *sayonara*.

SATURDAY 1st January 1994 – New Year's Day!

Alisa and I were delightfully cheered up by my sixty-one-year-old neighbour Jill, who kindly invited us into her lovely flat to toast in the New Year with a bottle of champagne.

On Big Ben's midnight *bong*, we three raised our glasses to 1994!

As we chatted, I said, "Jill, you must tell Alisa about your interesting show business connections."

"I'm retired now, Alisa, but in the 1960s and 70s I worked as a typist for an agency called Scripts Inc. It was run by an actor called Victor Maddern. Peter said he's heard of him."

"Oh, when I was growing up, he was never off the box. He popped up in all kinds of TV comedies and dramas. But he also set up a script-printing business and Jill typed manuscripts for a lot of his famous clients."

"I did. I took their scribbled originals and gave them a professional look. There was Antony Shaffer; he wrote the play *Sleuth*, a funny chiller-thriller. And his brother Peter Shaffer; his play *Equus* was filmed and nominated for several Academy Awards. I did *Noises Off* too, for Michael Frayn. And they all said the same thing. 'Can you have it ready for me by tomorrow, please? Yesterday, if possible.' Of course, this was long before word processors. They made us lot redundant. Now, authors can run off neat-looking copies of their own manuscripts at the press of a button."

"Did you type any musicals, Jill?" Alisa asked.

"Yes. I did two shows for Leslie Bricusse and Anthony Newley. Big hits. You might have heard of them: *Stop the World – I Want to Get Off* and *The Roar of the Greasepaint – The Smell of the Crowd*."

"Oh yes, of course. They transferred to New York."

"Jill also typed for a weird English comic genius, Spike Milligan. He wrote and performed in a BBC radio comedy series called *The Goon Show*. His crazy jokes saved my tormented teenage sanity. He was once asked, 'How long were you in the army?' He said, 'Five foot eleven.' But you've never told me, Jill; what was Spike Milligan like to work for?"

"Dreadful. Could be polite, but was moody, and kept drawing lavatories in the margins of his pages, which wasn't very helpful. I also typed novels for Barbara Taylor Bradford. Plays for Harold Pinter, including *Landscape* and *Betrayal*. Harold was great fun and relaxed, until he met Antonia Frazer. Then he went all posh and pompous. I typed *Up the Junction* for Nell Dunn. That became a film directed by Ken Loach. I also did films for Philip Saville; he was Diana Rigg's partner for a few years. And for Robert Bolt I typed his play *A Man for All Seasons,* and his film, *Ryan's Daughter*."

I said, "Jill also typed *Lawrence of Arabia* for the film director David Lean."

"I did several versions of that; it won an Academy Award. And novels for the Irish author Edna O'Brien; a very lovely lady to work for, beautifully spoken. What else? I typed *Confessions of an Actor*, Sir Laurence Olivier's autobiography." Jill smiled coyly. "He was extremely charming. And there was Joan Collins, her autobiography as well. I greatly admire Joan and we're still in touch. She says I'm the only person who can read her handwriting."

"Good Lord!" I said. "I do envy you knowing Joan Collins. She's a total delight in TV interviews. A friend of mine, the actress Jean Marsh, said to me that Joan Collins is one of the most beautiful women she's ever met."

"She really is. Her facial bone structure is perfect."

Alisa said, "She's very famous in America for playing Alexis Carrington in *Dynasty* on TV."

Jill then dropped another name. "And I also worked for Tom Stoppard. He's been a frequent visitor here in my flat. I typed out several versions of the script Tom wrote for the Steven Spielberg film, *The Empire of the Sun*."

"What?" I exclaimed. "You typed that as well, Jill? I can't believe my ears. Alisa, I played Mr Victor in that movie, seven years ago. And Jill lives only two doors away from me! What are the chances of that?"

THURSDAY 17th February 1994

7 p.m.

Tannoy: "This is a message for Peter Gale. Please go to Patti's dressing room. She wants to speak to the company Equity representative."

Poor Patti was beside herself, shaking, tears pouring down her cheeks. Between gasps and sniffs, she said, "Peter, the Really Useful Group have broken the terms of my contract. They have betrayed me! They promised me that I would create the role of Norma Desmond in London, New York and San Francisco. But friends of mine who live in New York have just rung me and said they've read a press announcement in the New York Times saying Glenn Close will play Norma when *Sunset Boulevard* opens on Broadway, and then in San Francisco. This management has betrayed me! I feel completely humiliated!"

I could barely take in what Patti was saying. Clearly, something has gone seriously wrong between Andrew Lloyd Webber and Patti. But what? They are old working colleagues. She was the original Evita in his musical *Evita* on Broadway. Sacking her so brutally will cause her great distress and the bad publicity might harm her professional status. Patti's wholehearted commitment to her work is very impressive. She takes it one hundred percent seriously, and that passion fuels her raw emotion in front of an audience. Have the mixed reviews for her performance and the poor bookings soured her relationship with Sir Andrew?

I noticed Patti's husband Matthew was in the room, leaning with his back against the wall, unable to give her practical help or advice any more than I could. As the humble Equity representative, I suddenly felt plunged fathoms out of my depths in shark-infested waters. This private, contractual dispute that can only be sorted out between Sir Andrew's production company, Patti's agent and, presumably, both their lawyers. There was only one way that I could think of helping Patti.

"I completely understand how you must be feeling and I'm shocked to hear Andrew's company has treated you so appallingly. Speaking as your Equity rep, this complex matter will probably take some time to be resolved. Meanwhile, you can't possibly perform tonight, Patti, so I suggest the best thing would be for you to go home. I'll tell the company manager that your understudy, Alisa, will have to go on this evening."

As Patti began to remove her make-up, I reeled out of that room. It's bizarre. Andrew knows he can't just tear up his contract with Patti and walk away. Her lawyers are bound to come chasing after him waving lawsuit papers citing breach of contract. It's bizarre. Oh boy.

7:15 p.m.

At fifteen minutes to curtain-up, Patti left the theatre in emotional shreds, sobbing. And again, dear Alisa – with practically no warning – played the leading role of Norma Desmond. And again, she received a terrific ovation.

In three weeks' time, the first year of *Sunset Boulevard* ends. After only a three-week re-rehearsal gap *Sunset* will re-open with several new actors in the cast. I wonder if Sir Andrew has prepared for this and already engaged another actress to take over the role of Norma Desmond?

FRIDAY 18th February 1994

11:15 a.m. Adelphi Theatre

I auditioned to take over the role of Cecil B. DeMille if Michael Bauer leaves the show. As I walked onto the stage, I smiled and said, "Hello".

Trevor and *Sunset*'s production team were sitting in the stalls. No reply. I noticed Andrew Lloyd Webber wandering about aimlessly in the back row. No welcome from him either. I wasn't sure what to do next.

The pianist began to play my audition number. I sang it. No response.

Then I did my two audition speeches. Again, no response.

A muted "Thank you" came from someone. I walked off. Not the best house I ever played to.

I've a strange feeling they've serious reservations about my suitability for DeMille. If that's the case, why aren't they sharing?

1 p.m. Home

Mark Piper rang me. He runs the Theatre Royal at Windsor.

"Peter, I know you're busy but we'd like to offer you a little job. We're presenting a one-off show called *60 Years of Musicals*, an evening of selected songs from musicals performed here since the 1930s, with numbers like 'I Could've Danced All Night' from *My Fair Lady* and 'Memory' from *Cats*. We'd also like you to be its master of ceremonies. It's going to be on Sunday, April 3rd. Would you be free to do it? Rehearsals at 2 p.m., the show at 8 p.m. And it would be splendid if you would sing a couple of songs. What about 'We Said We Wouldn't Look Back' from Sandy Wilson's *Salad Days*? According to our records, the leading role of Timothy was your first appearance here in 1967. Twenty-six years ago."

"Good heavens, Mark. So it was. Yes, I was twenty-something!"

"Our musical director is Tom Wakely. Helen Hobson and Graham Bickley will be your co-artists, both West End stars. Helen appeared in Andrew Lloyd Webber's musical, *Aspects of Love*, and Graham was in the original production of *Miss Saigon* at Drury Lane. We also have a local boy, Eddie Redmayne. He could sing 'Memory' from Lloyd Webber's *Cats*, and 'Where Is Love' from Lionel Bart's musical *Oliver*. Eddie could partner Helen in the charming duet from that show: 'I'd Do Anything for You'. Eddie is very young; only twelve years old, but extremely good. Would you be free to do it?"

"Oh yes, thank you. It sounds like a wonderful idea."

9:40 p.m.

Got home and stupidly drank a whole bottle of red wine with my supper.

My inner voice said: "It's getting to be a habit, Peter. Better watch it."

MONDAY 21st February 1994

It's a notoriously slippery slope, drinking alone of an evening after work so I'm putting myself on a strict wine-watch from now on.

I rang my agent, Roberta Kanal, about a second year in *Sunset*.

"Yes, Peter, I understand your mixed feelings about it. When I spoke to RUG's general manager he said, 'Unfortunately, we can't offer Peter the role of DeMille, but will he stay if we pay him £25 a week more?'"

I couldn't believe my ears. "Roberta, that's got to be a joke. A £25 rise? For a major production in the West End? Three fifty a week? It's appalling. They've got to be kidding."

"Yes, I'm not surprised to hear you say that. To be honest, my reaction was similar but, of course, in our discussions I used more diplomatic terms. What I suggest for the moment, Peter, is that you think this over and let me know later. There's no rush right now."

My gut feeling is to make RUG wait. Then tell them to stick it.

No wine tonight.

TUESDAY 22nd February 1994

Johnathan Brown rang, the Theatre Royal Windsor's general manager. He offered me £400 for their *60 Years* show on April 3rd. It means a massive amount of research, writing the script, narrating the show and learning and performing numbers. But I shall definitely do it. A labour of love.

Drank half a bottle of wine.

My inner voice said to me, "Peter, I thought you were going to stop…"

I said, "Just shut up."

WEDNESDAY 23rd February 1994

I rang my agent.

"Please say no to RUG's latest miserly offer of £350 a week."

Now, let's wait and see.

Then I had a really brilliant idea. "Come on, Pete! Get drunk! Crack open a bottle. That'll show RUG and their crap offer."

THURSDAY 24th February 1994

And like crap is how I feel this morning.

My inner voice said, "You've got a lot on your plate, Pete. Like it or not, no more drinking wine at night."

MONDAY 28th February 1994

11:30 a.m. Theatre Royal, Windsor. Johnathan Brown's Office
I designed and had printed a hundred leaflets for *60 Years of Musicals*.

Drove to Windsor and took them into Johnathan Brown's office. He'll set them out in the theatre foyer and have them distributed.

I phoned Andrew McBean, Trev's assistant and described the piddling salary rise RUG have offered me for a second year in

Sunset.

"An extra £25 a week! Honestly, Andrew. It beggars belief. That's the same money they're paying kids in the ensemble who are straight out of drama college! And after all the effort I've put into *Sunset* over this past year – as an actor, understudy, Equity deputy, company liaison officer and goodwill RUG ambassador. It's unacceptably stingy, and a depressing, bare-faced insult to someone of my experience."

Andrew said, "Peter, I agree with you. It is shocking. I shall tell Trevor about RUG's proposed contractual terms. Believe me; Trevor will be very angry on your behalf."

No wine. Feel better. But, Pete, do *not* lapse!

Chapter 11

MARCH 1994

TUESDAY 1st March 1994

Andrew McBean called me. "Peter, I spoke to Trevor about the new salary offer you've had from RUG. Your phone will ring tomorrow at 4 p.m. They will make you a better offer."

No wine.

WEDNESDAY 2nd March 1994

5:30 p.m.

4 p.m. came and went and no word of any kind from RUG. It's like trying to communicate with a dense fog. I must get out!

My mate Stephanie Cole rang me to see how things were going. "I do sympathise, Petey. Just to let you know, Ned Sherrin is going to direct me in a revival of a Ben Travers comedy, *A Bed Before Yesterday*. I shall mention your name to Ned for one of the roles. And to our producer, David Pugh, as well."

That was kind of Steph but I shan't hold my breath.

8:30 p.m. Interval

Alisa and I had a Chekhov moment.s

"What's it all about?" I asked her, gazing into the middle distance with inscrutable profundity. "They say it's a great life if you don't weaken – or lose your sense of humour. But in the name of knitted pink knickers, what is our existence on this planet all about?"

It seems Alisa has already grappled with this existential mystery. "Life is ten percent what you are given and ninety percent what you make of it."

No wine.

THURSDAY 3rd March 1994

My agent rang. "RUG would now like to offer you £450 a week."

No wine.

FRIDAY 4th March 1994

I called my agent. "Please say thanks to RUG but no thanks. I'm hugely grateful to *Sunset* for giving my bank balance the kiss of life, but the salary rise they've offered isn't worth the risk to my mental health."

"I shall convey your feelings to them, Peter. Politely but clearly."

So, that's it. I cannot face twelve more months performing these scrappy bits and pieces. I'm an actor. I want to act. I'm going to act.

And I've kicked the nightly booze habit.

MONDAY 7th March 1994

12 p.m.

I posted Trevor a letter wishing him well with his revised production of *Sunset*.

6 p.m. Stage Door, Adelphi Theatre

By coincidence, a letter from Trevor was waiting for me in my mail box. He says he kindly hopes that I will stay on for another year. I feel flattered. But no.

WEDNESDAY 9th March 1994

Roberta called. "Peter, I have spoken again to David Grindrod, RUG's production co-ordinator. He said, 'What does Peter want?' So, I told David that I would ask you. Have you made up your mind?"

"Yes, and after a lot of thought, I've decided I can only face another year doing walk-on and understudy in *Sunset* for at least £700 a week."

"Okay. What I shall do is this – ring David and say you want £750, but indicate that a near offer might be considered."

That sounded fine but, oh God, the thought of another twelve months of repeating my piddling bits and pieces 400 times is nightmarish.

Bronnie's advice keeps re-echoing in my head. "Think positive."

Okay. The good news is that if they agree to pay me £700 a week, I could save about £3,500.

THURSDAY 10th March 1994

RUG have offered me £700 a week starting next Monday. Just

two misgivings remain. I should have had the guts to sack Roberta and renegotiated this new contract myself. It would have saved me paying ten percent agent's commission to her on the terms I demanded and got. But I like Roberta and two years in *Sunset* might give her useful leverage later when she's bigging me up for better roles. Or will it?

When producers mount a show, their first job is usually to find a director. The next port of call is a casting director. That's when *type-casting* can step in. That's my second misgiving and the bane of many a versatile actor's career. Casting directors stick actors in pigeon holes; once a Pompous Bank Manager, always a Pompous Bank Manager. Likewise, once an understudy, always an understudy. Will this lower my status on the showbiz ladder? I guess that's a risk I'll have to take. I badly need this dough, and needs must when the devil drives.

FRIDAY 11th March 1994

I rang Roberta my agent. "Please say yes to RUG's £700 offer."

Meanwhile, in another part of *Sunset*'s weird wood, Patti and Sir Andrew are preparing to do battle. Patti now claims Andrew has broken her contract by engaging Glenn Close to star in the New York production of *Sunset* instead of Patti. She chatted to me during this evening's interval.

"Peter, if Andrew Lloyd Webber joins us at tomorrow night's final curtain call, I shall walk off the stage and I want everyone to follow me."

Her proposal astonished me. I sympathise with Patti but how can she expect us vastly lower-paid actors to take sides with her against Andrew, our employer, composer and notable West End producer? That's one helluva big ask, so I changed the subject. Boats' rowlocks and rowers' bollocks! It's tough at the top.

My exhausted brain is befuddled with these big shots' murky backstage politics. They are like the daft Red Knight and White Knight in *Alice in Wonderland*, preparing to do battle in her freaky forest. Alice says, "Curiouser and curiouser." And I echo her: "Furiouser and furiouser."

SATURDAY 12th March 1994

Sunset's First Year Run Ends

Two months ago, I wrote this in my diary…

Tonight is my last performance in Sunset.

Not quite. Far from leaving the show, I sent Trevor a "thank you" card for helping me get my salary upped to £700 a week. In my thrifty world, 700 smackers is an awesome improvement on £325.

Headline news: "Today Clovis the Cranky computer broke down twice."

The first time was during the matinee. Here's how Clovis waved goodbye before our five-week break. He crossed his arms, narrowed his eyes and said, "My gigabytes are feeling their age. When the show closes, I want some 'me time'. I'm thinking a fortnight's holiday in a five star B&B in Margate. Then a high-tech makeover – new microchips, a massage, and colonic irrigation; the lot. Think about it and call me."

I said to our chief electrician, David Donoghue, "Please threaten Clovis with a pick axe and a one-way ticket to a scrap metal yard."

He said, "I have."

The curtain was lowered and, as the minutes ticked by, Pippa voiced the usual apology to the audience for the hold up over the public address system: "Ladies and gentlemen, please remain seated till the problem is sorted out."

As Patti and I waited behind the front curtain listening to the audience chatting away, I was suddenly reminded of a similar incident.

Seventeen years ago, my partner Paulie and Ingrid Bergman were in a revival of N. C. Hunter's play Waters of the Moon at the Chichester Festival Theatre. In one scene, boarding house guests raise their glasses to toast in the new year singing "Auld Lang Syne" accompanied by someone playing a (dummy) grand piano. On the first night, there was a serious technical hitch. Dame Wendy Hiller ran her fingers over the keys... What came out? A loud silence. The culprit was the offstage tape recorder. It was switched on but it refused to play.

After an awkward pause, Ingrid Bergman turned to the audience. "Ladies and gentlemen, we have a slight technical problem with the piano. If you would wait a few moments, I'm sure we will be able to continue very soon. Thank you."

The audience were delighted. Instead of a tediously baffling hold up, they were treated to a charming apology from the show's famous leading lady.

Here's how they solved the "technical problem". Was the tape recorder switched on? Yes. Was it plugged into the wall? Yes. Was the wall plug switched on? No!

During our hold up today at the Adelphi Theatre, I thought, If Ingrid could do it, so could...

"Patti, why don't you go out onstage and sing the audience a song."

She looked at me, puzzled. "Sing? What song?"

"Not from this show but one you know really well and feel comfortable with. It doesn't matter very much what it is; they'd just love you to sing anything. Otherwise, they'll get the hump and start giving us the deadly slow hand-clap."

Patti considered the idea. She looked at me. "You think I could? On my own? Unaccompanied?"

"Yes, I do. It would be astonishing for them. They'll tell all their friends, 'Norma Desmond came onto the stage, apologised for the delay and then sang a song! Specially for us!'."

A second later, Patti did just that.

Our leading lady walked in front of the curtain to a warm round of applause, apologised sweetly for the hold up, thanked the audience for their patience and then said she would like to sing them a song called "A Hundred Years from Today". She started the number as a solo, but after a moment, our pianist picked up the melody, began to accompany her and very soon the whole orchestra joined in. Patti's charming love song was new to me. I discovered later that it was written in 1933 by Victor Young, Ned Washington and Joe Young, and stars like Frank Sinatra and Dean Martin recorded it.

"The moon is shining, and that's a good sign.

Cling to me closer and say you'll be mine.

Remember, darling, we won't see it shine

A hundred years from today."

As Patti sang, I just hoped our computer wasn't going to take a hundred years to get its act together.

When Patti ended the number, the audience went crazy! They cheered loudly and applauded her off-the-cuff number. Patti thanked them and left the stage to wait with us behind the curtain. The next moment, our stage manager gave Patti the all-clear to continue the performance, having provided our technical team with exactly enough time to fix the problem. Patti calls herself "just a broad". I would say a great broad, and one hell of a trouper.

Tonight was Patti's last performance as Norma Desmond in Sunset Boulevard but she did not leave without making her feelings about being sacked by Sir Andrew very clear.

She (allegedly) completely trashed her dressing room to express her rage. And when Betty Buckley took over the role of Norma Desmond, she (again allegedly) had the room spiritually cleansed, whatever that means. Perhaps it was sprinkled with holy water by a priest.

I once asked a priest in my local church, "Where does the holy water in the font came from?"

He said, "From the kitchen tap."

I was puzzled. "But what makes it holy?"

He said, "Because I have blessed it."

And there was I thinking it was water taken from streams in Jerusalem and shipped here in barrels from the Vatican in Rome.

The second computer failure today happened in the evening show. We were all told to wait in our dressing rooms till it was fixed. While this was going on, a niggling question popped up in my brain's front row seat.

Where is Nadia? I wondered. I can't recall the last time I saw her and have no idea where she's gone or why.

So, I asked one of her ensemble chums.

Their reply amazed me. "She's been let go by RUG."

"She's been what? You mean fired? Are you kidding? When was this?"

"Recently."

"But why wasn't I told? She's my co-Equity dep."

"You'll have to ring Nadia; or ask Richard Oriel."

I went to our company manager's office and had a quick word but Richard was strangely evasive. "It was a private matter, Peter, between her and the Really Useful Group. That's all I'm able to say." And that was it.

I know that RUG employed Nadia in Sunset on probation but people won't tell me the precise reason why she's been sacked. The phrase "pot smoking" cropped up but I've no idea if that was involved. In all theatres, cigarette smoking backstage of any kind is strictly forbidden.

This reminds me of my first theatre acting job. I was thirteen when I played a lost boy in Peter Pan at the Scala Theatre in London in 1954. The Canadian actress Barbara Kelly starred as Peter. I saw "No Smoking" painted on the walls in the wings in huge capital letters; hence the anagram stage name of a popular Victorian music hall artist, Nosmo King.

Today at the Adelphi Theatre, our health and safety inspectors would go nuts if they smelt cigarette smoke backstage. We're surrounded by complex scenery with restless leg syndrome; using any kind of flame to light a snorter could be horribly dangerous and puffing marijuana even lethal. Those pallets constantly slide under our feet, shifting furniture, stairs, walls and doors every which-way. The last thing we need in these pitch-dark wings is an actor swaying about, dazed on whacky baccy, muttering, "Hey, cool, man."

9:40 p.m.

Tonight, *Sunset Boulevard* ended its first year's run. The Adelphi will be dark for the next five weeks.

Well! Surprise-surprise. Tonight, Clovis the Cranky Computer broke down *again*. Yes, he stuck two binary fingers up and went AWOL for fifteen minutes.

Not only that, bizarrely, Nadia, sacked a couple of weeks ago, smuggled herself into the show's last scene to make a farewell appearance as a newspaper reporter. Her chums, who probably helped her, treated it as a big joke. The unprofessional behaviour of some ensemble members is astonishing; their lack of discipline and bare-faced contempt for the audience appalls me. And as if that wasn't enough, this evening a fire alarm went off in the auditorium for no reason whatsoever.

On Monday, we begin rehearsals for the second-year run. There are cast changes. Both Patti and Kevin will leave. Betty Buckley, a forty-six-year-old Texan actress, will play Norma Desmond, and John Barrowman, a twenty-seven-year-old Scottish born actor, will be Joe Gillis. John's American accent is authentic because, although he was born in Glasgow, his family emigrated to a town near Chicago when he was eight.

New ensemble artists joining us include Alasdair Harvey, Kim Ismay, Larissa Murray and Laurie Cartier Rose.

The prospect of repeating my humble walk-on scraps in *Sunset* another four hundred times is pretty daunting. Day after day, the same tube journeys, the same chorus numbers in the same unrewarding walk-on roles, the same gestures, the same moves, the same costume changes, week after week... But that's my choice.

Weirdly, I am reminded of the film *Groundhog Day*, about an arrogant TV weatherman who is doomed to wake up every morning on the same day again and again as a punishment for his bad behaviour. That plot rings a faintly familiar bell, but what did I do wrong?

SUNDAY 13th March 1994

This morning, I was rung by Mark Piper, the theatre manager at Windsor's Theatre Royal. I had been asked to write and present a one-off entertainment called *60 Years of Musicals*, starring Graham

Bickley and Helen Robson. It's going to be performed there on a Sunday in three weeks.

We'll have to stage it simply. We only have the afternoon to rehearse that evening's programme of songs. It's to celebrate the memory of John Counsell OBE who ran the theatre for forty-eight years (1938 to 1986), but it's also a tribute to his wife the splendid actress Mary Kerridge who will be the guest of honour. Mary was John's co-theatre manager and leading lady. Their achievement was astonishing. They ran the Theatre Royal with no local grant or government subsidy at all. John retired in 1987 and sadly died soon afterwards.

I was born and grew up nearby in Slough and as an adult appeared in some twenty-five productions at Windsor, including pantos, light comedies, musicals and plays by George Farquhar, Bernard Shaw, Oscar Wilde, Agathe Christie and Noel Coward. I've written a rough draft of my narration linking all the show's numbers. Now I must phone Helen and Graham to find out which songs they will sing.

MONDAY 14th March 1994

10:30 a.m. Royalty Theatre

Trevor is directing a revised version of *Sunset Boulevard*.

For the next two weeks, we rehearse here at the Royalty or at the BBC Acton Rehearsal Rooms.

THURSDAY 24th March 1994

11 a.m. to 1 p.m. St. Martin-in-the-Fields Church

Today, I took part in a memorial programme for the American actor Kenneth Nelson. Kenny died of AIDS last October aged sixty-three. It was organised by the director/choreographer Wendy

Toye CBE and also by Kenny's partner Dougie Squires OBE.

Dougie is a choreographer famous for creating the Young Generation singing and dance group specifically for BBC TV in the late 1960s. They included the actress Una Stubbs, a dear friend of mine since we were in the 1971 Noel Coward revue at the Mermaid Theatre, *Cowardy Custard.*

When Dougie rang me about this memorial he said, "I'd like you to sing the lovely song 'Try to Remember' from the musical *The Fantasticks.* Kenny played the Boy in the original 1960 off-Broadway production."

I said, "Of course. I'll be only too glad and honoured, Dougie."

"We've got an excellent accompanist, Kevin Amos."

Kevin and I managed to rehearse the number last Tuesday.

The Fantasticks became the world's longest running musical. It ran for forty-two years! That's more than 17,000 performances!

In 1969, Kenny moved to London to play the lead in the play *The Boys in the Band* – a ground-breaking comedy/drama about New York's gay scene. Five years later, I worked with him in *Cole* at the Mermaid Theatre in London, a hugely successful revue featuring Cole Porter's life story and his great songs.

8 p.m.

This evening, I watched myself on TV in *Newsnight* playing the Conservative MP Sir Nicholas Leyell. We shot my scene last week as part of a documentary called *Passing the Buck* about the 1980s Iran-Iraq War.

My verbatim dialogue was transcribed from the evidence Sir Nicholas gave in the courtroom during the notorious trial over the sale of British arms to Saddam Hussein's administration. Leyell was then the Attorney General. Transcribed verbatim speech can be difficult to learn and Leyell's dialogue was literally his word for word evidence as spoken in court, slightly uncrafted and fractured. After studying video extracts of him being interviewed, I think I nailed his hesitant delivery.

FRIDAY 25th March 1994

9:30 a.m.

I drove over to Dave and we made mad, passionate love. Alas, only half an hour but one hell of a lot better than nothing. His partner knows and doesn't mind, thank heaven. Our rendezvous keep me sane.

MONDAY 28th March 1994

10:30 a.m. BBC TV Rehearsal Rooms, Acton

Sunset re-rehearsals continue. I mustn't forget to photocopy and send scripts to Helen and Graham for the show at Windsor this coming Sunday.

TUESDAY 29th March 1994

2:30 p.m. BBC TV Rehearsal Rooms, Acton

Today, we did a full run of *Sunset Boulevard* with the new cast. We'll be working here all day tomorrow as well.

THURSDAY 31st March 1994

2 p.m. Adelphi Theatre

Today and tomorrow, we rehearse with the new scenery.

Chapter 12

APRIL 1994

SATURDAY 2nd April 1994

3 p.m. Royalty Theatre. Band Call

It's always a joy to hear the orchestra playing David Cullen and Andrew Lloyd Webber's arrangements of the songs. They sound absolutely terrific.

SUNDAY 3rd April 1994

2 p.m. Theatre Royal, Windsor

A rehearsal with Mark Piper's show tonight and then…

8 p.m.

60 Years of Musicals went great!

Both Graham Bickley and Helen Hobson were ace, young Eddie Redmayne was splendid and Mark Piper seemed pleased with it.

I concluded the show with this little speech: "Tonight, we've celebrated the stage musical in all its diversity and paid an affectionate tribute to this beautiful theatre, which John Counsell and his wife Mary Kerridge have kept going for forty-eight years, sometimes against terrific odds and with no government subsidy. As we pay tribute to John's memory, we can also say thank you to Mary, who is with us here tonight, by wishing Mary a happy eightieth birthday this very evening!"

Dear Mary stood up in the stalls and received a well-deserved ovation.

Author's note: I must add that I later rang Eddie Redmayne and fixed up tickets for him and his mum to see a matinee of Sunset Boulevard. In 2015, Eddie, my young co-star at Windsor, won Best Actor Oscar for his outstanding performance as the astrophysicist Stephen Hawking in the film The Theory of Everything. Hasn't young master Eddie done well?

WEDNESDAY 6th April 1994

7:30 p.m. Adelphi Theatre. A Run-Through of the Re-Directed Sunset

I had to stop this rehearsal in the first scene! I bashed my head on a baby spot doing my costume quick change. The lamp was moved to a much lower position on the redesigned set. The wings are pitch dark now and everything offstage is painted black, so the lamp (also painted black) was completely invisible. We weren't warned. Its sharp metal edge cut me and I bled.

THURSDAY 7th April 1994

Adelphi Theatre. First Preview of Sunset Boulevard. Year Two

Our two new leads are Betty Buckley playing Norma Desmond and John Barrowman playing Joe Gillis.

SATURDAY 9th April 1994

10:30 p.m. Adelphi Theatre. First Night of Sunset Boulevard. Year Two

A party in the theatre after the show. Didn't take a guest.

Left early. Bushed.

SUNDAY 17th April 1994

The London Palladium

It was a knackering day. In the afternoon (in full costumes and wigs), we rehearsed the finale for tonight's live BBC TV broadcast of the awards ceremony.

6:30 p.m. The Laurence Olivier Awards Ceremony

Sunset Boulevard was nominated for Best Musical. *City of Angels* won.

Patti was nominated for Best Actress in a Musical. My chum Julia McKenzie bagged it for her performance as Mrs Lovett in Steven Sondheim's *Sweeney Todd* at the National Theatre.

9 p.m. The Great Room, Grosvenor House, Park Lane

There was a champagne reception followed by a dinner. Coaches took the *Sunset* company all dressed up in their evening clothes to the awards banquet.

I didn't go because I'm bone tired and must focus on learning my dialogue for a corporate video I'm booked to shoot on Wednesday.

10 p.m. Home

Only half a glass of wine and a quick supper.

TUESDAY 19th April 1994

Sunset Boulevard Preview

This evening's preview kicked off the second year run of *Sunset*.

MONDAY 25th April 1994

During tonight's curtain call, a section of plastic fell off the "on the road" car unit. The damn thing landed with an almighty thump on the stage. It actually hit Larissa Murray but, miraculously, she wasn't seriously injured.

THURSDAY 19th May 1994

The backstage elevator that links our top floor dressing room to the stage wasn't working for both the matinee and evening shows. Aaaagh!

FRIDAY 20th May 1994

As we waited onstage to begin the show, Richard Tate said something odd.

"Barrowman keeps taking out his penis and showing it to everyone."

I said, "He hasn't shown it to me."

"Barrowman does it all the time," Richard added.

SATURDAY 21st May 1994

5:30 p.m.

And, lo and behold, what do I see between shows the next day but John Barrowman, stark naked, jogging past my open dressing room door, his joystick bobbing away.

Daniele Combe partnered him, more demurely wearing her bra and panties. They were trotting along the corridor in tandem like a pair of ponies. Is streaking now a "bonding" technique they teach in drama colleges?

I wonder if Sir Henry Irving and Dame Ellen Terry got up to this sort of hanky-panky in the 1870s. She was quite a goer. When Dame Ellen was sixty, she married an American actor called James Carew, twenty-nine years her junior. Jimmy said, "The only way to get on with Nell is not to live in the same house with her."

Their marriage, "till death us do part", lasted three years.

Sharing too much reminds me of something my sister Sylvia told me. Sylvia was a buyer of women's dresses in Debenhams in Clapham Junction.

"A man came up to one of my young female assistants in the make-up section, plonked his hampton on the counter and said to her, 'Match that with a lipstick'. Completely unfazed, the girl took one look and said, 'Hmm. If it was twice as big, I'd say it was a human penis. Kindly wait here, my supervisor will help.' Then she yelled, 'Mr Tompkins!' That got rid of him."

MONDAY 11th July 1994

I am playing DeMille in *Sunset* for the next two weeks while Michael Bauer is on holiday. Oh the joy! I feel like a real actor again.

THURSDAY 21st July 1994

Fixed up three complementary tickets for Pauline Collins, Helen Weir and Stella Tanner to see today's matinee.

Stella, now sixty-seven, has acted in gazillions of TV dramas, including the popular series *Take Three Girls*. In the 1970s, she used to share bevies and theatrical gossip with my partner Paulie in the Buxton Club. It was the actors' drinking hole behind the Haymarket Theatre.

Stella once said to me in her gravelly voice, "Men never grow up. They just go from the tit to the tit."

Pauline Collins and I went to Central School of Speech and Drama. I was studying acting and Pauline was on the teaching course but her attractive personality and sense of humour hinted she could well shine as an actor. One day in Central's foyer, Pauline and her chum Marie were clutching each other, helpless with laughter. Pauline told me they had been talking to a Dutch drama student, Evert Steen.

"Evert said to us, 'I want to tell you both something in the strictest confidence. But not in this corridor. Nobody must overhear us. It's got to be kept an absolute secret.' So, Marie and I obediently followed Evert along the corridors for a while. Then he stopped, shook his head and said, 'No. This won't do either.' So, we followed him again upstairs. 'Here is okay,' he finally whispered. We were all ears. 'How would you like,' Evert began, 'Never to have to shave under your armpits again?' We burst out laughing and couldn't stop. He's promoting some new cream that's not on public sale yet."

Pauline famously played the maid Sarah in the popular 1970s series *Upstairs Downstairs* and later married her co-star John Alderton. Her wonderful career has included international success in the one-woman play *Shirley Valentine* by Willy Russell in 1986. The 1989 film version won her a BAFTA Award and an Oscar nomination. Now fifty-two years old, Pauline remains as down to earth and friendly as ever.

The following week she sent me a jolly card:

"Thank you for the lovely comps to *Sunset Boulevard*. And

for the tea! You really were beautiful as Cecil B. DeMille. I only hope your agent gets his or her finger out! Your voice is wonderful, Peter, even better as the years go by. Long may it warble! Since we met, I got a surprise film – eleven weeks in Prague making *My Mother's Courage*. Isn't this an extraordinary business? Feast or famine. Much love."

That was very kind, but I've suddenly woken up to a huge snag. It's been staring me in the face! My wish to play DeMille is deeply misguided; the reason's obvious. The actor who plays DeMille must also understudy the role of Max, the German film director.

In the movie, it was played by Eric Von Stroheim! I'm completely wrong casting for that role. I lack the necessary heavy physical bearing and threatening presence. This is presumably what Trevor and the production team were thinking when I auditioned to take over the role of DeMille and didn't get it. I wish they had told me.

Chapter 13

AUGUST 1994

SATURDAY 13th August 1994

7:30 p.m. Adelphi Theatre

This is too good to leave out.

Tonight, during the opening number, "Let's Have Lunch", John Barrowman, who plays Joe Gillis, improvised (unwisely) an exchange of dialogue with Richard Tate, who plays Morino, Joe's literary agent.

Joe begs Morino for a money loan, but Morino resolutely refuses.

"Aw, come on," Barrowman pleaded.

Richard responded indignantly, "Don't you come on me!"

Several titters ran round the stage.

MONDAY 26th September 1994

Adelphi Theatre

I'm playing DeMille again for two weeks while Daniel Benzali is on holiday. His understudy Michael Bauer is playing Max – extremely well.

MONDAY 21st November 1994

2 p.m. Adelphi Theatre. Rehearsal Call

Tonight, Elaine Paige is taking over the role of Norma Desmond for the next six weeks. This evening will be Elaine's first show.

9:45 p.m.

Elaine was terrific.

SUNDAY 27th November 1994

Kahramana Hotel, Sharm el Sheikh, Egypt

I flew here today by Monarch Airlines for a five-day holiday. A treat for Pete. Sharm el Sheikh means "bay of peace". It's a resort town by the Red Sea that has sandy beaches and beautiful coral reefs.

I'm here on the advice of a gorgeous newcomer to the *Sunset* ensemble, Laurie Carter Rose from Cincinnati, US.

Two months ago, I said to Laurie, "I've got a week's break coming up and I don't know what to do with it."

Laurie said, "You should go on a scuba diving holiday."

I was astonished. "What? You mean – deep in the ocean? Like a hero in a Hollywood movie? With a breathing mask on my face? A bit scary, isn't it?"

Laurie smiled. "First," she explained, "They give you a quick course in a swimming pool; then you dive in shallow sea water with an instructor, and then you go deeper. It's wonderful. I've got a feeling you would really enjoy it."

MONDAY 28th November 1994

Divers Lodge in Naam Bay, Egypt

How right Laurie was! My hotel is dead posh and I'm having a fantastic break.

11:05 to 11:30 a.m. Ras um Sid

It means "cape mother of the Lord".

Today was my first go at snorkel swimming! On the shore, my instructor, Bernard, taught me how to scuba dive just below the surface in shallow water. I wore goggles and I breathed through a snorkel. A snorkel is just a tube; my mouth is on one end and the other end curves up to the surface. Easy-peasy.

2:40 to 3:02 p.m.

Once I was okay with that, on the boat Bernard helped me to strap a heavy tank of air on my back. This time my breathing tube was linked to the air tank.

"Next, we do an exercise, Peter," Bernard said. "You always dive with a 'buddy'. Never alone. Imagine I am your buddy, and we're well below the surface. Suppose you have trouble with your air supply. You signal to me and so I share my breathing mask with you. I take one deep breath from my mask then hand it to you. You breathe with my mask for a few seconds, take a deep breath and hand my mask back to me. And so on, while we make our way back to the surface." That went fine.

We then swam down head-first for about twenty feet. Everything was astonishingly beautiful and clear. Crowds of little fishes surrounded me, swimming inches close to my face and flashing gorgeous iridescent colours just to make friends.

"Hello, Pete. Fancy you coming all the way from the Adelphi Theatre specially to visit us! Hope you have a good time."

3:40 p.m.

A large Napoleon Wrasse also befriended me, keeping me company for quite a while. He or she looks like a blue human head with a very wide mouth and thick lips; instead of ears it has flapping fins.

TUESDAY 29th November 1994

11:15 a.m. Ras Nasrani

Ras Nasrani means "beautiful bay" and it certainly is.

Bernard was my dive buddy again.

A sunny, windy day. The boat was rocking and there was a strong current. The coral reefs in this shallow water are incredibly lovely, perfect for snorkelling.

11:40 a.m.

End of dive. We humans call our planet, Earth. We should call it Sea because only twenty-nine percent of it is land; seventy-one percent is covered with water.

Planet Sea is astoundingly beautiful and we don't need to spend astronomic sums of money flying vast distances into space to meet bizarre and fascinating aliens. They are living and swimming right here with us; most are magnificent and many are friendly. Sometimes, the cruel way we treat them breaks my heart.

3:03 p.m. The Gordon Reef

After lunch, Bernard and I explored this reef.

My guidebook says, "The Gordon Reef contains a vast plateau with stretches of white sand. A shallow garden of coral provides angelfish and clownfish with shelter from extremely dangerous lionfish; they have poisonous spikes and they prowl here. The reef's outer sandy banks are visited by turtles and zebra sharks."

Oddly, there are fish called "anemones", unrelated to the land flower. Each anemone can "put down a root to stay on a spot but can uproot and move on." Each one is like a fishy mobile home!

3:25 p.m.

We returned to the shore. Bernard wrote this in my diving logbook:

"Congratulations! You passed!"

WEDNESDAY 30th November 1994

12:18 to 12:40 p.m. Deep Dive Advance Course. The Tower Site Dive

Today, my diving buddy was Amr. It's Arabic for "live a long life".

While we were on the boat, Amr asked me to do a simple add-up sum: e.g. 12+16. It took me four seconds.

After descending 120 feet, a similar sum took six seconds longer *yet* it felt the same time.

3:30 to 3:53 p.m.

The Tower has an underwater cliff. Its walls descend 360 feet, spectacular for diving. The colourful landscape is rich in fishy life – moray eels, parrot fish and the weird boxfish. And yes, he really looks like a swimming box! A square face with an eye in each top corner!

THURSDAY 1st December 1994

11:25 a.m. to 12:16 p.m. A Navigation Dive. Red Sea Beach

Today, my dive buddy was Ali Baba – with no forty thieves.

I told him I was from England and he said, "My parents are Egyptian but I was raised in Huddersfield, Yorkshire."

I said, "Well, I'll go to the bottom of our stairs!"

Ali is deaf, poor lad. He is reasonably easy to follow, but his explanation of the complicated navigation stuff was a bit hard-going.

7 to 8 p.m. A Night Dive

Ali drew a smiley face in my logbook, and wrote: "Lots of interesting marine life." That is putting it mildly.

Laurie was right. This deep-sea experience was a gorgeous revelation and the perfect break. Tomorrow, I fly home.

SATURDAY 7th January 1995

10 p.m. Adelphi Theatre

Elaine Paige has played Norma for six weeks. After the show, the management threw a company party for her in the theatre.

As entertainment, some of the younger ensemble members put on a show called *Lampoon Sunset* while the rest of the cast and the stage staff sat in the stalls and watched. They impersonated various people, including Trevor Nunn and Betty Buckley. Sir Andrew featured only as an amusing voiceover.

Mercifully, I escaped mockery but Miss Buckley did not. Nadia Strahan, who was sacked weeks ago, made a personal reappearance impersonating Betty in a skit. Credit to her, Nadia did a fine job. Nadia's Betty arrived in her dressing room late for the half-hour call and held the curtain up for fifteen minutes, pacing back and forth, talking on the phone to her New York shrink, and shooing away appeals from a stage manager.

"Please, Miss Buckley, the whole company are waiting to start the show and the audience are slow hand-clapping."

Hard to believe but this actually happened quite a few times. Once, as we all stood on the stage waiting to begin, a stage manager told me something interesting about Betty's contract.

"It contains a special clause. It stipulates that the show can't begin until she is 'emotionally prepared' and gives the stage manager her permission for us to go ahead."

I was astonished. "How on earth could RUG have been so naïve to comply with that demand? It's ludicrous."

Several times I asked our stage manager, "So what's causing the hold up this time?"

He would give me an old-fashioned look. "Guess."

Tonight was no exception.

I said, "You mean Betty Buckley? Again? You're kidding."

He nodded. "She arrived late after the half-hour call. And now she's in her dressing room talking on the phone to her agent in New York."

I said, "She obviously never heard the old saying that punctuality is the politeness of princes."

And here's another reason Betty hasn't endeared herself to the company. Sometimes (when she manages to arrive early), she invites the cast to attend an energy circle in her dressing room with her pet dogs. Richard Tate is a regular guest but most of us don't bother. I've never gone and nor has Harry Ditson.

On one occasion, the stage management went to Harry's dressing room and said to him, "Miss Buckley has asked me to invite you to attend her energy circle this evening."

Harry replied, "Tell her I haven't got the energy."

Tonight, after the company's *Lampoon Sunset* cabaret, I was standing at the stage door about to head home when a tearful Betty approached me escorted by Trevor. She was sobbing. I think she felt humiliated by seeing Nadia's funny impersonation of her.

It reminded me of the karma principle: "What you put out into the world comes back at you."

Chapter 14

APRIL 1995

SATURDAY 1st April 1995

My Last Night in *Sunset*

10 a.m. London Weekend Television Studios, Southbank

Leaving *Sunset* feels weird, but it's a *good* weird.

My friend Jean Marsh made a cute remark on this subject. "When my mother talks about out of work actors she says, 'They are unindated with work.'"

Luckily, I've *two* acting jobs lined up. The first begins this very morning with the read-through of an episode in ITV's *Expert Witness* series directed by Nigel Miller.

And three weeks later, I play the vicar Reverend Clemens in Agathe Christie's *Murder at the Vicarage* at the Theatre Royal, Windsor. I've a particularly soft spot for it. I was born and grew up in Slough only three miles away and saw my first plays, musicals and pantos at Windsor. Since 1962, I've appeared in about twenty-five productions there.

Maybe I'm being unwise to risk months of unemployment but that's the nature of the beast. My lowly status as walk-on and understudy in *Sunset* was no fun but it put me back on my financial feet.

Talking of feet, I shall not miss climbing those eighty-four steps from the stage up to my dressing room.

And so, I bid *Sunset Boulevard* a final, coughing adieu. My doctor has diagnosed bronchitis and prescribed an inhaler.

Shot of spectacular sunset. Fade up closing music and...

The End

TUESDAY 11th April 1995

Two Letters from Trevor and Andrew

From Trevor:

Dear Peter,

Having persuaded you, to my delight, to stay on a year ago, I am not surprised, even though I am sad, to discover that two years were enough. You made a terrific contribution to the show and I shall miss your wise and human presence both on and off the stage. Thank you for two wonderful years and great good luck in what you undertake next.

From Andrew:

Dear Peter,

Thank you for your card and for all your loyal work in the company over the last two years. You will be greatly missed.

EPILOGUE

P. S. I am delighted to say my chest infection cleared up quickly and the prescribed inhaler still rests happily in the bedroom drawer, unused.

With its glitzy first night, we achieved lift-off. *Sunset Boulevard* spread its multimillion-pound wings and soared into British theatrical history. Sadly, the show only ran four years at the Adelphi, closing on the 5th April 1997 after 1,530 performances. According to a recent newspaper, *Sunset* never made money because of its expensive staging and the litigation fees Sir Andrew paid Patti when she sued him for tearing up her contract, firing her and starring Glenn Close in the New York production.

One press report said Patti was paid an "undisclosed financial settlement." Others claimed the sum was $1 million, quoting Patti saying, "That money paid for a beautiful swimming pool which I've installed in the back garden of my house in Connecticut. I've named it the Andrew Lloyd Webber Memorial Pool."

TUESDAY 9th September 2014

Royal Academy of Arts

Andrew Lloyd Webber has admitted in press interviews that, in spite of his terrific success and honours, he has a drink problem and struggles with depression. His fondness for fine wine was bizarrely confirmed to me by an engineer I met in the forecourt of the R.A. in London. He was assembling an art installation created by Anselm Kiefer. Two models of rusty German submarines dangled inside enormous transparent plastic fish tanks. Don't ask.

As we chatted, the engineer asked me what kind of work I did and I happened to mention *Sunset Boulevard*.

"What a coincidence," he replied. "I've just been working for Andrew Lloyd Webber in his country home. I fixed up an elaborate novelty clock in the living room for Lady Webber. It was a birthday present she bought Sir Andrew. Instead of chiming on the hour, the clock plays the recorded voice of his wife saying, 'Do you really think another bottle of wine is going to cure this?'"

I didn't get to know Andrew at all, but I felt a bit sorry for him. Our crew on *Sunset* told me Andrew drove them nuts during our interminable technical rehearsals.

"He constantly fussed over the sound levels, so, to keep him happy, we created a DFA button for Andrew to fiddle with. We said to him, 'It makes subtle alterations to the amplified sound balance in the theatre.' What we didn't tell Andrew was DFA stood for 'Does Fuck All'."

Yes, I did feel a bit sorry for poor Andrew, although poor is hardly the right word. Recent press reports allege that Sir Andrew is worth something around £1,200,000,000. Yes. That's one billion, two hundred million, several thousand pounds and about forty-eight pence. Allegedly.

The title of this book *Murder at the Adelphi* refers, of course, to the plot of *Sunset* which begins with a fatal shooting and homicide investigation.

By a strange coincidence, a real murder did take place at the Adelphi Theatre way back in 1897. There is a plaque on the wall by the stage door in Maiden Lane. It honours the memory of an actor, William Terriss. Born in 1847, he was a famous, dashingly handsome star who appeared in dramas and comedies at the Adelphi, some by Shakespeare.

Being kind-hearted, William helped an out-of-work supporting actor called Richard Prince. William Terriss gave Richard Prince small roles in several productions, unaware that Prince had dangerous mental problems. William soon became exasperated by Prince's ingratitude, alcoholism and insulting behaviour and he finally sacked him.

Shockingly, in December of 1897, the insane Richard Prince lurked in the shadows near the stage door and, when William Terriss emerged, Prince stabbed him to death. Prince was soon caught and arrested.

Reports of the murder in the London press caused a sensation. During Prince's trial, the judge found him guilty but insane. Murder was then a hanging offence but instead Prince was sent to Broadmoor Criminal Lunatic Asylum where he died forty years later in 1937. The great Victorian actor Sir Henry Irving expressed the fury of the entire acting community.

"The victim William Terris was an actor, so the man who murdered him will not be executed."

It could make a powerfully dramatic play, especially if presented at the Adelphi Theatre.

TUESDAY 9th September 2014

The Tate Gallery

I met two chums for a jolly lunch, the actor Stephen Carlile and his wife, the actor/director Emily Kempson.

After saying goodbye, I crossed Waterloo Bridge and by chance walked along Maiden Lane. Near the Adelphi Theatre's stage door, its huge dock doors were wide open. Lighting equipment was being delivered. I stopped dead in my tracks and beheld a surreal vision – the theatre's entire stage, also its stalls seats, dress circle and upper circle, all silent and empty.

"What's happening?" I asked the lighting rig guys on the pavement.

"We're doing the get-in for a new musical called *Made in Dagenham*."

"Years ago, I was in *Sunset Boulevard* here. We had terrible problems with our computer. I called it Clovis. It was programmed to move the scenery around the stage at the press of a button, but sometimes Clovis refused to obey for no apparent reason, so the sets kept getting stuck and the show ground to a halt."

He said, "The latest AI technology has made that a rare problem now. But the amazing thing is the Adelphi is still using the original hydraulic stage lifts specially installed to move the scenery in *Sunset Boulevard*. And they're working perfectly."

MONDAY 3rd January 2022

Last Words

I'm happy to say my fabulous acting career was not at all damaged by my "walk-on and understudy" status in *Sunset*. In fact, for the next twenty-five years I kept myself busy as an actor, singer, composer, orchestrator, producer, director, journalist, publisher, novelist and poet.

My final acting role was Master Shallow in Christopher Luscombe's wonderfully successful 2008 production of *The Merry Wives of Windsor* at Shakespeare's Globe Theatre. In 2010, it was revived at the Globe.

Returning home after the last night, I sat on the train, thinking, *Next year, I shall be seventy. My acting career began when I was twelve, playing the boy David in a live BBC TV drama called* A Little Stone *directed by Dorothea Brooking. I killed Nigel Green (Goliath) with my lethal sling.* Merry Wives *is a lovely way to say goodbye to show business. Don't become an old actor who can't remember his lines. Leave the party while you're having fun, Pete.*

So, I did. Now aged eighty, I have no regrets, hordes of happy memories, feelings of intense gratitude and several interesting projects to keep me busy.

One of them is to publish a book I've written called *Murder at the Adelphi.*

Printed in Great Britain
by Amazon